T0311828

Climate Change, Migration and Human Rights

Climate change is already having serious impacts on the lives of millions of people across the world. These impacts are not only ecological, but also social, economic and legal. Among the most significant of such impacts is climate change-induced migration. The implications of this on human rights raise pressing questions, which require serious scholarly reflection.

Drawing together experts in this field, *Climate Change, Migration and Human Rights* offers a fresh perspective on human rights law and policy issues in the climate change regime by examining the interrelationships between various aspects of human rights, climate change and migration. Three key themes are explored: understanding the concepts of human dignity, human rights and human security; the theoretical nexus between human rights, climate change and migration or displacement; and the practical implications and challenges for lawyers and policy-makers of protecting human dignity in the face of climate change and displacement. The book also includes a series of case studies from Alaska, Bangladesh, Kenya and the Pacific islands which aim to improve our understanding of the theoretical and practical implications of climate change for human rights and migration.

This book will be of great interest to scholars of environmental law and policy, human rights law, climate change, and migration and refugee studies.

Dimitra Manou is Senior Researcher in the School of Law, Aristotle University of Thessaloniki, Greece.

Andrew Baldwin is Associate Professor of Human Geography in the Department of Geography, Durham University, UK.

Dug Cubie is Lecturer in the School of Law, University College Cork, Ireland.

Anja Mihr is Programme Director of the Humboldt–Viadrina Center on Governance through Human Rights, Berlin, Germany.

Teresa Thorp is CEO & Principal Insight International (International Trade & Environmental Lawyers & Economists).

Routledge Studies in Environmental Migration, Displacement and Resettlement

Climate Change, Migration and Human Rights

Law and Policy Perspectives

Edited by
Dimitra Manou, Andrew Baldwin, Dug
Cubie, Anja Mihr and Teresa Thorp

LONDON AND NEW YORK

First published 2017 by Routledge

2 Park Square, Milton Park, Abingdon, Oxfordshire OX14 4RN
52 Vanderbilt Avenue, New York, NY 10017

Routledge is an imprint of the Taylor & Francis Group, an informa business

First issued in paperback 2018

British Library Cataloguing in Publication Data
A catalogue record for this book is available from the British Library

Library of Congress Cataloging in Publication Data
A catalog record for this book has been requested.

ISBN: 978-1-138-65594-2 (hbk)
ISBN: 978-0-367-13616-1 (pbk)

Typeset in Goudy
by Taylor & Francis Books

Contents

Illustrations

Figure

Tables

Contributors

Brooke A. Ackerly is Associate Professor at Vanderbilt University. Her publications include *Political Theory and Feminist Social Criticism* (Cambridge 2000), *Universal Human Rights in a World of Difference* (Cambridge 2008) and *Doing Feminist Research* with Jacqui True (Palgrave Macmillan 2010; second edition forthcoming). *Just Responsibility: A Human Rights Theory of Global Justice* is forthcoming from Oxford University Press.

Mujibul Anam is Associate Professor in the Department of Anthropology at Jahangirnagar University, Bangladesh. His areas of interest include public health anthropology, social justice and environment.

Andrew Baldwin is Associate Professor in the Department of Geography, Durham University, and was Chair of COST Action IS1101 Climate change and migration: knowledge, law and policy, and theory. He is co-editor of *Life Adrift: Climate Change, Migration, Critique* (Rowman and Littlefield, 2017). Andrew's research examines the intersections of race, whiteness, migration and climate change, and appears in *Transactions of the Institute of British Geographers*, *WIREs Climate Change*, *Resilience*, and *Environment and Planning A*.

Robin Bronen is Human Rights Attorney and Senior Research Scientist at the University of Alaska Fairbanks, where she has researched climate-induced relocations in Alaska since 2007. She co-founded and currently works as the executive director of the Alaska Institute for Justice, a nonprofit agency that is a research and policy institute focused on climate justice issues. The Alaska Bar Association awarded her the 2012 International Human Rights Award. Soroptomist International awarded her the 2012 Advancing the Rights of Women Award.

Dug Cubie is Lecturer in the School of Law at University College Cork, Ireland. Prior to returning to academia, he worked for over ten years in refugee protection and humanitarian assistance, including for UNHCR in Nepal and the Republic of Congo; IOM in Dublin; and the Irish Red Cross.

Elizabeth Ferris is Research Professor with the Institute for the Study of International Migration at Georgetown University's School of Foreign

Service and also serves as Non-Resident Senior Fellow in Foreign Policy at the Brookings Institution.

Elisa Fornalé is SBSF Professor at the World Trade Institute. She is the Scientific Responsible of the newly launched Horizon 2020 Project "Climate Security with Local Authorities". She was awarded the SNSF Professorship for a project entitled "Framing Environmental Degradation, Human Mobility and Human Development as a Matter of Common Concern". She holds a law degree from the University of Trento and a Ph.D. in law from the University of Palermo.

Jonathan Gilligan is Associate Professor of Earth and Environmental Sciences and Associate Professor of Civil and Environmental Engineering at Vanderbilt University. His publications include more than 70 papers in physics, medicine, engineering, environmental science, law and policy. *Beyond Gridlock*, with Michael Vandenbergh, is forthcoming from Cambridge University Press.

Steve Goodbred is Professor of Earth and Environmental Sciences at Vanderbilt University. His research centres on the geologic development and response of coastal settings to natural and human-driven environmental change. He has published over 50 peer-reviewed articles and book chapters, with an emphasis on research in the Ganges–Brahmaputra River delta, Bangladesh.

Johannes Herbeck has studied Human Geography, Political Sciences and Sociology in Munich, Germany. Since 2008, he has been working as a Researcher at the Sustainability Research Center at the University of Bremen. In 2014, he received a Ph.D. for his thesis "Geographies of Climate Change: Vulnerability, Security, Translocality". Since then, he has been a researcher and scientific coordinator within the project "New Regional Formations: Rapid Environmental Change and Migration in Coastal Regions of Ghana and Indonesia", funded by the Volkswagen Foundation, Germany.

Silja Klepp is Professor of Geography at Kiel University. She is a trained social anthropologist. In her current research on climate change migration and adaptation she integrates postcolonial perspectives and critical theories in the study of the effects of climate change.

Dimitra Manou is Senior Researcher at the School of Law, Aristotle University of Thessaloniki. From 2011 to 2015, she was the co-leader of Working Group II "Law and Policy" of COST Action programme IS1101: "Climate Change and Migration: Knowledge, Law and Policy, and Theory". Her research focuses on aspects of international environmental law, including climate change and biodiversity conservation.

Benoît Mayer is Assistant Professor at the Faculty of Law in the Chinese University of Hong Kong and the managing editor of the *Chinese Journal* *of Environmental Law.* His research addresses diverse aspects of international climate change law, including migration, mitigation, loss and damage, and the relation of the climate regime to general international law.

Anja Mihr is founder and Programme Director of the Humboldt–Viadrina Center on Governance through Human Rights in Berlin, Germany. She has held professorships in public policy, international relations and human rights at the Willy Brandt School of Public Policy at Erfurt University, and at the Netherlands Institute of Human Rights (SIM) at the University of Utrecht.

Lennart Olsson, Professor of Geography at Lund University, was the founding director of LUCSUS, 2000–2016. His current research focuses on the politics of climate change in the context of poverty, food insecurity and ill-health in sub-Saharan Africa. He was coordinating lead author for the chapter on livelihoods and poverty in IPCC's *5th Assessment Report*, 2011–2014.

Jeanette Schade, Ph.D. (Bielefeld University), collaborated in the IOM-led research project "MECLEP – Migration, Environment and Climate Change: Evidence for Policy" and in "ClimAccount" on the EU's extraterritorial human rights obligations in funding climate projects in developing countries. From 2011 to 2015, she was the acting vice-chair of COST Action programme IS1101: "Climate Change and Migration: Knowledge, Law and Policy, and Theory". Her work focuses strongly on planned relocation and human rights.

Ezekiel Simperingham is an international lawyer with 13 years' experience working on human rights, rule of law, migration and displacement issues. He has a Masters of Laws (LLM) from New York University School of Law and has authored a number of publications on displacement, climate change and human rights. He is currently the Regional Migration Coordinator for IFRC, covering the Asia-Pacific region. All the views and opinions he expresses in this book are his alone and do not represent those of the IFRC.

Teresa Thorp is an economist, jurist and policy advisor with a background in diplomacy (former senior diplomat of the Commonwealth Secretariat (Britain and New Zealand), the South African Development Community, and others). She is also the founder of Insight International. Through Insight, Teresa has led trade and climate change programmes throughout Asia, Africa, the Caribbean and the Pacific since 1996; engaged more than 1,200 associates to work on trade, environmental and climate justice programmes over a twenty-year period; and been a delegation member of a number of African, Caribbean and Pacific states in the UNFCCC, UNGA and UN Climate Summit. She has published and presented widely on environmental matters and sets forth a universal and unified way to negotiate international climate accords in Climate Justice – A Voice for the Future (Palgrave-MacMillan 2014).

Foreword

Koko Warner

At the time this volume was being written and going to press, profound mismatches between the governance of economic interests, resource management, and social cohesion were rocketing migration and asylum to the top of the international agenda. Human mobility has taken center stage in the first two decades of the twenty-first century as a defining issue linked with a suite of interrelated challenges, including conflict, climate change, and international cooperation. Headlines routinely note how flooding, extreme storms, and drought drive people away from their homes and livelihoods in search of shelter. As civil war in Syria erupted, co-mingling forces of a significant drought and agricultural poverty drove many people[1] from the countryside into conflict-ripe urban areas like Aleppo and Damascus.

By 2015, escalating violence drove as many or more of these people out of Syria as refugees. At the same time as stressors like unexpected weather or conflict deteriorate living conditions and drive large numbers of people from their areas of origin, places that potentially could offer a safe haven to affected people manifest decreased appetite to receive newcomers. Anti-immigration sentiment has fueled widespread debate in national and subnational elections across a number of countries in recent years. In 2016, a slight majority of citizens who cast their votes in the United Kingdom carried the Brexit referendum to leave the European Union, in part over immigration and mobility issues. Immigration also played a significant role in the outcome of the 2016 US presidential election.

Since 2010, I have had the privilege to be part of COST Action programme IS1101: "Climate Change and Migration: Knowledge, Law and Policy, and Theory" – the scholarly network that has produced this volume. A topic we frequently discussed was that while these megatrends typify this new century, the institutions we have to manage migration and refugees, on the one hand, and the policy processes that shape them, on the other, remain rooted in past centuries. Members of the COST network and a blossoming research community around it have produced an impressive body of empirical research in which we are seeing four broad patterns of human mobility linked to climatic stressors beginning to emerge: so-called "disaster displacement," complex patterns of movements in conflict-affected areas, livelihood-related mobility, and longer-term movement related to issues of habitability. Each of these patterns has different implications for human rights, law, and policy that are not always matched to current governance structures for human mobility. **Understanding these different patterns of climate-related human mobility requires multiple perspectives.**

First, disasters such as floods and storms displace four times as many people worldwide today than conflicts, displacing around 20 million people each year in recent years.[2] Governance and institutions are currently dominated by crisis management paradigms. For example, the Nansen Initiative found that, worldwide, country approaches to manage displacement related to hazards focused on humanitarian assistance and protection measures. In the future, humanitarian efforts will need to be blended with future-oriented resilience measures that strive to move people, not least the most vulnerable, into a state of safety and well-being. This shift will require substantial rethinking of the management of extreme events.

Second, droughts, floods, and storms worsen the situation for people in conflict-torn areas and make it hard for them to access food, water, and humanitarian help. Current laws and norms for people on the move within and away from conflict-torn areas are guided by agreements such as the Geneva Convention, the asylum regulations of individual receiving states, and international refugee law. Yet the aforementioned drought in Syria as well as drought in the Horn of Africa and other areas of heightened political tension or war reveal complex roots of human movement that require new thinking about fragile states and managing exacerbating factors like climate stressors.

Third, drought, heatwaves, and changing rainfall patterns are making it increasingly hard for people like farmers and herders to make a living and feed their families. Current laws about cross-border migration focus on regular, documented labor migration. A handful of countries have policies addressing in-country moves, such as from one rural area to another, or from rural to urban areas. Already today, regional-scale shifts in weather patterns require a rethinking of institutions so that they are better suited to address future livelihoods under climate change in both areas of origin and potential areas of destination.

A fourth and final pattern emerging from the literature suggests that sea-level rise, glacial melt, desertification, and other global-scale climate-related changes this century could render large areas of the world less habitable than they are today. Changes in habitability such as shifts in coastlines or water availability linked to glacial melt, soil moisture, or salinization of groundwater may drive new types of border management and translocality, which may transcend current ways of thinking and governing in different regions of the world.

A look ahead

From a personal perspective, being part of the COST network convinced me of the importance of fostering multi- and interdisciplinary dialogue about the forces shaping human mobility as a vehicle of transformation. For example, the thousands of interviews from our research at the United Nations University as part of research consortia and part of the COST network helped us better understand the forces that already stress livelihood systems and how these may interact with weather-dependent livelihoods and food security. The critical analyses of political scientists, geographers, and legal scholars have elucidated further systemic ties between these stressors, such as trade agreements and agricultural policies. These system dynamics dramatically affect livelihoods in areas of origin, as well as attempts to manage risk through mobility to other places in search of work, a decent life, and safety.

Understanding and addressing the different needs of people on the move, those left behind, and receiving communities holds the key to actions that will shape and transport us into a climate-resilient future. With support from the European Commission, COST Action programme IS1101: "Climate Change and Migration: Knowledge, Law and Policy, and Theory" has explored the nuanced aspects of these debates, resulting in the current volume, which examines legal and policy perspectives across human rights theory and practice. Informed management of human mobility decisions will make the difference between a chaotic, "dangerous" future with fewer opportunities and a more resilient, sustainable future with expanding opportunities for the well-being of all people.

Across these emerging patterns of human mobility and climate change, different perspectives and approaches like those facilitated by the COST network are required to address the needs of people on the move, people in receiving communities, and people that stay behind. The rich exchange stemming from the COST network as well as the chapters presented in this volume suggest that effective laws, policies, and norms related to climate change and human mobility will share the following guiding notions:

- **Patterns**: Emerging rules should fit the majority of mobility patterns, particularly complex, multi-causal mobility that may include elements of migration (such as related to diminished livelihood possibilities), displacement related to extreme events, and seeking refuge from conflict.
- **People**: New ways of managing human mobility in the face of climate stressors should be better suited to address the needs of people on the move. This may require better empirical understanding of household profiles and needs, taking into account a variety of development characteristics including gender, age, and other household characteristics that affect the process and outcomes of human mobility. Similarly, empirical and theoretical research should play a role in supporting policy and actions that target underlying causes of mobility in ways that accentuate opportunity and innovation, and provide safe fallback options to prevent or avoid poverty traps that can be associated with people moving in highly vulnerable circumstances. Policies should ideally

ensure safe, dignified, resilience-building options for communities as they transition into and adapt to climate change.

- **Practice/institutions**: New rules will need to be aligned with institutions designed to manage the reality and processes of mobility, including preemptive measures and contingency plans. This will require innovation and shifts over time from current "divided" thinking about the management of development processes, humanitarian affairs, risk reduction, and other processes related to inter-border and cross-border adaptation measures. Substantial new thinking that reaches beyond and integrates issues like human mobility will be characteristic of new practices in the face of managing climate change and other significant trends shaping the twenty-first century.
- **Political realities**: Finally, new ways of governing the interrelationships between different patterns of human mobility linked with climatic stressors will require alignment with the realities of twenty-first-century geopolitical dynamics. As early as we are in this new century, these trends may include peaking world population around midcentury and redistribution of demographics and these populations, corresponding pressures of large populations in the Global South, and other megatrends like urbanization in areas prone to climatic hazards.

For me, participating in the COST network was a highly rewarding experience that helped put policy makers into dialogue with academic research. We all have much to learn from one another. Looking ahead to midcentury, the governance of human mobility will be a yardstick of progress against the aspirations of the Sustainable Development Goals, the Sendai Framework on disaster risk reduction, and the Paris Agreement towards climate-resilient sustainable development. The ideas presented in this volume point the way towards a new period of innovation and rethinking the governance of climate, migration, and human well-being.

Koko Warner, Ph.D.
Manager, Impacts, Vulnerabilities and Risks Subprogramme
Adaptation Programme
Climate Change Secretariat
United Nations

Notes

1 The actual numbers remain unclear. While the IRIN noted, "The drought also forced 250,000–300,000 families" (at least 1.25–1.5 million people) to leave their villages and they are now concentrated in the suburbs of Damascus and other cities like Aleppo and Daa'ra, according to Mohamad Alloush, director of the environment department at the State Planning Commission (SPC), "There was nothing left for these people in their villages and they are living now in very poor conditions" IRIN, 'Drought Response Faces Funding Shortfall' (2009) www.irin

news.org/news/2009/11/24/drought-response-faces- funding-shortfall accessed 1 February 2017). The UNOCHA Consolidated Appeals Process in 2009 reported: "A third consecutive year of drought has hit north-eastern Syria. According to Government and UN estimates, 1.3 million inhabitants are affected and 800,000 severely affected, over 95% of whom live in the three governorates of Al-Hassake, Dayr az Zawr and Ar-Raqqa. The effects of the drought are being exacerbated by the impact of high food and fuel prices, and the global financial crisis. The result is a dramatic decrease in communities' resilience and coping capacity. The rural population directly affected by the drought has lost almost all sources of livelihood and faces extreme hardship" (United Nations, Office for the Coordination of Humanitarian Affairs (UNOCHA), 'Syria Drought Response Plan 2009–2010' www.unocha.org/cap/appeals/syria-drought-response-plan-2009-2010 accessed 1 February 2017).

2 Internal Displacement Monitoring Centre (IDMC), "Global Report on Internal Displacement 2016" (2016) www.internal-displacement.org/globalreport2016/#home accessed 1 February 2017.

Part I
Introduction

1 Climate change, migration and human rights

Dimitra Manou[1] and Anja Mihr[2]

Global warming and environmental change are already having serious impacts on the lives of millions of people all across the world. Changes to our climatic system, such as floods, droughts, rising sea levels, glacial melting, deserts shrinking or expanding, and rainfall patterns changing, to name but a few, impose huge stresses on livelihoods. Scientists raise their voices to warn that parts of the world may become completely uninhabitable not only due to severe environmental degradation but due to climate change as well. Consequently, the impacts on livelihoods are not only ecological but also social, economic and legal. Overall, they are man- and woman-made and, thus, the anticipated global and local solution to decrease the negative impact of climate change on our livelihoods will depend on how men and women agree legally and politically binding agreements, and develop instruments, mechanisms and procedures to safeguard and protect human rights standards for climate change-affected people.

The potential climate change-induced migration of millions of people is currently one of the most disputed impacts of climate change and is increasingly becoming an issue of great concern for governments and policy makers. Whether as so-called 'climate refugees', 'economic migrants' or 'displaced people', climate change-induced migration has many faces. Climate change affects everyone in the world in different ways. For example, disputes over scarce natural resources such as water or fertile ground can cause violent conflicts; droughts can cause displacement and prompt people to seek refuge; and the seepage of cliffs and fertile grounds and the flooding of coastal areas force or encourage people to move and migrate. Some do so through legal channels, but many more do so outwith a specific legal framework. Human rights and the concept of climate justice aim to fill the legal and political gap for millions of migrants who do not benefit from international legal protection as the cause of their migration is not yet fully enshrined in either international or regional law.

However, both migrants and those who decide to remain in environmentally degraded areas face a range of humanitarian challenges and the potential deprivation of basic human rights, such as the rights to health, property and adequate housing. Despite extensive discussions and analysis of international and internal human mobility, the issue of protecting the rights of people who decide to stay and those who are left behind has not been sufficiently analysed in the academic literature. This is where this volume aims to make a difference. Our prime concern in this book is that the implications of climate change-induced migration affect or violate basic international human rights norms and standards and thus raise pressing questions requiring serious scholarly reflection about both those who move and those who stay. Such civil, political, social, economic and cultural human rights include the right for all to live a dignified life, the right to self-determination and participation of those most affected, the right to livelihoods thay are threatened when livestock and farms vanish or are destroyed, the right to adequate housing and the right to seek education and professional development if one is forced to migrate.

Furthermore, climate change-induced migration interacts in complex ways with human rights protection. People's ability to enjoy their rights is severely affected by climate change, which has been recognised by the UN Office of the High Commissioner for Human Rights as one of the greatest human rights challenges of our generation.[3] Citizens not only lose assets, but rights. Discrimination in gender and ethnic relations may be triggered by climate change-induced migration. Economic and social balance/relations are also affected, leading to new patterns of inequality. All these diverse challenges create increased pressure on human rights. In fact, all human rights may be undermined as a result of the impacts of climate change.

That being said, human rights, as universally accepted in the 1948 Universal Declaration of Human Rights, can offer a normative direction for addressing climate change-induced migration. As advocated by the Mary Robinson Foundation, incorporating human rights considerations into climate policies can contribute to achieving actions that benefit both the needs of people and the planet.[4] Throughout this book, a distinction will be made regarding the status of the people who are moving: internal migration within the borders of a state gives rise to internally displaced persons who are entitled to enjoy the full range of their human rights (as recognised by both international and domestic law) in that state; while international, cross-border migrants often face a serious protection gap, which is highlighted and explored throughout the book's chapters. For both categories of migrant, it is a necessity for states of origin, transit and/or destination to design, adopt and enforce effective policies, strategies and legislative solutions at the national level.

Development of new, more effective governance mechanisms requires a deep knowledge of existing climate- and migration-related policies and a solid understanding of the reasons why such policies may lead to more inequalities instead of mitigating them. In light of the pitfalls that accompany climate change-induced migration, the human rights-based approach pro-vides a strong conceptual and practical framework to protect human rights in the context of climate change.

Over the past twenty years, proposals have been advanced for new legal frameworks, such as a new international convention to protect climate-displaced persons or amendments to the 1951 Refugee Convention or the 1992 UN Framework Convention on Climate Change. Yet we remain without a clear, internationally binding framework for many people who migrate due to the negative impacts of climate change. The widely endorsed 2015 Paris Agreement at the UNFCCC COP21 meeting may serve as an example of how complicated and difficult it is to include relevant clauses on population movement arising from climate change in international agreements.[5]

In 2016 in Marrakech, COP22 confirmed the goals and plans of COP21 in Paris. The COP22 Agreement identifies not only states' responsibilities, in particular the joint efforts of Global North and Global South nations, but also those of NGOs, CSOs and businesses. Marrakech focused on initiatives to reinforce existing plans, with some countries promising to review their 2020 targets. Timelines and roadmaps for reviewing states' and stakeholders' achievements were agreed. Primarily, however, the meeting secured a commitment to implementation and answered at least some technical questions. Subsequent annual meetings will reinforce the agreements and also assess, evaluate and if necessary penalise and apply pressure to those countries that do not comply.

Clearly, identifying environmental or climate migrants has not been an easy task. Therefore, it seems unlikely that proposals on population movement arising from climate change will gain the necessary political support in the near future with regard to drafting, amending, endorsing or adopting an entirely new legal framework. On the other hand, at the national level, there have been governmental and civil society efforts to respond to legal, policy and administrative gaps with regard to climate migration, as is demonstrated in the case studies within this book.

The suffering of many people in the so-called Global South who face the worst of climate change's impacts, such as inhabitants of the Marshall Islands, Bangladesh, Chile, Kenya, Sudan and many other sub-Saharan countries, has led to large-scale cross-border movements and internal displacements. However, it is now clear that the impacts of climate change are of concern not only for people in the South (who have contributed least to the root causes of climate change) but for the North as well, such as Europe, North America, China and Japan, where climate change-induced floods, hurricanes and other natural forces have led to displacement and resettlement of thousands of people and industries. As a result, injustice, adaptation and mitigation strategies, as well as reallocation decisions (individual or community), have evolved to become concerns across the globe. Thus, new challenges have arisen for national, regional and international agencies, including UN bodies, the African Union, the European Union and the Organization of American States, resulting in a need for appropriate programmes and initiatives to reduce and minimise people's vulnerability to the negative impacts of climate change and forced displacement.

Decision-making processes and the design and adoption of new policies and laws have been difficult in the contexts of global climate change and especially climate change-induced migration. Aside from the lack of an appropriate legal framework (at the national, regional or international level), uncertainty about the precise numbers of people who will eventually move and about the forms that this human movement will take put much more pressure on policy makers, international and regional agencies, and national and local authorities. The development of new legal and policy frameworks, which may address the harmful impacts of climate change as associated migration and human rights violations, still seems a long way ahead. New ways of thinking are necessary for the international community to support those most in need, recognising that the main goal remains helping existing (and future) victims of climate change by offering them adequate legal and policy tools to support their adaptation and mitigation activities. Adaptation mechanisms must therefore be created and enhanced, including supporting migration away from climate change-affected areas or providing support to those who are unable or unwilling to leave their homes.

Therefore, this book addresses issues such as:

- What theoretical frameworks will help us to understand the links between human rights, climate change and migration?
- Is the current legal framework for human rights protection adequate to address climate change-induced migration?
- Is a human rights-based approach the most appropriate method for responding to climate change-induced migration?
- What other responses might there be?
- And what lessons may be learned from countries or regions that are already obliged to address the issue of displacement due to environmental and climatic stressors?

This edited volume aims to respond to some of these pressing questions and has thus encouraged interdisciplinary approaches between social, legal and political scientists to offer a fresh look at the interlinkages between climate change, migration and human rights. The nexus between human rights, climate change and migration policy has been explored and analysed. This volume has also encouraged transnational approaches, highlighting the differences and/or commonalities of people on the move. Issues covered by the chapters include, inter alia, planned relocation, questions of asylum, humanitarian policies, climate justice and adaptation strategies. Questions of implementing human rights standards in existing and emerging policies and governance mechanisms (i.e. for climate change adaptation and disaster risk reduction) and their relation to migration strategies have been also explored.

This book arose from the EU's COST Action programme IS1101: 'Climate Change and Migration: Knowledge; Law and Policy, and Theory', and in particular from the Working Group II on 'Law and Policy', which met on four occasions between 2012 and 2015. All of the contributors have been members of – or have worked closely with – this COST Action to establish a network of researchers in this field, with the aim of sharing their knowledge and building upon and extending research on the legal and policy perspectives of climate change-induced migration.

The adequacy of existing legal and policy frameworks, and how they may apply to people on the move due to climate change, raises fundamental questions for policy makers and practitioners (Ferris, Thorp), as does the possibility of designing and adopting new legal frameworks that could respond to human rights and climate-induced displacement. Discussions on international legal frameworks under the European and international law regimes with regard to climate change and migration highlight the fact that soft law initiatives may play a crucial role in addressing climate change-induced migration, such as the development of guidelines to meet the needs of specific groups affected by climate change (Ferris). If existing frameworks prove inadequate for this purpose, there may be a need to modify the existing – or develop new – legal architecture to govern the rights of migrant populations displaced due to climate change, including the international and regional legal frameworks for international climate change, sustainable development and disaster risk reduction measures (Thorp).

The challenges of identifying a satisfactory legal definition of environmental or climate migrants (or refugees) seem insurmountable, due to the difficulties of isolating the causal links of environmental factors as the sole cause for migration (Mayer). Nevertheless, climate change and human rights are strongly interlinked and the concept of climate justice may offer a way to conceptualise these links (Mihr).

The necessity to ensure protection and respect of housing, land and property rights of climate change-displaced persons is underlined in the case study of Bangladesh, one of the countries that is most vulnerable to climate change, where thousands of people have been displaced internally (Simperingham). Individuals in environmentally stressed areas are faced with three stark choices: forced migration, pre-emptive migration or in-situ adaptation (Cubie). Therefore, the issue of non-migration as a coping strategy in response to climate change also needs to be addressed. Adapting or migrating with dignity should be promoted through the application of key procedural rights, such as the right to information and the right to participate (Cubie). The potential links between climate change and the social impact of migration with armed conflicts are clearly highlighted (Olsson).

The importance of policy strategies at the international and domestic level for the reallocation of resources is exemplified through case studies from Alaska and Kenya (Bronen, Schade), as well as suggestions for climate change adaptation policies (Cubie). While relocation appears to be the only durable solution to protect the inhabitants of many vulnerable communities, tribal, state and national government agencies are struggling to respond in Alaska (Bronen). In addition, environmental change, climate policies and land regulations may lead to additional disadvantages for already vulnerable groups and prevent them from enjoying basic human rights to water, food and housing (Schade).

The methods whereby rights and resources are negotiated in transnational law-making processes through informal actors and forums is highlighted, offering another view on global law-making processes which localises respective negotiations on innovative migration strategies and new rights in the Global South (Klepp and Herbeck).

A human rights lens is essential when thinking about the injustices caused by climate change, and that the threat to human rights may also come from less acknowledged factors, like the dynamics of the political economy, which may affect people's ability to resist or overcome these threats (Ackerly *et al.*). Finally, existing avenues and tools to facilitate mobility are explored, in particular the option to consider labour mobility as an adaptation strategy to environmental change (Fornalé).

The dialogue that is presented here will hopefully generate new synergies and understanding between social scientists, legal scholars and policy makers as well as new opportunities for stronger and more effective responses to these interlinked global agendas: climate change, migration and human rights. Thus, this book offers state-of-the-art legal and policy research on climate change-induced migration and human rights as a means of adding to the international policy dialogue and to serve as a basis for expanding research capacity in the field of climate change and migration. It also provides useful guidance to legal practitioners and policy makers working at the cutting edge of the subject.

Notes

1 Senior Researcher, School of Law, Aristotle University of Thessaloniki, Greece.
2 Programme Director, Humboldt–Viadrina Center on Governance through Human Rights, Berlin, Germany.
3 United Nations, Office of the High Commissioner for Human Rights (OHCHR), 'Human Rights and the Environment: Our Generation Must Meet the Great Challenge – UN Experts' press release (5 June 2015) www.ohchr.org/EN/NewsEvents/Pages/DisplayNews.aspx?NewsID=16052&LangID=E accessed 21 October 2016.
4 Mary Robinson Foundation – Climate Justice, 'Incorporating Human Rights into Climate Action', Version (1 October 2014) www.mrfcj.org/wp-content/uploads/2015/09/2014- 10-20-Incorporating-Human-Rights-into-Climate-Action.pdf accessed 21 October 2016.
5 UNFCCC, *Paris Agreement Concluded at the 21st Conference of the Parties to the UN Framework Convention on Climate Change* (adopted 12 December 2015, entered into force 4 November 2016) FCCC/CP/2015/L.9/Rev.1.

Part II
The theoretical nexus

2 Governance and climate change-induced mobility

International and regional frameworks

Elizabeth Ferris

Introduction

Since the very first report of the Intergovernmental Panel on Climate Change (IPCC) in 1990, there has been recognition that climate change is likely to increase human mobility.[1] However, there is little evidence on who, when, where, why, how or how many people will move. Dire warnings of the potential for climate change to displace millions or even hundreds of millions of people seem to have given way to a realisation that the relationship between migration and climate change is a complex process influenced by factors that do not lend themselves well to estimates generated by statistical projections and models.[2]

This chapter looks at international and regional approaches to the governance of climate change mobility from the perspective of assessing the ability of existing mobility regimes to meet the needs and uphold the rights of those who are moving or who will move because of the effects of climate change. The applicability of various existing governance models depends in large part on whether the movement is voluntary or forced, internal or cross-border, and temporary or permanent.

The international system that has emerged over the past seventy-five years is primarily based on the causes of movement; people who are forced to leave their countries because of persecution or conflict may be considered refugees and are treated differently from those who leave their countries for other reasons. There is a well-regarded body of international law governing the treatment of refugees; governments that have signed up to the relevant conventions are obligated to allow refugees to enter their territories. While there are many shortcomings in practice and the system rarely works as well as it should, there is at least an international regime governing refugee movements.

The world of migration governance is a different animal. The international system is built on the principle of national sovereignty, and the bedrock of that system is the right of national authorities to decide who can enter their territories. While they are constrained by international refugee law and the Convention against Torture to accept those fleeing persecution, and to refrain from returning people to places where they might be tortured, beyond those limitations there are no restrictions on their decisions about whom to admit in all other categories. While the refugee system – as discussed in more detail below – is characterised by a common definition, a binding international treaty and a designated UN agency, the system of migration governance – also discussed in more detail below – is much less institutionalised and has fewer internationally accepted norms and frameworks.

In looking at the governance of climate change mobility, the issue of whether people are forced – or voluntarily choose – to move is crucial. If they are seen as being forced to leave their communities, then the international refugee system – and the much less institutionalised system for dealing with internally displaced persons (IDPs) – may offer some guidance on how they should be treated. If, on the other hand, they are seen as migrants (who under international law are presumed to move voluntarily), then there are fewer international legal prescriptions governing their treatment. We return to this question after discussing the 'elephant in the room' – the question of understanding the causes of movement in the context of climate change.

The elephant in the room

The most serious obstacle to developing a system for climate change-related mobility is the multi-causal nature of population movements. The line between 'voluntary' and 'forced' – while clear in international law – is not so clear when it comes to people's motivation for movement. While climate change may act as a force multiplier, intensifying the effects of disasters, it is impossible to make the case that a particular storm was the result of climate change, much less to assess the role of climate change in prolonging drought. As Mayer remarked, '[a]fter all, there were hurricanes, desertification and sinking islands before climate change, and greenhouse gas emissions do not bear the responsibility for all of these phenomena happening today'.[3] It is even more difficult to determine the role played by climate change in any given situation, given the interplay of political, social, demographic and economic factors. For example, wealthy families living in a coastal area affected by sea level rise may be able to make physical changes to their homes which would allow them to remain, while poor families affected by the same sea level rise may have no option but to leave. Or poverty may make it impossible for those most affected by climate change to move. A recent survey of Pacific islanders by the UN University found that 23 per cent of those moving from Kiribati and 8 per cent of those migrating from Tuvalu cited climate change as the reason. Many more inhabitants of those island states said they would move if conditions worsened, although one-quarter also said they didn't have the economic means to do so.[4] It also may be that global warming makes an area uninhabitable for the present population but could support a smaller population. The specific role of climate change and environmental factors needs to be carefully drawn.

While it is relatively easy to see the connections between climate change and conditions in small island states, it is more difficult to assess the role of climate change in slow-onset disasters, such as droughts. Overall patterns seem to demonstrate that droughts, desertification and heatwaves are increasing around the planet as a result of climate change, but, again, it is hard to attribute changes in any one particular situation to climate change and even more difficult to assess the role of climate change in comparison with other environmental and economic factors in individuals' decisions to move.

The difficulties in assessing the specific impact of climate change on mobility make it difficult to develop governance models for all those whose movements are determined or affected by the effects of climate change.

Voluntary or forced movement?

The present systems for the governance of international mobility are largely based on the motivation for movement, distinguishing between involuntary or forced movement, on the one hand, and voluntary migration, on the other. The assumption in much of the literature on climate change and mobility is that people will be **forced** to leave their homes because of the effects of climate change. Hence the term 'climate change refugees' is widely used and the referent legal standard for cross-border movements is international refugee law and, for those moving within the borders of their country, normative frameworks around IDPs.

But in fact, in addition to those who are indisputably compelled to move, it is likely that many people whose habitats are being destroyed by the effects of climate change will see the writing on the wall and will move to other countries in anticipation of the negative effects of climate change. They will be considered to be voluntary migrants even if their reason for moving is directly or indirectly due to the negative effects of climate change. It is likely that this will be a large number of people, that they will move through existing migration channels and that the scope of this movement will not be known.

For example, a pastor from Kiribati told the author in 2010, 'Because of climate change, there is no future for my children on our island. I sent my son to school in Australia, hoping that he can find a job and settle down there. It breaks my heart, but there is no future for him here.' Even though the reason why the son stays in Australia may be due to climate change, and even if the son feels that he cannot return to his country, he will likely be considered to be an economic migrant. It is not unreasonable to expect that those who move in anticipation of the likely effects of climate change – before the situation becomes catastrophic – will be financially better off, and perhaps younger and healthier, than those who – although they recognise the worsening conditions – are simply unable to move. The UNU Pacific survey found the median income of those living in Kiribati, Nauru and Tuvalu to be just 12 US dollars per month.[5]

As will be seen below, this issue of causation has been a thorn in the side of those seeking to come up with new governance models for climate-induced mobility, as evidenced by initiatives such as the Peninsula Principles[6] and Robin Bronen's call for a framework to respond to 'climigration'.[7] But it is hard to distinguish between a climate-displaced person and one whose livelihood prospects were diminished in part because of climate change but also because he/she was living in poverty. In these circumstances, even a relatively minor change in the environment – such as a change in rainfall patterns – might be enough to push them over the edge and lead them to leave their communities and join others who are leaving the same communities in search of better opportunities elsewhere.

While there is a robust debate about the terms to be used to describe those who leave because of the effects of climate change, there are also questions about whether all those who move because of some connection to climate change should be lumped together. As Mayer asks,

> But is there *anything* in common between a retired Canadian deciding to go and live in Florida to avoid Canadian winters, a desperate fisher family from a 'sinking' island, a Nigerian farmer migrating to town to earn some revenue during the dry season, and a Bangladeshi family taking refuge in a shelter during a cyclone? What rationale could justify protection of those individuals and not, say, of any [other] individual suffering in their home country and sufficiently desperate to risk their lives crossing seas on overcrowded rafts or travelling in freight trains?[8]

The refugee regime

If individuals are forced to leave their countries of origin because they can no longer live there due to the effects of climate change, then perhaps the most applicable normative framework is the international refugee regime. This regime was developed in the mid-twentieth century for a different purpose – to protect people who were outside their countries of origin and unable to avail themselves of their governments' protection. Over the past sixty-five years, the refugee regime has proven to be remarkably adaptable to new circumstances, but there are problems with extending its reach to those displaced by the effects of climate change.

The 1951 Refugee Convention and its 1967 Protocol define a refugee as 'a person who, owing to well-founded fear of being persecuted for reasons of race, religion, nationality, membership of a particular social group or political opinion, is outside the country of his nationality and is unable, or owing to such fear is unwilling, to avail himself of the protection of that country'.[9] Clearly, an individual fleeing his or her country because of the effects of climate change is not facing persecution for one of the five reasons given in this definition. Indeed, the one case that has been tried in New Zealand courts of a family from Tuvalu claiming refugee status because of the effects of climate change was rejected on those grounds (although the family was later allowed to remain for humanitarian reasons).[10] The 1951

Refugee Convention was originally developed to protect individuals (rather than groups) fleeing persecution by governments. Over the years, it has been applied to groups having *prima facie* claims to refugee status and to those fleeing persecution by non-state armed groups, including criminal gangs. The central thrust of the Convention is that refugees need international protection because their governments are unable or unwilling to protect them for one of the five named reasons for persecution. While it can be argued that those leaving their countries because of the effects of climate change are doing so because their governments cannot protect them from those effects, the narrow scope of the five reasons for persecution makes it difficult to apply the refugee convention to this group of people.

Moreover, refugee advocates and experts in refugee law have resisted expanding the definition to include those displaced by the effects of climate change because of the fear that such an expansion would weaken the applicability of the Convention to those in need of protection for one of the five grounds. There are also concerns on the part of some countries, particularly developed countries, that if the door is opened, they could be inundated with large numbers of people arriving on their borders. Considering those who move as forcibly displaced is also complicated because of its potential linkage to contentious discussions over loss and damage taking place in the context of climate change negotiations. It is not unreasonable to expect in this context that the countries responsible for the carbon emissions that are forcing people to leave their countries might be expected to have a responsibility to accept these individuals in their territories.

While the term 'climate change refugee' is thus not accepted under international law and is staunchly opposed by refugee advocates and governments of potential receiving countries, it does have a certain popular resonance that other – more nuanced – terms do not. Indeed, François Gemenne makes the case that in spite of its legal uncertainties, the term is applicable precisely because of its emphasis on the forced nature of displacement.[11]

While UNHCR has resisted calls to expand the refugee definition, it has been active in tracing the connections between climate change and displacement, producing a number of studies,[12] convening meetings,[13] participating in the Climate Change negotiations[14] and playing an active role in interagency processes to advance understanding. Given its experience with refugees, it is likely that UNHCR will be called to play a role in responding to those who are displaced because of the effects of climate change, regardless of their legal status.

At the present time, the 1951 Refugee Convention cannot be applied to people who have been displaced because of the effects of climate change because it is limited to five specific types of persecution, none of which applies directly or could even be stretched to include those who move because of climate change.

The question then arises: might the Refugee Convention be expanded? In 2006, the Maldives proposed amending the 1951 Refugee Convention to extend the definition of 'refugee' to include climate refugees.[15] While this would be the most straightforward way of coming up with an international regime for protecting those displaced by the effects of climate change, it seems highly unlikely, at least in the present context. There is widespread opposition to reopening discussions on the Refugee Convention because of a fear that the Convention itself might be rejected. Countries of potential destination are opposed to expanding the definition of refugees, and there are many conceptual difficulties in determining the role of climate change in forcing people to leave their home countries.

A new global treaty?

Given the resistance to amending the 1951 Refugee Convention, there have been several efforts in recent years to come up with a new global convention on 'climate change refugees'. Biermann and Boas suggested a new UN Framework Convention on Climate Change (UNFCCC) Protocol on the Recognition, Protection and Resettlement of Climate Refugees.[16] A group of legal scholars from the University of Limoges published a Draft Convention on the International Status of Environmentally Displaced Persons,[17] which was updated in 2010. A Harvard initiative spells out a new legal instrument on climate change refugees.[18] Hodginkson *et al.* have also attempted to elaborate a draft convention for persons displaced by climate change which would establish an international regime for the status and treatment of such persons.[19]

Such proposals face several obstacles. On the conceptual level, it has so far proven impossible to determine the extent to which climate change is a driver of migration – and hence to prove the degree of compulsion. The challenge for these proposals is how to prove – or at least make a convincing case – that people are forced to leave their countries because of the effects of climate change and not, say, because of poverty. However, as the effects of climate change intensify in the coming years and decades, it may well be that it becomes obvious when people are displaced primarily because of climate change and thus there will be more receptivity to developing a binding legal instrument to ensure their protection in other countries.

Another obstacle to the development of a global treaty on cross-border movement is that it is likely that most of those who are displaced because of the effects of climate change will move within the borders of their own countries. Before considering the normative frameworks that are available for responding to internal displacement, however, we briefly look at the possibility of using refugee instruments at the regional level.

Using regional refugee instruments

The 1969 Organisation of African Unity (OAU) Convention incorporates those refugees who fall within the 1951 definition but extends this to persons who flee their country 'owing to external aggression, occupation, foreign domination or events seriously disturbing public order'.[20] Similarly, the 1984 Cartagena Declaration expands the definition to a broader set of beneficiaries in Latin America, including people who flee because their 'lives, safety or freedom have been threatened by generalised violence, foreign aggression, internal conflicts, massive violation of human rights or other circumstances which have seriously disturbed public order'.[21]

These two regional definitions are usually referred to in the context of the 1951 Refugee Convention as part of the international refugee regime. However, both include provisions to treat those fleeing their home country because of 'events seriously disturbing public order' as refugees. So far, this has not been used in the case of climate change, although one might imagine that a massive sudden-onset disaster – such as Hurricane Mitch in 1998 – or even desertification leading to mass migration could be the basis for national decisions to allow people to enter a receiving country in those two regions. The case would have to be made, however, most likely in the courts. It is telling, perhaps, that the regions most likely to experience massive displacement because of the impact of climate change – Asia and the Pacific – have no regional convention or instrument on refugees (and, indeed, many Asian states have not ratified the 1951 Convention).

Internal displacement

While the international refugee system applies only to those who have crossed an international border, far larger numbers of people are displaced within the borders of their own countries. These are known as internally displaced persons (IDPs). As Susan Martin has noted, 'Since internal migration is the most likely outcome for those affected by climate change and other environmental hazards, highest priority should be given to policies and programs aimed at managing these issues within the most affected countries.'[22] Thus, we turn to a brief discussion of the existing legal regime for those forcibly displaced within the borders of their own countries.

Unlike refugees, for whom there is a UN convention and a UN agency for their protection, there is no specific treaty on IDPs. Rather, individual national governments are responsible for the well-being of IDPs under the Guiding Principles on Internal Displacement,[23] which offer guidance on their protection. While the Guiding Principles do not, in themselves, comprise a binding instrument, they are compiled from existing international human rights and humanitarian law and, by analogy, refugee law. They were also affirmed by the 2005 World Summit as an 'important international framework for the protection of internally displaced persons'.[24] The Guiding Principles define internally displaced persons as

> persons or groups of persons who have been forced or obliged to flee or to leave their homes or places of habitual residence, in particular as a result of or in order to avoid the effects of armed conflict, situations of

generalised violence, violations of human rights or natural or human-made disasters, and who have not crossed an internationally recognised State border.[25]

Although they do not explicitly mention climate change, the Guiding Principles do apply to those forced to move because of 'natural or human-made' disasters, and the case could certainly be made that displacement because of the effects of climate change is a human-made disaster.

The connection between climate change and displacement is much more explicit in the African Union's Convention on the Protection and Assistance of Internally Displaced Persons in Africa, commonly known as the Kampala Convention. This was adopted at the first ever African Union Summit, held in October 2009, and constitutes the first binding regional instrument covering internal displacement. Abebe notes that the development of this convention is rooted in Africa's tradition of looking for regional solutions to migration and displacement.[26] In examining the precursors of the Kampala Convention, he notes the 2006 adoption by the African Union of a regional strategy on migration in which the link between environment and migration was acknowledged.

The Kampala Convention builds on the definition of an IDP in the Guiding Principles, but also specifically refers to those displaced by climate change, stating in Article 4: 'States Parties shall take measures to protect and assist persons who have been internally displaced due to natural or human-made disasters, including climate change.' In Article 1(K), the Convention also defines as IDPs those who are 'forced to flee as a result of events including natural or manmade disasters but also those who do so in anticipation or in order to avoid the effect of disasters'. In addition, it seeks to prevent and mitigate displacement, and provides for the establishment of national and regional mechanisms for early warning and disaster risk reduction.

Both the Guiding Principles and the Kampala Convention offer specific guidance for those displaced internally by the effects of climate change. Given the reality that most of those displaced by the effects of climate change will remain within their own countries, much more work is needed to draw the connections between these frameworks and those people who are displaced by climate change.

An additional set of guidelines – the Peninsula Principles – was developed by an international group of experts to provide guidance on climate displacement within states.[27] The Principles are intended to provide a comprehensive normative framework to uphold the rights of climate-displaced persons. They define 'climate displacement' as 'the movement of people within a State due to the effects of climate change, including sudden and slow-onset environmental events and processes, occurring either alone or in combination with other factors', and 'climate displaced persons' as 'individuals, households or communities who are facing or experiencing climate displacement'.[28]

While providing important guidance on both conceptual and practical issues, the thorny issue of definitions limits the utility of the Peninsula Principles in their present form as it is far from clear in most cases that climate change is the principal driver of movement, and 'in combination with other factors' opens the door to a very wide group of people.[29]

As an aside, it is interesting that so much attention has been devoted to the need for global instruments to deal with cross-border movements when most of those likely to be displaced will remain within their own countries. Benoît Mayer attributes this to a difference between developed and developing countries. He suggests that even though developing countries are likely to be more vulnerable to the effects of climate change – and hence to experience more displacement and mobility – most studies of environmental migration governance are carried out within Western institutions.[30] He suggests that this may be rooted in a Western concern that 'those individuals could come and "invade" "our" countries'.[31] He also notes that academic research carried out in the Global North often calls for a top-down implementation of universal standards or international treaties, while those writing in the Global South emphasise the paramount need for climate change mitigation measures that will reduce people's need to move and enable them to stay in their homes.

Both the international refugee regime and the much less institutionalised IDP regime address those who are forced or compelled to leave their homes, but the international migration regime potentially applies to many more people. Presently there are an estimated 240 million international migrants, 20 million refugees and 40 million IDPs in the world.[32] It is also a more complex and fragmented system of governance than the regime that applies to refugees.

The international migration regime

As is the case with those who are forcibly displaced from their homes because of the effects of climate change, those who migrate are likely to do so internally, within the borders of their own countries. Internal migration policies are clearly the responsibility of the state in question.

The migration system stands in sharp contrast to the international refugee regime, which has a common legal definition of the group of concern, a binding convention signed by most countries and a central UN agency that not only interprets the Convention but is also operational in providing direct support to refugees at the request of states.

In contrast, the international migration regime does not have a common definition, a comprehensive binding convention signed by most countries or a central UN agency with a mandate to protect all migrants. Rather, it has a set of bilateral and regional agreements on migration, a central migration agency that is outside the United Nations, no mandate to set norms (although it is evolving in that direction) and a plethora of international bodies, including UN agencies, that deal with various aspects of migration.

Definitions

There is no universally accepted legal definition of a migrant or an international migrant, although there are agreed definitions under International Labour Organization (ILO) conventions and recommendations for migrant worker and migrant for employment. There is also a UN definition for statistical purposes[33] and a further definition formulated by the Office of the United Nations High Commissioner for Human Rights (OHCHR).[34]

While these definitions include those who migrate for all reasons, the International Organization for Migration (IOM) has also come up with a definition of environmental migrants as

> persons or groups of persons who, for compelling reasons of sudden or progressive change in the environment that adversely affects their lives or living conditions, are obliged to leave their habitual homes, or choose to do so, either temporarily or permanently, and who move either within their country or abroad.[35]

This definition includes those moving both within and across borders and both voluntary and involuntary migrants.

Legal frameworks

All migrants are entitled to the respect, protection and full enjoyment of their human rights under the core international human rights treaties, regardless of their migration status. In addition to the nine basic human rights instruments,[36] several international legal instruments grant specific protections to migrant workers, such as the 1990 Convention on the Rights of All Migrant Workers and Members of Their Families, and relevant ILO conventions, including Convention 97 on Migration for Employment, Convention 143 on Migrant Workers and the recently adopted Convention on Domestic Workers. Moreover, migrants also enjoy rights and protection under various branches of international law, including refugee, labour, humanitarian, maritime, law of the sea, transnational criminal, criminal, nationality and consular law.

However, none of these instruments covers all of those who migrate across international borders. The 1990 Convention has only forty-eight states parties, none of which is a major migrant-receiving country. Nor do any of these legal instruments make specific provisions for those who migrate because of the effects of climate change. Migration policy is still largely determined by national political processes, and, as Susan Martin has noted, 'no major destination country has a proactive policy designed to resettle persons adversely affected by environmental hazards'.[37]

Institutions

While UNHCR is universally recognised as the international institution with a mandate for the protection and assistance of refugees, there is no single organisation recognised as playing a similar role in the migration regime. IOM, an intergovernmental body that is outside the UN, is the pre-eminent international body dealing with migrants, but it was originally conceived as a service organisation that would provide support for states, and it has no mandate to develop normative standards.[38] However, these limitations are changing as IOM's membership continues to grow (it now has 165 member states) and its global presence increases (it boasts some 8,000 staff working in 150 countries). More than any other international body working on migration, IOM has played a leadership role since 1992 in creating a forum for discussion of environmental migration, and it has published numerous working papers and books on the relationship between climate change and migration.[39]

In 2015, IOM's Governing Council adopted a Migration Governance Framework.[40] Although this framework mentions climate change and environment only in the context of trends that affect migration, it offers a promising approach for dealing with migration due to the effects of climate change in its principles and objectives. Indeed, if one were trying to come up with a global framework for dealing with migration due to the effects of climate change, this would be a promising starting point.

While IOM is the only intergovernmental organisation working exclusively on migration, many others – ILO, DESA, OHCHR, UNODC – include migration as part of their portfolio of concerns. Apart from IOM, none of these agencies has displayed particular interest in the interconnections between climate change and their specific areas of responsibility. The Global Migration Group (GMG), established to promote coordination and identify gaps in the international migration system, has not taken up the issue of environmental migration (and does not include among its eighteen members either the UN Environment Program or the Secretariat of the UNFCCC).

In addition to these UN agencies, the Special Representative of the UN Secretary-General for Migration and Development played a leadership role in establishing the Global Forum for Migration and Development (GFMD) – a voluntary, informal, non-binding and government-led process. The World Bank established the Global Knowledge Partnership in Migration and Development (KNOMAD) as a global hub of knowledge and expertise to complement the work of the GFMD and the GMG. KNOMAD brings together experts from around the world in thirteen working groups on specific issues, including one on Environmental Change and Migration which aims to strengthen scholarship on environmentally induced migration.

Other promising initiatives at the global level

Several other global initiatives are relevant to future migration governance and/or building on the work on forced displacement. The Migrants in Countries in Crisis Initiative has identified the roles and responsibilities of countries of origin in protecting and assisting their nationals abroad, and highlights promising practices in doing so, such as enhanced consular capacity, and bilateral and regional consular cooperation, particularly in emergencies.[41] While this does not focus on environmental or climate change causes of migration, it is useful as an example of a process by which guidance that is developed to respond to particular needs can contribute to the development of normative migration frameworks. Furthermore, the crises under consideration include disasters.

Similarly, the Nansen Initiative has been a state-led consultative process looking at cross-border disaster displacement. In 2012, the Norwegian and Swedish governments took the lead in launching this initiative with the intention of exploring ways to address the specific legal gap for those displaced across borders by disasters. The Nansen Initiative commissioned a number of studies, held consultations with governments and other stakeholders in all regions, engaged civil society and in late 2015 mobilised a broad consensus in support of its Agenda for Protection. This Agenda does not propose a new framework for cross-border disaster displacement, nor even a set of loose guidelines, but rather offers a set of good practices and practical tools that governments may use to respond when people are displaced across borders by disasters. The Nansen Initiative has already been successful in putting the issue of cross-border disaster displacement on the international agenda and highlighting concrete ways that governments may address these issues.[42]

A third example is the joint effort by Georgetown University, UNHCR and the UN University's Environmental and Human Security Programme to work on the issue of planned relocations.[43] Through a series of consultations, studies and expert workshops, this initiative developed a common definition of planned relocations and draft guidelines to be used by governments and others when planned relocations are necessary to protect people because of disasters and environmental change, including the effects of climate change.

These three initiatives, which use different methodologies and address different issues, all have the potential to shape future governance of climate change mobility. To varying degrees, all three have grappled with the difficult issue of defining the particular groups of concern, have engaged a range of actors, including states, international organisations, academic experts and civil society, and have focused on current practices as a basis for developing guidance for future policies and practices. All three are ongoing projects that have engaged both IOM and UNHCR in common efforts.

Policies and processes

Historically, engagement with migration at both the national and the international level has been ad hoc and fragmented. At the national level, many governments lack comprehensive migration policies. Instead, they usually focus on only one aspect of migration, such as the return of irregular migrants or advocacy on behalf of their citizens who are working in other countries. In recent years, however, there has been a move towards greater interstate cooperation on migration issues at both the regional and the global level. In addition to the global processes mentioned above, Regional Consultative Processes on Migration (RCPs) have been developed in every region, and the Regional Economic Communities and various inter-regional fora are focusing increasingly on migration-related initiatives.

In some cases, efforts to promote free movement of people within a particular region are particularly relevant for those moving between countries because of changes in the environment, including climate change. For example, the Economic Community of West African States (ECOWAS) is working to produce a regional biometric identification card to facilitate intra-regional mobility and residence rights under its Free Movement Protocol. Although it does not specifically reference environmental or climate change, this agreement will be enormously beneficial if and when people leave their countries because of the effects of environmental change, including climate change. In fact, by sidestepping the issues of whether people are forced or voluntarily choose to migrate and whether climate change is the primary cause of their movement, these measures avoid many of the dilemmas faced by other efforts to strengthen the normative framework around environmentally induced movement.

The way forward

Most discussions of the governance of migration and displacement resulting from the effects of climate change have focused on the global level – on the need either to expand the reach of existing global instruments or to develop new normative frameworks. This study reaches a different conclusion. As discussed above, efforts to include such movements in the present international refugee regime are unlikely to succeed. At the same time, governance of international migration is fragmented and uneven; while there are promising developments in the area of migration and development, it is unlikely that progress will be made in developing new global frameworks related to mobility resulting from the effects of climate change. There is presently little appetite to develop binding international treaties in any field and there are simply too many pitfalls in defining 'climate change-induced mobility' to anticipate much progress in this direction.

In order to move forward on the issue of governance, mobility and climate change, this chapter suggests areas where more research and conceptual work are needed and then outlines three areas where progress may be made to strengthen the governance of mobility resulting from climate change.

First, there is a need for further research and conceptual thought on the way in which different drivers of migration interact and the relative role of climate change in shaping individual decisions to move. Further work is needed to synthesise scientific projections of the impact of climate change on human habitats. More conceptual work by academics and policy-makers alike is needed to agree on terminology relating to climate change mobility. This should include further reflection on the tricky issue of how to situate those who move because of the effects of climate change into the broader context of population movements undertaken for other reasons. As the author has written elsewhere, 'should people displaced by the effects of climate change receive preferential treatment compared to those displaced by volcanoes or tsunamis? In comparison with those forced to leave their communities because of wars or grinding poverty?'[44] Given the difficulties in determining the role of climate change in mobility, perhaps it is time to drop the focus on the 'causes' of movement and focus instead on the specific needs of those who move. As Jane McAdam has asked, '[s]hould displacement be addressed in terms of what drives it, or rather in terms of the needs of those who move?'[45]

In addition to much-needed research and conceptual work, there are three areas that offer potential ways forward to strengthen the governance of mobility associated with the effects of climate change.

First, much more work is needed on the dynamics of internal displacement and existing and potential policies and practices. This could include further work on issues such as the relevance of the Guiding Principles on Internal Displacement,[46] analysis of best practices in responding to internal movements, ways to translate the Kampala Convention into policies at the national level and efforts to analyse how affected communities are working to reduce the risk of displacement. Given that most of those who move because of the effects of climate change will probably do so within the borders of their own countries, this should be a priority area for further research and policy development.

Second, more work is needed at the regional level. There are uneven but promising efforts to develop regional protocols for free movement of people, which might well be the most productive means to address future cross-border movements resulting from the effects of climate change. Efforts to consolidate regional understandings and practices around disaster risk reduction and climate change adaptation could serve as springboards for the development of regional guidance on people moving internally or within a region because of climate change or environmental change. It could well be that regional organisations will be able to make at least 'incremental progress' on specific issues related to climate change-induced mobility. The African Union stands out as one regional organisation that has dared to include climate change-induced mobility into a binding regional convention.

Although there are difficulties in the implementation of the Kampala Convention, it is possible to imagine eventual regional or sub-regional agreements within Africa on the cross-border movement of people because of the effects of climate change. Other regions – such as the Pacific and Latin America – may also develop regional understandings, which could constitute a movement toward enhanced regional governance of climate change-related mobility.

At the global level, rather than developing new 'top-down' treaties (which would probably never gain ratification), it would be more fruitful to focus on individual initiatives – such as the Migrants in Countries in Crisis (MICIC) Initiative, the Nansen Initiative and the work on planned relocation – which are likely to lead to more concrete and practical results on specific aspects of migration. While not as flashy as a new convention, governments are much more likely to adopt and utilise such initiatives when responding to those who move, in some measure, because of the effects of climate change. Making incremental progress in developing guidance with respect to specific groups of people might contribute in the long run to a more robust normative framework for others who migrate or are displaced because of the effects of climate change.

Notes

1 J. T. Houghton, G. J. Jenkins and J. J. Ephraums (eds), *Climate Change: The IPCC Scientific Assessment* (1990) report prepared for IPCC by Working Group I ch. 5–10; M. L. Parry, O. F. Canziani, J. P. Palutikof, P. J. van der Linden and C. E. Hanson (eds), 'Impacts, Adaptation and Vulnerability, Appendix 1: Glossary' in *Contribution of Working Group II to the Fourth Assessment Report of the Intergovernmental Panel on Climate Change* (Cambridge University Press 2007).

2 N. H. Stern, *The Economics of Climate Change: The Stern Review* (Cambridge University Press 2007); Norwegian Refugee Council, *Climate Changed: People Displaced* (2009); Christian Aid, *Human Tide: The Real Migration Crisis* (2007); R. Zetter, *Protecting Environmentally Displaced People: Developing the Capacity of Legal and Normative Frameworks* (Refugees Studies Centre, University of Oxford 2011); J. McAdam, 'Swimming against the Tide: Why a Climate Change Displacement Treaty Is Not the Answer' (2011) 23(1) *International Journal of Refugee Law* 2; UN Development Programme (UNDP), *Fighting Climate Change: Human Solidarity in a Divided World* [Human Development Report] (2007); UK Government Office for Science, *Migration and Global Environmental Change: Future Challenges and Opportunities* (2011).

3 B. Mayer, 'Environmental Migration: Prospects for a Regional Governance in the Asia-Pacific Region' (2013) 16 *Asia Pacific Journal of Environmental Law* 77, 84.

4 UN University (UNU), *Climate Change and Migration in the Pacific: Links, Attitudes and Future Scenarios in Nauru, Tuvalu and Kiribati* (2015).

5 Ibid. 2.

6 Displacement Solutions, *Peninsula Principles on Climate Displacement within States* (2013) http://displacementsolutions.org/wp-content/uploads/FINAL-Peninsula-Principles-FINAL.pdf accessed 25 October 2016.

7 R. Bronen, 'Climate-Induced Community Relocations: Creating an Adaptive Governance Framework Based in Human Rights Doctrine' (2011) 35(2) *NYU Review of Law and Social Change* 101.

8 Mayer, 'Environmental Migration' 83–84.
9 United Nations, *Convention Relating to the Status of Refugees* (adopted 28 July 1951, entered into force 22 April 1954) 189 UNTS 137.
10 J. McAdam, 'No "Climate Refugees" in New Zealand' (13 August 2014) *Brookings Planet Policy Blog* www.brookings.edu/blogs/planetpolicy/posts/2014/08/13-climate-refugees-new-zealand-mcadam accessed 25 October 2016.
11 F. Gemenne, 'One Good Reason to Speak of Climate Refugees' (2015) 49 *Forced Migration Review*.
12 UNHCR, *Planned Relocations, Disasters and Climate Change: Consolidating Good Practices and Preparing for the Future* (2014) background document for San Remo consultation.
13 UNHCR, *Summary of Deliberations on Climate Change and Displacement* (2011) www.unhcr.org/542e95f09.html accessed 25 October 2016.
14 UNHCR, *Climate Change and Disasters* www.unhcr.org/pages/49e4a5096.html accessed 25 October 2016.
15 Cited in McAdam, 'Swimming against the Tide' 6.
16 F. Biermann and I. Boas, 'Preparing for a Warmer World: Towards a Global Governance System to Protect Climate Refugees' (2010) 10(1) *Global Environmental Politics*.
17 CRIDEAU and CRDP, Faculty of Law and Economic Science, University of Limoges, *Revue Europeene de Droit de l'Environnement* (2008) 375.
18 B. Docherty and T. Giannini, 'Confronting a Rising Tide: A Proposal for a Convention on Climate Change Refugees' (2009) 33 *Harvard Environmental Law Review* 349.
19 D. Hodgkinson, T. Burton, H. Anderson and L. Young, '"The Hour When the Ship Comes In": A Convention for Persons Displaced by Climate Change' (2010) 36(1) *Monash University Law Review*.
20 African Union, *Convention Governing Specific Aspects of Refugee Problems in Africa* (1969) Article 2 www.achpr.org/instruments/refugee-convention/#1 accessed 10 January 2017.
21 Colloquium on the International Protection of Refugees in Central America, Mexico and Panama, *Cartagena Declaration on Refugees* (1984) Conclusion III.3 www.oas.org/dil/1984_Cartagena_Declaration_on_Refugees.pdf accessed 10 January 2017.
22 S. F. Martin, 'Climate Change, Migration, and Governance' (2010) 26 *Global Governance* 397, 410.
23 United Nations, *Guiding Principles on Internal Displacement* (1998).
24 UN General Assembly, *World Summit Outcome Document* (2005) para. 132.
25 UN, *Guiding Principles*.
26 A. M. Abebe, 'The Kampala Convention and Environmentally Induced Displacement in Africa' (2011) paper presented at the IOM Intersessional Workshop on Climate Change, Environmental Degradation and Migration, Geneva 2 www.iom.int/jahia/webdav/shared/shared/mainsite/microsites/IDM/workshops/climate-change-2011/SessionIII-Paper-Allehone-Mulugeta-Abebe.pdf accessed 25 October 2016.
27 Displacement Solutions, *Peninsula Principles*.
28 Ibid. Principle 2.
29 For further discussion of the Peninsula Principles, see Chapter 6, this volume.
30 Mayer, 'Environmental Migration' 88–89.
31 Ibid. 89.
32 United Nations, Department of Social and Economic Affairs (DESA), 'Population Facts: Trends in International Migration' (2015) www.un.org/en/development/desa/population/migration/publications/populationfacts/docs/MigrationPopFacts 20154.pdf accessed 25 October 2016.

33 United Nations, Department of Social and Economic Affairs (DESA), 'Recommendations on Statistics, Revision 1' (1998) http://unstats.un.org/unsd/publication/SeriesM/seriesm_58rev1e.pdf accessed 25 October 2016.

34 United Nations, Office of the High Commissioner for Human Rights (OHCHR), *Recommended Principles and Guidelines on Human Rights at International Borders* (2015).

35 International Organization for Migration, *Discussion Note: Migration and the Environment* (2007) MC/INF/288.

36 United Nations, Office of the High Commissioner for Human Rights (OHCHR), *The Core International Human Rights Instruments and Their Monitoring Bodies* (2014) www.ohchr.org/EN/ProfessionalInterest/Pages/CoreInstruments.aspx accessed 25 October 2016.

37 Martin, 'Climate Change' 410.

38 Ibid. 407.

39 International Organization for Migration, Environmental Migration Portal www.environmentalmigration.iom.int accessed 25 October 2016.

40 International Organization for Migration, *Migration Governance Framework* (2015) C/106/40.

41 Migrants in Countries in Crisis (MICIC), *Migrants in Countries in Crisis* (2016) https://micicinitiative.iom.int accessed 25 October 2016.

42 Nansen Initiative, *The Nansen Initiative: Disaster-Induced Cross-Border Displacement* (2015) www.nanseninitiative.org accessed 25 October 2016.

43 Brookings Institution, Georgetown University and UNHCR, 'Guidance on Protecting People from Disasters and Environmental Change through Planned Relocation' (2015) www.brookings.edu/research/planned-relocations-disasters-and-climate-change accessed 4 January 2017.

44 E. Ferris, *On Climate Change, Migration and Policy* (Center for Migration Studies 2015) 3 http://cmsny.org/climate-change-migration-policy accessed 25 October 2016.

45 McAdam, 'Swimming against the Tide' 14.

46 Gemenne, 'One Good Reason'; R. Cohen, 'Lessons Learned from the Development of the Guiding Principles on Internal Displacement' (2013) www.brookings.edu/research/papers/2013/10/guiding-principles-on-internal-displacement-cohen accessed 25 October 2016.

3 Critical perspective on the identification of 'environmental refugees' as a category of human rights concern

Benoît Mayer[1]

Introduction

Much has been written over the last few years on migration induced by environmental or (more specifically) climate factors, particularly with an emphasis on normative prospects. Thus, it is quite natural that the rapid development of this new literature trend has led to a certain academic hubbub. Merryman's words recounting the birth of comparative law in the 1960s resonate here: 'in a new field unsure of its identity a certain amount of conceptual and semantic chaos is unavoidable'.[2] It may nonetheless be that, beyond the inherent difficulty of disciplining academics, the phenomenon at issue here – be it referenced through notions such as 'environmental refugees', 'climate change-induced displacement' or any comparable terms – lacks the necessary conceptual consistency that its specific 'governance' would imply. In the present chapter, I question the relevance of identifying 'environmental migration' as a distinct governance issue. I conclude that it may be more relevant to address climate and environmental migration as *part of* (Forced) Migration Studies (and, possibly, within Climate Change Studies).

The great semantic heterogeneity in the literature on environmental migration reflects initial disagreements as to the object of the studies: displacement *or* migration (the latter implying perhaps less spontaneity, more permanency and perhaps more internationality), caused by any factor linked to the environment *or*, more specifically, by global environmental change (i.e. 'climate' change), forced and/or voluntary, etc. Besides, ongoing conceptual debates reflect essential questions relating to the *scope* and the *nature* of the phenomenon at issue. Thus, following the publication of alarmist reports and academic papers in the second half of the 1980s,[3] largely influenced by Malthusian theories,[4] several authors developed what was called a minimalist (or 'sceptical') critique, starting in the early 1990s.[5] The next two decades witnessed continued opposition between the maximalist and the minimalist schools.[6] On the one hand, the maximalist notion of 'environmental refugees' assumed a strict, perceivable distinction between people displaced because of environmental factors and those displaced by other (e.g. economic, social, political) causes. Myers, for instance, distinguished 'people who are driven by environmental problems outright' from 'economic migrants who are voluntary opportunists rather than refugees'.[7] On the other hand, the minimalists maintained that the distinction is not so neat, for economic factors can result from underlying environmental causes: the environmental causation of a displacement is often indirect and complex.[8]

Morrissey recently noted that 'far less literature comes out of the maximalist school, save from Myers who continues to cite enormous figures for environmental refugees without addressing the criticisms put forward by the minimalist school'.[9] Yet, if empirical research has abandoned the simplistic terms of the maximalist school, the latter remains particularly influential, not only within the media, but also within research on law and governance and advocacy materials. Thus, in recent years, several proposals have been put forward for an international treaty to be adopted for the protection of 'climate refugees' that were deeply rooted in maximalist ideas.[10] Furthermore, several leading international researchers supported the 2004 Toledo Initiative on Environmental Refugees and Ecological Restoration, which was based on maximalist concepts.[11] By contrast, relatively few authors have tried to take into account the minimalist critique in an extensive discussion on the normative aspects of environmental migration.[12]

A decade ago, Castles questioned the surprising success of the maximalist school, despite the development of the minimalist critique.[13] Certainly, the limpid simplicity of the maximalist estimations and previsions exerts a certain attraction, providing a simplistic, media-friendly and policy-relevant message that also draws on 'deep-seated fears and stereotypes of the dark-skinned, over-breeding, dangerous poor'[14] – a discourse that is more effective than the half-tone, prudent voices of the minimalists. Also contributing to the perseverance of the maximalist school, White recently identified the 'tendency for circular citations' and a form of escalation of statistic estimations based on little scientific methodology,[15] while Betts highlighted the '"common sense" assumption of an unambiguous causal relationship'.[16] Yet other sociological factors may be suggested, such as the huge geographic disconnection between the research, which almost exclusively carried out in the West, and its object, perceived as mainly occurring in the developing world.[17] In addition to geographical distance, disciplinary compartmentalisation may have impeded the diffusion of minimalist ideas from empirical to normative works.

This chapter attempts to form what Chimni called a 'critique of critique',[18] considering not only the insufficiencies of existing governance, but also the flaws and weaknesses of reform proposals. The first section looks through the 'conceptual and semantic chaos' and shows why notions such as 'environmental refugees' and 'environmental migrants' are fundamentally flawed and practically unhelpful. In turn, the second section argues that, normatively, there seems to be no justification for distinguishing between 'environmental' and 'climate' migration rather than, for instance, addressing all forms of migration.

A 'conceptual and semantic chaos': 'environmental refugees' or 'environmental migrants'?

The notion of 'climate refugees' or 'environmental refugees' has been repeatedly denounced, but I argue that this was not always for good reasons. A positivistic stance that rejects this notion as a 'legal misnomer' or the fear that 'distorting the definition … would risk reducing still further states' responsibility for, and standards of, protection and assistance for refugees'[19] discards the intended progressivity of the international refugee protection regime. The drafters of the 1951 Convention on the Status of Refugees avoided setting in stone any restrictive definition; on the contrary, they expressed the hope that the Convention would gain 'value as an example exceeding its contractual scope and that all nations [would] be guided by it in granting so far as possible to persons in their territory as refugees and who would not be covered by the terms of the Convention, the treatment for which it provides'.[20] Thus, international refugee law does not claim the *exclusive* use of the term of 'refugee' as a positivistic notion. Complementary protection does, indeed, recognise unconventional 'refugees'.[21]

More fundamentally, if one follows Bourdieu's perspective on the use of language as symbolic power,[22] the misnomer argument seems particularly conservative – a reaffirmation of a given power relation in favour of the dominant classes. On the other hand, labelling environmental migrants as 'refugees' may contribute to emancipatory strategies for their protection. If social notions may evolve, the same is true of legal ones. There is a continuum rather than a dichotomy between the 'legal' and the 'sociological' notion of 'refugee':[23] in the course of one judgement, a judge will be influenced by the meaning she/he, as a judge but also as a social individual, actually gives to a word. The 'legal misnomer' argument is based on a misunderstanding of law as an immutable set of given norms. On the contrary, Levi recalled in a classic methodological manual that 'legal rules are never clear':[24] interpretations are necessarily creative, and legal notions are constantly refined. In fact, the inherent ambiguity of any legal term is not only inevitable, but also instrumental in adapting law to social changes through constant terminological adjustments. Legal notions are, and *must be*, open to renegotiation.

Nonetheless, I believe that the real issue with the notion of 'refugee' when applied in the context of environmentally induced migration is that precisely the analogy between environmentally induced migrants and conventional refugees is impeded by the minimalist critique. Unlike the 'legal misnomer' objection, this is a conceptual rather than semantic issue – an issue that is not addressed merely by replacing 'refugee' with another substantive term (e.g. 'migrant', 'displaced person') as long as the underlying argument remains based on the analogy with conventional refugees[25] (*contra* DIDCE 2012). Without denying the environmental inducement of migration, the minimalist critique has demonstrated that the circumstances in which environmental migration occurs do not support an analogy between environmental migrants and conventional refugees.

A 'refugee' can be broadly defined as 'someone in flight, who seeks to escape conditions of personal circumstances found to be intolerable'.[26] Thus, *forcedness* is inherent in the notion of a 'refugee'. Naturally, the distinction between 'forced' and 'voluntary' migrants is always subtle, be they induced by environmental factors or by a well-founded fear of persecution. Hugo suggested that 'population mobility is probably best viewed as being arranged along a continuum ranging from totally voluntary migration, in which the choice and will of the migrants is the overwhelmingly decisive element encouraging people to move, to totally forced migration, where the migrants are faced with death if they remain in their present place of residence'.[27] Environmental circumstances are *sometimes* life-threatening, in particular in the case of natural disasters (e.g. cyclone, flood). Yet, in many cases, slow-onset environmental changes (e.g. sea-level rise, desertification) affect people's livelihoods without necessarily posing a direct threat to their lives.[28] If 'voluntary' and 'forced' environmental migrants had to be distinguished, many would fall within the 'voluntary' category, as the threshold of an immediate threat similar to that of persecution would generally not be met for all migrants induced to move by slow-onset environmental changes. Such a distinction is misleading, however, as situations triggered by slow-onset environmental change are perhaps more likely than persecution to worsen: if 'voluntary' environmental migrants are unable to move, they may well become 'forced' migrants when environmental constraints increase. On the other hand, early but limited migration may foster development and adaptation while decreasing environmental stress, thus possibly preventing further 'forced' migration.

Yet, beside *forcedness*, the concept of 'refugee' remains inherently attached to *internationality*. Whereas Cernea argued in favour of the recognition of 'internal refugees',[29] the notion was excluded from soft-law and regional instruments on the protection of internally displaced persons (IDPs). The question was arguably not semantic as much as it was conceptual: the protection of IDPs is situated within the affected states' primary responsibility to protect their citizens, whereas the protection of refugees is conceived as substituting for the protection that the state of origin fails to provide. So, here again, environmental migrants should be distinguished from refugees, and compared more closely with IDPs.[30] Substantial empirical evidence reveals that environmental migration is 'mainly internal and seldom international'.[31] Even in a 4°C+ world, Gemenne predicted, 'climate change-induced migration ... is not expected to become more international'.[32]

Furthermore, although empirical evidence shows that *some* environmental migrants are forced to leave, and *some* environmental migrants cross international borders, it does not necessarily follow that *all* environmental migrants are *forced to leave their countries* – i.e., that there are no reasonable internal flight alternatives. Regarding conventional refugees, internal flight is generally excluded because of the involvement of national authorities in the persecution (either through the conduct of the state, or as a result of its incapacity to protect individuals from non-state actors). In contrast, environmental migrants flee a region affected by environmental conditions, not the political space of a state: nothing, in principle, opposes a reasonable internal flight alternative.

Two main scenarios allow us to consider forced, international environmental migration without a reasonable internal flight alternative. On the one hand, the whole territory of a state may be affected by an environmental phenomenon, leaving no safe area. This eventuality seems limited to a few small, developing, island states, such as the Maldives, Kiribati and Tuvalu.[33] On the other hand, the demographic density of the part of the state that is unaffected may reach a threshold beyond which human dignity is not respected. This scenario may apply to Bangladesh and (in an earlier stage) to some small, developing, island states, such as the Maldives. Yet, this argument relies on the conception of a threshold of 'bearable' human density, which would arguably be contingent upon the levels of development and economic activity.

Even in these limited scenarios the analogy between environmental migrants and refugees faces one more conceptual issue, as the nature of internationality – the relationship between the state of origin and the state of destination – would be substantially different. In the international refugee regime, it may generally be assumed that the state of origin is unwilling to cooperate in the resettlement of outgoing refugees as it is often involved in their persecution.[34] In such circumstances, arguably to avoid tension with the state of origin, international refugee protection is limited to those who have already left their country,[35] excluding those who are unable to leave. By contrast, in circumstances of environmental migration, there is no ground for assuming the hostility of the state of origin. On the contrary, empirical evidence reveals that states of origin are often committed to push for the international governance of environmentally induced migration and for the protection of their outgoing nationals.[36] The difference is of significant practical importance in terms of possible governance. It is well recognised that those who do not have the necessary resources to move and who are invisible to international scrutiny may be the most vulnerable – and this applies similarly to individuals who are moved by political circumstances[37] or by environmental factors.[38] Thus, limiting the protection of environmental migrants to those already outside their country of origin would be unjustified,[39] resulting in significant differences with the protection of the refugees.

However, at the end of the day, the most fundamental impediment to any category of 'environmental refugees' may be a practical hurdle: the impracticability of such a legal category. Notions always reduce complex realities to black and white, and, as mentioned above, all legal notions have a 'grey zone'. The conventional refugee is no exception; the determination of the threshold of persecution, for instance, must be somewhat arbitrary. Yet, if the category of 'refugee' remains relatively workable, it is because persecution and risk can *generally* be assessed without insurmountable difficulties. In particular, membership of a certain group may often establish a prima facie claim for 'refugee' status. Unfortunately, though, prima facie determination seems impossible in the case of most environmental migration, except for very localised, small-scale natural disasters. Other environmental factors affect neither specific individuals nor specific groups, but only broad populations who live in specific areas. Although some individuals may be more vulnerable to environmental phenomena, their sufferings are diffuse and they affect practically every member of a society. One may argue that all migrants coming from a shortlist of overcrowded countries (or, internally, from specific regions) should be recognised as 'environmental refugees' without individual assessment, but an authorisation for anyone from specific countries to migrate could exceed the capacity of any receiving country (or region), except perhaps in the case of small, developing, island states.

Without group determination, an individual determination of 'environmental refugee' status would be impossible. Indeed, fieldwork shows that very few migrants spontaneously identify environmental factors as determining their migration strategy.[40] This surely does not mean that the environmental inducement to migration is a 'myth'.[41] Rather, it suggests that it is, in practice, extremely difficult to determine causation in an individual case. For instance, assessing that drier years induce greater numbers of Mexican migrants to the United States[42] does not necessarily mean that a border official would be able to determine those migrants who would not have travelled if there had been no drought. The effect of environmental factors must be conceived as part of a cluster of causes and, regarding international migration in particular, causation may be indirect: accelerated rural–urban migration may worsen conditions in large cities and influence rich urbanites to go abroad.[43] Replacing 'environmental refugees' with 'climate refugees' creates an additional difficulty, as the causal relation between climate change and local circumstances should then be assessed: while climate change increases the likelihood of certain phenomena, it cannot be considered as 'the cause' of an individual environmental phenomenon. The causal relation between climate change and local environmental circumstances, just like that between local environmental circumstances and individual migration, is about probabilities, not about unequivocal causation.

More than a decade ago, Black wrote, 'in a multi-dimensional world in which people's decisions to migrate (or stay) are influenced by a huge range of factors, an adequate definition [of "environmental refugee"] does not seem very likely'.[44] Only in specific cases of sudden-onset disasters affecting specific geographical areas could a status of 'environmental refugee' be determined. In all other cases, for lack of a general and enforceable definition, environmental migrants could not be granted an individual status. A working definition similar to that of IDPs could be applied to develop some non-binding guidelines,[45] but the inoperability of such a definition would significantly reduce its legal value.

Rationales for international governance: environmental migration, climate migration or simply migration?

Beyond the superficiality of the analogy-based argument and the practical difficulty of determining a status of 'environmental migrant', this section questions the possible rationales for any policy (in particular, protection policy) on environmental migration. It argues that environmental inducement should not be relevant in terms of protection, as no rationale justifies distinguishing 'environmental migrant' as a category of migrant who is *specifically* entitled to a certain form of protection.

First of all, the analogy between refugees and environmental migrants does not reveal any rationale for the protection of the former that would apply to the latter. If an analogy is to be used as an argument for the extension of a rule, the assessment of similitude between two situations must be completed by a teleological interpretation of the rule at issue. In particular, it is necessary to determine the rationale of the rule and to question the possibility of applying it to the new situation. For instance, in a classic case, an American tribunal extended the responsibility of innkeepers to a steamboat company by analogy, as it considered that the rationale for the responsibility of the innkeeper – the 'great temptation to fraud and danger of plunder' – equally applied to the officers of the steamboat with respect to its cabin passengers.[46]

The discourse on 'environmental refugees' is based on the implicit assumption that the rationale for the protection of conventional refugees is a sense of solidarity. Accordingly, the same solidarity that the refugee protection embodies with respect to refugees should justify a protection of 'environmental refugees'. Yet, this assumption of a solidarity-based rationale is not supported by further scrutiny. In another context, Hathaway identified the 'rejection of [a] comprehensive protection' by the drafters of the Refugee Convention as a challenge to such a naïve conception. Accordingly, rather than the protection of humanitarian or human rights principles, the underlying premise of refugee law is the intention of states to 'govern disruptions of regulated international migration' in accordance with their own interests.[47]

In fact, the neatly circumscribed definition of a 'refugee' has certainly been instrumental to state participation in a binding regime. In the words of Louis Henkin, 'the categories of refugees coming under the convention should … be clearly and specifically determined' and 'the definition should … be precise, so that the United Nations and the Governments concerned would know exactly to whom the benefits of the convention would be extended'.[48] Besides, the exceptional protection of refugees might have been motivated by a desire among states' representatives to confirm the rule: the general principle of a sovereign right to accept or reject migrants. These elements impede any extension of the protection of conventional refugees to further categories of (forced) migrants. At the very least, if one agrees that the international refugee regime is not motivated primarily by solidarity but by a more pragmatic understanding of state interests, the argument based on analogy is considerably weakened: the protection of environmental migrants can be justified on its own grounds only if it is in states' perceived interests.

Besides the analogy with refugees, proposals for a protection of climate or environmental migrants are based on two alternative ethical considerations. The first possible ethical ground, which is at the core of the analogy, is grounded in a principle of solidarity and distributive justice.[49] Solidarity arguments have the strength of the evidence – there is no doubt that environmental migrants, or at least some of them, are in great need of international support. Yet, one should not overestimate the influence of such arguments in international relations. In Rizki's crude words, 'there is a large gap between assertions of international solidarity in theory and their reflection in practice'.[50] States often have a limited willingness (to say the least) to help foreigners, especially when doing so touches on the control of their borders. Regarding environmentally induced migration, only limited unilateral measures, such as the temporary suspension of expulsions to a country facing a natural disaster, have yet been adopted, under the pressure that civil societies put on receiving states.[51]

The second possible ethical ground for reform proposals is rooted in concepts of corrective justice, and more specifically in the principle of a common but differentiated responsibility for climate change.[52] Yet, here again, such arguments have only limited influence on international politics. As a legal argument, they face a number of hurdles, such as the absence of compulsory jurisdiction, the necessary threshold of harm, the difficulty of proving the causation between a given 'responsible' state and a given 'injured' state, and so on. Nonetheless, responsibility-based arguments may be recycled as ethical arguments. The principle of a common but differentiated responsibility has already been raised to justify substantial adaptation funds that may soon be used in support of migration projects.[53]

Instead of assessing the influence of solidarity- and responsibility-based arguments in international relations, I would like to look at the internal coherence of these normative arguments. Yet, neither solidarity nor responsibility is sufficient to convince me of the desirability of a specific effort to address environmental or climate migration *as such*. Instead, both types of argument seem to highlight the need for international efforts to address broader issues within a larger conceptual framework, or perhaps smaller issues more specifically.

On the one hand, solidarity-based arguments raise important issues related to the needs of migrants, especially those of forced migrants. Yet, I do not see any reason why these issues would be contingent upon environmental inducement, or, in other words, why *environmental* migrants should be treated differently from other (forced) migrants. Solidarity-based arguments could justify the protection of categories such as 'survival migrants' or 'vulnerable irregular migrants'.[54] Focusing on 'environmental migrants' instead of 'vulnerable migrants' would make sense if the environmental inducement of migration were an indicator of protection need. Public policies are often based on such indicators, allowing approximate categorisations to be made when reliable information is unavailable. Famous examples in England and Wales, France and Spain used the number of windows as a convenient indicator of an individual's capacity to contribute to the public purse, for lack of better accessible information. Such indicators, while certainly imperfect, are useful if they are easy to use and reliable. Yet, precisely, environmental inducement is neither a convenient nor a reliable indicator of a migrant's protection needs. On the one hand, as was argued in the previous section, the role of environmental factors in individual migration is not always easy to perceive. On the other hand, there is no necessary correlation between environmental inducement and vulnerability.

If unjustified as a convenient indicator, conditioning the protection of (forced) migrants to environmental inducement might make sense if the protection needs of environmental migrants were qualitatively different from those of other migrants, thus calling for *specific* forms of action. Yet, this is obviously not the case, as there is no common denominator for all forms of environmental migration (e.g. temporary or permanent, individual or collective, planned or unplanned, and so on). Solidarity-based arguments may support specific norms relating to particular *forms* of migration, but here again the environmental *cause* of migration is irrelevant. For instance, I do not understand why norms on preventive resettlement of a population facing a risk should differ according to whether that risk is environmental or (directly) human-made.[55] Why should migrants fleeing the Fukushima nuclear disaster be dealt with differently from those fleeing a volcanic eruption? Why should protection be offered to those fleeing land degradation but not to those leaving disastrous living conditions caused exclusively by politico-economic conditions?

On the other hand, responsibility does not seem to be a more convincing rationale for the international governance of climate or environmental migration as such. Migration may arguably be one of the most important harms caused by climate change. Yet, questions of 'climate justice' are discussed more generally by a specific literature.[56] These authors address, in particular, the issue of imputability of harms caused by climate change, not only in the case of climate *migration*.[57]

Here again, I do not see why climate migration should be addressed separately from other climate justice issues, as – in the most frequent case of *internal* migration – there is no necessary relationship between inter-state responsibility and a state's responsibility to protect its own population. On the one hand, international responsibility is based on a horizontal relationship between states. Here, migration is only one of the 'injuries' suffered by a state; the affected state's governance of internal migration is not relevant to the determination of intergovernmental responsibility. On the other hand, the management of internal migration, despite international responsibility, is an internal matter, implying a relationship between a state and its population. Of course, international standards could apply, but I do not see why they should be influenced by international responsibility: such solidarity-based standards should apply to any similar form of migration. Overall, these standards of treatment need not be linked to the framework on responsibility, as there is no ethical ground for those responsible for climate change to determine the treatment of those affected by climate change.

The case of *international* migration is certainly different. The responsibility of a state for creating the conditions that make international migration necessary raises a host of specific questions relating, inter alia, to the nature of the harm and to the appropriate forms of reparation. (Could restitution or compensation include a duty to resettle?) But, here again, these issues are not specific *stricto sensu* to environmental migration. In fact, similar issues may be – and have been – raised in non-environment-related circumstances, for instance following the resettlement of the population of Diego Garcia to allow the development of a US military base[58] or regarding the possible resettlement of the inhabitants of Nauru following the extensive exploitation of the nation's phosphate deposits.[59] Similar issues have been raised in cases of international conflict, in particular the United States' responsibilities with respect to Iraqi refugees after the 2003 invasion.[60] Thus, even in the – very limited – case of forced international migration, it does not seem that environmental migration brings distinct normative issues.

Conclusion

In this chapter, I articulated a critical perspective on the normative discourse on 'environmental refugees' around three main ideas. First, environmental migration cannot be governed by analogy with refugees, as they are rarely forced and rarely international migrants, and are not distinct from other migrants. Second, there is no ethical justification for the protection of environmental (or climate) migrants as such: solidarity-based arguments rather argue for the protection of (forced) migrants, whereas responsibility-based arguments call for a form of 'climate justice' for all those affected by climate change.

These two arguments concur in a sceptical consideration of the normative discourse on environmental migration. One may hope that this normative literature on environmental migration will generally contribute to raising awareness of global migration challenges, in particular the lack of protection for migrants. Yet, for this critique to succeed, its advocates must be aware of the underlying challenges: 'environmental refugees' are not unfortunate migrants who have been overlooked by an otherwise fair and protective world order; rather, they are members of a large category of vulnerable migrants, induced to move by a cluster of causes, who are generally not protected under either international or national law. A warming world will certainly exacerbate existing social and political tensions, but these tensions are neither new nor specific to climate change: they should be addressed in their totality, using existing knowledge and experience. Climate change may provide the impetus to rethink global migration governance, not only for the sake of a blurred (and potentially very limited) category of environmentally induced migrants, but also to protect all other (forced) migrants.

Notes

1 Assistant Professor, Chinese University of Hong Kong Faculty of Law; http://www.benoitmayer.com.
2 J. H. Merryman, 'Comparative Law and Social Change: On the Origins, Style, Decline and Revival of the Law and Development Movement' (1977) 25 *American Journal of Comparative Law* 457.
3 E. El-Hinnawi, *Environmental Refugees* (United Nations Environment Programme 1985); J. L. Jacobson, 'Environmental Refugees: A Yardstick of Habitability' (1988) 8 *Bulletin of Science, Technology and Society* 257; N. Myers, 'Environmental Refugees in a Globally Warmed World' (1993) 43 *BioScience* 752.
4 P. L. Saunders, 'Environmental Refugees: The Origins of a Construct' in P. Scott and S. Sullivan (eds), *Political Ecology: Science, Myth and Power* (Arnold 2000).
5 R. E. Bilsborrow, 'Rural Poverty, Migration and the Environment in Developing Countries: Three Case Studies' (1992) World Bank Policy Research Working Paper No. 1017; G. Kibreab, 'Environmental Causes and Impact of Refugee Movements: A Critique of the Current Debate' (1997) 21 *Disasters* 20; R. Black, *Refugees, Environment and Development* (Longman 1998).
6 F. Gemenne, *Environmental Changes and Migration Flows: Normative Frameworks and Policy Responses* (2009) Doctorate in Political Sciences, Institut d'Etudes Politiques de Paris and the University of Liege 117; J. Morrissey, 'Environmental Change and Forced Migration: A State of the Art Review' (2009) paper prepared for the Refugee Studies Centre, Oxford Department of International Development.
7 N. Myers, 'Environmental Refugees: A Growing Phenomenon of the 21st Century' (2002) 357 *Philosophical Transactions of the Royal Society: Biological Sciences* 610.
8 R. Black *et al.*, 'Migration and Global Environmental Change' (2011) 21 *Global Environmental Change* S1–S2.
9 Morrissey, 'Environmental Change and Forced Migration' 5.
10 F. Biermann and I. Boas, 'Preparing for a Warmer World: Towards a Global Governance System to Protect Climate Refugees' (2010) 10(1) *Global Environmental Politics* 60; DIDCE, 'Draft Convention on the International Status of Environmentally Displaced Persons' in J. Bétaille and M. Prieur (eds), *Les Catastrophes Écologiques et le Droit: Échecs du Droit, Appels au Droit* (Bruylant 2012); B. Docherty and T. Giannini, 'Confronting a Rising Tide: A Proposal for a Convention on Climate Change Refugees' (2009) 33 *Harvard Environmental Law Review* 349; D. Hodgkinson, T. Burton, H. Anderson and L. Young, '"The Hour When the Ship Comes In": A Convention for Persons Displaced by Climate Change' (2010) 36(1) *Monash University Law Review*.
11 H. Wijnberg and S. M. Leiderman, *The Toledo Initiative on Environmental Refugees and Ecological Restoration* (Living Space for Environmental Refugees and Environmental Refugees & Environmental Restoration Environmental Response/4th World Project 2004).
12 B. Mayer, 'The International Legal Challenges of Climate-Induced Migration: Proposal for an International Legal Framework' (2011) 22 *Colorado Journal of International Environmental Law and Policy* 357; J. McAdam, *Climate Change, Forced Migration, and International Law* (Oxford University Press 2012) 5; G. White, *Climate Change and Migration: Security and Borders in a Warming World* (Oxford University Press 2011).

13 S. Castles, 'Environmental Change and Forced Migration: Making Sense of the Debate' (2002) UNHCR Working Paper on New Issues in Refugee Research No. 70 2.

14 B. Hartmann, 'Rethinking Climate Refugees and Climate Conflict: Rhetoric, Reality and the Politics of Policy Discourse' (2010) 22 *Journal of International Development* 238.

15 White, *Climate Change and Migration* 22.

16 A. Betts, 'Substantive Issue Linkage and the Politics of Migration' in C. Bjola and M. Kornprobst (eds), *Arguing Global Governance* (Routledge 2012) 92; C. Jakobeit and C. Methmann, '"Climate Refugees" as Dawning Catastrophe? A Critique of the Dominant Quest for Numbers' in J. Scheffran *et al.* (eds), *Climate Change, Human Security and Violent Conflict* (Springer 2012) 301.

17 B. Mayer, 'Environmental Migration in Asia and the Pacific: Could We Hang Out Sometime?' (2013) 3(1) *Asian Journal of International Law* 101.

18 B. S. Chimni, 'The Birth of a "Discipline": From Refugee to Forced Migration Studies' (2009) 22(1) *Journal of Refugee Studies* 14.

19 R. Zetter, 'The Role of Legal and Normative Frameworks for the Protection of Environmentally Displaced People' in F. Laczko and C. Aghazarm (eds), *Migration, Environment and Climate Change: Assessing the Evidence* (IOM 2009) 397; A. Guterres, *Climate Change, Natural Disasters and Human Displacement: A UNHCR Perspective* (UNHCR 2009) 9.

20 Final Act of the UN Conference of Plenipotentiaries on the Status of Refugees and Stateless Persons (1951) Recommendation E.

21 J. McAdam, *Complementary Protection in International Refugee Law* (Oxford University Press 2007).

22 P. Bourdieu, 'Sur le Pouvoir Symbolique' (1977) 32 *Annales Économies, Sociétés, Civilisations* 405.

23 A. Suhrke, 'Environmental Degradation and Population Flows' (1994) 47 *Journal of International Affairs* 482; Zetter, 'Role of Legal and Normative Frameworks' 397.

24 E. H. Levi, *An Introduction to Legal Reasoning* (University of Chicago Press 1948) 1.

25 DIDCE, 'Draft Convention'.

26 G. S. Goodwin-Gill and J. McAdam, *The Refugee in International Law* (3rd edn, Oxford University Press 2007) 15.

27 G. Hugo, 'Environmental Concerns and International Migration' (1996) 30(1) *International Migration Review* 107.

28 EACH-FOR, *Synthesis Report* (2009) 71; J. T. Locke, 'Climate Change-Induced Migration in the Pacific Region: Sudden Crisis and Long-Term Developments' (2009) 175 *The Geographical Journal* 171.

29 M. M. Cernea, 'Internal Refugee Flows and Development-Induced Population Displacement' (1990) 3(4) *Journal of Refugee Studies* 320.

30 The UN's Guiding Principles on Internal Displacement (Introduction, para. 2) and the African Union's Kampala Convention (Article 1(k)) apply to persons or groups of persons displaced by 'natural or human-made disasters'. Yet, the persons displaced by slow-onset environmental changes are not included in this definition.

31 EACH-FOR, *Synthesis Report* 72.

32 F. Gemenne, 'Climate-Induced Population Displacements in a 4°C+ World' (2011) 369 *Philosophical Transactions of the Royal Society A: Mathematical, Physical and Engineering Sciences* 188.

33 C. A. Johnson, 'Governing Climate Displacement: The Ethics and Politics of Human Resettlement' (2012) 21 *Environmental Politics* 308; A. Sherbinin *et al.*, 'Preparing for Resettlement Associated with Climate Change' (2011) 334 *Science* 456.

34 The exception concerns the case where a state is willing but unable to protect a national: e.g. *Canada (Attorney General) v. Ward* (1993) 2 S.C.R. 689.

35 United Nations, *Convention Relating to the Status of Refugees* (adopted 28 July 1951, entered into force 22 April 1954) 189 UNS 137, Article 1A(2).

36 Climate Vulnerable Forum, *Dhaka Ministerial Declaration* (2011).

37 E.g. S. C. Lubkemann, 'Involuntary Immobility: On a Theoretical Invisibility in Forced Migration Studies' (2008) 21(4) *Journal of Refugee Studies* 454.

38 E.g. UK Government Office for Science, *Foresight: Migration and Global Environmental Change: Final Project Report* (2011) 104; M. Hollifield, M. T. Fullilove and S. E. Hobfoll, 'Climate Change Refugees' in I. Weissbecker and A. Marsella (eds), *Climate Change and Human Well-Being* (Springer 2011) 135.

39 M. Wahlström, 'Chair's Summary' (2011) Nansen Conference on Climate Change and Displacement in the 21st Century, Oslo, (2011) Principle 2.

40 L. Chappell, 'Drivers of Migration in Household Surveys' (2011) Foresight Report WP4.

41 R. Black, 'Environmental Refugees: Myth or Reality?' (2001) UNHCR Working Paper on New Issues in Refugee Research No. 34.

42 S. Feng, A. B. Krueger and M. Oppenheimer, 'Linkages among Climate Change, Crop Yields and Mexico–US Cross-Border Migration' (2010) 107(32) *Proceedings of the National Academy of Sciences* 14257.

43 See, generally, UK Government Office for Science, *Foresight*.

44 Black, 'Environmental Refugees' 1414.

45 W. Kälin, *Guiding Principles on Internal Displacement: Annotations* (American Society of International Law 2008) 4.

46 *Adams v. New Jersey Steamboat Co* (1896) 151 NY 163, 45 NE 369.

47 J. C. Hathaway, 'A Reconsideration of the Underlying Premise of Refugee Law' (1990) 31 *Harvard International Law Journal* 129, 133, 144.

48 United Nations, 'Record of the Third Meeting of the Ad Hoc Committee on Statelessness and Related Problems Held on 17 January 1950 at 3pm' UN Doc. E/AC.32/SR.3 para. 40.

49 S. Byravan and S. C. Rajan, 'The Ethical Implications of Sea-Level Rise due to Climate Change' (2010) 24 *Ethics and International Affairs* 239; C. A. Johnson, 'Governing Climate Displacement: The Ethics and Politics of Human Resettlement' (2012) 21 *Environmental Politics* 308; P. Penz, 'International Ethical Responsibilities to "Climate Change Refugees"' in J. McAdam (ed), *Climate Change and Displacement: Multidisciplinary Perspectives* (Oxford University Press 2010) 155.

50 R. M. Rizki, *Report of the Independent Expert on Human Rights and International Solidarity* (UN 2010) UN Doc. A/HRC/15/32 para. 6.

51 B. Mayer, 'Fraternity, Responsibility and Sustainability: The International Legal Protection of Climate (or Environmental) Migrants at the Crossroads' (2012) 56 *Supreme Court Law Review* [Canada] 723.

52 D. Jamieson, 'Climate Change, Responsibility, and Justice' (2010) 16 *Science and Engineering Ethics* 431; Penz, 'International Ethical Responsibilities' 162.

53 United Nations, *The Cancun Agreements: Outcome of the Work of the Ad Hoc Working Group on Long-Term Cooperative Action under the Convention* (2011) FCCC/CP/2010/7/Add.1 para. 14(f); K. Warner, 'Climate Change Induced Displacement: Adaptation Policy in the Context of the UNFCCC Climate Negotiations' (2011) UNHCR Legal and Protection Policy Research Series.

54 A. Betts, 'Survival Migration: A New Protection Framework' (2010) 16 *Global Governance* 361; A. Betts, 'Towards a "Soft Law" Framework for the Protection of Vulnerable Irregular Migrants' (2010) 22 *International Journal of Refugee Law* 209.

55 Sherbinin *et al.*, 'Preparing for Resettlement'.

56 E.g. M. Grasso, *Justice in Funding Adaptation under the International Climate Change Regime* (Springer 2010); F. Soltau, *Fairness in International Climate Change Law and Policy* (Cambridge University Press 2009).

57 For further discussion of the concept of climate justice, see Chapter 4, this volume.
58 P. H. Sand, 'Diego Garcia: British–American Legal Black Hole in the Indian Ocean?' (2009) 21 *Journal of Environmental Law* 113.
59 G. M. Tabucanon and B. Opeskin, 'The Resettlement of Nauruans in Australia: An Early Case of Failed Environmental Migration' (2011) 46(3) *Journal of Pacific History* 337.
60 R. Bettis, 'The Iraqi Refugee Crisis' (2010) 19 *Transnational Law and Contemporary Problems* 261; R. Cohen, 'Iraq's Displaced: Where to Turn?' (2008) 24 *American University International Law Review* 301.

Part III

Legal and policy approaches

4 Climate justice, migration and human rights

Anja Mihr[1]

Introduction

Anthony Giddens has argued that climate change differs from any other problem that the world has faced so far, because it affects all of humanity and therefore challenges the whole spectrum of human rights.[2] The world community is currently struggling to find answers and solutions to the rapidly growing changes and violations of human rights induced through climate change. Climate justice, meanwhile, encompasses all human rights-based approaches towards adaptation and mitigation efforts and measures in the context of climate change – for example, adopting a gender-equality approach to policies that deal with the consequences of climate change. If we aim to prevent people from migrating, losing their homes and work, and not being able to access school or to participate in decision-making processes concerning climate change, a climate justice approach argues that we need to do this with a human rights lens. Through the human rights-based or – centred approach, state and non-state actors are required to safeguard the rights of the most vulnerable people and share the burdens and benefits of climate change and its resolution equitably and fairly. Moreover, climate justice acknowledges the need for equitable stewardship of the world's resources.[3]

In this context, obtaining agreement from all 193 UN member states, and identifying the duties, entitlements and responsibilities of each stakeholder involved in the climate regime, is a diplomatic challenge of its own. In 2015, the 21st Conference of the Parties to the UN Framework Convention on Climate Change (UNFCCC), held in Paris (COP21), thus had a record number of state and non-state participants that pushed for major changes and progress within the climate regime. The importance and urgency of this meeting was underlined by the presence of 150 presidents and prime ministers, in addition to other key stakeholders and non-state actors, representing the largest ever single-day gathering of heads of state. Apart from agreeing (again) on limiting global temperature increase to less than 2°C and other relevant measures, what was most significant for our understanding of the concept of climate justice was the agreement on 'loss and damage' policies adopted at

COP21. This agreement decrees that the international community will address 'loss and damage' resulting from climate change by naming actors and those responsible for implementing the required changes.

However, this chapter argues that this naming of actors will not 'involve or provide a basis for any liability or compensation', but simply identifies existing obligations and those private or public actors who are responsible for the effects that lead to climate change. Even though liability and compensation is off the table, the identification of who has been responsible for the causes of climate change is already a step ahead. The agreement on 'loss and damages' therefore helps to identify root causes and consequences and helps to 'repair' some of the damage and avoid similar consequences in the future.[4] Central to this idea is to help vulnerable countries and groups to cope with unavoidable impacts, including extreme weather events and slow-onset events, such as sea-level rise. These measures include early warning systems and risk insurance. It also helps to identify how to compensate for this damage with international and national human rights policies aimed at minimising the potential violations of basic rights, such as to adequate housing, clean water and livelihood.

In recent years, apart from COP21's far-reaching results, of similar importance for the concept of climate justice are the Sustainable Development Goals (SDGs), likewise agreed in 2015. Combating climate change and its impacts is one explicit goal among the seventeen SDGs, and directly connects the climate change debate to human rights.[5] Through this goal, stakeholders jointly aim to:

1   strengthen the resilience and adaptive capacity to climate-related hazards and natural disasters in all countries, including increasing the capacity of people to participate in decision-making processes concerning climate change;
2   integrate climate change measures into national policies, strategies and planning; and
3   improve education, awareness-raising and human and institutional capacity on climate change mitigation, adaptation, impact reduction and early warning.

Such objectives will be met only if gender equality is guaranteed, access to education is increased, and information and the right to participate, regardless of citizenship or other ethnic or religious background, are guaranteed. Human rights are therefore now clearly part of the climate change regime, and help define the concept of climate justice.[6]

Based on such recent developments, achieving climate justice will require action by all stakeholders, not least those in control of the root causes of climate change and those affected by it. And this is the particular novelty in the UN climate change regime, which endorsed the concept of climate justice as an additional notion and motivation to encourage all actors and stakeholders involved to find common and joint solutions. This has dramatically changed the way in which we govern, namely more jointly and less nationalistically: the climate regime has not been affected by renationalisation tendencies across the globe. Moreover, this regime will affect the international human rights and justice regime as it stands today within the UN, EU or AU. It therefore requires a concept of climate justice that reflects the consequences for all humanity, across many ideological, religious, ethnic, economic and physical borders.

Climate change has divided societies but also generated avenues to unify them – for example, a human rights-based approach to climate migration can support the most affected communities. But what does this mean? Climate justice is about how resources, wealth and access to a good quality of life are guaranteed under dramatically changing conditions that do not stop at borders of any kind. It endorses the human rights of people to development, freedom and a healthy and sustainable environment, and reflects the full spectrum of international human rights law.

Climate change is perceived as an environmental as well as a socio-ecological and economic threat that causes human rights violations, particularly against the poor and the marginalised.[7] In its synthesis report, the Intergovernmental Panel on Climate Change (IPCC) concluded that climate change is an unequivocal, accelerating and very likely anthropogenic phenomenon.[8] It is reinforcing the intensity and frequency of extreme weather events, including floods, storms, heatwaves, droughts and tornadoes. These, in turn, have profound consequences on human development and human rights. Women's and indigenous people's rights, along with the more general rights to life, food, health, water, adequate housing, culture and self-determination, are all affected by climate change.[9] Calling these dramatic changes a 'human tragedy in the making', UNDP has warned that allowing such a tragedy to develop would cause a systematic violation of the human rights of the world's poor and future generations and represents a step back from universal values.[10] Therefore, in this chapter, I will elaborate how a human rights-based and multi-stakeholder approach, incorporating corporate social responsibility, has emerged within the concept of climate justice.

Climate justice

Climate justice envisages international human rights standards that are governed and implemented in the most accountable, transparent and participatory way. This concept of justice aims to treat all people equally and to uphold their human rights in the face of the multiple threats that climate change may create. Climate justice aims to hold stakeholders accountable and recognises duty-bearers at various levels of society, including private, corporate, public and individual actors. Even though liabilities have not been defined thus far, the first step towards achieving climate justice is to identify the duty-bearers who carry the responsibility for the causes and impacts of climate change.

Although assessing the liability of companies or state actors is still in its infancy, this issue was high on the agenda at COP21. For example, if natural forces directly or indirectly linked to climate change result in the violation of an individual's rights, such as the loss of housing or work, or their right of access to water and food or property, then the different duty-bearers or stakeholders should be held accountable for these violations. But who are these duty-bearers? And how should they be held accountable? In order to understand the difficult debate about climate justice, it is worth looking at these questions.

One way of approaching this is to link climate justice to the concepts of intergenerational justice and the 'human right to a green future.' Intergenerational justice calls upon all of us to consume, act or behave more responsibly towards our environment in order to safeguard the basis for dignified living for future generations. Richard Hiskes argues that this concept of justice can therefore best be pursued within democratic societies, because these allow all citizens to participate and take responsibility for their own actions. Only under democratic governance can substantive and procedural human rights be protected and guaranteed for all generations, present and future.[11] Climate justice will not be achieved unless those who are most affected by climate change are allowed to participate in the debate along with those who are contributors to climate change. David Griffin has appealed to the moral obligations that humanity has towards future generations.[12] He compares the necessity to change global politics and behaviour towards climate change with the campaign to abolish slavery in the nineteenth century, regardless of its economic or other consequences. Griffin argues that our human obligations regarding global warming are implicit in our understanding of human rights as well as religious principles. For him, it is intergenerational justice that calls upon today's generation to act fast and decisively in order to save the planet for our descendants. This means we ought to transcend our narrow physical and political boundaries, and our mindsets of narrowly defined self-interest, and act globally. There is thus a moral obligation for climate protection, and Griffin suggests that with our capacity for morality we can make a difference at all levels. Consequently, he concludes that not only human rights and security issues but also climate change should be included in ongoing campaigns for global justice.

Climate justice thus refers to the causes and effects of climate change upon the individual – that is, all of us – when creating injustice and inequality through migration, poverty or the loss of territory and professional or personal development. It refers to the violations of human rights if access to justice or compensation is denied, or if duty-bearers deny freedom of speech and protest against the reckless behaviour of companies or governments that fail to protect people from climate change-induced disasters. Consequently, climate justice refers to lost livelihoods and opportunities resulting from migration or other changes to our way of life that under normal circumstances we would not have to make.

The different concepts of justice, particularly environmental justice (i.e. the right to a healthy environment) and social justice (i.e. guaranteed development for all), can help us understand the kind of injustice that climate change causes. A people-centred approach, which delivers outcomes that are fair, effective and transformative, thus serves as a tool to overcome great injustice and violations of human rights induced by climate change. Or, as Mary Robinson puts it, 'climate justice is a human-centred approach linking human rights and development. It protects the rights of the most vulnerable and aims at sharing the burdens and benefits of climate change and its resolution equitably and fairly.'[13] It is about ensuring, both collectively and individually, that we have 'the ability to prepare for, respond to and recover from climate change impacts and the policies to mitigate or adapt to them by taking account of existing and projected vulnerabilities, resources and capabilities'.[14]

The human rights-based approach

Climate justice therefore encompasses the full spectrum of human rights and its mechanisms, in the form of global, regional and domestic human rights regimes, including the UN's human rights monitoring bodies, regional structures, such as the African Union, the Organization of American States, the European Union and the Council of Europe, and national human rights institutions around the world. When founded in 1948, the international human rights law regime was meant to offer protection against autocratic states and (mainly) governments and state authorities that violate and abuse human rights. The need to protect and enhance human rights in the face of natural disasters, floods, desertification, sea-level rise or droughts was not explicitly considered at the time. Therefore, the 'perpetrators' or violators of human rights arising from climate change were not clearly named or identified. Who can and will take responsibility for human rights violations, and who can or should be held accountable for the consequences of climate change?

Appeals to morality, ethics and responsibility will not be enough. Clear facts and data, as well as causal links between climate change and disasters and economic breakdown, are already persuasive but have to be linked to human rights. Otherwise, sustainable and long-lasting decisions for future generations cannot be taken effectively. Over the past decade, the UN Office of the High Commissioner for Human Rights (OHCHR) has repeatedly emphasised the urgent need to combine the climate change and human rights regimes, and thus to identify the 'perpetrators' as well as the victims of violations of human rights. Although we know the root causes of climate change today, we do not know whom to hold legally – let alone politically – accountable. Neither do we know where to file claims against or how to prosecute or indict those who are responsible. National judicial and political accountability is insufficient in many states. Governments often view issues such as forced resettlement either as state charity or under the auspices of 'natural disasters' or 'emergencies' caused by natural forces. In other cases, international public law or private law is applied, but this is insufficient to hold accountable all those responsible for the specific losses an individual or family may face. The UN Human Rights Council has recognised this in its many resolutions on human rights and climate change. The first resolution, in 2008, states that climate change poses an immediate and far-reaching threat to individuals, families and communities around the world. It thus asked the OHCHR to prepare a study and demand immediate *joint* action (and jurisdiction) among its member states that would establish clear responsibilities for governments, as well as private companies, with respect to human rights violations.[15]

Thus, the global human rights regime, with its plethora of international human rights agreements, conventions, covenants, treaties and declarations, has had to be adapted and reconciled with the challenges posed by climate change. It has to respond to victims and violators alike. The main challenge in this is that climate change-induced violations are partly human-made and partly environmental. While the change is to a large extent human-made, humans cannot entirely alter physics, biology or the dynamics of nature. Thus, who should be held accountable? Moreover, climate change is first and foremost a cross-border issue, not a national one.

The global human rights regime elaborates norms and standards for all humans, not just for states. In this context, the first forms of human rights to be named in the context of climate change are usually economic, social and cultural, including the rights to health, to a healthy environment, to establish and raise a family, to adequate housing, to clean water and food, to property, to education and to work. Uprooted people – those who have to flee and migrate or resettle – are often deprived of some or all of these rights. They live in unfamiliar territory where they cannot exercise their skills or utilise their professional qualifications – for example, farmers who suddenly have to move to the city and cannot return to their land. Generally speaking, uprooted people are those who are forced to migrate to other regions of their own country or another country. Families are separated by force. People who move within their home countries and territories often have no access to proper housing and good living conditions, and they may be driven into poverty. The list of consequences that qualify as human rights violations is long.

If, after flooding, people have no access to clean water, food or income because their land is under water, as happens frequently in India's and Bangladesh's rural areas, governments must respond urgently. Giving these people shelter and food as an act of charity is a short-term solution and by no means a sustainable policy. Indigenous people who enjoy specific rights under international human rights law – for example, with respect to language, culture, territorial abduction and cultural heritage – can claim them if their governments violate them. But these human rights are unprotected if they are violated by natural disasters that are not clearly linked to human-made environmental change or global warming. Islanders in the Pacific, the Sami and Inuit in northern latitudes and Amazonians in South America all claim massive land losses and loss of traditional ways of life because of environmental change, and thus argue that their grounds for living, farming and culture have been violated and destroyed.[16]

Once people are forced to leave their homes as a result of flooding, submersion or erosion, the problem of accountability and legal entitlement begins. These people are often called climate refugees, environmental refugees or climate migrants in an attempt to give them some form of legal status.[17] But their legal status is far from clear. Their rights and entitlements are not (yet) clearly covered under international law, nor by international refugee law, which defines 'refugees' as persons who have a well-founded fear of persecution based on one of five enumerated grounds. Moreover, the UN definition indicates that if the situation in their homeland or territory improves and is pacified, then the refugee may return to their land, home and workplace. This condition may be impossible if people migrate due to climate change, because their land, homes and workplaces may not exist any more – unless they can manage to farm under the sea or on desert sand.

The result is that violations of these human rights generate new categories of marginalised or vulnerable groups who do not have legal status either domestically or internationally. I call them 'climate victims'. At present, we define marginalised or vulnerable groups according to their ethnic, sexual or religious backgrounds and orientations; or we define them according to their specific human rights needs, such as women, children, people with disabilities and so on. They all enjoy specific international human rights protection via conventions and agreements that are overseen by international and domestic monitoring bodies or enforcement mechanisms, such as national human rights institutions, UN human rights committees or regional bodies, such as the European Court of Human Rights. The specific challenges arising from climate change are only slowly being acknowledged by such mechanisms or procedures.

The fact that climate change victims may be found in democracies as well as conflict-torn or autocratic societies run by dictators or warlords (although climate is often a root cause of conflict) adds a new dimension to the debate about global justice. Climate change equally affects people in peaceful and democratic societies, in both developed and less developed states; for example, coastal erosion, frequent flooding or droughts and desertification have led to the resettlement of people in the US, the UK, Australia, the Czech Republic and Spain in recent years. But these societies have the advantage of established mechanisms of democratic participation and conflict resolution that allow those affected by climate change to express themselves and participate in finding solutions to their problems at the national or international level. They are also able to manage resettlement and compensation, and thus avoid large-scale uncoordinated internal migration. Such governments have introduced programmes that enable dispossessed farmers to find work in the urban labour market; or compensation for lost land and housing. Most uprooted people do not benefit from such support, however, because they live in less democratic and poorer societies. Therefore, we hear about victims of climate change in societies such as Bangladesh, Kenya, the Pacific islands and Nigeria, and not so much about those in the UK or the Czech Republic. Thus, the question may arise whether climate change adaptation and mitigation policies are less about climate justice and more about good climate governance.

From a worst-case-scenario perspective, it has been estimated that around 150–200 million people will be uprooted due to climate change by around 2040. Most of them will be from poor and/or less democratic countries in Asia and Africa, and they will amount to around 2 per cent of world's population. The consequences of this for human rights, good governance and consequently global justice will be dramatic. The UN Intergovernmental Panel on Climate Change (IPCC) reported in 2007 that global warming was rooted in human-made greenhouse gas emissions. Consequently, those responsible need to be identified and held accountable, which COP21 recognised as a key issue in climate justice. Furthermore, the IPCC has stated that global warming is affecting the basic elements of life for millions of people around the world and thus is not an issue of 'only' national interest. Effects include an increasing frequency of extreme weather events, rising sea levels, droughts, increasing water shortages and the spread of tropical and vector-born diseases.[18]

In addition, the ongoing migration has affected civil, political and economic human rights, and thus our fundamental freedoms. Uprooted people who seek refuge in other countries may lack basic citizenship rights and are often treated as asylum seekers rather than refugees, because the 1951 UN Convention on Refugees offers insufficient guidance on how to define and classify climate change-induced and forced migration. These uprooted people are deprived of participatory rights and entitlements, so they cannot participate in decision-making processes and cannot express themselves or even assemble freely because they are held in camps and denied basic citizenship rights because of their foreign status. Women and children generally suffer most, because they tend to remain in devastated areas and territories far longer than men, farming and/or protecting their households until the very last moment. For instance, in Bangladesh, women and children have remained in flooded areas until the water is literally up to their hips. They are less mobile than men because of their traditional farming and childcare duties and their relatively poor education, so they are less able to find alternative forms of income elsewhere.[19] Therefore, specific human rights for migrant workers rarely apply to them. By contrast, men usually have the flexibility to leave vulnerable rural areas and seek work in urban areas. Hence, the death rate tends to be much higher among women and children when the floods come. These examples and reactions to them illustrate that the full spectrum of human rights – social and political alike – apply to the concept of justice in the climate change regime.

Yet, climate justice differs from other individual or social justice concepts in one fundamental respect. It does not pose a new justice concept in comparison to certain ideological, religious or extremist ideas, such as neo-liberal, Marxist, Platonist or Hobbesian, but rather calls upon the general definition of justice in the context of climate change. Generally, the nature of justice is both a moral character virtue and a desirable quality of political society. It marks social regimes and how they apply justice to ethical and social decision-making for the well-being of society across generations.

Thus, climate justice – or rather good climate governance based on human rights – aims to provide an alternative to the irresponsible, if not reckless, 'environmental mismanagement regime' that governments, businesses and consumers alike have supported since the Industrial Revolution of the nineteenth century. Its concept is somewhat different in character from social or individual justice. Nevertheless, the traditional Habermasian or Rawlsian liberal concept of justice is based upon the (human) rights and duties of the individual person and their claims against duty-bearers, such as governments, companies or other individuals. It aims to resolve conflicts between individuals or between institutions and private enterprises that possess some form of legal status. The environment and climate do not yet have such legal status. Individuals, including those who represent companies or governments, can suffer or perpetrate wrongdoing. Individuals can be punished, protected or granted restitution. Individual and social justice aims to uphold that which is right and due between persons or groups. In this context, both individual and social justice concepts apply to climate justice, or vice versa; climate justice adapts elements from both individual and social justice. Adapting individual responsibility for the concept of climate justice means that a person should not be disadvantaged or punished except for intentional, reckless or negligent fault or wrongdoing, such as reckless carbon-dioxide emissions or mono-agriculture in fragile environments. Thus, companies or individuals are strictly liable and accountable for the consequences of their actions. Penalties or prison sentences are applied to governments, companies and individuals alike, with the aim of changing these actors' behaviour in the future. Adherence to fairness and equal opportunity is a principle that is often highlighted by the IPCC and other stakeholders, such as the Mary Robinson Foundation, on the premise that climate justice has to safeguard the dignity of people as the underlying/overarching principle of all human rights.

Adapting climate justice to social justice and John Rawls' theory of justice, we find the idea of a social contract among humanity that should lead to socio-economic equity and thus to fair and equal development for all. Without this equity, which encompasses all fundamental freedoms and social and economic human rights, there is no social peace and thus no justice at all. Translated to climate justice, the idea of social justice aims to reduce the potential harm and inequality that climate change might bring about for people's development. Consequently, it can be interpreted that governance regimes, which are based on 'nations' and statehood, ought to be revisited and adapted. The creation of a multitude of inter*national* organisations at both the governmental and non-governmental levels over the past two decades is a first sign that this is happening. At the same time, as observed by Beth Simmons, governments have become increasingly accountable to their own people. She links the human desire for more and better justice to the democratisation waves of the 1980s and 1990s. In return, democratisation provides institutions and procedures that not only hold governmental agencies but also corporations and individuals to account.[20] Thus, the recent moves towards climate justice based on human rights build upon the democratisation waves and the call for more 'good governance' practice of the last two decades. At the same time, social movements and networks claim that climate justice is cross-border and global in nature, and about the people who suffer. Last but not least, climate justice combines elements of individual and social justice. If we identify people's rights and entitlements, then we can also identify and define duty-bearers and their responsibilities, be they other individuals, companies or governments.

As illustrated, climate justice has strong ties to human rights due to the rising general awareness of these rights and democratisation over recent decades. But calls for climate justice have also led to more expectations of equity by people. People become aware that forced resettlement, the denial of fresh water or the erosion of their land is a human rights violation. They start protesting and claiming compensation and participatory ways of solving the problem, which are best guaranteed in democratic systems. In doing so, they often form interest or victim groups across borders, because, for instance, floods that affect Bangladesh also affect communities in India and Myanmar. They object jointly in front of the UN or other international and intergovernmental bodies, courts or organisations. This enhances their transnational visibility and thus their chance of generating reactions among the global community. A new form of international, multi-level governance is born and exercised as a result of climate change. It also enhances democratisation through active citizenship participation and demands for transparency and accountability. A side-effect of climate justice is thus the creation of new forms of governance that seek global equity and multi-level and multi-stakeholder accountability based on good governance principles.

The practical application of a climate justice approach

There are various ways to identify and include stakeholders in the global climate change and climate justice regime, not least the multi-stakeholder approach and corporate social responsibility (CSR). Corporations are important elements within the multi-stakeholder concept. They also aim to increase the level of responsibility and action of stakeholders that are directly involved in climate change, either as contributors to the change or as consumers who benefit and victims who suffer from that change. Generally speaking, the majority of the world's population are contributors, consumers and potentially victims of climate change. Therefore, we cannot accuse only one audience or group of responsibility for our lost opportunities or claim compensation from one institution or organisation for our losses. We are collectively responsible in terms of rights-holders and duty-bearers and therefore it is an issue of collective humanity, as Giddens has claimed. Thus, the multi-stakeholder approach identifies all those private, public, international, national, local and individual actors who have 'something to do' with climate change – and there are many of these, of course.

While recognising multiple stakeholders, CSR focuses more on private enterprises and their responsibilities towards customers, citizens or the environment.

The multi-stakeholder approach

Global climate change summits,[21] climate change conferences, court decisions, CSOs and action networks[22] have never received so much coverage, attention and hope for change as they do today. There is an urge and a need to find local- and multi-stakeholder-based solutions to a global threat that affects us all. One way of approaching this is to address more comprehensively the root causes of climate injustice, such as in the final agreement on 'loss and damages' reached during COP21. Which human rights are violated and why is this violation connected to climate change? Who is the duty-bearer or responsible party for this? How can we share this responsibility among the various stakeholders involved? How can good climate governance, embedded in a human rights-based legal, economic and political framework, solve this issue?

Mary Robinson, formerly the UN Secretary General's Special Envoy for Climate Change, has argued that 'climate justice is founded in legal and moral imperatives of human rights and respect for the dignity of the person, making them the indispensable foundation for action in the area of climate change induced poverty, inequality or violations'.[23] For Robinson, a safe and sustainable environment that does not hamper personal and societal development is central to people's dignity. Such an approach is novel as it links a healthy and sustainable environment with a dignified life, which can be achieved only if human rights are respected.

Supporters of climate justice therefore highlight a people-centred approach that attains fair, effective and transformative legal and political tools to face injustice and the violation of human rights.[24] Some groups are more affected than others, such as women, children and indigenous people, because they are less mobile or have particularly strong ties to a certain territory. But all people may be forced to migrate when remaining becomes untenable. Yet, their legal status remains unclear. They are neither refugees nor emigrants in the traditional definitions of those terms. The closest we can get to a definition is that they are forced migrants due to climate change. Nevertheless, they face the problem that they cannot hold anyone accountable for their losses and displacement, because there is no single duty-bearer and no binding law that would clearly link the person's poverty or miserable situation to all the different actors and factors that created global warming in the first place. Although we know who these actors are – governments, companies and all of us who move about by car or plane and consume food, electronics and clothes from around the world – existing international and domestic law does not adequately reflect all of these 'perpetrators' in a balanced and equal manner. In short, any climate change-induced migrants ought to be entitled to hold 'us' – global citizens from industrial countries who produce an average of 10 tons of carbon dioxide per person each year – accountable for their misery. A global limit of just 2 tons per person per year is required to hold the climate where it is now. Efforts to address this injustice through legal methods have failed so far. In May 2014, a landmark decision by New Zealand's Court of Appeal refused refugee status to a family from Kiribati, a Pacific island that is sinking rapidly beneath the rising sea, because the causal link between the rights-holder and the duty-bearer was not sufficiently clear to fit within the 1951 UN Refugee Convention's definition of 'refugee'.[25]

When thinking about future generations, the expectation is that human rights-based approaches can contribute to widen the notion and understanding of climate justice and trigger urgent legislative, policy and political reforms at the national and international levels. This can be achieved only in a multi-level and multi-stakeholder environment which recognises the interests of future generations, where governments, polluters and advocates all sit at the same table to draft new legal and political ways of dealing with it. Such an approach calls for various actors to react, decide and implement decisions that overcome injustice. However, the existing approach relies upon international and national governmental actors and agencies to solve problems and set up legal and political frameworks that are best suited to dealing with the challenges that climate change poses. Conversely, a multi-stakeholder approach includes businesses and corporations, politicians, civil society and interest groups comprising people who are directly affected by climate change, including climate change-induced migrants and those who have lost their assets and property.[26]

The two global regimes – the climate change regime on the one side and the human rights regime on the other – are especially difficult to reconcile. In our current justice concept, human rights violations are stakeholder-made, but climate-induced violations are of a global nature and their direct link to state responsibilities and/or obligations is not always clear or linear. Of course, climate change is also human-made, as are the violations of human rights that are directly related to it; the problem is that the duty-bearer is difficult to identify. Without a duty-bearer treaty-based regime – as in the human rights or refugee regime – it will be difficult to grant people compensation or reparations, let alone legal status.[27] Other than the rule of law, which is a legal practice and societal adherence to common rules and regulations, the reference to justice raises the fundamental questions of what justice is, in essence, and more importantly to whom and for whom it is directed. Justice is not merely an ethical or moral imperative, but rather a source of reasoning for what is considered legitimate.[28]

Two main dichotomies can be applied to the environmental debate to define the concept of justice. The first of these is between distributive justice and procedural justice. Distributive justice seeks to determine who is affected by and who benefits from climate change and who should pay for adaptation and mitigation policies. Procedural justice reflects whose voices are heard when decisions are made.[29] Current climate negotiations largely revolve around distributive justice, including core principles of equality, compensation and proportionality.[30] The second dichotomy is between intergenerational justice[31] and intragenerational justice. The former protects the rights of future generations while the latter is concerned with the rights of the current generation.[32]

Many efforts have nonetheless been undertaken under the UN umbrella in the form of the UNFCCC and frequent intergovernmental meetings that have tried to reconcile the consequences that climate change can have not only in negative terms of violating human rights but also as an opportunity to enhance human rights. The UNFCCC and the Kyoto Protocols in 1997 largely created what is known today as the 'climate change regime'. In 2010, the member states of the UNFCCC acknowledged that all climate-related actions should also respect international human rights norms. Since then, they have continued to stress the need for a more human rights-based approach to tackle climate change-affected societal problems. However, the signatory states of the UNFCCC are not yet obliged to base or benchmark their actions against human rights fulfilment. Thus, the fulfilment of human rights rests chiefly on existing agreements within the international human rights regime. Above all, this refers back to the UN High Commissioner for Human Rights in Geneva, but he himself has recognised that the multi-stakeholder approach might be the best way forward.

Climate change affects all stakeholders and causes great discrepancies and inequalities among people(s) and countries, regardless of political regime or ideology. People who lose their homes or livelihoods through climate change-induced natural disasters, such as droughts and floods, address their demands for human rights to housing, development, food and access to clean water – to name but a few – to various duty-bearers. So far, their level of compensation depends entirely on the charity and benevolence of their governments or international aid organisations. Most of these human rights claims have a social, economic or cultural basis. Uprooted or displaced people face not only material but often cultural losses, such as the destruction of religious, ancestral or heritage sites. Climate change-induced migrants, as defined by the International Organization for Migration,[33] also often suffer the loss of native languages and traditions when they are forced to adapt and survive in alien territory.

Individual governments' attempts to combat the consequences and effects of climate change on their own have proved futile. One government, state or country cannot address the challenges of climate change effectively. Thus, climate change has the potential to be a driver for positive change. It encourages people and governments – including even the most authoritarian regimes – to collaborate with others in the field – private or public, local or global – to solve collective action problems. In other words, climate change forces us to leave our cultural, legal and political comfort zones. Regional organisations, such as the European Union[34] and the African Union,[35] have responded to the challenge by calling for a more multi-stakeholder-based regime. Although they have focused on environmental issues, migration and adaptation, their efforts show governments' political willingness to promote a healthy environment that will allow people to enjoy human rights across borders.

Many of these efforts are motivated by good intentions to reconcile the consequences of climate change and a desire to meet international human rights norms and standards, in particular economic, social and cultural rights. However, at the global level climate change still induces human rights violations, such as the forced migration of refugees from Kiribati and the Marshall Islands to Australia and New Zealand. Furthermore, after natural disasters linked to climate change have occurred, millions of people remain without social and human security. They also sometimes lose a territorial base where they can claim residency, and so lose the right to participate in decision-making, along with access to adequate housing, clean water, professional development and citizenship. But here again the question remains: among the many stakeholders, who should be held accountable in the search for justice in the context of climate? One response that has come close to defining responsibilities has been that governments can only set legal and political frameworks and offer incentives, such as through taxes, to encourage all of us duty-bearers to change our behaviour, in particular our consumption habits. Consumers turn into advocates, advocates turn into human rights defenders and political actors and vice versa. That said, this means that we find ourselves in various positions during our lifetimes which make us either active or passive stakeholders in the climate change regime. We are all co-responsible for the consequences of climate change and therefore can be held accountable for it (some more than others, depending on their share of responsibility and contribution to climate change). Consequently, we all have a responsibility to contribute to the development of adaptation strategies that will allow the people who suffer most from human rights abuses to recover and resettle in a different environment.

As a result, the full spectrum of international human rights law applies to climate change-affected people and societies. Thus, one of the ways ahead to tackle it is through the concept of climate justice based on human rights in order to enhance an international rule of law culture that allows us to comply with common norms and standards to bring justice to those most in need and most affected by climate change.

Consequently, climate justice is a process that calls for various actors to react, decide and implement decisions that overcome injustice. The multi-stakeholder approach to climate change aims to overcome most of these obstacles because it includes all relevant actors within the climate game. Its goal is to solve problems and set up a legal and political framework that is best suited to deal with the challenges that climate change poses. This raises the question of who the primary and secondary stakeholders may be. Generally, states are perceived as the main duty-bearers as they have power and control over the main legislative tools to regulate and define a clear framework for climate change.

Efforts have been made under the UN umbrella in the form of the oft-cited UNFCCC and the intergovernmental meetings at the Lima and Paris Climate Change Conferences (COP20 and COP21, which took place in 2014 and 2015, respectively). In Lima and Paris, for the first time since the start of negotiations twenty years ago, a legally binding and universal agreement on climate was on the agenda. The Paris Agreement is considered a step forward, but again it lacks liabilities that would deter actions leading to more climate change. Yet, the trans-boundary effects of climate change continue to move on rapidly. States regulate through domestic legislation, but in the context of global challenges such as climate change domestic politics ought to have a transnational component and global outreach. Prior to the Lima summit, twenty-eight UN Special Rapporteurs and independent experts advising the OHCHR on special procedures at the Human Rights Council wrote an open letter to the parties to the UNFCCC. They stressed that climate change threatens to undermine the protection of human rights, and that the UNFCCC has a crucial role in effectively protecting human rights for all. They therefore urged governments to include references to human rights in the climate agreement that was expected to result from the Paris meeting the following year.[36] Specifically, they suggested that the state parties should, in all climate change-related actions, respect, protect, promote and fulfil human rights for all, as this would be a first step towards clearly defining and iden-tifying right-holders and duty-bearers in the future. Thus far, though, there has been no agreement over what should be included in 'international climate law', let alone who should accept responsibility for climate change and who is entitled to reparations or compensation. Environmental law alone cannot serve the purpose of what climate justice aims to achieve.

Another concept that has come close to climate justice based on human rights and the multi-stakeholder approach is that of John Ruggie, the former UN Special Representative of the Secretary-General on Human Rights and Transnational Corporations and Other Business Enterprises. He stated that governments have a duty to protect people against non-state abuses and that this obligation is part of the very foundation of the international human rights regime. Meanwhile, the International Bar Association stated that it is incumbent on states and international organisations to agree coherent and consistent standards to regulate corporations and multinationals within their jurisdiction as part of their efforts to mitigate and adapt to climate change.[37] Thus, the challenges that climate change poses for international law and the way people claim their rights are not new. But they can be solved.

A government's environmental agenda might vary depending on the population's primary concerns (in terms of prioritisation of policies and resources), and its policies on climate change may be amended depending on the political party that currently holds power. Furthermore, environmental, human rights and trade regulations are inconsistent and might be deemed ineffective.[38] However, it could be argued that the private sector has an immediate interest in solving climate change.[39]

It goes without saying that climate change can have a significant impact on business activity. In the agricultural sector, for instance, scarcity of water caused by extreme drought may lead to reduced food supplies. Subsequently, climate change becomes a cost factor as well as a risk factor because it affects the cost of everything in the production line.[40] Most large multinational companies have been either indifferent or hostile to advocacy on climate change. Now, though, an increasing number are pressing for action and calling for clear government signals and policy options to support mitigation.[41]

This and other issues highlight the need for a multi-stakeholder approach to solve the pending problems and answer the questions of duty-bearers and rights-holders. If governments, CSOs, business, science, NGOs and international organisations join this effort on equal terms, the answers to these questions are likely to be more holistic and, I would add, more realistic. There is an urgent need to respond to citizens' needs, in particular those who have already moved or otherwise made severe compromises in their lives due to climate change.

Taking action on climate change will likely benefit corporations by allowing them to improve their reputations and brand values, make financial savings over the long term and reduce the risk of climate change-induced economic downturns in the future.[42] Many business leaders have finally realised that they need to steer their investment decisions in a more sustainable direction in order to keep up with their more forward-thinking competitors. Indeed, it has been argued that ecological sustainability could become the main social responsibility challenge for business.[43] Meanwhile, public and governmental actors will gain more credibility and legitimacy if they start to take decisive action. And CSOs and NGOs already represent their constituencies, often victims of climate change as well as donors, and benefit from the fact that their involvement is seen as giving citizens a voice in the climate change regime.

Nevertheless, the multi-stakeholder approach will work only if all parties involved in the 'multi-round-table' debates have at least the perception that they will benefit from the joint decisions they reach and the responsibilities they accept. These responsibilities vary from stakeholder to stakeholder, depending on their level of involvement and share in the root causes or consequences of climate change.

Corporate social responsibility[44]

Within the context of climate justice and the multi-stakeholder approach, the concept of corporate social responsibility (CSR) is sometimes used to fill a governance gap in state-centric international law, which has allowed corporations to escape accountability for their human rights abuses in countries with weak governance.[45] CSR is defined as the 'responsibility of enterprises for their impacts on society',[46] a perspective that clashes with the traditional view that firms exist primarily to make profits. CSR emphasises both a company's responsibility towards its shareholders to make profits *and* its responsibility to other stakeholders to interact ethically with the surrounding community. Hence, it marks a shift from 'bottom line' to 'triple bottom line' – from 'profit' to 'people, planet and profits'.[47] Two of CSR's cornerstones are: companies have a responsibility for their impact on society and the environment and thus the climate; and they have a responsibility for the behaviour of those with whom they do business. Private enterprises' CSR activities are usually not legally enforceable; rather, they are voluntary.[48] But this may be changed through an international, legally binding framework on climate change that identifies these actors' responsibilities.

According to the UN's Guiding Principles on Business and Human Rights (the Ruggie Principles), all corporations have a responsibility to respect human rights. However, whether and how they are held accountable if they violate them depend on the national jurisdiction and enforcement mechanism of the country in which they are legally based or in which they operate. There are many expectations of private enterprises, but their compliance with the human rights to safety, security, housing, healthy environment and assembly is rarely even monitored, let alone enforced. They are expected to exercise due diligence when carrying out all of their commercial activities (see below for more details of what this entails),[49] but the obligation to respect human rights remains a legal rather a moral and ethical responsibility that is owed to society.[50]

Responsibility and due diligence

In order to avoid being perceived as complicit in adverse human rights impacts caused by climate change induced by other parties, every business should conduct appropriate human rights due diligence. Due diligence in the concept of climate justice is defined as the diligence – or rather the care – that one can reasonably expect from, and should ordinarily be exercised by, a person who seeks to satisfy a legal requirement or discharge an obligation.[51] When a company, government or CSO can argue that they have taken every reasonable precaution to avoid involvement with the abuse, they ensure some (but not necessarily full) protection against lawsuits.

Overall (not merely in the climate change regime), there is much room for improvement in the area of due diligence and human rights. But it has a contribution to make in improving our definition of the concept of climate justice. The Ruggie Principles are a good place to start and may show the path towards more concrete guidance on climate change.[52] According to these Principles, due diligence is an operational principle that business enterprises should undertake in order to identify, prevent, mitigate and account for how they address their adverse human rights impacts. It should include assessing actual and potential human rights impacts, integrating and acting upon the findings, tracking responses and communicating how impacts are addressed.[53] Hence, in order to apply CSR in the context of climate change, every corporation should have in place measures to prevent or mitigate adverse climate change impacts linked to its operations. Such measures should include the due diligence process in both the company's and its affiliates' practices.

Further relevant international guidance frameworks include the OECD's Guidelines for Companies, inspired by the Ruggie Principles, which also call on multinational corporations to respect human rights and carry out due diligence.[54] The process is ongoing, in recognition of the fact that human rights risks may change over time as an enterprise's operations and operating context evolve. As in Ruggie's Guiding Principles, once enterprises have acknowledged that they have caused or contributed to an adverse impact, the OECD's Guidelines recommend remedying this through operational-level grievance mechanisms.[55] Although companies are not expected to solve all of the world's problems, their responsibilities in countries where human rights are violated will largely depend on their intentions, awareness of the situation and proximity to the misdeed. And at the end of the chain, once again, it is us – the consumers and clients – who will decide what and when to consume from companies that are known for their human rights violations or reckless behaviour when it comes to carbon emissions. Ideally, they should be aware of every local human rights issue and understand that there are bigger risks of human rights violations in conflict areas and fragile states.[56] It should come as no surprise that those companies, factories and enterprises that are most responsible for high carbon emissions and thus climate change operate in countries with a weak or no independent judiciary. There is a correlation between the industrial countries that today have the highest greenhouse gas emissions and/or consumption per capita and those with the most people at risk, such as China, India, the US and Russia. However, the distribution of emissions and people at risk is not equal across the world; for example, carbon-dioxide emissions have the most serious effect on East Asian and sub-Saharan African countries and put their citizens at high levels of risk.[57] Corruption should also be taken into account, as state actors may protect companies with high emission rates and justify their actions on the basis that industrial development is of paramount importance, regardless of the costs, up to and including human right violations.[58]

In one of his reports, John Knox, Independent Expert to the UN Human Rights Council on the issue of human rights obligations relating to the enjoyment of a safe, clean, healthy and sustainable environment, asserts that the private sector has a responsibility to apply the 'Protect, Respect and Remedy' framework set out in the Guiding Principles.[59] He states that business enterprises should carry out thorough human rights due diligence, as described above.[60] Moreover, when assessing their violations of the rights to life, food, health, water and adequate housing, he says that companies must consult properly with the affected communities.[61]

Human rights due diligence can be implemented via a company's risk-management systems, providing that it is an inclusive process whose scope extends to other rights-holders.[62] It is important to consider commercial transactions, such as mergers and acquisitions, in which human rights risks may be inherited through contracts and agreements.[63] Due diligence should be applied not only to the company itself but to its affiliates, main contractors and suppliers.[64] The Ruggie Principles recognise that, especially for businesses with a large number of entities in their value chain, conducting due diligence for adverse human rights impacts may be an extremely complex process. Hence, they suggest that such businesses should identify the general areas where human rights impact is most significant and prioritise whichever suppliers or clients are involved in those sectors.[65]

Both CSR and the multi-stakeholder approach allow for more proper consultation with affected and vulnerable communities, which lies at the heart of human rights due diligence and allows public and private actors, such as municipalities and companies, to improve their assessment of potential and actual human rights violations and, ultimately, remedy them. As has been mentioned, climate justice is a people-centred approach that aims to deliver fair, effective and transformative outcomes. Such results rely on adoption of the bottom-up approach. The idea is that a mix of stakeholders will result in a pooling of expertise so that any problem will be addressed effectively and the best possible solution will be reached. The bottom-up approach can be seen as the first step in the human rights due diligence process, and it should inform every subsequent step.[66]

The OECD's Guidelines also contain a section on the environment, in which they advise enterprises to pay appropriate attention to environmental issues in order to achieve the ultimate goal of sustainable development. Section VI, part 2(b) advocates adequate, timely communication and consultation with any community that is directly affected by the enterprise's environmental, health and safety policies and their implementation.[67]

Conclusion: ways ahead

Executing a climate justice approach entails more than governments and corporations being held accountable and changing their behaviour. The

International Bar Association has recommended that private enterprises should adopt and promote the UN's Guiding Principles as they pertain to human rights and climate change, particularly taking into account the due diligence process.[68] In addition, states must clarify regulatory mechanisms relating to climate change, including extra-territorial violations, and demand increased transparency from corporations in the form of more detailed reporting of greenhouse gas emissions. The recently published technical specifications on carbon footprint measurement should help with this. Third, international governmental organisations, such as the UN, WTO, EU, AU and OECD, should support these initiatives by increasing their external monitoring of corporations and endorsing those corporations that take the most proactive measures. Fourth, sector-specific initiatives promoting human rights – and especially environmental rights – as seen in the banking and financial sector, should be encouraged.[69] Finally, civil society should be involved in the formal process, particularly in the monitoring of corporations and naming and shaming any non-compliant corporations. This could be achieved by encouraging them to lobby multinational organisations.

Climate justice is a concept of justice that incorporates principles such as the right to recognition and genuine participation for all relevant actors, including marginalised groups. Therefore, private and public actors should have open communication with affected communities by investing in green technologies for those communities affected by climate change (open patent technology) and so on. Much has been said on fast-mitigation projects that focus on reducing greenhouse gas emissions, rather than investing in local technology capacities in developing countries, similar to the UNFCCC's Clean Development Mechanism.[70] Within the UNFCCC, the Green Climate Fund receives its finances from developed country parties to the Convention, but it can also receive inputs from other public or private sources.[71] Contributions from non-public sources are accepted by the Secretariat after a due diligence review is undertaken in accordance with the Board's approved policies and procedures.[72] In addition to the Green Climate Fund, more and more initiatives – such as AdMit, an initiative of the International Institute for Environment and Development – are being launched with similar aims.[73]

Finally, climate justice in the context of migration and human rights is a way to conceptualise path dependencies assessing what climate change-affected migrants and other communities undergo in terms of human rights. The climate change and human rights regimes are closely linked to each other, although the latter is treaty based and can hold stakeholders and 'perpetrators' to account. Therefore, both depend strongly on each other in the context of climate justice. The UN is thus by far the largest umbrella organisation that fosters this approach, as it recognises the importance of global versus national solutions to address climate change in a human rights-based manner.

Notes

1 Many thanks for the thorough investigative research and support from Charlotte Divin and Marcella Mizzi at The Hague Institute for Global Justice.
2 A. Giddens, *The Politics of Climate Change* (John Wiley & Sons 2009).
3 Mary Robinson Foundation – Climate Justice, 'Rights for Action' (2014).
4 Center for Climate and Energy Solution, 'Outcomes of the UN Climate Change Conference in Paris' (2015).
5 United Nations, 'Goal 13: Take Urgent Action to Combat Climate Change and Its Impacts' (2016) www.un.org/sustainabledevelopment/climate-change-2/ accessed 27 September 2016.
6 Mary Robinson Foundation – Climate Justice, 'Zero Carbon, Zero Poverty the Climate Justice Way' (2014).
7 E. Cameron, T. Shine and W. Bevins, 'Climate Justice: Equity and Justice Informing a New Climate Agreement' (World Resources Institute and Mary Robinson Foundation – Climate Justice 2013) 2.
8 Intergovernmental Panel on Climate Change (IPCC), *Climate Change 2014: Synthesis Report* (Intergovernmental Panel on Climate Change 2014).
9 Cameron *et al.*, 'Climate Justice' 3–6.
10 UN Development Programme (UNDP), *Fighting Climate Change: Human Solidarity in a Divided World* [Human Development Report] (2007) 4.
11 R. P. Hiskes, *The Human Right to a Green Future: Environmental Rights and Intergenerational Justice* (Cambridge University Press 2008) 143.
12 D. R. Griffin, *Unprecedented: Can Civilization Survive the CO_2 Crisis?* (Clarity Press 2015) ch. 14.
13 Mary Robinson Foundation – Climate Justice, 'Principles of Climate Justice' (2015) 1.
14 I. Preston *et al.*, 'Climate Change and Social Justice: An Evidence Review' (Joseph Rowntree Foundation – Centre for Sustainable Energy 2014).
15 M. Wewerinke, 'The Role of the UN Human Rights Council in Addressing Climate Change' (2014) 8(1) *Human Rights and International Legal Discourse* 10.
16 C. Heyward, 'Climate Change as Cultural Injustice' in T. Brooks (ed), *New Waves in Global Justice* (Palgrave Macmillan 2014).
17 For a discussion of the various terminologies, see Chapter 3, this volume.
18 United Nations, Office of the High Commissioner for Human Rights (OHCHR), 'Human Rights and Climate Change' (2016) www.ohchr.org/EN/Issues/HRAnd ClimateChange/Pages/HRClimateChangeIndex.aspx accessed 27 September 2016.
19 R. W. Yavinsky, 'Women More Vulnerable than Men to Climate Change' (Population Reference Bureau 2012).
20 B. A. Simmons, *Mobilizing for Human Rights: International Law in Domestic Politics* (Cambridge University Press 2009) 24–25.
21 United Nations, 'UN Climate Summit 2014' (2014) www.un.org/climatechange/ summit/ accessed 27 September 2016.
22 J. Silva, 'Purposes of Trust in Trust Law' (2016) www.climate-justice-now.org/ purposes-of-trust-in-trust-law/ accessed 11 January 2017.
23 Mary Robinson Foundation – Climate Justice, 'Home' (2016) www.mrfcj.org accessed 27 September 2016.
24 S. Kartha and P. Baer, 'Zero Carbon Zero Poverty, the Climate Justice Way: Achieving an Equitable Phase-Out of Carbon Emissions by 2050 while Protecting Human Rights' (Mary Robinson Foundation – Climate Justice 2014) www.mrfcj. org/wp-content/uploads/2015/02/MRFCJ-Zero-Zero-short-doc-v3.pdf accessed 20 October 2016.
25 M. Godfery, 'New Zealand Refuses Climate Change Refugees: Mass Action Is Now Needed' (5 December 2014) *Guardian* www.theguardian.com/commentisfree/

2014/may/12/new-zealand-refuses-climate-change-refugees-mass-action-is-now-needed accessed 27 March 2016.

26 Mary Robinson Foundation – Climate Justice, 'Human Rights and Climate Justice' (2014).
27 See, for example, *Teitiota v. Chief Executive of the Ministry of Business Innovation and Employment* (2014) NZCA 173, NZAR 688.
28 T. Forsyth, 'Climate Justice Is Not Just Ice' (2014) 54 *Geoforum* 230.
29 Preston *et al.*, 'Climate Change and Social Justice'.
30 R. Hardin, 'From Bodo Ethics to Distributive Justice' (1999) 2 *Ethical Theory and Moral Practice* 399.
31 As the UN Secretary-General pointed out in his Report on Intergenerational Solidarity and the Needs of Future Generations, '[f]uture generations are politically powerless, with the representation of their interests limited to the vicarious concern of present generations'. As such, climate justice by necessity incorporates intergenerational equity as a consideration in mitigating the effects of climate change not just on the living but on generations yet unborn.
32 Forsyth, 'Climate Justice'.
33 International Organization for Migration (IOM), 'Migration and Climate Change' (2015) www.iom.int/migration-and-climate-change-0 accessed 27 September 2016.
34 European Commission, 'European Climate Change Programme' (2016).
35 ClimDev-Africa, 'Home Page' (2013) www.climdev-africa.org accessed 27 September 2016.
36 M. Robinson, 'Climate Justice: Human Rights Informing Climate Action – Development that Also Grows Those at Risk and Those in Poverty' (10 December 2014) *Stakeholder Forum* www.stakeholderforum.org/fileadmin/files/OUTREACH COP20DAY8.pdf accessed 12 January 2017.
37 International Bar Association (IBA), 'Achieving Justice and Human Rights in an Era of Climate Disruption' (2014) Climate Change Justice and Human Rights Task Force Report 147.
38 Ibid.
39 J. Bacchus, 'What Does Climate Change Mean for Business?' (World Economic Forum 2014) 2.
40 ICIMOD Foundation, 'Help Save the Third Pole' (2016) www.icimod.org/?q= 3491 accessed 27 September 2016.
41 UN Development Programme (UNDP), *Work for Human Development* (2015) Human Development Report 160.
42 Practical Action, 'Corporate Social Responsibility and Our Changing Climate' (2014) http://practicalaction.org/climate-change-3 accessed 27 September 2016.
43 M. Orlitzky, D. S. Siegel and D. A. Waldman, 'Strategic Corporate Social Responsibility and Environmental Sustainability' (2011) 50 *Business and Society* 6, 7.
44 The author is grateful for the research assistance of Marcella Mizzi (The Hague Institute for Global Justice) in this section.
45 R. McCorquodale, 'Corporate Social Responsibility and International Human Rights Law' (2009) 87 *Journal of Business Ethics* 385, 391.
46 European Commission, 'Communication from the Commission to the European Parliament, the Council, the European Economic and Social Committee and the Committee of the Regions: A Renewed EU Strategy 2011–14 for Corporate Social Responsibility' (2011) COM (2011) 681 final.
47 D. McBarnet, 'Corporate Social Responsibility beyond Law, through Law, for Law: The New Corporate Accountability' in A. Voiculescu, T. Campbell and D. McBarnet (eds), *The New Corporate Accountability: Corporate Social Responsibility and the Law* (Cambridge University Press 2009).
48 J. G. Frynas, 'Corporate Social Responsibility or Government Regulation? Evidence on Oil Spill Prevention' (2012) 17 *Ecology and Society* 2.

49 United Nations, Office of the High Commissioner for Human Rights (OHCHR), *UN Guiding Principles on Business and Human Rights* (2011) ch. 2.
50 J. Ruggie, *Just Business: Multinational Corporations and Human Rights* (W. W. Norton & Company 2013) 91–94, 112–116.
51 OHCHR, *UN Guiding Principles* para. 25.
52 The Ruggie Principles embody the bottom-up approach in paragraph 18, where it is stated that in order to gauge human rights risks, business enterprises should identify and assess any actual or potential adverse human rights impacts with which they may be involved either through their own activities or as a result of their business relationships. The latter process should, inter alia, involve meaningful consultation with potentially affected groups and other relevant stakeholders, as appropriate to the size of the business enterprise and the nature and context of the operation. The involvement of the affected stakeholders through consultation is vital to enable companies to assess their human rights impacts.
53 OHCHR, *UN Guiding Principles* II.
54 OECD, 'OECD Guidelines for Multinational Enterprises' (2011) Guideline IV http://dx.doi.org/10.1787/9789264115415-en accessed 27 September 2016.
55 Ibid. 45, 46.
56 A. Sitkin and N. Bowen, *International Business: Challenges and Choices* (Oxford University Press 2013) 194.
57 Kiln, 'The Carbon Map' (2013) www.carbonmap.org/#Extraction accessed 27 September 2016.
58 Sitkin and Bowen, *International Business* 194.
59 J. H. Knox, 'Report of the Independent Expert on the Issue of Human Rights Obligations Relating to the Enjoyment of a Safe, Clean, Healthy and Sustainable Environment' (General Assembly of the United Nations 2012) A/HRC/22/43.
60 OHCHR, *UN Guiding Principles* II, 17.
61 Ibid.
62 Ibid.
63 Ibid.
64 IBA, 'Achieving Justice' 148.
65 OHCHR, *UN Guiding Principles* II, 17.
66 Ibid.
67 OECD, 'OECD Guidelines' Guideline IV, 2(b).
68 To this end, Hoffmann, together with the Pew Center on Global Climate Change, drafted a highly practical and comprehensive report (a how-to manual) for companies interested in developing effective climate strategies: Andrew Hoffmann, *Getting Ahead of the Curve: Corporate Strategies that Address Climate Change* (Pew Center on Global Climate Change 2006) www.c2es.org/publications/getting-ahead-curve-corporate-strategies-address-climate-change accessed 11 January 2017.
69 IBA, 'Achieving Justice' 148.
70 Forsyth, 'Climate Justice' quoting E. Boyd, H. Osbahr, P. J. Ericksen, E. L. Tompkins, M. C. Lemos and F. Miller, 'Resilience and "Climatizing" Development: Examples and Policy Implications' (2008) 51 *Development* 390–396.
71 United Nations, *The Cancun Agreements: Outcome of the Work of the Ad Hoc Working Group on Long-Term Cooperative Action under the Convention* (2011) FCCC/CP/2010/7/Add.1.
72 Green Climate Fund, 'Home Page' (2016) www.greenclimate.fund/home accessed 27 September 2016.
73 International Institute for Environment and Development (IIED), 'AdMit' (2016) www.iied.org/admit#about accessed 27 September 2016.

5 Transitional law in the climate change context

Teresa Thorp[1]

Introduction

Transitional legal frameworks have been widely applied to redress the legacies of human rights abuses. Crimes against humanity, for instance, marked the genesis for countries to implement transparent judicial, quasi-judicial or non-judicial measures with a view to moving from violent instability to living in peace under a stable rule of law. In this sense, tribunals, truth commissions and hybrid frameworks of domestic and international composition have exemplified political choices made by states to redress human rights violations committed by former governments and non-state actors.

The desire to redress historical responsibility and promote possibilities for climate justice has also gained momentum under climate change and migration talks. Notwithstanding this, commentators, jurists and climate change negotiators alike have given little attention to transitionary legal frameworks. A new wave of transitional legal justice to protect the individual and collective rights of current and future generations in the climate change context may, however, at least partially remedy existing and potential harms while advancing solidarity.

This chapter attempts to explore these issues. The first half provides a springboard for assessing the potential for transitional legal frameworks in the climate change context. It lays out what have become well-known positions in the climate change–migration debate and assesses them in a succinct and direct manner. In the second half, the chapter moves beyond discussions about forced migration and adaptation in the climate change context and may add something new to the various accomplishments of others.

In contradistinction to previous work, the chapter presents a broader framework in terms of climate change and human security. It fleshes out how 'transitional justice' and 'transitional law' could contribute to a progressive normative architecture for *climigration*. And it concludes that a hybrid composition for addressing climate change is not necessarily flawed due to multi-causality but may work successfully only if there is active international support and a genuine will to facilitate the protection of present and future generations in a unified and universal way.

In terms of terminology, 'legal transition' refers to moving from one legal condition to another; 'normative plurality' infers bringing a multitude of legal norms and systems into the frame and governing them in a collective and ubiquitous way.

Overview of *climigration* and legal frameworks

The contemporary literatures on climate change and migration seem to contribute a common set of conclusions. Climate-induced migration *en masse*, or failure to respond to a climate-related disaster, could signal a failed international legal system. In turn, a failed international legal system may indicate a failure to protect human dignity. To avoid failure, legal architecture ought to evolve by responding to climate-induced migration. But how should such legal architecture evolve?

It is obviously impossible to address all of the topics that arise from this interesting question. Nevertheless, some of them will be touched upon here in an attempt to frame a general overview. Amongst the various ideas proposed, and the various routes travelled, one thing is clear: potential modalities by which to evolve international legal architecture at the climate change–migration nexus are not without controversy.

Extending the interpretative scope of the 1951 Geneva Refugee Convention is politically sensitive.[2] According to the United Nations Refugee Agency, an extension of existing obligations may 'place a potentially unbearable strain on current standards and practices'.[3] An approach of this nature may not be desirable anyhow.[4] On the one hand, the term 'refugee' remains subject to academic debate. On the other, resources may simply not cope with a controversy that seeps across the global commons.

On the subject of definition, refugee status is triggered by the Geneva Refugee Convention of 1951 due to persecution, or 'a well-founded fear of being persecuted', on the grounds of race, religion, nationality, membership of a particular social group or political opinion, subject to certain temporal and geographic restrictions.[5] Irrespective of having grounds to question the applicability of 'persecution' (or a well-founded fear thereof) to 'climate-induced' displacement, the 'Convention shall not apply to persons who are at present receiving from organs or agencies of the United Nations other than the United Nations High Commissioner for Refugees protection or assistance'.[6] In practice, several UN organs and agencies already assist existing and potential victims of climate-induced displacement. (The chapter gives examples later.)

Interpretative arguments may also stem from whether refugee status is triggered only when people cross a border. Commentators often make arguments for ex post proviso tests. What should we do with people once they arrive on our shores?

Ex ante interests are equally – some might say more – important. Roughly speaking, what should we do before they depart? Answers to this latter question may entail a pre-emptive response, a pre-emptive self-defence or a pre-emptive anticipatory defence action.

Thus, right from the beginning, there is a sort of continuum. A progression from ex ante to ex post responses to climate-related disaster arises. For the purposes of this chapter, rather than try to disaggregate the transitions from a mono-causal perspective, the task is to assess whether there is any role for the law to help charter progressive responses to them.

Review of the climate change–migration debate usually starts ex post. What happened after disaster struck? We could have done better with hindsight. Yet, hindsight is only a positive stimulant to foresight. Pre-emption may therefore provide a useful starting point for a more thorough investigation.

Notwithstanding the difficulties of distinguishing one pre-emptive right from another, the parties may still lift restrictions on temporal and geographical specificity. This idea is not new and at first sight it is not so objectionable. In recognition of the 1951 Geneva Refugee Convention restricting its application to refugees resulting from events occurring before 1 January 1951, the 1967 Protocol on the Status of Refugees redefined the term 'refugee'. Three main requirements now trigger refugee status.[7] First, the person must be outside his or her country of origin, and unable or unwilling to return to that country of origin or to avail himself or herself of its protection. Second, once it is established that the person is 'outside' his or her country of origin, the reason for being 'outside' has to be due to past, present or future persecution, or 'a well-founded fear of being persecuted'. Third, the risk of persecution must be on the grounds of race, religion, nationality, membership of a particular social group or political opinion.

Barriers remain, and hands on both sides of the border have erected them. Not least of these hurdles is that refugee status is triggered only if a person crosses a border. Yet, many so-called climigration victims do not actually want to cross a border. Pre-emption is chief amongst their concerns.

'Persecution' also has its own particular meaning in general international law. The Rome Statute of the International Criminal Court recognises persecution as a crime against humanity,[8] whereas, for the present discussion, 'persecution' means the 'intentional and severe deprivation of fundamental rights contrary to international law by reason of the identity of the group or collectivity'.[9]

In *Prosecutor v Simic*, the Trial Chamber considered the crime of persecution in two parts. First, the *actus reus*: there is discrimination in fact, which denies or infringes upon a fundamental right laid down in international customary law or treaty law. Second, the *mens rea*: the act (or deliberate inaction) was carried out with the express intention to discriminate on one of the listed grounds, specifically race, religion or politics.[10]

However, when it comes to climate change, a certain degree of vagueness hovers around stretching the meaning of 'persecution' beyond the original definition. Commentators may, for example, still try to redefine 'climate refugee' by suggesting an international climate crime could equate to persecution. Inaction may even inflame a broader discussion about climate genocide.[11] While there is little doubt that the very threat of severe flooding or desertification may invoke serious mental harm on members of the affected group. In the context of this chapter, however, other pertinent questions arise. What is deprivation in the climate context? What are fundamental rights? And what about other crimes? Are they relevant too?[12]

Even if the answers to these questions have a certain degree of validity, the actual persecutor remains unclear. It would, for example, be difficult, if not implausible, to argue that governments of small developing island states are responsible for global warming. More often than not, people feel that the core and substance of the problem is that industrial countries are at fault, or that those with larger territorial responsibilities are accountable, or even that historical responsibility to historically unimaginable populations puts stress on the environment. The legal validity of such claims is questionable.

Most developing countries have benefited from international assistance. The construction of infrastructure, roads and public services, for example, would have been virtually impossible without industrial processes. Many people are arguably far better off than they would have been if states had not displayed a common concern of humankind.

Reasons other than climate change may account for poor states or failed states. Corruption, penurious governance, class divides, systemic organisational failings and the lack of national motivation to support local communities may all have a bearing on trade, development and economic human rights. Economic interests and individualism may play larger roles than the weather in persuading people to flee a country.

What is clear, though, is that once a person becomes a refugee, the Refugee Convention prevents that person's forcible return (*refoulement*) to a country of persecution.[13] Once a refugee has crossed a border, and is within a state, state practice is that he or she may have recourse to that state's legal system. If the rationale for return to the home state were civil strife, political instability, a crime against humanity or the migrant falls into one of the accepted categories of refugee, then return to the persecuting home state would be inconsistent with accepted state practice.

Why then, when it comes to distinguishing a climate crime – which allegedly induces civil strife, political instability or a crime against all citizens of a particular country – from other crimes, are the hurdles legendary? A decision made by New Zealand's Refugee Status Appeals Authority sheds some light on the issue. In 2000, the Authority found:

> Clearly, none of the fears articulated by the appellants vis-à-vis their return to Tuvalu, can be said to be for reason of any one of the five Convention grounds in terms of the Refugee Convention, namely race, religion, nationality, membership of a particular group and political opinion ... All Tuvalu citizens face the same environmental problems

and economic difficulties living in Tuvalu. Rather, the appellants are unfortunate victims, like all other Tuvaluan citizens, of the forces of nature leading to the erosion of coastland and the family property being partially submerged at high tide. As for the shortage of drinkable water and lack of hygienic sewerage systems, medicines and appropriate access to medical facilities, these are also deficiencies in the social services of Tuvalu that apply indiscriminately to all citizens of Tuvalu and cannot be said to be forms of harm directed at the appellants for reason of their civil or political status.[14]

When referring to the 'forces of nature', the New Zealand decision does not explicitly refute the notion that third-party actions may contribute to climate harm. However, the decision highlights how legal decision-making may omit transitionary analysis when assessing problems that seep across the global commons. Deforestation, loss of species and pollution associated with private-sector prospecting, mining and drilling activities in the Pacific, and elsewhere, may trigger slow-onset self-harm. Such investments may be incentivised internally, motivated politically or exist in the absence of free, prior and informed consent. Other considerations may therefore hold true, especially regarding appropriate remedies for loss and damage.

Even if commentators were to see an emerging viability of persecution at the national level on the grounds of climate-induced harm, the strict textual interpretation is that persecution has to be on the grounds of race, religion, nationality, membership of a particular social group or political opinion. Persuading those with conferred powers, such as judges, that climate harm falls into one of these categories is unlikely to be easy.

Redress at the regional level may prove more promising. The African Union's 2009 Convention for the Protection and Assistance of Internally Displaced Persons in Africa (hereinafter the 'Kampala Convention') formally recognises that displacement triggers criteria other than the conventional five identified by the 1951 Geneva Refugee Convention and the 1967 Protocol on the Status of Refugees. Like the UN's Guiding Principles on Internal Displacement of 1998, the Kampala Convention recognises displacement resulting from natural or human-made disasters. It also extends obligations on the parties in a far broader way: 'States Parties shall take measures to protect and assist persons who have been internally displaced due to natural or human made disasters, including climate change.'[15] The state parties are obligated to 'devise early warning systems' and 'establish and implement disaster risk reduction strategies'.[16]

At the international level, however, there appear to be few new solutions to a very sticky global commons problem. Constitutional reform within and across existing governmental and non-governmental organisational structures is one option. However, few organisational leaders are likely to want to cede their authority entirely to a hybrid national, regional and international framework.

In reference to defining the term 'refugee', 'for the purposes of the 1951 Geneva Refugee Convention, the term "refugee" shall apply to any person who has been considered a refugee under the Constitution of the International Refugee Organization'.[17] It therefore makes sense to look not only at the Refugee Convention but also at the Constitution of the International Refugee Organization. Under scrutiny, the mandate of the Constitution of the International Refugee Organization extends to refugees and displaced persons in accordance with the principles, definitions and conditions set forth in Annex I, which forms an integral part of the Constitution.[18] There is provision for amendment,[19] but here again, a codified amendment hinges as much on the will of the parties as to whether they wish to interpret, adjust or mobilise the constitution to encompass so-called 'climate refugees' or 'displaced persons' as it does on the will of the people.

As far back as 1946, the UN General Assembly recognised that the problem of refugees and displaced persons of *all categories* was one of immediate urgency and referred the problem to the Economic and Social Council for thorough examination and report.[20] Some studies have a helpful bearing. Renaud *et al.* (2007)'s study on environmental-related mass movement is noteworthy because it outlines a three-pronged classification scheme that could inform a transitionary legal framework.[21] First, environmentally motivated migrants are people who may have to pre-empt the worst and leave because of an environmental stressor. Second, environmentally forced migrants are people who, due to an environmental stressor, have to leave to avoid the worst. Third, environmental refugees (including disaster refugees) involuntarily flee the worst, and their displacement can be either temporary or permanent.[22] The authors refrain from endorsing an amendment to the 1951 Refugee Convention as they feel that would defeat the purpose of the Convention and weaken protection for those traditionally categorised as refugees. Instead, they propose a separate, discrete convention or the anchorage of a legal framework in intergovernmental environmental treaties. A discrete convention could face near-insurmountable challenges if it were to respond to real legal situations, which are hybrid in nature. Normative anchorage in first principles and consequential norms, however, could be useful, if not essential.[23]

For example, the International Refugee Organization's transcendent principle is to bring about a rapid, positive, just and equitable solution to the problem of bona fide refugees and displaced persons.[24] That responses are rapid, and interventions occur independent of circumstances, facilitates anchoring first principles so that consequential norms may enter through migration and refugee law or climate law, or through several different doors at the same time. A similar anchorage concerns epikeia (legal equity) and solidarity, from which derive the consequential norms of substantive fairness, procedural fairness, distributive fairness, the law of compensation and so on.

In other words, a hybrid normative interpretation at the nexus of relevant legal regimes could be invaluable and a logical corollary when considering normative plurality. It should also enhance cohesion between different institutions. The UN Refugee Agency, the UN Office for the Co-ordination of Humanitarian Affairs, the International Organization for Migration and the Conference of the Parties to the United Nations Framework Convention on Climate Change (hereinafter 'UNFCCC COP') are of note.[25] (See also the Paris Agreement, adopted under the UNFCCC.[26])

Although implicit, the Stern Review also recognises normative plurality. At a stretch, Stern went as far as to suggest that

> the United Nations Refugee Agency, United Nations Office for the Co-ordination of Humanitarian Affairs, and the International Organization for Migration (UNHCR, OCHA, and IOM) should take on expanded roles for resettlement if others do not step forward to do so, given the permanent nature of such migration in response to climate change.[27]

The parties to the UNFCCC could still append a new protocol to the UNFCCC[28] or the Paris Agreement. Some may oppose this view as yet another discrete solution. Others may argue that neither the UNFCCC legal framework nor its institutional structures are fit for purpose; or that the UNFCCC COP has not taken sufficient action so far. Notwithstanding these arguments, in adopting the Cancun Agreements, the parties thereto demonstrated a degree of initiative at UNFCCC COP16 that may be indicative of 'assistance' and lead to acknowledging attribution of conduct or 'best effort' via the Paris Agreement.

To recap, the Cancun Agreements (reached in 2010) invited action on 'measures to enhance understanding, coordination and cooperation with regard to climate change induced displacement, migration and planned relocation, where appropriate, at national, regional and international levels'.[29] The Paris Agreement (2015) requires all parties to undertake 'ambitious efforts' through 'nationally determined contributions' (NDCs) and to strengthen these efforts in the years to come.[30] While the Paris Agreement does not refer to transitionary law, it does refer to progression. Article 3 provides, 'The efforts of all Parties will represent a progression over time, while recognizing the need to support developing country Parties for the effective implementation of this Agreement.'

At the human rights end, like the discrete approaches mentioned above, a new protocol on climigration sounds reasonable, but may not eventuate.[31] (Being reasonable in law does not always equate to being reasonable in fact.) By 'reasonable', a rationale analysis founded in normative legal reason is meant. In practice, the UNFCCC COP is not an expert body on displacement any more than the United Nations Refugee Agency is an expert agency on international climate law. On these grounds alone, it is therefore difficult to argue that a legal instrument should emerge in isolation from a hybrid nexus of normative interpretation.

Advocates like Hodgkinson *et al.* (2010),[32] Docherty and Giannini (2009)[33] and Biermann and Boas (2008),[34] amongst others, do not entirely agree.

(They argue for a new, virtually stand-alone, legal instrument by which to govern climate migration.) But nor do they entirely reject harmonising existing legal frameworks. According to them, incorporating human rights concerning climate migration in a new treaty is one of the easiest ways to give universal applicability to a system of rights and responsibilities.

McAdam (2011), like Mayer (2011), contests this view. Mayer suggests a UNGA resolution could endorse a framework that recognises the rights of climate migrants, and mandate a new institutional structure.[35] McAdam does not reject a rights-based approach outright but contends that the international community should continue to conduct thorough 'needs assessments' before deciding on the type of protection required.[36] A new treaty instrument may therefore not be the answer, or it may not be the answer just yet.

One set of academics says negotiators are moving too slowly; another group suggests they are moving too fast. Clearly, the adverse effects of climate change may evolve progressively over a long period. Hence, legal processes may need to evolve in parallel, progressively, transitionally, over time. But just how much time is needed? A day, a week, a month, many years? A piece here, a piece there, a bit more after that?

The Commonwealth has been talking about climate change and migration since at least 1988, when it completed its 'needs assessments' so that the Commonwealth heads of government, representing a quarter of the world's population at the time, could adopt the Langkawi Declaration on the Environment at the Langkawi Conference in 1989. The Langkawi Declaration supported a Commonwealth Expert Group's findings on climate change and called for the early conclusion of an international convention to protect and conserve the global climate.

This said, migration and radicalisation remain real issues for the global community to grapple with, especially in terms of how displacement may impinge gravely and inappropriately upon human security if we do not cope with them now. Global organisations have made considerable progress in raising awareness of the challenges. Yet, more is to be done with respect to advancing a unified and universal call for solidarity. Here again, the Heads of Commonwealth and Francophone Governments may act as a catalyst for a new dialogue that includes everyone.

Underlying this approach is that each person is endowed with basic and inalienable rights. For sure, endeavours to develop an international legal framework that links climate-induced migration to individual climate crimes may be some way over the horizon. In the meantime, however, it is not enough to enforce a discrete solution, individual fault or state attribution in the absence of causal proximity. Protecting the climate system is a common concern of humankind. As such, a holistic transitionary approach must take account of multi-causal and multi-layered dimensions. Potential solutions also have something to do with African solutions that impose obligations on people, as a type of collective attribution.

As far as the second part of this chapter is concerned, the idea of legal transition has a bearing. It is, however, worthwhile taking stock before turning to examine transitional legal frameworks' bearing upon the problem. In sum, therefore, this chapter has thus far examined a number of existing and potential normative responses to the climate–migration debate. All of these responses are discrete in some way, unsound in themselves for dealing with normative plurality or inconclusive. In terms of transition, everything is closely related and requires a holistic approach. Yet, on the score of practicality, two types of specificity stand out. The first is geographical specificity (governing transitions between location); the second is temporal specificity (governing transitions from ex ante to ex post settlement).

With these findings in mind, the chapter now proceeds to examine constructive ways forward that have not yet been evident in the climate change context. First among these is transitional legal protection. What is it? And how could it be adapted to human rights and climimigration?

The evolution of transitional legal protection

Transitional justice associated with the Nuremberg and Tokyo trials after the Second World War perhaps marks the genesis of transitional law.[37] A new wave of transitional reform processes accompanied its progressive development from retributive to restorative justice. Restorative justice primarily aims to restore the situation before violation. It has its defects. For example, amnesty processes may undermine the overall process and numerous challenges arise with respect to causation when sourcing hidden or obsolete evidence. As Gooley notes, instead of putting the majority of blame on society's highest echelons, sidestepping collective complicity and neglect, and putting perpetrators of some of the most heinous crimes known to humankind to death, South Africa aimed to reconcile a whole country and, in the words of Nelson Mandela, 'bind the wounds' of a nation.[38]

Argentina's Human Rights Commission, known as Conadep (Comisión Nacional sobre la Desaparición de Personas, or National Commission on the Disappearance of Persons), which was founded in 1983, and public accountability by the South African Commission following the abolition of apartheid in 1994 exemplify restorative justice. Similarly, more recently, Sir John Chilcot's report into the United Kingdom's part in an invasion and full-scale occupation of a sovereign state (Iraq) may trigger a different legacy for Westminster. Given its inter-generational and global implications, responses to Sir John's inquiry may also trigger a new wave of transitional justice.

Akin to recent developments in global commons issues, such as radicalisation, climate change–migration issues may also have broader implications. Determining at whom or what to point the finger is not easy when injustices seep into the global commons and affect everyone. Perpetrators may be children or they may have passed away. Victims may not have been born. Governing these transitions may well have consequences for transitional justice.

The notion of transitional justice – broadly defined in a 2004 report of the UN Secretary-General to the UN Security Council – is the 'full range of processes and mechanisms associated with a society's attempts to come to terms with a legacy of large-scale past abuses, in order to ensure account-ability, serve justice and achieve reconciliation'.[39] Examples include filling a rule of law vacuum, truth-seeking and reconciliation mechanisms and the establishment of international and hybrid tribunals when national justice systems shatter.

Hybrid or mixed tribunals, such as the Special Court for Sierra Leone (SCSL), the Extraordinary Chambers in the Courts of Cambodia (ECCC) and the Special Tribunal for Lebanon (STL), typically fuse substantive and procedural law with domestic and international law. Besides institutional matters, however, normative transitional plurality could, and does tend to, give effect to international humanitarian law, international human rights law, international criminal law and international refugee law, as founded in the Charter of the United Nations itself. To these, the international community may add a fifth pillar: international climate change law. But climate change is far from being an integrated pillar of transitional law at present.

Climate change differs from traditional transitional justice contexts, but there may still be ways to use recognised practice to inform international climate negotiations, rectify past wrongs and improve the protection for present and future generations. From addressing the vulnerabilities facing small states and indigenous people to the implications for the Syrian crisis, the cases described below reveal how transitional law may help govern the linkages between climate change, displacement and migration.

Climate change poses an existential threat to all states, but especially small and vulnerable states. Some small island states are in danger of submerging below the sea. For others, relocation is already happening.[40]

Alaska's Division of Homeland Security and Emergency Management has already made a clear distinction between a transitional response and an emergency one.[41] For example, after the failure of erosion control and a democratic community vote to leave, the Newtok Traditional Council planned the community's relocation to a new site. Three points are of note in the management of this transition. First, human rights bind a community together, and relocation plans must embed human rights principles to help address transitionary problems as they occur. Second, human rights instruments can help build resilience after relocation. Third, the experience ought to help others. In brief, if we do not plan for the issues before they arise, we are unlikely to be able to respond to them when they do.

Another problem arises from trying to disaggregate the real threats climate change, migration and armed conflict pose to us jointly so we can see what is happening and respond to them. Turning to the Syrian crisis,[42] a significant part of the problem was looking at the pressure climate change imposed on migration. Droughts exacerbated by climate change put pressure on water supplies, destroyed crops, killed livestock, displaced Syrian farmers and led to large flows of people seeking safe havens in Syria's cities. While droughts and stresses on food security played major roles in the Syrian crisis, they were certainly not the only factors. Persecuted Syrians had to flee the country.

Nevertheless, ambiguities remain regarding the relative importance of migration in human security and radicalisation. In an IPCC report, Adger *et al.* (2014) write, 'Climate change has the potential to increase rivalry between countries over shared resources. However, there is high scientific agreement that this increased rivalry is unlikely to lead directly to warfare between states.'[43] With respect to Darfur, the authors point to studies disputing climate change as the primary cause of the conflict.[44] Causation is multifarious, based on past legacies, manipulation of ethnic divisions by elites, limited economic development, misuse of official development assistance, and so on. In sum, Adger *et al.* believe 'confident statements about the effects of future changes in climate on armed conflict are not possible given the absence of generally supported theories and evidence about causality'.[45]

While this finding is interesting, a main reason why some social researchers have found a direct positive relationship between global warming and armed conflict while others have found none may be that the two groups have different ways of viewing the subject. Then again, the reason why direct causal links are almost never found may simply be that there are few direct relationships or mono-causal correlations between climate and conflict. Dynamic multi-causal relationships require a multiple causation theory rather than a domino theory.

Furthermore, from a legal perspective, IPCC report findings, while influential, do not necessarily mean that the proximity of causation is so remote that the international community should not respond to it. As awareness of the stresses migration places on radicalisation increases, guiding transitional legal frameworks of human rights linked to climigration, whether internal to a state or external, may be highly relevant. After all, all countries face a set of significant problems due to increasing threats of terrorism. And it is already clear that if we fail to respond to the jurisprudential issues, a huge security challenge will occur.

Other issues exist at the institutional level. In terms of systemic problems, the United Nations and its respective agencies are among a burgeoning plethora of international actors conducting needs assessments and developing humanitarian responses to climigration (including the UN Trust Fund for Human Security, the Food and Agriculture Organization of the United Nations (FAO), the International Labour Organization, the United Nations High Commissioner for Refugees (UNHCR), the United Nations Children's Fund (UNICEF), the United Nations Development Fund for Women (UNIFEM), the Red Cross, the Sovereign Order of Malta, the International Organisation of the Francophonie, and numerous private-sector foundations). On the one hand, it is perhaps neither just nor legitimate for the UNHCR to intervene if several organs and agencies of the United Nations are already assisting existing and potential victims of climate-induced displacement. On the other, the UNHCR has built myriad competencies in assisting displaced persons.

A further pressing institutional concern is that a mixed bag of uncoordinated calls to action may do more harm than good. If climate, food and water form part of the common concern, then a collective and cooperative response would be beneficial. Put differently, it is one thing to disaggregate the link between human security and climate migration into concepts in search of a legal duty; it is another to give effect to transitionary legal duties in a coordinated and cohesive manner.

Explaining how a transitional model of pre-emptive international climate law may be positioned alongside the Guiding Principles on Internal Displacement and the 1951 Geneva Refugee Convention is another interesting task.[46] (A similar hybrid analysis is of merit with respect to other human rights conventions and disaster law.)

While on the subject of transitional law, normative instruments may evolve to respond to slow-onset climate events, such as drought, or rapid-onset events, such as extreme weather. Distinguishing between slow- and rapid-onset events could help when tailoring the most appropriate transitional policy and legal response. Research into the linkages between transitional law and the responsibility to protect at the climigration nexus may be another useful enterprise. In all these endeavours, however, using a common legal language about climate justice is necessary for lawyers and essential for advocates. It may also be possible to build upon an established jurisprudential approach, which, as agreed by all states at Rio in 1992, puts human dignity at the core of climate justice and is founded on legal principles and consequential legal norms.[47]

Human dignity manifests itself, inter alia, in human security and human rights (individual and collective rights). The observed phenomena represent a sort of kaleidoscopic normativity. Normative dynamics arise because the separation angle between the fractals of human dignity, human rights and human security that bound the legal system reduces to zero, resulting in an undefined number of norms. So, in addition to investing in research that tries to disentangle and model an infinite number of causes, one use – some may say better use – of scarce research funds could be to address the jurisprudential challenge.

In terms of jurisprudential norms relating to pre-emption, much more can be said. Some may argue that the lack of interest in tackling climate change and drought played a significant role in the lead-up to the Syrian and other crises. The Syrian conflict in itself is sufficient to look at transitional legal protection through the lens of pre-emption. In doing so, the following paragraphs explore potential jurisprudential developments and introduce three potential doctrines. These three doctrines may then be brought together when sketching a hybrid framework of national and international composition for responding to pre-emptive climate change-induced displacement. Finally, some mechanisms for implementation may be suggested.

Questions about proximity plainly arise throughout any discourse on transitional law and pre-emptive climate change-induced displacement and relate closely to questions about causation. As seen above, while a proximate cause could be either dominant or direct, this is misleading in terms of temporal specificity (time). Another simplified illustration helps to clarify.

Hence, with respect to rapid-onset weather-related disasters, it is easier to prove causation insofar as the relationship between a disastrous event and injury is often tangible. A cyclone strikes, homes are destroyed, people are harmed or even die. In such tragic circumstances, there is a certain proximity between a so-called direct cause (the weather) and the effect (the disaster). Uncertainty between the antedated cause, often referred to as a 'remote cause', which occurs before the weather-related disaster, and the effect remain. Did sea warming due to climate change cause the ocean's rising heat energy to form a cyclone?

The proof of causation concerning slow-onset disasters vis-à-vis rapid-onset disasters is clearly far more difficult. The origin of a single factor of 'remote' harm is less evident. The antedated cause may be invisible to the naked eye, or there may be no 'rules of origin', but that does not necessarily mean that we do not have faith in its existence. Slow-onset events are more likely to loosen a spring of ex ante reactions of an economic, social or cultural nature, thus obscuring the objective proof of causation.

One may rely on the best available science as a guideline for future greenhouse gas emissions reductions, but the legal issue of tackling an antedated cause still entails a pre-emptive undertaking. Building on the Paris Agreement, one prescription is to develop a doctrine of proximity as a supporting legal instrument that could help address pre-emptive climate-induced displacement. Such a doctrine could align to the fundamental transcendent principle of equity and 'responsibility' as provided for in Article 3(1) of the UNFCCC, rather than an inventory of infinite causes. The parties thereto may infer necessary actions from the circumstances surrounding the 'potential' disaster. Here again, bringing together many of the needs assessments undertaken so far would add value to a doctrine of probability.

As science advances, the parties to the UNFCCC and the Paris Agreement, intermediary actors, NGOs, private-sector investors and so on are likely to increase their understanding of the conditions creating the potential consequences of the antedated cause. The word 'potential' is pivotal. Potentiality implies a varying degree of probability. The more predictable the outcome, the more likely it is to occur.

Any reasonable person will try to do 'no harm' to others and will respond when harm occurs or is likely to occur. The consequential rules that may stem from the prescription of a doctrine of probability concerning climate and displacement derive, inter alia, from the good-neighbour principle embodied in Article 3(5) of the UNFCCC. (This article evokes two auxiliary constructs: no harm and cooperation.)

Another interesting question is how to give effect to the doctrines of proximity and probability. The answer lies, in part, in determining operational control. To determine 'effective' control – or 'effective' governance – the response may concern a third doctrine, such as a doctrine of determination.

Concerning determination,[48] a collective choice of humanity ought to be made as to which antedated causes merit a supporting normative framework. Merit in this sense should relate to the decision of the parties in terms of governing transcendent principles (those of the UNFCCC, disaster law, humanitarian law and so on, as discussed earlier). Certain factors will influence the determination in terms of consequential norms. For example, connecting factors may relate to durability. In other words, the likely consequence of the disaster resides on a sliding scale from 'temporary' to 'permanent'. Environmentally induced migration may be anticipatory (precautionary), whereas environmentally induced displacement may result from an outbreak of force. Ex ante, transitionary legal instruments engage a responsibility to anticipate the cause. Ex post, legal instruments infer a responsibility to mitigate the consequences.

Other ideas that may inform a transitional legal protection model at the ex ante or pre-emptive stage of climate protection may include introducing a construct of pre-emption rights and then applying this model to pre-emptive climate change-induced displacement. Pre-emption is typically an instrument of private international law, but negotiators could still work with it and adapt it to help govern climate harm, and it could be extended to responses that regulate natural disasters. Here, a distinction could be made between transactional interests (contractual division of humanitarian aid) and substantive equitable interests (human rights). In return, the rights-holder may be obligated to do certain things to legitimise his or her claim. For example, a person may need to uphold the tenets of good citizenship. Different actors (states and non-state) have certain obligations, irrespective of whether the response is ex ante or ex post climate-induced disaster.

The financial crisis may also provide an opportunity to survey and potentially integrate other normative responses. Responsible investment is required whatever the response to pre-empt climate-induced displacement. In this regard, the UN-backed Principles for Responsible Investment (hereinafter 'PRI') could be a helpful comparator if one is to invest to pre-empt climate-induced displacement.[49]

For clarity, PRI does not exemplify transitional law in and of itself, but PRI tools could help transitional law progress towards climate-resilient development. For example, incorporating environmental, social and corporate governance (hereinafter 'ESG') issues into climate change–migration analysis and decision-making processes could be helpful.[50] Signatories to the PRI could link the three proposed legal doctrines to ESG issues and incorporate them into their ownership policies and practices. They could also disclose where investment is likely to fuel climate-induced displacement as part of due diligence. And they could promote the importance of pre-emptive climate-induced displacement with respect to human security and transitional legal protection. The effectiveness principle ought to link to shared responsibility and integration. Myriad actors could share best practices and work together on these issues to implement them at the local and regional levels. And, as a final example, reporting could convey best practices. Webinars and social media could showcase areas where collaboration has been successful in responding to pre-emptive climate-induced displacement.

In brief, responding to pre-emptive climate-induced displacement may be attributed to a state's conduct if embedded in international law. (One of the essential conditions for the international responsibility of a state is that the conduct in question is attributable to the state under international law.) But attribution is not an issue for states alone. Taken together, the instruments outlined highlight the potential for shared responsibility.

In determining the constituents of any such framework, it would be helpful to identify the categories of persons who need protection, assess their needs, classify and recognise the types of protection that the international community should provide on a transitional basis, and do something about it. Part of transitional legal protection is specifying and implementing minimum standards of protection (a common responsibility shared by states and non-state actors). The scheduling of differentiated legal protection for those whose livelihoods may be significantly impacted by the adverse effects of climate change, and, as a result, forced to consider alternative lifestyles, is important too. States and non-state actors may develop new and varied mechanisms for implementing differentiated responsibility. Mobilising the UN-backed Principles for Responsible Investment is but one example. At the local level, implementing the principles of integration and subsidiarity would help develop more tailored solutions and ensure the right results.

To build on these constructs, a certain transition is required if society is to move from legally binding conduct to legally binding result. In this regard, the December 2015 Paris Agreement is pivotal to binding conduct ('intended contributions'). But future endeavours will also need to take stock and bind result. There is therefore a certain continuum. In other words, transitional law may have a key role to play if the parties to the Paris Agreement make restricting the increase in the global average temperature to less than 2°C more than pre-industrial levels not just an aim but a result.[51]

Conclusion

Whatever the doubts over multi-causality, there are some valid arguments for introducing transitional legal protection in the climate change context. If discrete normative solutions or single bodies of law are insufficient, then a hybrid composition may be valid. A hybrid composition for addressing climigration is not necessarily flawed due to unresolved challenges about causation but may work successfully only if there is active international support and a genuine will to facilitate the protection of present and future generations. The question now is this: what relevance do transitional normative tools have for achieving the goals agreed in Paris?

Notes

1 Group Principal, Insight International (www.insight-int.org), Climate Change Negotiator and Member of UN Climate Summit, UNGA and UNFCCC delegations. This chapter, first presented in 2012 under the COST network on 'Transitional Legal Protection', introduced the terms 'transitional justice' and 'transitional law' in the climate change context and explored normative tools to support the implementation of a new climate change agreement. I would like to thank Professor Marleen van Rijswick and Professor Fred Soons of Utrecht University's School of Law for the opportunity to engage with the pan-European COST Action Programme on climate change and migration, the EU for supporting research in this area and Andrew Baldwin, Chair of the COST Action IS1101.

2 United Nations, *Convention Relating to the Status of Refugees* (adopted 28 July 1951, entered into force 22 April 1954) 189 UNTS 137; United Nations, *Protocol Relating to the Status of Refugees* (adopted 31 January 1967, entered into force 4 October 1967) 606 UNTS.

3 UNHCR, *Climate Change, Natural Disasters and Human Displacement: A UNHCR Perspective* (2009) 6.

4 S. Park and United Nations High Commissioner for Refugees, 'Climate Change and the Risk of Statelessness: The Situation of Low-Lying Island States' (2011) PPLA/2011/04.

5 United Nations, *Convention Relating to the Status of Refugees* Article 1.

6 Ibid. Article 1D.

7 United Nations, *Protocol Relating to the Status of Refugees* Article 1A. Paragraph 2 of the Convention is now read in conjunction with the 1967 Protocol without temporal and geographical restrictions. The 1967 Protocol limited application by the parties to Articles 2–34 of the Geneva Refugee Convention of 1951 to refugees redefined in Article 1 of the 1967 Protocol.

8 *Rome Statute of the International Criminal Court* (concluded 17 July 1998, entered into force 1 July 2002).

9 Ibid. Article 7(2)(g), 'for the purpose of Article 7(1)(h)'.

10 International Tribunal for the Prosecution of Persons Responsible for Serious Violations of International Humanitarian Law Committed in the Territory of the Former Yugoslavia since 1991 (ICTY), *Prosecutor v. Blagoje Simić, Miroslav Tadić, Simo Zarić* (judgement 17 October 2003) para. 47. See also ICTY, *Statute of the International Tribunal for the Prosecution of Persons Responsible for Serious Violations of International Humanitarian Law Committed in the Territory of the Former Yugoslavia since 1991* (concluded 25 May 1993) Article 5(h). (The Statute established the ICTY and was appended to and adopted by UN Security Council Resolution 827.)

11 G. Polya, 'Climate Racism, Climate Injustice and Climate Genocide: Australia, US and EU Sabotage Copenhagen COP15' (2009) http://bellaciao.org/en/spip.php?article19422 accessed 25 October 2016; J. Parnell, 'Island States Appeal for COP17 Ministers to Avert "Climate Genocide"' (2011) www.rtcc.org/policy/island-states-appeal-for-cop17-ministers-to-avert-%E2%80%9Cclimate-genocide%E2%80%9D/ accessed 25 October 2016.

12 C. M. Bassiouni, *Crimes against Humanity in International Criminal Law* (2nd edn, Kluwer Law International 1999).

13 K. Wouters, *International Legal Standards for the Protection from Refoulement: A Legal Analysis of the Prohibitions on Refoulement Contained in the Refugee Rights and the Convention against Torture* (Intersentia 2009).

14 Refugee Status Appeals Authority, New Zealand, Refugee Appeal Nos. 72189/2000, 72190/2000, 72191/2000, 72192/2000, 72193/2000, 72194/2000, 72195/2000 at Auckland (judgement 17 August 2000) para. 13.

15 African Union, *African Union Convention for the Protection and Assistance of Internally Displaced Persons in Africa* (adopted 22 October 2009) Article 4(4), 'Obligations of States Parties relating to Protection from Internal Displacement.'
16 Ibid. Article 4(2).
17 United Nations, *Convention Relating to the Status of Refugees.*
18 United Nations, *Constitution of the International Refugee Organization* (adopted 15 December 1946) Article 1.
19 Ibid. Article 16 (amendment).
20 UN General Assembly Resolution A/RES/8(I), Doc A/45, 'Question of Refugees' (adopted 12 February 1946) (Annex III of United Nations, *Constitution of the International Refugee Organization*).
21 F. Renaud, J. J. Bogardi, O. Dun and K. Warner, 'Control, Adapt or Flee: How to Face Environmental Migration?' (UNU Institute for Environment and Human Security 2007).
22 Ibid. 29–30.
23 United Nations, *Constitution of the International Refugee Organization* Annex III, para. (c) ii, 'Principles'.
24 Ibid. Annex I, 'General Principles'.
25 United Nations, *United Nations Framework Convention on Climate Change* (UNFCCC) (concluded 9 May 1992, entered into force 21 March 1994) Article 3(1).
26 UNFCCC, *Paris Agreement Concluded at the 21st Conference of the Parties to the UN Framework Convention on Climate Change* (adopted 12 December 2015, entered into force 4 November 2016) FCCC/CP/2015/L.9/Rev.1.
27 N. H. Stern, *The Economics of Climate Change: The Stern Review* (Cambridge University Press 2007) 566.
28 F. Biermann and I. Boas, 'Protecting Climate Refugees: The Case for a Global Protocol' (2008) *Environment: Science and Policy for Sustainable Development* www.environmentmagazine.org/Archives/Back%20Issues/November-December%202008/Biermann-Boas-full.html accessed 25 October 2016; F. Biermann and I. Boas, 'Preparing for a Warmer World: Towards a Global Governance System to Protect Climate Refugees' (2010) 10(1) *Global Environmental Politics* 60.
29 UNFCCC, *Cancun Agreements Adopted by COP16 of the UNFCCC* (2010) para 14(f), http://unfccc.int/meetings/cop_16/items/5571.php accessed 25 October 2016. See also K. Warner, 'Climate and Environmental Change, Human Migration and Displacement: Recent Policy Developments and Research Gaps' (United Nations University 2011) UN/POP/MIG-9CM/2011/10.
30 UNFCCC, *Paris Agreement.*
31 M. Ammer, 'Climate Change and Human Rights: The Status of Climate Refugees in Europe' (Ludwig Boltzmann Institute of Human Rights 2009) 72.
32 D. Hodgkinson, T. Burton, H. Anderson and L. Young, '"The Hour When the Ship Comes In": A Convention for Persons Displaced by Climate Change' (2010) 36(1) *Monash University Law Review* 69.
33 B. Docherty and T. Giannini, 'Confronting a Rising Tide: A Proposal for a Convention on Climate Change Refugees' (2009) 33 *Harvard Environmental Law Review* 349.
34 Biermann and Boas, 'Protecting Climate Refugees'.
35 B. Mayer, 'The International Legal Challenges of Climate-Induced Migration: Proposal for an International Legal Framework' (2011) 22 *Colorado Journal of International Environmental Law and Policy* 357.
36 J. McAdam, 'Swimming against the Tide: Why a Climate Change Displacement Treaty Is Not the Answer' (2011) 23(1) *International Journal of Refugee Law* 2; J. McAdam, *Climate Change, Forced Migration, and International Law* (Oxford University Press 2012).

37 A. Costi, 'Hybrid Tribunals as a Viable Transitional Justice Mechanism to Combat Impunity in Post-Conflict Situations' (2008) 22(2) *New Zealand Universities Law Review* 213.

38 B. Gooley, 'Nuremberg or the South African TRC: A Comparison of the Retributive and Restorative Models of Justice' (2012) University of Connecticut Honors Scholar Theses Paper 270; R. E. Conot, *Justice at Nuremberg* (Harper & Row 1983) 498; N. Mandela, *Long Walk to Freedom: The Autobiography of Nelson Mandela* (Little, Brown & Company 1994) 619–620.

39 UN Security Council, 'The Rule of Law and Transitional Justice in Conflict and Post-Conflict Societies' (2004) report of the Secretary-General, S/2004/616, para. III.8.

40 R. Bronen, 'Climate-Induced Community Relocations: Creating an Adaptive Governance Framework Based in Human Rights Doctrine' (2011) 35(2) *NYU Review of Law and Social Change* 357.

41 For information about Alaska's Division of Homeland Security and Emergency Management, see Alaska Division of Homeland Security and Emergency Management, 'Home Page' (n.d.) http://ready.alaska.gov accessed 25 October 2016.

42 UN Human Rights Council, *11th Report of the Commission of Inquiry on Syria* (2016) UN A/HRC/31/68 (report of the Independent International Commission of Inquiry on the Syrian Arab Republic).

43 W. N. Adger, J. M. Pulhin, J. Barnett, G. D. Dabelko, G. K. Hovelsrud, M. Levy, Ú. Oswald Spring and C. H. Vogel, 'Human Security' in C. B. Field, V. R. Barros, D. J. Dokken, K. J. Mach, M. D. Mastrandrea, T. E. Bilir, M. Chatterjee, K. L. Ebi, Y. O. Estrada, R. C. Genova, B. Girma, E. S. Kissel, A. N. Levy, S. MacCracken, P. R. Mastrandrea and L. L. White (eds), *Climate Change 2014: Impacts, Adaptation, and Vulnerability. Part A: Global and Sectoral Aspects. Contribution of Working Group II to the Fifth Assessment Report of the Intergovernmental Panel on Climate Change* (Cambridge University Press 2014) 755, 772.

44 Ibid. 773.

45 Ibid.

46 United Nations, *Protection of and Assistance to Internally Displaced Persons* (adopted 19 December 2011, distributed 22 March 2012) A/RES/66/165.

47 T. Thorp, *Climate Justice: A Voice for the Future* (Palgrave Macmillan 2014).

48 F. Gemenne, 'Migration Doesn't Have to Be a Failure to Adapt: An Escape from Environmental Determinism' in J. Palutikof *et al.* (eds), *Climate Adaptation Futures* (John Wiley & Sons Ltd 2013).

49 Principles for Responsible Investment (PRI), 'Information on the UN-Backed Principles for Responsible Investment' www.unpri.org accessed 25 October 2016. See also Climate and Clean Air Coalition to Reduce Short Lived Climate Pollutants, 'Home Page' (n.d.) www.ccacoalition.org accessed 25 October 2016.

50 C. Cha-Sartori, 'Environmental Refugees: The Latest Enterprise of Corporate Social Responsibility' (2011) 34(1) *Houston Journal of International Law* 109.

51 UNFCCC, *Paris Agreement* Article 2.1(a).

6 State responsibility to prevent climate displacement

The importance of housing, land and property rights

Ezekiel Simperingham[1]

Introduction

Climate displacement – the forced movement of individuals and communities as a result of natural hazards and the effects of climate change[2] – is set to be among the greatest humanitarian, human rights and potentially existential challenges of the twenty-first century.[3]

In order to address climate displacement effectively, states and stakeholders must design and implement a range of measures to prevent climate displacement from occurring, respond to the humanitarian needs of climate-displaced persons and ensure that climate displacement is effectively resolved.

Ensuring that climate displacement is addressed in this 'prevent, respond and resolve' framework will necessarily involve integrated and inclusive interventions across a broad range of sectors, including the economic, legal, social, health, cultural, educational, environmental, technological, political and institutional spheres.

While acknowledging the interrelated nature of interventions to address climate displacement, this chapter focuses primarily on the responsibility of states to *prevent* climate displacement from occurring.[4] It also focuses on climate displacement that occurs *within* states – where the vast majority of climate displacement is already occurring and where it is expected to continue to occur[5] – rather than climate displacement across borders.[6]

The chapter begins by examining the nature of the global challenge of climate displacement, including the potential scale of climate displacement and the specific vulnerabilities of climate-displaced persons. It then examines the normative foundation of state responsibility to prevent climate displacement and outlines specific measures that states may take to meet this responsibility. There is also an analysis of the emerging focus of states and stakeholders on preventative planned relocations, the importance of a human rights-based approach and, crucially, the importance of housing, land and property (HLP) rights.

The challenges of climate displacement

It is now well accepted that one of the major impacts of climate change will be on human mobility.[7] This mobility is expected to take a variety of forms, including voluntary and forced movement, movement across and within national borders, temporary and permanent movement and spontaneous and planned movement. Of these types of movement, forced displacement is of particular concern due to the projected scale of the displacement and the vulnerability of those displaced.

The projected scale of climate displacement

Natural disasters are already leading to the displacement of an average of 26.4 million people every year,[8] with the vast majority of these disasters related to weather and climatic hazards.[9] This number is expected to increase as climate change leads to increasingly intense and frequent weather events.[10] The likelihood of being displaced by a disaster is already 60 per cent higher than it was four decades ago.[11]

Displacement from sudden-onset disasters will be combined with displacement from slow-onset events associated with climate change, including salinisation, land degradation, desertification and, critically, sea-level rise. Sea-level rise alone could displace tens or hundreds of millions of people from low-lying coastal areas, deltas and small island states.[12] The risk is clear: already more than 150 million people are living within one metre of sea level.[13]

The combination of displacement from sudden- and slow-onset events associated with climate change has led to widely reported predictions of the displacement of hundreds of millions of people this century.[14] However, it is exceptionally – and perhaps distractingly[15] – difficult to provide accurate estimates of the numbers of people who will be displaced by climate change. This is due at least in part to the inherent difficulties of isolating environmental factors or climate change as the motivation behind an individual's displacement.[16] It is also difficult to discern how effective states will be at mitigating and adapting to climate change in the coming decades.

Despite the difficulties in developing accurate projections of the likely scale of climate displacement, a consensus has emerged that climate change is already having and will continue to have a dramatic impact on human displacement;[17] that the majority of displacement will occur within countries, rather than across international borders;[18] and that the least developed and developing countries will be most affected.[19]

Already 95 per cent of displacement due to natural disasters is occurring in developing countries.[20] However, climate displacement is not just a challenge for the developing world; developed countries are also – and will be increasingly – affected. In 2014 alone, around 1.8 million people were displaced by natural hazards in high-income countries.[21] A 2015 report noted that, in the event of unabated climate change, the land where more than 20 million people live in the United States will be at risk from sea-level rise.[22]

The vulnerability of climate-displaced persons

In all countries it is the poor and marginalised who suffer disproportionately from climate displacement. They are the most exposed to climate hazards and have the least capability to adapt to the effects of climate change. Sick and wounded people, children,[23] women,[24] people with disabilities, older people, migrants, indigenous peoples and those who do not fully enjoy HLP rights[25] are often among the most seriously affected by climate hazards and displacement.

Once displaced, vulnerability often increases. Climate-displaced persons are at greater risk of HLP losses,[26] impoverishment and discrimination; livelihood insecurity; economic, social and psychological marginalisation; food and water insecurity; and increased morbidity and mortality through trauma and vulnerability to insanitary conditions. Critically, for the resolution of their displacement, they face disruption or destruction of social and economic support networks.[27]

State responsibility to prevent climate displacement

The scenario of hundreds of millions of vulnerable persons being displaced by climate hazards – increasing their risk of socio-economic deprivation and denial of their basic human rights – does not need to be a foregone conclusion. Much can and should be done to identify and protect communities at risk from climate displacement.

However, this will require states – as part of their responsibility to reduce the risk of disasters[28] and to respect, protect and fulfil the human rights of those within their territories[29] – to take a range of proactive measures to prevent climate displacement.[30]

Furthermore, states and stakeholders must recognise that climate displacement rarely occurs due to the impact of climate hazards alone. More often, it is exposure to climate hazards combined with the vulnerability of an individual or community that leads to displacement.

In other words: exposure + vulnerability = climate displacement.

Measures to prevent climate displacement

Effectively preventing climate displacement will require a range of legislative, policy and practical actions spanning disaster risk reduction, climate change adaptation and general development.[31]

Specific measures and actions to prevent climate displacement will necessarily be context specific, but, for example, may include: comprehensive hazard and vulnerability mapping to identify populations most at risk of climate displacement;[32] restricting human habitation or requiring climate-resilient housing and infrastructure in high-risk regions, for example through climate-sensitive land-use planning and building codes and controls;[33] protective mechanisms, including physical infrastructure, such as sea walls and embankments; and ecosystem-based measures, such as the planting of protective mangroves. Early warning systems and protection of lifeline infrastructure may also help prevent long-term displacement.[34] Information about the nature and risk of climate hazards and the function of such preventative measures must be clearly communicated to affected communities.

More generally, resilience to climate hazards (both sudden and slow onset) can be enhanced through general development measures as well as specific measures to protect and diversify livelihoods[35] and to ensure food and water security,[36] including, for example, developing drought-resistant seeds and salt- and flood-resistant crops.

A *rights-based approach to preventing climate displacement*

Critically, all measures to prevent climate displacement must address the human rights of affected communities. This is not only in accordance with the responsibility of states under human rights law, but also, at a practical level, ensures full respect for human rights has been shown to reduce the risk of displacement in the context of climate hazards.[37]

In practice, a human rights-based approach suggests that all measures to prevent climate displacement should ensure that the rights of affected communities are respected, protected and fulfilled; that all measures are designed and implemented with the meaningful participation of affected communities; that non-discrimination is ensured across all measures; and that the particular needs of the most vulnerable are addressed.[38]

The importance of housing, land and property rights in the prevention of climate displacement

As part of a rights-based approach, states and stakeholders must also address the central importance of HLP rights in the prevention of climate displacement.

The HLP sector is particularly vulnerable to climate hazards, which in turns increases the risk of displacement. For example, homes and lands are lost to river erosion in Bangladesh, displacing tens of thousands every year;[39] the town of Gramalote, Colombia, was completely destroyed by flooding and landslides in 2010, leading to the displacement of thousands;[40] Typhoon Haiyan led to massive storm surges, the destruction of over one million homes and the displacement of over four million people in the Philippines in 2013;[41] and in Ontong Java, in the Solomon Islands, sea-level rise and soil erosion are destroying homes, leading to displacement and forcing whole communities to consider permanently abandoning their homes and lands.[42]

Furthermore, persons with weak HLP rights are themselves more vulnerable to displacement from both sudden- and slow-onset climate events.[43] Persons living without adequate housing are often among the first to be displaced during a climate hazard – for example, those who were living in informal settlements and inadequate housing along the coast of Typhoon Haiyan-affected areas of the Philippines. Persons with weak HLP rights are often forced to live on marginalised land, which is most at risk of climate hazards – for example, people living on the vulnerable *chars* of Bangladesh.[44] Those living without security of tenure may be unwilling or unable to improve their housing to become more climate resilient.[45]

To address the clear links between HLP rights and preventing climate displacement, states and stakeholders should seek to remove existing vulnerabilities in the HLP sector. This includes ensuring that HLP rights are respected, protected and fulfilled, for example by reviewing legislation and policies to ensure that the HLP sector is free from discrimination; designing and implementing programmes to ensure that suitably located, secure, safe and affordable housing is accessible to all; and enhancing security of tenure by recognising a variety of forms of tenure, not solely freehold ownership.[46]

States and stakeholders should also ensure that specific measures are taken to respect, protect and fulfil the HLP rights of those who are most vulnerable to climate displacement. States should take targeted measures to enhance the adequacy of housing in vulnerable regions and among the most vulnerable communities, including unaccompanied children, single women or female-headed households, unaccompanied older persons, households headed by older persons, disabled persons, ethnic or religious minority groups, and families who do not own land or property. Affected communities should be able to upgrade their housing in high-risk regions to become more climate resilient, and measures should be taken to ensure that government and non-government HLP support programmes are available to all, not just to those with formal legal title.[47]

Planned relocations and preventing climate displacement

As the sudden- and slow-onset effects of climate change intensify and the limits of adaptation, resilience, disaster risk reduction and other measures are realised, states and stakeholders are increasingly expected to consider the pre-emptive planned relocation of entire communities away from areas at high risk of climate hazards.

It is also expected that the vast majority of planned relocations associated with climate hazards will occur within national borders. Such planned relocations in the context of climate hazards are already being considered and implemented in the Philippines,[48] Fiji,[49] the Solomon Islands,[50] the United States[51] and elsewhere.[52]

Planned relocations can also be an important means to avoid situations of protracted displacement,[53] notably for those individuals and communities who have been displaced but cannot return to their former homes and lands[54] and have not yet arrived at durable solutions.[55] A community-based initiative to support planned relocations for climate-displaced persons is already occurring in south-eastern Bangladesh, focusing on the key challenge of finding domestic land solutions.[56]

When done well, planned relocations can be important tools when tackling disaster risk reduction and climate change adaptation.[57] They may also allow states to meet their responsibilities to prevent climate displacement and to take proactive measures to safeguard life, physical integrity, health and HLP rights, among other human rights implicated in the context of climate hazards. However, it is important to stress that every planned relocation is a complex process, with the potential to exacerbate an already parlous situation, for instance by depriving affected communities of their human rights. Therefore, any planned relocation should generally be considered as a measure of last resort, to be implemented only when all reasonable in-situ alternatives have been explored – or when communities themselves have identified relocation as their preferred option.[58]

International law is clear on the subject of planned relocations. They must be sanctioned in law, only carried out to protect the safety of the persons concerned (and necessary and proportional to this end) and only resorted to when less intrusive measures are infeasible.[59] The feasibility of alternatives was a key challenge in the planned relocations of affected populations after Typhoon Haiyan, when it was unclear whether less intrusive measures, which would have allowed displaced communities to return to their homes in safety, had been fully explored and assessed.

When planned relocations are involuntary, human rights standards on forced evictions must be observed.[60] Such relocations should also draw on best-practice guidelines, including the Peninsula Principles on Climate Displacement within States[61] – which provide a normative framework for all states and stakeholders that are grappling with the question of whether and/or how to undertake planned relocations – and the guidance provided by the Brookings Institution, Georgetown University and the UNHCR.[62] These standards and guidelines suggest, inter alia, that all relocations must ensure an adequate standard of HLP rights, including that shelter, water and sanitation, infrastructure and other facilities are available at the relocation site, and that the relocation site itself is adequate. Adequate livelihood and social support should also be provided, including access to healthcare and education. Affected communities should be properly consulted as part of the planning and implementation process;[63] relocation plans should be sensitive to community, ethnic and cultural identity issues; and they should take measures to avoid tension with the host community. Non-discrimination must be ensured throughout the relocation process, and the special needs of the most vulnerable people must be addressed and their rights protected.

A variety of perspectives and inputs will be required if a planned relocation is to proceed smoothly, including from development, humanitarian, human rights, disaster risk reduction, environment and climate change actors and stakeholders. Financial and technical support from the international and regional communities may also be required, especially as the majority of climate displacement is expected to continue to affect the most marginalised and vulnerable people within the least developed and developing countries. The fact that the communities and countries most affected by climate displacement are the least responsible for contributing to climate change is often cited as a matter of 'climate justice'.

Planned relocations and land use planning: the Solomon Islands

In 2014, town planners from Australia played an integral role in the development of a climate change adaptation strategy for Choiseul, a provincial capital in the Solomon Islands, which included a detailed plan for the relocation of the capital from Taro Island to the mainland.[64] The recommendation to relocate the capital was based in part on the increasing risk of sea-level rise, tsunami, storm surge and coastal erosion on Taro, a small coral atoll lying mostly less than two metres above sea level.[65]

The final climate change adaptation plan included a mapping of existing and future hazards and other land constraints, which informed a community-driven vulnerability and risk assessment and the development of a number of adaptation options to improve community resilience, one of which was to relocate the entire Taro Island community, including all housing and infrastructure, to the adjacent mainland.[66] The involvement of land use planning experts in the development and assessment of climate change adaptation options, including the detailed relocation plan, was seen as highly positive and beneficial.[67]

However, a number of clear challenges were identified for the suggested planned relocation – should it go ahead – including continuity of provincial and social services, continuity of employment, financial capacity of individuals and families to relocate (and to adhere to the land use planning regulations and building controls at the new site), maintenance of access and connection to the sea, and loss of family homes and assets.[68]

More generally, including land use planning in planned relocations can be hazardous. When a land use plan is implemented in a country or region with no real tradition of land use planning, or method of enforcement, some or all of the community may not follow the plan, creating further financial, social and safety strains at the relocation site. Land use plans must therefore take the local context and realities into account, and must not be overly burdensome, in terms of both cost and expertise. Support must be provided when the intended community is unable to observe the land use planning and building code requirements; otherwise, informal rather than planned settlements may arise at the relocation site, which will then need to be addressed systematically (and sensitively) by the government.[69]

The importance of a domestic legal, policy and institutional framework to prevent climate displacement

More broadly, an effective approach to preventing climate displacement must build on state responsibilities at the international level by ensuring domestic legal and policy regulation, institutional support and the effective engagement of a range of stakeholders, including regional and international communities.

In order to develop effective laws and policies to prevent climate displacement, states should undertake legal and policy review and reform processes.[70] Effective laws and policies should ensure a rights-based approach, which includes ensuring accountability mechanisms are in place and accessible when human rights standards are not met. In developing national legal and policy measures to prevent climate displacement, states should draw on international standards and guidelines, including the Guiding Principles on Internal Displacement and the Peninsula Principles on Climate Displacement within States[71] – as recently happened in the drafting of Bangladesh's *National Strategy on the Management of Disaster and Climate Induced Internal Displacement.*[72]

Such laws and policies must also be supported by a strong, clear and accountable institutional structure.[73] In turn, this institutional structure must ensure effective coordination and a clear articulation of responsibilities – for example, between national and local government[74] and between disciplines that are commonly seen as disparate, such as disaster risk reduction and climate change adaptation.[75]

While states have the primary responsibility to *protect* persons at risk of climate displacement, *preventing* climate displacement should be seen as a shared responsibility between states and stakeholders.[76] This responsibility should also be shared by the regional and international communities, who should play an active role in supporting any state affected by or at risk of climate displacement.[77] Regional and international support should include the provision of financial and technical cooperation and the sharing of climate and hazard data. Climate displacement is a global challenge and those states that are most affected should not be left to face and resolve this challenge alone.

Notes

1 International Legal Consultant, Displacement Solutions www.displacementsolutions. org.
2 There is no formally agreed upon of 'climate displacement', nor indeed of the best term to characterise displacement associated with natural hazards and climate change. While cognisant of the debates over definitions and terminology, for the purposes of this paper the term 'climate displacement' will be used.
3 'The greatest single impact of climate change could be on human migration with millions of people displaced by shoreline erosion, coastal flooding, and agricultural disruption a crisis in the making' (European Commission, 'Priorities, Energy Union and Climate, Climate Action – Emission Reduction' in *COP21 UN*

Climate Change Conference, Paris http://ec.europa.eu/priorities/energy-union-and-climate/climate-action-emission-reduction/cop21-un-climate-change-conference-paris_en accessed 25 October 2016; 'Forced displacement related to disasters, including the adverse effects of climate change, is a reality and among the biggest humanitarian challenges facing States and the international community in the 21st century' (Nansen Initiative, *Agenda for the Protection of Cross-Border Displaced Persons in the Context of Disasters and Climate Change*, Volume 1 (2015) 14). The United Nations Human Rights Council has expressed 'concern that climate change has contributed to the increase of sudden-onset natural disasters and slow-onset events, and that these events have adverse effects on the full enjoyment of all human rights' (UN Human Rights Council, *Human Rights and Climate Change* (2015) A/HRC/29/L.21 2); 'Disasters caused by natural hazards are now among the greatest threats to long-term development worldwide. Over the last 20 years, they have killed 1.3 million people, affected 4.4 billion, and caused over US$ 2 trillion in economic losses' (International Federation of Red Cross and Red Crescent Societies (IFRC) and UN Development Programme (UNDP), *Effective Law and Regulation for Disaster Risk Reduction: A Multi-Country Report* (2013) Foreword); 'The entire populations of low-lying states such as the Maldives, Tuvalu, Kiribati and the Marshall Islands may in future be obliged to leave their own country as a result of climate change. Moreover, the existence of their State as such may be threatened' (UNHCR, IOM and NRC, *Climate Change and Statelessness: An Overview – Submission to the 6th Session of the Ad Hoc Working Group on Long-Term Cooperative Action (AWG-LCA 6) under the UN Framework Convention on Climate Change (UNFCCC)* (2009)).

4 For an analysis of state responsibility *to respond to and resolve* climate displacement, see, for example, E. Simperingham, 'The Responsibilities of States to Protect Climate Displaced Persons' in S. Leckie and C. Huggins (eds), *Repairing Domestic Climate Displacement: The Peninsula Principles* (Routledge 2016).

5 'It has long been recognized that the effects of climate change will displace people and that most of this displacement will be within national borders' (Brookings–LSE Project on Internal Displacement, *Climate Change and Internal Displacement* (2014) 1).

6 For an examination of state responsibility relevant to climate displacement across international borders, see, for example, Nansen Initiative, *Agenda*. See also Displacement Solutions, *Judicial Approaches to the Protection of Climate Displaced Persons: A Guide for the Legal Profession* (2016).

7 The links between climate change and human mobility have been increasingly recognised since the First Assessment Report of the IPCC – Intergovernmental Panel on Climate Change (IPCC), *Climate Change: The IPCC Scientific Assessment: Final Report of Working Group I* (Cambridge University Press 1990). Since 1990, international recognition of human mobility and displacement associated with climate change has been included in the Cancun Adaptation Framework (United Nations, *The Cancun Agreements: Outcome of the Work of the Ad Hoc Working Group on Long-Term Cooperative Action under the Convention* (2011) FCCC/CP/2010/7/Add.1); United Nations, *Doha Decision on Loss and Damage* (2013) FCCC/CP/2012/8/Add.1; United Nations, *Sendai Framework for Disaster Risk Reduction 2015–2030* (2015) A/CONF.224/CRP.1; and United Nations, *UN 2030 Agenda for Sustainable Development* (adopted 21 October 2015).

8 Norwegian Refugee Council/Internal Displacement Monitoring Centre (NRC/IDMC), *Global Estimates 2015: People Displaced by Disasters* (2015) 8.

9 Ibid. See also UNISDR, *The Human Cost of Weather Related Disasters 1995–2015* (2015) 5.

10 W. N. Adger, J. M. Pulhin, J. Barnett, G. D. Dabelko, G. K. Hovelsrud, M. Levy, U. Oswald Spring and C. H. Vogel, '2014: Human Security' in IPCC, C. B. Field, V. R. Barros, D. J. Dokken, K. J. Mach, M. D. Mastrandrea, T. E. Bilir,

M. Chatterjee, K. L. Ebi, Y. O. Estrada, R. C. Genova, B. Girma, E. S. Kissel, A. N. Levy, S. MacCracken, P. R. Mastrandrea and L. L. White (eds.), *Climate Change 2014: Impacts, Adaptation, and Vulnerability. Part A: Global and Sectoral Aspects. Contribution of Working Group II to the Fifth Assessment Report of the Intergovernmental Panel on Climate Change* (Cambridge University Press 2014) 755–791.

11 NRC/IDMC, *Global Estimates* 8.

12 Adger *et al.*, 'Human Security' 770.

13 ABC, 'World Sea Levels Set to Rise at Least One Metre over Next 100–200 Years, NASA Says' (26 August 2015) www.abc.net.au/news/2015-08-27/sea-levels-set-to-rise,-nasa-says/6728008?site=esperance accessed 25 October 2016.

14 See, for example, Al Jazeera, 'Where Will the Climate Refugees Go?' (23 December 2015) www.aljazeera.com/indepth/features/2015/11/climate-refugees-151125093146088. html accessed 31 December 2015.

15 See, for example, S. Leckie and E. Simperingham, 'Focusing on Climate-Related Internal Displacement' (2015) 49 *Forced Migration Review*.

16 It is difficult, if not impossible, to prove the causal link between climate change and an individual's displacement. For example, where a person is displaced due to an extreme weather event such as a cyclone or flood, it is very difficult to prove decisively that the cyclone or flood was a 'climate change'-related hazard, rather than a so-called 'normally occurring' hazard that would have occurred irrespective of climate change. Furthermore, when a person moves due to the slower-onset effects of climate change, the decision to move will often be determined by the individual's socio-economic and other circumstances just as much as by their ability to cope or adapt to the effects of climate change. In this way, climate change will often act as an amplifier of existing vulnerabilities, rather than the sole driver of displacement. This has been termed the 'causation conundrum' (ibid.).

17 Adger *et al.*, 'Human Security'.

18 Brookings–LSE Project on Internal Displacement, *Climate Change*.

19 For an interactive, online map of where these events are occurring globally, see Displacement Solutions, *World Climate Displacement Map* (2016) http://displacementsolutions.org/world-displacement-map accessed 25 October 2016.

20 NRC/IDMC, *Global Estimates* 9.

21 Ibid. 25.

22 'For unabated climate change, we find that land that is home to more than 20 million people is implicated' (B. H. Straussa, S. Kulpa and A. Levermann, 'Carbon Choices Determine US Cities Committed to Futures below Sea Level' (2015) *Proceedings of the National Academy of Sciences* www.pnas.org/content/early/2015/10/07/1511186112.full.pdf accessed 25 October 2016.

23 'Children, in particular, are highly vulnerable during population displacements' (UNICEF, *The Impact of Climate Change on Children* (2015) 30).

24 'There are well-documented gender differences in displacement from extreme events, especially when women lose their social networks or their social capital, and women are often affected by adverse mental health outcomes in situations of displacement' (Adger *et al.*, 'Human Security' 767).

25 See, for example, R. Rolnik, *Report of the Special Rapporteur on Adequate Housing as a Component of the Right to an Adequate Standard of Living, and on the Right to Non-Discrimination in This Context* (United Nations 2010) A/HRC/16/42.

26 UN Habitat, *Land and Natural Disasters: Guidance for Practitioners* (2010).

27 See, for example, E. Simperingham, 'The Urgent Need for Rights Based Solutions to Climate Displacement in Bangladesh' (10 October 2015) *Dhaka Tribune* www.dhakatribune.com/feature/2015/oct/10/urgent-need-rights-based-solutions-climate-displacement-bangladesh accessed 25 October 2016.

28 The responsibility of states to reduce the risk of disasters has been affirmed, for example, in United Nations, *Sendai Framework* para. 19(a) and International Law

Commission, *Draft Articles on the Protection of Persons in the Event of Disasters* (2014) A/CN.4/L.831. For an analysis of the history of the development of the concept of disaster risk reduction and 'prevention as a principle of international law', see also E. Valencia-Ospina, *Sixth Report on the Protection of Persons in the Event of Disasters* (United Nations 2013) A/CN.4/66.

29 'States are under a permanent and universal obligation to provide protection to those on their territory under the various international human rights instruments and customary international human rights law' and 'each human right [entails] the duty to respect (i.e. refraining itself from violating), protect (i.e. protecting rights holders from violations by third parties) and fulfil (i.e. taking affirmative actions to strengthen access to the right)' (E. Valencia-Ospina, *Preliminary Report on the Protection of Persons in the Event of Disasters* (United Nations 2008) A/CN.4/598 para. 25).

30 The responsibility to 'protect' human rights 'does not only relate to actual violations of human rights but also entails an obligation for States to prevent their occurrence' (Valencia-Ospina, *Sixth Report* para. 42). The European Court of Human Rights has affirmed that the reduction of disaster risks and vulnerabilities is a human rights obligation and that states have a positive obligation to take measures to prevent or mitigate the consequences of foreseeable disasters. See: *Budayeva and Others v. Russian Federation* (European Court of Human Rights 20 March 2008) and *Öneryildiz v. Turkey* (European Court of Human Rights 30 November 2004).

31 'Strengthening the resilience of people and communities in the context of natural disasters and other environmental events is a multidisciplinary task and requires addressing a multitude of economic, social, technical and developmental challenges' (W. Kälin, 'A Human Rights-Based Approach to Building Resilience to Natural Disasters' (2011) www.brookings.edu/research/a-human-rights-based-approach-to-building-resilience-to-natural-disasters/ accessed 12 January 2017).

32 See Displacement Solutions, *Preventing and Resolving Climate Displacement: The Critical Role of Land Use Planning* (forthcoming).

33 Ibid.

34 'Land use planning can help to ensure that lifeline infrastructure and critical facilities remain operational and functional, preventing the need for displacement. This can be achieved through structural improvements and technology upgrades, including the construction of hazard-resistant infrastructure, the protection of water, sewer and power lines, and ensuring that critical facilities, including hospitals, shelter and evacuation locations are located out of high-risk areas and protected' (ibid.).

35 'In the case of slow-onset disasters both environmental adaptation measures (e.g. preventing soil erosion) and social issues are likely to be needed [including] developing different forms of livelihoods, addressing issues of management of natural resources or establishing safety nets for the most vulnerable people' (Brookings–LSE Project on Internal Displacement, *Climate Change* 12).

36 Ibid. 12.

37 See, for example, B. Docherty, 'General Obligations in Repairing Domestic Climate Displacement' in Leckie and Huggins, *Repairing Domestic Climate Displacement*.

38 For example, 'Disaster risk reduction requires … empowerment and inclusive, accessible and non-discriminatory participation, paying special attention to people disproportionately affected by disasters, especially the poorest. A gender, age, disability and cultural perspective should be integrated in all policies and practices, and women and youth leadership should be promoted' (United Nations, *Sendai Framework* para. 19(d)).

39 See, for example, Displacement Solutions and Young Power in Social Action, *Guidance Note on New Land for Climate Displaced Persons in Bangladesh* (2015) http://displacementsolutions.org/wp-content/uploads/2010/03/Guidance-Note-New-

Land-for-Climate-Displaced-Persons-in-Bangladesh-FINAL.pdf accessed 25 October 2016.

40 Displacement Solutions, *Climate Displacement and Planned Relocation in Colombia: The Case of Gramalote* (2015) http://displacementsolutions.org/wp-content/uploads/2015/08/Colombia-final-Redux1.pdf accessed 25 October 2016.

41 USAID, 'Fact Sheet on Typhoon Haiyan/Yolanda in Philippines' (2014) http://iipdigital.usembassy.gov/st/english/texttrans/2013/11/20131112286248.html#ixzz3yyeFWGPR accessed 25 October 2016.

42 Displacement Solutions, *Climate Displacement in Ontong Java, Solomon Islands* (2015) http://displacementsolutions.org/wp-content/uploads/2015/11/DIS4231-Ontong-Java-Photo-journal-v2_1-WEB.pdf accessed 25 October 2016.

43 Rolnik, *Report of the Special Rapporteur*.

44 See, for example, Displacement Solutions, *Regulatory Obstacles to Rapid and Equitable Emergency and Interim Shelter Solutions after Natural Disasters* (2011).

45 See, for example, Chapter 10, this volume.

46 Rolnik, *Report of the Special Rapporteur* para. 58.

47 Often persons who do not have formal property ownership are not eligible for or receive lesser shelter or humanitarian assistance from governments or NGO agencies, despite their clear needs (Displacement Solutions, *Regulatory Obstacles*).

48 See, for example, Brookings–LSE Project on Internal Displacement, *Resettlement in the Wake of Typhoon Haiyan in the Philippines: A Strategy to Mitigate Risk or a Risky Strategy?* (2015).

49 See, for example, *Sydney Morning Herald*, 'Escaping the Waves: A Fijian Village Relocates' (3 October 2015).

50 See Reuters, 'Solomons Town First in Pacific to Relocate Due to Climate Change' (15 August 2014).

51 See, for example, Brookings–LSE Project on Internal Displacement, *Climate-Induced Displacement of Alaska Native Communities* (2013).

52 Displacement Solutions, *World Climate Displacement Map*.

53 'As climate change displacement continues, the urgency of finding solutions and avoiding marginalization, instability and other problems with protracted displacement become national, and potentially regional, security imperatives' (Brookings–LSE Project on Internal Displacement, *Climate Change* 15).

54 For example, due to damage or destruction of their homes and lands, or the risk of future climate hazards.

55 For example, individuals and communities displaced after Cyclone Aila in Bangladesh (2007), who remain without durable solutions (NRC/IDMC, *Global Estimates*).

56 See, for example, the work of the Bangladesh HLP Initiative: Displacement Solutions, 'Bangladesh HLP Initiative: Updates and Developments' (2014) http://displacementsolutions.org/bangladesh-hlp-initiative-updates-and-developments accessed 25 October 2016.

57 Brookings–LSE Project on Internal Displacement, *Climate Change*.

58 Ibid. See also Chapter 7, this volume.

59 Kälin, 'A Human Rights-Based Approach'.

60 See, for example, UN Committee on Economic, Social and Cultural Rights, *General Comment No. 7: The Right to Adequate Housing (Art.11.1): Forced Evictions* (1997) E/1998/22.

61 In particular, 'Principles 9–11' in Displacement Solutions, *Peninsula Principles on Climate Displacement within States* (2013) http://displacementsolutions.org/wp-content/uploads/FINAL-Peninsula-Principles-FINAL.pdf accessed 25 October 2016.

62 Brookings Institution, Georgetown University and UNHCR, 'Guidance on Protecting People from Disasters and Environmental Change through Planned Relocation' (2015) www.brookings.edu/research/planned-relocations-disasters-and-climate-change accessed 25 October 2016.

63 See, for example, 'Principle 10(B)', Displacement Solutions, *Peninsula Principles*: 'to enable successful preparation and planning for climate displacement, States should: ensure that no relocation shall take place unless individuals, households and communities (both displaced and host) provide full and informed consent for such relocation'.

64 Buckley Vann Town Planning Consultants, *Newsletter*, *Climate Change Adaptation Planning for Choiseul Bay Township, Solomon Islands* (2014) www.buckleyvann.com.au/wp-content/uploads/2015/11/BV-Newsletter-20-Aug-14-Climate-change-adaptation-Solomon-Is.pdf accessed 25 October 2016.

65 Ibid.

66 P. Haines, K. Rolley, S. Albert and S. McGuire, 'Empowering Solomon Islands Communities to Improve Resilience to Climate Change' (2015) 55(1) *Queensland Planner, Journal of the Planning Profession*.

67 Displacement Solutions interview with Buckley Vann Town Planners, August 2015.

68 Haines *et al.*, 'Empowering'.

69 A. McNeil, 'Solomon Islands Planners' Four-Day Intensive' (2015) 55(1) *Queensland Planner, Journal of the Planning Profession*.

70 See, for example, 'Each State shall reduce the risk of disasters by taking the necessary and appropriate measures, including through legislation and regulations, to prevent, mitigate, and prepare for disasters' (International Law Commission, *Draft Articles*).

71 See, for example, the recent comment by Mary Robinson: 'States facing climate-related displacement within their borders require significant financial support and technical expertise to develop solutions that provide for the rights of those affected. The Peninsula Principles provide a normative framework, based on human rights, to address the rights of internally displaced people' (G. Canzi, 'Q&A with Mary Robinson: What Is Climate Justice?' (2015) *The Road to Paris* http://roadtoparis.info/2015/07/29/qa-with-mary-robinson-what-is-climate-justice accessed 25 October 2016).

72 Comprehensive Disaster Management Programme (CDMP II) and Ministry of Disaster Management and Relief (MoDMR), *National Strategy on the Management of Disaster and Climate Induced Internal Displacement* (2015).

73 See, for example, the analysis contained in Displacement Solutions, *Climate Displacement in Bangladesh: Stakeholders, Laws and Policies – Mapping the Existing Institutional Framework* (2014) http://displacementsolutions.org/wp-content/uploads/Mapping-Study-Climate-Displacement-Bangladesh.pdf accessed 25 October 2016.

74 'While the enabling, guiding and coordinating roles of national and federal state governments remain essential, it is necessary to empower local authorities and local communities to reduce disaster risk, including through resources, incentives and decision-making responsibilities, as appropriate' (United Nations, *Sendai Framework* para. 19(f)).

75 See, for example, M. Burger, *Towards an Integrated Approach to Disaster Risk Management and Climate Change Adaptation* (Sabin Center for Climate Change Law 2015).

76 See note 74.

77 Paragraph 14(f) of the Cancun Adaptation Framework recognises the need for national, regional and international cooperation regarding adaptation strategies for displacement, migration and relocation (United Nations, *The Cancun Agreements*).

7 In-situ adaptation

Non-migration as a coping strategy for vulnerable persons

Dug Cubie[1]

Introduction

The contentious debate surrounding so-called 'climate migrants' often revolves around a fear of vast hordes of 'environmental refugees'[2] flooding into our (generally prosperous Western) states, as sea levels rise and arable land turns to desert. Yet the reality is that not only is every country in the world likely to be affected to some degree by climate change, but that many more people will remain in or close to areas of environmental degradation than will risk treacherous and expensive cross-border journeys. Empirical research in Malawi has found that rural communities generally wish to remain in their homes even in the face of severe climate risks, except for limited numbers of younger farmers from better-off households. However, crucially, unchecked climate stresses may erode those same communities' human, financial and social capital, consequently reducing their capacity to migrate in the future.[3] Likewise, the negative impacts of climate change can be seen in the UK National Trust's 2015 annual report into coastal erosion, which noted that erosion and flooding around the UK coastline (where large numbers of people live) was becoming more apparent and widespread as a result of climate change.[4] For this reason, the National Trust has advocated for the UK to 'rethink our approach to coastal protection. We must embrace adaptive responses to managing coastal change as an equally valid approach to engineering responses – investing in adaptation where it's shown to be the best approach.'[5]

Such an approach reflects the Department of Environment, Food and Rural Affairs' advice to UK local councils: 'The first step has to be accepting that some form of climate change is happening, assessing the risks and then taking action within your own community to reduce your vulnerability to these changes.'[6] Few people would choose to live in a severely environmentally degraded area, whether in Malawi or the UK, and so it is recognised that some individuals and communities will be forced to leave areas that become uninhabitable as a result of climate change.[7] However, not everyone will be willing or able to leave areas of high risk, so this poses certain challenges for policy-makers to ensure that the rights of those who remain behind are respected through the application of in-situ adaptation measures.[8]

This chapter therefore examines the application of international human rights standards to the protection of vulnerable individuals, families and communities faced with the need to undertake adaptation to the negative impacts of climate change. Migration from environmentally stressed areas, either internally or cross-border, is widely recognised as an important adaptation mechanism – yet not all individuals or families are willing or able to move from their homes.[9] A case in point occurred in October 2014 when a campaign group called Pacific Climate Warriors, comprising members of twelve small Pacific island states, undertook direct action by blockading Australian coal ships to protest against the impact of climate change and to highlight their desire to remain in their homes and traditional lands.[10]

Indeed, apart from localised situations of catastrophic environmental degradation or habitat loss, in the short to medium term few parts of the world will become completely uninhabitable due to climate change. It therefore follows that non-migrants who remain in areas of increasing, but not catastrophic, environmental stress may face a range of humanitarian and human rights challenges, including livelihood erosion, deteriorating health and reduced life expectancy.[11] So, although certain community members (particularly those who are economically active) may migrate as a personal coping strategy and subsequently act as external support for family and community who remain behind, the issue of non-migration as a coping strategy to climate change also needs to be considered.[12] At its core, the discussion revolves around the right to stay and the right to leave.[13] Therefore, this chapter argues that states need to establish procedures in conjunction with local affected communities to determine which measures can and should be taken to strengthen their resilience so that the right to stay is an effective and meaningful option, rather than simply a right to be poor and hungry.[14]

After setting out four key premises regarding the relationship between climate change, migration and human rights, this chapter examines the concepts of vulnerability, state obligations to respect, protect and fulfil human rights, and human rights-based approaches to climate change. Next, the chapter examines non-migration as a coping strategy in the face of climatic risks and environmental degradation, before arguing that human rights principles should be applied in all actions affecting individuals, families and communities that are unable or unwilling to leave their homes in the face of such hazards. The chapter concludes by highlighting the key role played by procedural rights (in particular the right of access to information, the right to participate in decision-making and the right to effective access to justice and administrative proceedings) to allow communities to make informed decisions as to whether to stay or leave. Such rights must be implemented in conjunction with structural and non-structural adaptation measures by states to ensure that communities can adapt or migrate with dignity.[15]

The relationship between climate change, migration and human rights

Considering the complex and evolving nature of both the anthropogenic source of global climate change and the difficulty in identifying the causal linkages between climate change and migration, this chapter takes as its starting point four key premises:

1 Climate change is already creating negative impacts in many parts of the world.
2 Climate change and human rights are interlinked.
3 Counter-measures in the form of mitigation and adaptation are required to offset these negative impacts.
4 Climate change is not necessarily the sole driver of migratory decisions.

These statements can be backed up by both scientific data and social science research. So, before commencing substantive discussion of in-situ adaptation as a coping strategy, it is beneficial briefly to summarise the basis for these premises. First of all, the comprehensive Intergovernmental Panel on Climate Change (IPCC) SREX report on extreme weather and climate events concluded that there is evidence of changes in the frequency and severity of extreme weather and climate events, alongside increased economic losses from weather- and climate-related disasters.[16] Moreover, the IPCC has stressed that warming of the climate system is taking place and that it is extremely likely that the majority of this warming arises from anthropogenic activities.[17]

Second, if climate change is creating negative impacts at the local, national, regional and international levels, it follows that actual and potential violations of well-established human rights are already taking place. Indeed, the December 2015 Paris Agreement under the UN Framework Convention on Climate Change (UNFCCC) acknowledged that when taking action to address climate change, states should respect, promote and consider their respective human rights obligations, including for people in vulnerable situations.[18] Likewise, the UN High Commissioner for Human Rights has highlighted that a wide range of human rights may be breached by climate change, including the rights to life, adequate standard of living, food, water, health and housing.[19] Therefore, it is important to consider human rights principles, such as participation, empowerment and accountability, in developing any adaptation measures.[20] It follows that it is necessary to minimise the impact of climate change through mitigation measures tackling its root causes (i.e. the emission of greenhouse gases), while simultaneously recognising that climate change is not just a future threat, so we must adapt to these increased threats and vulnerabilities today. Such an approach was adopted in the 2010 Cancun Adaptation Framework, which argues that 'climate change represents an urgent and potentially irreversible threat to human societies and the planet', noting that 'adaptation must be addressed with the same priority as mitigation and requires appropriate institutional arrangements to enhance adaptation action and support'.[21] While this chapter primarily focuses on adaptation processes, the symbiotic relationship between adaptation and mitigation activities cannot be ignored.[22]

Finally, while there is strong evidence that increased risks from sudden-onset hydro-meteorological hazards such as hurricanes, storm surges and flooding, or from slow-onset environmental degradation such as droughts, desertification or salt-water intrusion, will lead to population movements away from high-risk areas,[23] determining the causal factors leading to domestic and international migration is complex. As noted by Renaud *et al.* (2007), it can be difficult to disaggregate the root causes of migration, as economic, social, environmental and security factors may all play roles,[24] thereby presenting one of the first challenges in determining the appropriate legal and policy responses to climate-induced migration. Nevertheless, the Cancun Adaptation Framework invites parties to the UNFCCC to undertake 'measures to enhance understanding, coordination and cooperation with regard to climate change induced displacement, migration and planned relocation, where appropriate, at the national, regional and international levels'.[25]

Therefore, it is necessary to consider how these four premises should underpin our understanding of the negative impacts of climate change, and guide our policy responses in regard to the migratory options available for persons facing climatic stress. The following section introduces some of the key concepts required to apply these four premises on the ground, namely: the need to differentiate between structural and non-structural adaptation policies; the interconnected questions of vulnerability and capacity; and a state's obligations under international human rights law.

From theory to practice: advancing policy coherence

Adaptation, mitigation and resilience

The generally accepted definition of 'adaptation' of human systems to climate change is 'the process of adjustment to actual or expected climate and its effects, in order to moderate harm or exploit beneficial opportunities'.[26] Adaptation can then be broken down into a variety of different forms. For example, *planned* adaptation takes place as a result of a deliberate policy action, while *anticipatory* or *proactive* adaptation occurs before the impacts of climate change are observed.[27] Geographically, adaptation can occur in-situ, when measures are taken to minimise the need for people to leave a particular area in the first place; or ex situ, which involves the movement of people, systems and/or assets from a place of vulnerability.[28] In terms of substantive activities, structural adaptation measures include physical constructions such as dams, dykes and strengthened housing stock, while non-structural adaptation measures include changes to land use regulations, early warning systems and improved disaster management institutions, policies and procedures.[29]

In contrast to adaptation measures to reduce the impacts (or symptoms) of climate change, 'mitigation' refers to 'anthropogenic interventions to reduce the anthropogenic forcing of the climate system'[30] – in other words, measures to tackle the root causes of climate change through reductions in greenhouse gas emissions.[31]

Finally, 'resilience' refers to the 'capacity of social, economic, and environmental systems to cope with a hazardous event or trend or disturbance, responding or reorganising in ways that maintain their essential function, identity, and structure, while also maintaining the capacity for adaptation, learning, and transformation'.[32] So, while it is recognised that certain changes may need to be made to everyone's daily life as a result of climate change, adaptation and mitigation measures are aimed at ensuring that the basic structure and functioning of societies are not fundamentally destroyed. Generally speaking, the greater an individual's or community's level of resilience, the less vulnerable they are to the negative effects of climate change due to limitations in their own adaptive capacity.

Understanding vulnerability and capacity

Vulnerability and capacity assessment techniques (VCAs) were developed by practitioners in the 1990s as a means of collecting, analysing and systematising information on a given community's vulnerability to hazards in a structured and meaningful way.[33] Reflecting global trends, organisations such as the Red Cross Movement now include hazards associated with climate change in their analyses.[34] From a more academic perspective, Terry Cannon from the UK Institute of Development Studies examined the issue of human vulnerability to natural hazards and identified five interrelated components to an individual's vulnerability, namely: livelihood strength and resilience; well-being and baseline status; self-protection; social protection; and governance.[35] Frank Thomalla et al. (2006) have additionally highlighted that the underlying causes of vulnerability have been ignored by both disaster risk reduction and climate change adaptation practitioners and academics, noting that these disciplines have largely developed and operated in isolation from each other.[36] Thomalla et al. argue that the extended timescale for the long-term threats posed by climate change, compared with more immediate threats posed by disasters and forced displacement, mean that lawyers and policy-makers need to examine ways to develop effective frameworks that take the social complexities of at-risk populations into account through an interdisciplinary approach that bridges the various research and policy communities. Cannon is likewise keen to stress that vulnerability is only one aspect of the equation; so, rather than simply focusing on individuals' or communities' perceived vulnerabilities, academics and policy-makers alike must also look to their pre-existing capacities and determine ways to strengthen these to foster resilience and positive coping strategies.[37]

A cogent example of differential vulnerabilities and capacities is provided by Barnett and Webber (2009), who cite the similar environmental stressors faced by farmers in parts of Australia and northern Ethiopia during periods of drought. The fact that families in northern Ethiopia may well have to migrate to avoid the effects of hunger, while Australian families do not, highlights the complex relationship between poverty, vulnerability, resilience and ultimately the calculated decision to stay or leave an area facing environmental stress.[38] Barnett and Webber conclude that 'social processes that create poverty and marginality are more important determinants of likely migration outcomes than environmental changes *per se*'.[39] Thus, tackling the root causes of poverty and vulnerability wherever possible will positively impact on individual and family capacities and so their need to undertake coping migratory strategies in the first place.

However, it is essential that those most affected are allowed to participate in the decision-making process. The Mary Robinson Foundation – Climate Justice (MRFCJ) has developed an understanding of the concept of climate justice as one that links human rights and development to achieve a 'human-centred approach, safeguarding the rights of the most vulnerable and sharing the burdens and benefits of climate change and its resolution equitably and fairly'. Key to this approach is a set of principles of climate justice that draw on international human rights law to argue that the dignity of the person is at the core of climate justice.[40] Moreover, the principles recognise both the horizontal obligations between states at the international level and the vertical relationship between a state and persons on its territory, particularly the most vulnerable members of society.[41] The principles therefore highlight that 'The opportunity to participate in decision-making processes which are fair, accountable, open and corruption-free is essential to the growth of a culture of climate justice. The voices of the most vulnerable to climate change must be heard and acted upon.'[42] This leads us to consider the role that human rights law plays in influencing the policy and resource decisions of states and the international community in attempting to minimise the negative impacts of climate change.

State obligations to respect, protect and fulfil human rights

The now well-established tripartite typology of a state's obligations to respect, protect and fulfil all human rights was initially proposed by UN Rapporteur Asbjørn Eide in the context of the right to food. In his 1987 report, Eide set out that, at the primary level, states must respect the freedom of individuals to take action relating to the resources necessary for their livelihoods. Moreover, states should protect individuals' freedom of action and use of resources when these are challenged by third parties; while, as a last resort, the state has an obligation to fulfil individuals' expectations in relation to the enjoyment of their rights.[43] This understanding of a state's obligations has since been widely accepted, and has been credited with encouraging the justiciability of economic, social and cultural rights (ESCRs), such as the rights to water, health and housing.[44] In its General Comment 14 on the right to the highest attainable standard of health, the UN Committee on Economic, Social and Cultural Rights reaffirmed the applicability of these three levels of obligation to all human rights, not just ESCRs.[45]

In low-income areas, non-migration in the face of environmental degradation may actually be an indication of extreme vulnerability as individuals are *unable* to migrate, rather than simply do not wish to migrate.[46] If this is the case, these particularly vulnerable people may need priority access to a wide range of in-situ agricultural, economic and income-generating programmes as well as social protection measures, such as access to healthcare, education and climate forecasts.[47] François Gemenne has justifiably argued that the most vulnerable members of society may also need specific assistance to leave so that they are not forced to stay in an area of environmental degradation.[48] In other words, different migratory decisions will be taken based on an individual's or family's livelihood strength and well-being, overall baseline status and resilience to an actual or perceived hazard, as supplemented by self-protection strategies such as facilitating the migration of economically active family members to create a remittance stream to support those who have remained. As states have obligations to minimise potential human rights violations arising from the negative effects of climate change through concrete measures to respect, protect and fulfil international human rights law, of equal importance in whether people are ultimately forced to move from their homes are the concomitant state-supported measures of social protection and good governance (or lack thereof) to minimise expected or actual negative impacts. It is therefore pertinent to consider what role, if any, non-migration plays as a coping strategy in the face of environmental stressors.

Non-migration as a coping strategy

The International Organization for Migration (IOM) has stressed that there are no reliable figures for the projected number of potential 'environmental migrants'. Estimates of the number of people displaced by 2050 for environmental reasons vary by a factor of 40 – from a low of 25 million to a high of 1 billion.[49] This understandably creates problems for policy- and decision-makers in determining the correct measures to put in place. However, it is not an excuse for inaction. Individuals in environmentally stressed areas face three stark choices: forced displacement, pre-emptive migration or in-situ adaptation. While there has been a level of discussion and debate around the first two choices, encompassing issues such as expanding the definition of 'refugee' to encompass 'climate refugees', voluntary and involuntary relocation programmes, and improved work visa mechanisms,[50] there has been insufficient analysis of those who choose – or are forced – to remain at home despite threats to their livelihoods and health. Graeme Hugo (1996) stressed the continuum between voluntary and forced migration, and the difficulty in determining the exact causal factors influencing a decision to migrate.[51] Individuals may flee in advance of a major natural disaster, only to return soon afterwards to help with reconstruction. Alternatively, an economically active family member may migrate internally within a country from a rural to an urban setting on a seasonal basis to augment family income, while others may be in a position to follow established international migration routes.[52] Such pre-emptive migration can act as an advance party for future migration by other family members or as a means of securing remittances for those remaining in the stressed environment. The multifaceted reasons behind people's differential migratory decisions must therefore be recognised, and Gemenne has highlighted the risk of environmental determinism, whereby environmental factors are seen as the sole driver of decisions to migrate.[53]

However, there is also a tendency for different groups, such as environmental scientists, the humanitarian community and demographers, to articulate their concerns regarding climate-induced migration from their own disciplinary perspectives. Bardsley and Hugo (2010) argue that this can result in policy-makers focusing exclusively on the socio-economic drivers of migration, in other words the human mobility side of the equation, while neglecting the most effective adaptation measures and the importance of the environment's impact on socio-economic well-being.[54] The application of in-situ adaptation measures may delay or negate the need for individuals to leave their homes, and therefore delay or negate the corresponding need to rely on ex situ adaptation measures – in other words reduce the need to migrate from a place of vulnerability.[55] Nevertheless, Bardsley and Hugo caution that a threshold, or tipping point, may be crossed, whereby in-situ adaptation measures either fail or are perceived as inadequate. When this occurs, migration as an adaptation strategy becomes a realistic – or indeed the only – viable option.[56] Of note, the IPCC has argued:

> If disasters occur more frequently and/or with greater magnitude, some local areas will become increasingly marginal as places to live or in which to maintain livelihoods. In such cases, migration and displacement could become permanent and could introduce new pressures in areas of relocation. For locations such as atolls, in some cases it is possible that many residents will have to relocate.[57]

Notwithstanding alarmist reports and statistics generated around the potential numbers of 'environmental migrants', Barnett and Webber argue that the total number of persons who remain in places of environmental stress may in fact be far greater. Particular challenges will therefore arise not just because the people who remain are more likely to be vulnerable members of society as a result of poverty, remoteness, ill-health or age, but also because those who remain will be less visible than large groups of forcibly displaced people.[58] As noted by the UNHCR, 'most people do not want to leave their communities and those who are unable to leave may be particularly vulnerable. Adaptation strategies must thus support both those who leave and those who stay.'[59] Due to the disproportionate impact on women from climate change, gender-sensitive vulnerability assessments are specifically required as part of this process for both migrant and non-migrant women.[60] Moreover, it is important to recognise that in-situ adaptation measures can strengthen the linkages between climate change adaptation and disaster risk reduction to minimise the negative impacts for those persons who remain, or to assist them to return and rebuild following catastrophic events, such as hydro-meteorological disasters.[61]

It follows that if non-migration as a coping strategy, coupled with effective in-situ adaptation measures, is a realistic and viable option for at least some of those individuals and communities facing environmental stress, it is important to ensure that the process of determining the needs of the community, and the structural and non-structural adaptation measures required, complies with general human rights standards. Jane McAdam (2012) has noted the different approaches taken by the governments of Kiribati and Tuvalu to the question of migration or non-migration.[62] The authorities in Kiribati have stressed the need for managed migration avenues, as opposed to refugee protection regimes, as an adaptation strategy over the next thirty–fifty years. Meanwhile, the authorities in Tuvalu are fighting hard to allow people to remain in their homes through a range of in-situ adaptation measures, such as disaster risk reduction and sustainable development programmes. Interestingly, other Pacific islanders who already have viable migration options, such as Micronesia and the Marshall Islands, are also arguing for in-situ adaptation before large-scale migration is considered.[63]

Undoubtedly, there is a range of political, economic, social and cultural reasons behind the different stances taken by various Pacific island states on the front line of climate-induced migration. However, this simply highlights the need to ensure the lead role of the affected communities themselves in any discussions about their future, and the importance of ensuring that all viable migration avenues remain open.

Another example of the differential perspectives of local communities comes from the Arctic. The Inuit Circumpolar Council has strongly publicised the negative impact of climate change on their traditional culture and lifestyles across Canada, Alaska and Greenland, including filing an unsuccessful petition before the Inter-American Commission of Human Rights.[64] However, the retreating polar icecap also presents economic opportunities, not least increasing access to potential fossil fuel deposits. The Greenland Prime Minister, Aleqa Hammond, has noted: 'Climate change and this resultant new industrialisation brings new risks. We must understand that the effects will be both positive and negative ... We are vulnerable but we know how to adapt.'[65]

Reflecting the intertwined root causes of migration, Gibb and Ford (2012) have highlighted that, for many communities, adaptation is required not just to climate change but also to other stressors, such as rapid urbanisation and unsustainable development processes.[66] As a result, those vulnerable communities most likely to be impacted by climate change face particular challenges for in-situ adaptation, through living within marginal ecosystems or other high-risk locations, their dependence on natural resources for livelihoods, an overall limited adaptation capacity, and greater risk of human rights violations (including a lack of participation, equality or accountability mechanisms).[67]

Therefore, it is important to reiterate that non-migration following effective in-situ adaptation measures is not an appropriate coping strategy for all scenarios. Living in a flooded environment is not a dignified way of life, even if one is able to adapt one's house by adding stilts and designing a floating garden.[68] Hence, measures taken to promote in-situ adaptation capacity need to recognise the differential resilience and vulnerabilities of specific communities. In particular, measures need to increase the social capital of individuals and communities to make their own decisions; ensure acceptable, diversified livelihoods and income sources; avoid involuntary resettlement or relocation; and respect, protect and fulfil the inherent dignity of all persons through participatory and accountable processes.[69] The final section of this chapter will therefore consider the forms that such processes may take.

Adaptation with dignity

Applying a human rights-based framework to climate-induced migration means in practice that all actions regarding both migration and non-migration decisions fully respect, protect and fulfil international human rights law and principles, not least the principle of human dignity.[70] As with human rights themselves, the concept of human dignity has both a legal and a more general application. While an enforceable 'right to dignity' may not exist,[71] the International Law Commission (the UN body responsible for the codification and progressive development of international law) has recognised that human dignity is 'the core principle that informs and underpins international human rights law'.[72] Jane McAdam has noted the similarity between the need to ensure migration with dignity and the need to ensure adaptation with dignity.[73] Therefore, recognising that an individual legally binding right to dignity may not exist per se, it is nevertheless argued that principles of international human rights law are directly applicable to ensuring that persons who are unable or unwilling to migrate in the face of environmental degradation are still treated with dignity and respect.

Rather than elaborating on the substantive content arising from such an approach, this section will briefly focus on the principles and governance processes required for understanding and applying human rights-based approaches to in-situ adaptation by the relevant authorities. It is contended that applying a human rights-based approach would help ensure that the negative impacts of climate change on particularly vulnerable people can be minimised by focusing on the vertical relationship between a state and all persons on its territory, and the explicit identification of the rights-holders and duty-bearers who are responsible for delivering the associated rights. As set out in discussions on the post-2015 frameworks for sustainable development,[74] human rights-based frameworks are built on the principles of participation, accountability, non-discrimination, empowerment and the rule of law.

Of particular importance in the context of climate change and migration are those procedural rights set out in Principle 10 of the Rio Declaration on Environment and Development: the right to access information; the right to participate in decision-making; and the right to effective access to justice and administrative proceedings, including redress and remedies.[75] Such rights go to the heart of participation and empowerment for local communities.[76] Moreover, as Marc Limon (2009) has argued, accountability mechanisms linked to such procedural rights are crucial to ensure effective, legitimate and sustainable policy responses in environmental matters.[77] The UN Office of the High Commissioner for Human Rights (OHCHR 2012) has likewise noted that improved accountability helps 'strengthen political commitment and justifications for resource allocations, and improves incentives for the fair delivery of social services'.[78]

So, if one accepts that large numbers of people will remain in environmentally stressed areas, whether by choice or otherwise, it is necessary for authorities to ensure adequate information as to the potential risks, as well as concrete measures to minimise those risks, while providing redress and remedies for the negative impacts of climate change on their homes, livelihoods and land. Structural and non-structural in-situ adaptation measures, developed in consultation with the local community, therefore provide an important (but not exclusive) course of action. Nevertheless, successful in-situ adaptation is dependent on a range of factors, not least: the speed of climate change globally and in particular regions; individuals' and communities' psychological and physical adaptation capacities and vulnerabilities; sufficient human and financial resources; political will at the national, regional and international levels; and the development of holistic preparatory and response frameworks (in particular those relating to disaster risk reduction, sustainable development and climate change).[79] Moreover, in addition to tackling the root cause of climate change (i.e. reducing greenhouse gas emissions via effective mitigation measures), it is necessary to identify the interlinking reasons behind particular migratory flows and to take action on underlying drivers of migration, such as poverty, vulnerability, lack of infrastructure and lack of preparedness.

As noted by the Mary Robinson Foundation – Climate Justice (2011), 'the idea of human rights points societies towards internationally agreed values around which common action can be negotiated and then acted upon'.[80] By instituting a human rights-based approach that embraces participation, empowerment through access to information, and accountability mechanisms, in-situ adaptation can be undertaken in a manner that respects the dignity of those most affected by climate change. If such an approach is adopted before a situation of catastrophic land loss or environmental degradation comes to pass, should such a tipping point occur and involuntary relocation be subsequently required, processes and governance structures will already be in place to ensure that individuals and communities are able to migrate with dignity.

Conclusions

This brief analysis is not intended to provide detailed examples of in-situ adaptation measures that may be undertaken to promote non-migration as a coping strategy. What has been identified is the need for human rights-based approaches that recognise that individuals, families and/or communities may be unable or unwilling to migrate in the face of environmental stressors. This may be particularly true for people who are specifically vulnerable due to age, gender, ill-health, poverty or other reasons. If this is the case, drawing on the principles of climate justice elaborated by the Mary Robinson Foundation – Climate Justice, and a state's obligations under international human rights law to respect, protect and fulfil all human rights, key actions must be taken as part of a participatory process whereby governments, local authorities and communities decide what is best for their futures. Is it remaining in place with appropriate adaptation measures implemented, or is it support for internal or international migration programmes? The principles of participation, empowerment and accountability must therefore be incorporated into all policy and decision-making processes to ensure that local communities face neither forced relocation nor forced adaptation, and that they can migrate or adapt with dignity.

Notes

1 Lecturer in Law, School of Law, University College Cork, Ireland. I would like to thank Mary Dobbs and Anja Mihr for their insightful comments on an early draft of this chapter.
2 For discussion of the terminology, see Chapter 3, this volume.
3 N. Suckalla, E. Fraser and P. Forster, 'Reduced Migration under Climate Change: Evidence from Malawi using an Aspirations and Capabilities Framework' (2016) *Climate and Development* www.tandfonline.com/doi/full/10.1080/17565529.2016.1149441 accessed 25 October 2016.
4 National Trust, *Shifting Shores* (2015) 12.
5 Ibid.
6 Department of Environment, Food and Rural Affairs (DEFRA), *Adapting to Climate Change: A Guide for Local Councils* (2010) 11 www.gov.uk/government/uploads/system/uploads/attachment_data/file/218798/adapt-local councilguide.pdf accessed 25 October 2016. For a discussion of the role of local and regional authorities in tackling climate change, see K. H. Hirokawa and J. Rosenbloom, 'Climate Change Adaptation and Land Use Planning Law' in J. Verschuuren (ed.), *Research Handbook on Climate Change Adaptation Law* (Edward Elgar 2013) 325.
7 For a comprehensive discussion of migration as a form of adaptation, see R. McLeman and B. Smit, 'Migration as an Adaptation to Climate Change' (2006) 76 *Climatic Change* 31.

8 Suckalla *et al.* ('Reduced Migration' 10) have cautioned climate scientists 'not to underestimate people's capacity or willingness to remain rooted in their home environment'.

9 For a discussion of different migration strategies in Nepal and Thailand, see D. Bardsley and G. Hugo, 'Migration and Climate Change: Examining Thresholds of Change to Guide Effective Adaptation Decision-Making' (2010) 32 *Population and Environment* 238.

10 See H. Fair, 'Not Drowning but Fighting: Pacific Islands Activists' (2015) 49 *Forced Migration Review* 58, who argues: 'the Pacific Climate Warriors present a grassroots message of hope and agency, in contrast to narratives of inevitable climate-induced population displacement. They remind us that all is not lost in Oceania and that, with committed effective action on climate change, mass forced migration in the Pacific may never come to pass.'

11 J. Barnett and M. Webber, 'Accommodating Migration to Promote Adaptation to Climate Change' (2009) policy brief prepared for the Secretariat of the Swedish Commission on Climate Change and Development and the World Bank World Development Report 2010 team 12–13.

12 C. Gibb and J. Ford, 'Should the United Nations Framework Convention on Climate Change Recognize Climate Migrants?' (2012) 7(4) *Environmental Research Letters*.

13 Barnett and Webber, 'Accommodating Migration' 6: 'In any decision to move, perceptions of the risks of staying and the risks of moving are important variables.'

14 See, for example, D. Bacon, 'The Right to Stay Home' (14 July 2008) *Truthout* www. truthout.org/article/the-right-stay-home accessed 25 October 2016.

15 The terms 'displacement with dignity' and 'adaptation with dignity' come from J. McAdam and B. Saul, 'Displacement with Dignity: International Law and Policy Responses to Climate Change Migration and Security in Bangladesh' (2010) Sydney Law School, Legal Studies Research Paper No. 10/113. See also 'Facilitating Migration with Dignity' in Nansen Initiative, *Agenda for the Protection of Cross-Border Displaced Persons in the Context of Disasters and Climate Change* (2015) Vol. 1, 47–48.

16 Intergovernmental Panel on Climate Change (IPCC), 'Summary for Policymakers' in C. B. Field *et al.* (eds), *Managing the Risks of Extreme Events and Disasters to Advance Climate Change Adaptation: A Special Report of Working Groups I and II of the Intergovernmental Panel on Climate Change* (Cambridge University Press 2012) 6–7 (hereafter the 'SREX Report').

17 The IPCC stated in 2013: 'Warming of the climate system is unequivocal, and since the 1950s, many of the observed changes are unprecedented over decades to millennia … It is extremely likely that more than half of the observed increase in global average surface temperature from 1951 to 2010 was caused by the anthropogenic increase in greenhouse gas concentrations and other anthropogenic forcings together' (Intergovernmental Panel on Climate Change (IPCC), 'Summary for Policymakers' in T. F. Stocker *et al.* (eds), *Climate Change 2013: The Physical Science Basis: Contribution of Working Group I to the Fifth Assessment Report of the Intergovernmental Panel on Climate Change* (Cambridge University Press 2013) 4, 17).

18 UNFCCC, *Paris Agreement Concluded at the 21st Conference of the Parties to the UN Framework Convention on Climate Change* (adopted 12 December 2015, entered into force 4 November 2016) FCCC/CP/2015/L.9/Rev.1.

19 United Nations, Office of the High Commissioner for Human Rights (OHCHR), *Report of the Office of the UN High Commissioner for Human Rights on the Relationship between Climate Change and Human Rights* (2009) A/HCR/10/61 8–15. See also M. M. Naser, 'Climate Change and Forced Displacement: Obligation of States under International Human Rights Law' (2010) 22(2) *Sri Lanka Journal of International Law* 117.

20 For a discussion of the connections between climate change and human rights, see M. Wewerinke, 'The Role of the UN Human Rights Council in Addressing Climate Change' (2014) 8(1) *Human Rights and International Discourse* 10; D. Cubie,

'Promoting Dignity for All: Human Rights Approaches in the Post-2015 Climate Change, Disaster Risk Reduction and Sustainable Development Frameworks' (2014) 8(1) *Human Rights and International Discourse* 36–51.

21 United Nations, *The Cancun Agreements: Outcome of the Work of the Ad Hoc Working Group on Long-Term Cooperative Action under the Convention* (2011) FCCC/ CP/2010/7/Add.1 Article 2(b) (hereafter 'Cancun Adaptation Framework').

22 J. Verschuuren, 'Introduction' in Verschuuren (ed.), *Research Handbook* 8–9.

23 See, for example, SREX Report 14.

24 F. Renaud, J. J. Bogardi, O. Dun and K. Warner, 'Control, Adapt or Flee: How to Face Environmental Migration?' (UNU Institute for Environment and Human Security 2007) 10.

25 Cancun Adaptation Framework Article 14(f).

26 SREX Report 3.

27 See Intergovernmental Panel on Climate Change (IPCC), 'Glossary A–D' (2007) in *Climate Change 2007: Working Group II: Impacts, Adaptation and Vulnerability* www.ipcc.ch/publications_and_data/ar4/wg2/en/annexessglossary-a-d. html accessed 25 October 2016.

28 Bardsley and Hugo, 'Migration and Climate Change' 241–243.

29 Ibid. 254.

30 See IPCC, 'Glossary A–D'

31 Key to future mitigation efforts will be the December 2015 Paris Agreement.

32 Intergovernmental Panel on Climate Change (IPCC), 'Summary for Policymakers' in C. B. Field, V. R. Barros, D. J. Dokken, K. J. Mach, M. D. Mastrandrea, T. E. Bilir, M. Chatterjee, K. L. Ebi, Y. O. Estrada, R. C. Genova, B. Girma, E. S. Kissel, A. N. Levy, S. MacCracken, P. R. Mastrandrea and L. L. White (eds), *Climate Change 2014: Impacts, Adaptation, and Vulnerability. Part A: Global and Sectoral Aspects. Contribution of Working Group II to the Fifth Assessment Report of the Intergovernmental Panel on Climate Change* (Cambridge University Press 2014) 5. It should be noted that definitions of 'resilience' are contested. See L. Olsson *et al.*, 'Why Resilience Is Unappealing to Social Science: Theoretical and Empirical Investigations of the Scientific Use of Resilience' (2015) 1(4) *Science Advances*; S. Levine *et al.*, *The Relevance of 'Resilience'?* (Overseas Development Institute 2012) Humanitarian Policy Group Policy Brief 49.

33 International Federation of Red Cross and Red Crescent Societies (IFRC), *What Is VCA? An Introduction to Vulnerability and Capacity Assessment* (2006) 4–5.

34 See, for example, International Federation of Red Cross and Red Crescent Societies (IFRC), *Integrating Climate Change and Urban Risks into the VCA: Ensure Effective Participatory Analysis and Enhanced Community Action* (2014).

35 T. Cannon, 'Reducing People's Vulnerability to Natural Hazards: Communities and Resilience' (United Nations University, World Institute for Development Economic Research 2008), Research Paper No. 2008/34 2–3.

36 F. Thomalla *et al.*, 'Reducing Hazard Vulnerability: Towards a Common Approach between Disaster Risk Reduction and Climate Adaptation' (2006) 30(1) *Disasters* 39, 41–44.

37 Cannon, 'Reducing People's Vulnerability' 2.

38 Barnett and Webber, 'Accommodating Migration' 6.

39 Ibid.

40 Mary Robinson Foundation – Climate Justice, Principles of Climate Justice (2011) www.mrfcj.org/pdf/Principles-of-Climate-Justice.pdf accessed 25 October 2016. The principles were developed following an expert consultative process. For further discussion of the concept of climate justice, see Chapter 4, this volume.

41 For a discussion of the impact of climate change on the human rights of specific groups, such as women, children and indigenous peoples, see UN OHCHR, *Report on Climate Change and Human Rights* 15, 18.

42 Mary Robinson Foundation – Climate Justice, Principles of Climate Justice.

43 UN Commission on Human Rights, Sub-Commission on Prevention of Discrimination and Protection of Minorities, *Report on the Right to Adequate Food as a Human Right Submitted by Mr Asbjørn Eide, Special Rapporteur* (1987) E/CN.4/Sub.2/1987/23, paras. 112–114.

44 O. De Schutter, *International Human Rights Law* (Cambridge University Press 2010) 248. See also M. Dennis and D. Stewart, 'Justiciability of Economic, Social and Cultural Rights: Should There Be an International Complaints Mechanism to Adjudicate the Rights to Food, Water, Housing and Health?' (2004) 98 *American Journal of International Law* 462.

45 UN Committee on Economic, Social and Cultural Rights, *General Comment No. 14: The Right to the Highest Attainable Standard of Health* (2000) E/C.12/2000/4 paras. 33–37.

46 Suckalla *et al.*, 'Reduced Migration'.

47 Barnett and Webber 'Accommodating Migration' 40.

48 F. Gemenne, 'Migration Doesn't Have to Be a Failure to Adapt: An Escape from Environmental Determinism' in J. Palutikof *et al.* (eds), *Climate Adaptation Futures* (John Wiley & Sons 2013) 240. See also Chapter 8, this volume, on the impact of heatwaves on the most vulnerable.

49 International Organization for Migration (IOM), 'Brief 5: State of Knowledge on Migration, Environment and Climate Change' in IOM, *Outlook on Migration, Environment and Climate Change* (2014) 38. See also E. Ferris, 'Climate Change Is Displacing People Now: Alarmists vs. Skeptics' (21 May 2014) www.brookings.edu/blogs/planetpolicy/posts/2014/05/21-climate-change-displacement-ferris accessed 25 October 2016.

50 See, for example, M. Gromilova and N. Jägers, 'Climate Change Induced Displacement and International Law' in Verschuuren, *Research Handbook* 70; J. McAdam, 'Swimming against the Tide: Why a Climate Change Displacement Treaty Is Not the Answer' (2011) 23(1) *International Journal of Refugee Law* 2.

51 G. Hugo, 'Environmental Concerns and International Migration' (1996) 30(1) *International Migration Review* 105, 113–118. See also Chapter 2, this volume.

52 See Bardsley and Hugo, 'Migration and Climate Change'; Suckalla *et al.*, 'Reduced Migration'.

53 Gemenne, 'Migration Doesn't Have to Be a Failure to Adapt' 236.

54 Bardsley and Hugo, 'Migration and Climate Change' 240.

55 Ibid. 243.

56 Ibid.

57 SREX Report 14.

58 Barnett and Webber, 'Accommodating Migration' 12–13.

59 UNHCR, 'Summary of Deliberations on Climate Change and Displacement' (2011) 23(3) *International Journal of Refugee Law* 561, 573.

60 N. Chindarkar, 'Gender and Climate Change-Induced Migration: Proposing a Framework for Analysis' (2012) 7(2) *Environmental Research Letters* 1.

61 As noted by the IPCC (SREX Report 9): 'Closer integration of disaster risk management and climate change adaptation, along with the incorporation of both into local, sub-national, national, and international development policies and practices, could provide benefits at all scales.'

62 J. McAdam, *Climate Change, Forced Migration, and International Law* (Oxford University Press 2012) 200–201. See also Chapter 11, this volume.

63 As Hannah Fair ('Not Drowning but Fighting' 58–59) has argued: 'the Pacific Climate Warriors present a grassroots message of hope and agency, in contrast to narratives of inevitable climate-induced population displacement. They remind us that all is not lost in Oceania and that, with committed effective action on climate change, mass forced migration in the Pacific may never come to pass.'

64 Inuit Circumpolar Conference, *Petition to the Inter-American Commission on Human Rights Seeking Relief from Violations Resulting from Global Warming Caused by Acts and Omissions of the United States* (2005). See also Chapter 9, this volume.

65   J. Vidal, 'Climate Change Brings New Risks to Greenland, Says PM Aleqa Hammond' (23 January 2014) *Guardian* www.theguardian.com/environment/2014/jan/23/climate-change-risks-greenland-arctic-icecap accessed 25 October 2016.

66   Gibb and Ford, 'Should the UNFCCC Recognize Climate Migrants?' 5.

67   Ibid.

68   McAdam and Saul, 'Displacement with Dignity' 28.

69   For a discussion of 'pro-poor approaches' to climate change adaptation, see R. Heltberg, P. B. Siegel and S. L. Jorgensen, 'Social Policies for Adaptation to Climate Change' in R. Mearns and A. Norton (eds), *Social Dimensions of Climate Change: Equity and Vulnerability in a Warming World* (World Bank 2010).

70   As noted in the preambles to both the International Covenant on Civil and Political Rights and the International Covenant on Economic, Social and Cultural Rights, 'Recognising that these rights derive from the inherent dignity of the human person.'

71   For a discussion, see C. O'Mahony, 'There Is No Such Thing as a Right to Dignity' (2012) 10(2) *International Journal of Constitutional Law* 551.

72   For text of the commentaries regarding human dignity, see UN General Assembly, 'Chapter IX: Protection of Persons in the Event of Disasters' in *Sixty-Sixth Session, Supplement No. 10* (2011) A/66/10 258–260.

73   McAdam and Saul, 'Displacement with Dignity'; McAdam, *Climate Change* 201. David Ritter, CEO of Greenpeace Australia, has likewise advanced the concept of 'climate change migration with dignity (CCMD)'. He argues that to satisfy the requirement of dignity, CCMD would need to 'reflect criteria which includes being legal, planned, orderly, safe, timely and respectful' (D. Ritter, 'Climate Change and Human Rights: The Imperative for Climate Change Migration with Dignity (CCMD)' in M. Di Paola and D. Kamal (eds), *Climate Change and Human Rights: The 2015 Paris Conference and the Task of Protecting People on a Warming Planet* (Global Policy 2015)).

74   United Nations, Office of the High Commissioner for Human Rights (UN OHCHR), *Towards Freedom from Fear and Want: Human Rights in the Post-2015 Agenda* (2012).

75   United Nations, *Rio Declaration on Environment and Development* (1992) A/CONF.151/26 Volume 1, Principle 10.

76   Of note, in the Budayeva case, the European Court of Human Rights highlighted the public's right to information regarding the potential risk to human life in the context of the regulation of dangerous activities (*Budayeva and Others v. Russian Federation* (European Court of Human Rights 20 March 2008) para. 132).

77   M. Limon, 'Human Rights and Climate Change: Constructing a Case for Political Action' (2009) 33 *Harvard Environmental Law Review* 439, 451.

78   UN OHCHR, *Towards Freedom from Fear and Want* 6–7.

79   For a discussion, see Cubie, 'Promoting Dignity for All'.

80   Mary Robinson Foundation – Climate Justice, Principles of Climate Justice.

Part IV

Case studies

8 Climate migration and conflicts

A self-fulfilling prophecy?

Lennart Olsson[1]

Introduction

This Will Change Everything is the title of Naomi Klein's recent book on climate change. This is an interesting proposition which may be correct in some senses. The climate will definitely change and its impacts on nature and society as well. But will our responses to climate impacts change? Will they change in a direction that is conducive to better adaptation to climate change impacts? Will they change in ways that are compatible with social and intergenerational justice? In this chapter I will explore the potential links between climate change and social impacts on migration and conflicts.

Research on climate change and its impacts on society and nature provides dire projections for the near and medium-term future. Making projections about future climate impacts on natural systems such as low-lying coastal regions, drylands, river basins and permafrost is easier than predicting the social repercussions and responses to such climate impacts. In contrast to predictions of responses in natural systems, there is a risk that the way in which we discuss social responses to climate change may contribute to self-fulfilling prophecies. For example, if we reiterate on a weak scientific foundation that climate change will lead to more frequent thunderstorms, there will be no impact on the frequency of thunderstorms. But if we do the same for the link between climate change mass migration and armed conflicts, this may lead to policies that actually trigger such responses. The concept of self-fulfilling prophecy, elaborated scientifically by Robert Merton,[2] is well suited for discussing issues like climate-induced migration and conflicts. The self-fulfilling prophecy is 'a false definition of the situation evoking a new behaviour which makes the originally false conception come true'.[3]

Preparing for war?

In the public debate we often hear about strong links between climate change impacts and mass migration and/or armed conflicts. One of the most vivid descriptions is found within Gwynne Dyer's 2010 book *Climate Wars: The Fight for Survival as the World Overheats*.[4] Dyer talks about future scenarios of galloping climate change, but the contemporary climate change discourse is already rife with examples of preparations for conflicts and even war. Perhaps the most salient and spectacular example is in President Obama's speech when receiving the Nobel Peace Prize in 2009:

> There is little scientific dispute that if we do nothing [about climate change], we will face more drought, famine and mass displacement that will fuel more conflict for decades. For this reason, it is not merely scientists and activists who call for swift and forceful action – it is military leaders in my country and others who understand that our common security hangs in the balance.[5]

In his speech, Obama not only makes the link between climate change and conflict but also alludes to the potential role of military forces in responding to this threat. The notion of 'swift and forceful action' seems to be borrowed from the military vocabulary.

More recently, we have seen examples of how climate change enters the military realm more concretely. In a recent directive from the US Department of Defense (DoD) on climate change adaptation and resilience, we see what could be understood as preparations for war: 'Collaborates with allies and partners to optimize joint exercises and war games incorporating climate change considerations, including factors contributing to geopolitical and socioeconomic instability and long-term planning.'[6] It is interesting to see how climate change adaptation is discussed and understood in the context of national security. Military forces can play important roles in disaster management and relief, but it is also obvious that climate change is discussed in terms of combat:

> Incorporate climate change impacts into plans and operations and integrate DoD guidance and analysis in Combatant Command planning to address climate change-related risks and opportunities across the full range of military operations, including steady-state campaign planning and operations and contingency planning.[7]

Preparedness for war is of course a key task for military forces, but we also notice how other, presumably peaceful actors contribute to linking climate change (or the environment writ large) with armed conflict. There is an increasing collaboration and even integration of international development agencies and the military. In the USA, over 20 per cent of official development aid (ODA) was channelled through the Pentagon in 2007,[8] and this figure has probably increased since then. The more recent policy of collaboration between USAID and the Department of Defense is very explicit about this: 'The global challenges we confront – from violent extremism to climate change and global health security – are so large and complex that no single agency can handle them all alone.'[9] And the collaborators are quite explicit about their goals: 'we shoulder the same mission: to safeguard not only our nation's borders, but our national creed, which upholds the dignity of every individual.'[10] The two organisations are attempting to 'align development and defense and leverage the unique capabilities of USAID and DoD to achieve better development outcomes in pursuit of national security goals and national values'.[11]

In this context, and to conclude this section, it is worth highlighting what Gregory White (2011) describes in his book on climate change and migration.[12] He compares the perceived and the actual costs, the political payoff (Donald Trump's presidential election may be a good illustration of this) and the long-term efficacy of various approaches to climate-induced migration. I have added a fifth category: the potential risk to society of the approaches. By this, I mean the risk that such actions will result in '[w]orld society becom[ing] world risk society',[13] with all its ramifications.

Scientific (non-)support for linking climate and conflicts

In contrast to the public debate, the scientific debate is much less certain about climate impacts on migration and conflicts. The comprehensive report on migration and global environmental change commissioned by the UK government comments on the various numerical estimates of environmental migrants: 'these estimates are methodologically unsound, as migration is a multi-causal phenomenon and it is problematic to assign a proportion of the actual or predicted number of migrants as moving as a direct result of environmental change.'[14] Nevertheless, the scientific community is divided. There seems to be a methodological dividing line where those in favour of quantitative methods argue for a causal link between climate variability[15] and armed conflict while other scholars are highly sceptical about such links.

The quantitative approaches to link climate variability to armed conflict are problematic for several reasons. First, we can count the frequency and intensity of historical armed conflicts but we cannot count the opposite: the instances when a conflict did *not* happen because of collaboration. This means that the data itself is highly biased towards conflicts. Second, causality

Table 8.1 Comparison of various state-led approaches to climate-induced migration

	Perceived cost	*Actual cost*	*Political payoff*	*Long-term efficacy*	*Potential risks*
CC mitigation	High	Low	Low	High	Low
Adaptation of affected populations	High	Low	Low	High	Low
Building fences	Low	High	High	Low	High
Enhancing capacity of transit states	Low	High	High	Low	Extreme

Source: Modified from White (2011)[16]

cannot be inferred from a statistical correlation. Third, to claim causality across a very long time period and a very large region (Hsiang *et al.* (2013)[17] used 10,000 years and the entire world) implies that the mechanisms of linking climate and war are consistent over time and space, and across political regimes and cultural domains. Fourth, it serves to depoliticise and naturalise armed conflicts.

In the midst of these alleged linkages between climate change impacts and social unrest resulting in displacement and armed conflict, it is sobering to think about historical evidence on how scarcity and crises do not necessarily imply violent conflict. The concept of 'earthquake diplomacy'[18] was coined after the severe earthquakes in Turkey and Greece in 1999, when these two former arch-enemies came to each other's aid after they were hit by a pair of devastating earthquakes that occurred only days apart. 'Disaster diplomacy', a more general concept suggested by Ilan Kelman,[19] describes the more widespread phenomenon of questioning the common 'hardship determinism' that says that hardship leads to conflict. Kelman describes several examples of collaboration in contexts dominated by hostility: for example, in southern Africa in the early 1990s; between Ethiopia and Eritrea during the drought of the early 2000s; and between China and Taiwan after a severe earthquake in 1999. It is also interesting to note that the armed conflict in Aceh (Sumatra) ended rather abruptly after the Indian Ocean tsunami of 2004, a fact that could be attributed to the severe impact the tsunami had on livelihoods in the region.[20] Another reason to question a strong causal link between climate change and conflict relates to what Aaron Wolf and colleagues have been describing for many years: water scarcity is more often a source of cooperation than a source of conflict.[21]

A comparison of two severe climate-related events in the USA serves as an illustration that a disaster may precipitate either cooperation or conflict. In August 2005, New Orleans was hit by Katrina, a category 1–3 (out of 5) hurricane when it made landfall, which resulted in over 1,400 deaths, massive flooding and significant loss of property. But Katrina also resulted in wide-spread violence, looting and vandalism in which marginalised groups suffered disproportionately. To quote Tomlinson: 'Katrina uncovered the ugly realities of New Orleans, and in particular the position of its poor African-American population.'[22] The effects of Katrina can be juxtaposed with the aftermath of Superstorm Sandy, which hit New York City and nearby coastal areas in New Jersey on 29 October 2012. Thanks to a unique dataset, which collated a large sample of affected people's responses and attitudes after the disaster,[23] we have an important insight into the question of collaboration or cooperation as a response to disaster. Superstorm Sandy affected large swaths of coastal New Jersey and New York, causing 130 immediate deaths as well as economic damage that ran into tens of billions of dollars. Most affected people reported that they turned to family, friends and neighbours for help, and an astonishing 77 per cent of them felt that 'Superstorm Sandy brought out the best in people', while only 7 per cent said that it brought out the worst in their neighbourhoods. Looting and stealing were rare (only 11 per cent of respondents reported seeing such incidents), as was vandalism of property (with only 7 per cent witnessing that).[24]

If we turn to the psychological literature on how people cope with disasters, there is little support for the claim that disasters cause conflicts. Overall, the vast majority of disaster survivors, typically more than 70 per cent, recover fully in terms of mental health, and some even report improved mental health as a result of living through a disaster.[25] Those affected by disasters often receive immediate help from family, relatives or friends, and many survivors claim that the disaster brought them closer together[26] (as was seen in the case of Superstorm Sandy). Overall, however, the existing literature shows mixed results in terms of social relationships. There is empirical evidence of improved social relationships after a disaster, but a majority of the empirical studies show that disaster can erode both social relationships and a sense of community.[27]

An important lesson can be learned from the severe heatwave in Chicago in July 1995. It was very intense but short-lived – only four days.[28] Nevertheless, many people suffered and died. The extreme mortality rate was much higher in 1995 than the city had suffered in any previous heatwave. The heatwave was also characterised by conflicts and even fierce street battles, with news media calling it a 'water war'.[29] But a closer look at how the disaster evolved reveals that many of the deaths were actually attributable to social and political causes.[30] Social segregation and high crime levels prevented citizens from accessing safe outdoor spaces, which explained much of the differentiated exposure and sensitivity to the heat, while the city's recent implementation of neoliberal policies, including the privatisation and downsizing of many social support functions, explained why the authorities were unable to respond to the crisis in an effective manner.[31]

Hotspots for potential displacement and conflict/cooperation

Even if the evidence for climate-induced migration and conflict is weak and ambiguous, we must acknowledge that the bleak outlook for climate change, in combination with other change processes, raises concerns about the future habitability of some parts of the globe. Below, I describe three important potential climate change hotspots. These areas may also become hotspots of outmigration, and conflicts – or cooperation – may arise in them, too.

Coastal deltas

Climate-induced migration is often discussed in the context of climate change adaptation, and an important aspect of adaptation funding is the concept of additionality. This means that only impacts from anthropogenic climate change are recognised[32] that is, natural climate variability or any other process of change is not recognised as eligible for adaptation funding. If we take an anthropocentric perspective, this can become tricky, as in the case of river deltas.

We have always assumed, quite correctly, that low-lying coastal areas are hotspots of climate change impact because of ongoing and future sea-level rise. Hence, they are places where people will be displaced due to the combined effect of sea-level rise and intensified coastal erosion due to increasing hurricane activity. And yet, many coastal deltas are sinking for other reasons – just as they have for generations, in some cases.[33] For example, the Po river delta in Italy subsided by 3.7 metres in the twentieth century alone.[34] And if we go further back in history, geologists and geomorphologists note that similar anthropogenic processes can be detected thousands of years ago.[35] So, in essence, those who live on coastal deltas have evolved in highly dynamic settings since the very beginning of civilisation. This makes it very hard to distinguish between the impacts of anthropogenic climate change, other anthropogenic processes (such as delta subsidence) and natural variability.

Importantly, deltas develop through the balance of two forces: the constructive force of sediments transported by rivers and deposited on the delta and the destructive force of abrasion by ocean waves and currents. Depending on the balance of these two forces, a delta will either increase or decrease over time. In many deltas, a third force has also come to play an important role: subsidence due to various economic activities, such as pumping of ground water, soil mining and/or extraction of natural gas. The constructive forces have been under attack for many decades since dams have been built to harness water for hydro-power, irrigation and industrial and domestic water use. Such dams trap much of the sediment upstream, while irrigation reduces the amount of water flowing into the delta, and hence the rivers' transport capacity, which also reduces the amount of sediment that reaches the delta. In fact, many rivers no longer reach the sea.[36] Meanwhile, the destructive forces are increasing: sea-level rise is accelerating, from an average of 1.7 millimetres per year in the twentieth century to 3.2 millimetres per year over the last three decades; and the most severe hurricanes have increased in frequency.[37] Simultaneously, many deltas are now subject to intensive activities that are causing subsidence. In fact, most of the world's deltas are sinking even faster than the sea level is rising.

Syvitski *et al.* (2009)[38] selected thirty-three large deltas to represent the deltas of the world and found that 85 per cent of them had experienced severe flooding over the previous decade, resulting in over 260,000 square kilometres that were temporarily submerged – an area larger than the UK. Another study, by Ericson *et al.* (2006),[39] calculated the effective sea-level rise in forty coastal deltas around the world. About 300 million of the 500 million people who lived or worked on deltas at the time were included in their study.[40]

One of the principal hotspots of sea-level rise and risk of mass displacement is the Ganges–Brahmaputra delta in Bangladesh. With 170 million inhabitants, it is the most populous delta in the world. Human interference to stabilise the delta has in some cases made the situation worse. Islands that were reinforced by concrete in the 1960s are now 1–1.5 metres below natural wetlands in the area because the concrete embankments have prevented river sediments from reinforcing the islands naturally.[41]

From a migration point of view, there is no doubt that millions of people in these delta regions around the world will have to make major changes to their livelihoods. Many will have to move. So, will this be climate-induced migration? If, when the time comes, there is funding for assisting adaptation to climate change, there will certainly be strong attempts to frame it as such – even if subsidence is a much more potent driver of the changes. The impacts of sea-level rise and increasing storm damage are outside the control of the affected localities, while subsidence is a local driver that could and should be addressed. However, there is a risk that more attention will be paid to addressing the problem within the frame of climate change than to fighting subsidence locally.[42]

What can be done about subsidence as the most important driver of delta destruction? The local drivers are usually well known – extraction of ground water or methane as a source of energy – and should be addressed urgently and forcefully. The upstream drivers, related to the flow of water and transport of sediment, are more difficult to address in the local setting. Dams for hydro-power (trapping sediment and contributing to evaporation) and irrigation (trapping sediment and diverting water that is lost through evapo-transpiration) play an important role for social and economic life upstream. But, most importantly, there needs to be increased awareness of and pre-paredness for what will happen in the future. This could be achieved through public discussions about the drivers and consequences while recog-nising the complex web of causality within coastal river deltas.

Urban poverty

Traditionally, we have correctly associated poverty primarily with rural live-lihoods. According to a recent *Rural Poverty Report*, more than two-thirds of those who are living in extreme poverty are in rural areas.[43] However, this may change in the future. The world has experienced rapid urbanisation over the last few decades. Whether we rely on the neoclassical theories of migration[44] or the new economics of migration,[45] migration is understood as a process through which people seek better economic conditions. Even if sociological theories of migration are more nuanced, seeking better economic conditions is an important driver of rural–urban migration,[46] hence rural poverty has been a strong driver. One of the best-established economic theories of the twentieth century is Engel's law, which stipulates that the proportion of income spent on food is decreasing, even if actual expenditure on food is increasing.[47] This persistent condition has facilitated the shift from farming to non-farming because the risks associated with being a net buyer of food have decreased. But this situation is liable to change, or possibly has already changed. The rapid increase in food prices in 2007–2008, and the continuation of those high prices until 2013, has been seen as a harbinger of what to expect in the near or medium-term future. The IPCC has concluded that it is very likely that food prices will increase by 2050 due to the impact of climate change.[48]

Urban areas are increasingly centres for people who are poor and food insecure, and urban net buyers of food are particularly at risk when food prices increase. A recent study in Nairobi revealed an extremely high rate of urban food insecurity, with 85 per cent of the very large sample food insecure and 50 per cent suffering from 'severe' food insecurity.[49]

Urban slums have often been associated with violence and crime – a link that may become a self-fulfilling prophecy. It is important to refrain from making simple links between slums and crime, but there is good empirical support for linking food price increases with riots in cities in the Global South. The 1980s and early 1990s witnessed a reappearance of food riots across the developing world as a result of structural adjustments, and there was similar violence after the food price increases of 2007–2008. It is interesting to note that the political community, which calls climate change a security threat, did not label the structural adjustment programmes in the same way. If we want to reduce the risk of unrest and displacement, we will need to avoid further food price hikes.

Heat-sensitive groups in hot places

Heatwaves may well be the most predictable and also the most devastating manifestations of climate change. The number and intensity of heatwaves have already increased markedly, and this is likely to continue.[50] Well-known examples of devastating heatwaves with high mortality rates and economic losses are: Chicago 1995, France 2003 and 2006, Russia 2010, India, Pakistan and China 2013, and India, Pakistan and Egypt in 2015. There is even a risk of large parts of the planet becoming uninhabitable if the global mean temperature increases by 7°C or more.[51] Moreover, the economic effects of heatwaves – primarily in the forms of reduced labour productivity[52] and increased costs for social welfare and healthcare – could be huge.[53]

The relevance for migration and conflict is that heatwaves have been associated with a range of social and health-related predicaments in many countries, such as increasing violence,[54] emotional problems and low life satisfaction.[55] Urban areas are expected to suffer comparatively more due to the combined effect of climate and the urban heat-island effect.[56] The best way to endure a heatwave is either to escape (to cooled buildings or mountainous areas, for example) or to relax and do as little physical activity as possible. Therefore, those who are dependent on hard physical labour outdoors – such as farmers, fishermen and construction workers – are severely limited in their ability to make the necessary adaptations. In small-scale agriculture, women and children may be particularly at risk due to gendered divisions of labour and responsibilities.[57] With more frequent and more intense heatwaves, we can expect certain areas to become increasingly prone to out-migration. A recent study in Pakistan found that excessive heat was more often a causal factor of long-term and long-distance migration than floods.[58]

The increasing frequency, intensity and duration of heatwaves is probably the most serious threat to communities in heat-prone areas. They are particularly problematic because of their spatial extent (they can be subcontinental), their persistence (they can last for many weeks), their many impacts on society,[59] the differentials in vulnerability and poor people's very limited adaptation options.

Concluding remarks

Most aspects of climate change have been the subject of intensive research. Of all the global environmental challenges, climate change is the most scientifically informed, and the more we know about it, the worse it seems to affect us. The policy debate about climate change is generally well supported by science, not least due to the efforts of the IPCC. But there is one field within the vast area of climate change where science and policy are diverging: the relationships between climate change, on the one hand, and migration and conflict, on the other.

Powerful actors, such as military leaders and heads of state, have accepted a simple, deterministic view that climate change will inevitably lead to migration and conflict, even though the science is highly uncertain – and in some cases highly polarised – on this issue. This simplistic view runs the risk of generating a self-fulfilling prophecy. There is therefore an urgent need to increase the research into the possible link between climate change and migration and conflict, and improve the communication between the scientists and the policy-makers, if we are to avoid walking headlong into a terrible fate that is far from inevitable.[60]

If we are to reduce the risk of fulfilling the prophecy of mass displacement and armed conflict, perhaps we should focus on peaceful development in social justice and the creation of meaningful jobs, rather than boosting military capacity and erecting fences between nations.

Notes

1 LUCSUS, Lund University, Sweden.
2 R. K. Merton, 'The Self-Fulfilling Prophecy' (1948) 8 *The Antioch Review* 193.
3 Ibid. 195.
4 G. Dwyer, *Climate Wars: The Fight for Survival as the World Overheats* (Oneworld Publications 2010).
5 B. Obama, 'Nobel Peace Prize Lecture' (2009) www.nobelprize.org/nobel_prizes/peace/laureates/2009/obama-lecture.html accessed 25 October 2016.
6 Department of Defense, *Climate Change Adaptation and Resilience* (2016) 9 (instructions to the Chairman of the Joint Chiefs of Staff).
7 Ibid. (instructions to Combatant Commander).

8 S. Patrick and K. Brown, 'The Pentagon and Global Development: Making Sense of the DoD's Expanding Role' (2007) https://papers.ssrn.com/sol3/papers.cfm?abstract_id=1101526 accessed 17 December 2016.
9 USAID, 'New Policy Guides: USAID's Cooperation with Department of Defense' (2015) https://blog.usaid.gov/2015/06/new-policy-guides-usaids-cooperation-with-department-of-defense/ accessed 25 October 2016.
10 Letter from A. E. Lenhardt, Acting Administrator of USAID, July 2015 (Ibid. Foreword).
11 B. D. Kauffeld, *Analysis and Recommendations to Enhance Development–Military Cooperation* (USAID and DoD 2014) v.
12 G. White, *Climate Change and Migration: Security and Borders in a Warming World* (Oxford University Press 2011) 88.
13 U. Beck, *World at Risk* (Polity Press 2009) 146.
14 UK Government Office for Science, *Foresight: Migration and Global Environmental Change: Final Project Report* (2011) 11.
15 In this context, it is important to make distinctions between climate variability (i.e. the natural inter-annual variability without any secular trend), climate change (a secular trend) and anthropogenic climate change (a secular trend attributed to anthropogenic activity, such as increasing levels of greenhouse gases).
16 White, *Climate Change* 88.
17 S. M. Hsiang, M. Burke and E. Miguel, 'Quantifying the Influence of Climate on Human Conflict' (2013) 341 *Science*.
18 D. Keridis, 'Earthquakes, Diplomacy and New Thinking in Foreign Policy' (2006) 30 *Fletcher Forum of World Affairs* 207.
19 I. Kelman, 'Beyond Disaster, beyond Diplomacy' in M. Pellman (ed.), *Natural Disasters and Development in a Globalizing World* (Routledge 2003) 110.
20 I. Kelman, 'Tsunami Diplomacy: Will the 26 December, 2004 Tsunami Bring Peace to the Affected Countries?' (2005) 10 *Sociological Research Online*; P. Le Billon and A. Waizenegger, 'Peace in the Wake of Disaster? Secessionist Conflicts and the 2004 Indian Ocean Tsunami' (2007) 32 *Transactions of the Institute of British Geographers* 411; E. S. Yim *et al.*, 'Disaster Diplomacy: Current Controversies and Future Prospects' (2009) 24 *Prehospital and Disaster Medicine* 291.
21 A. T. Wolf, 'Conflict and Cooperation along International Waterways' (1998) 1(2) *Water Policy* 251–265.
22 S. A. Tomlinson, 'No New Orleanians Left Behind: An Examination of the Disparate Impact of Hurricane Katrina on Minorities' (2005) 38 *Connecticut Law Review* 1153.
23 T. Tompson *et al.*, *Resilience in the Wake of Superstorm Sandy* (Associated Press–NORC Centre for Public Affairs Research 2013).
24 Ibid.
25 G. A. Bonanno *et al.*, 'Weighing the Costs of Disaster: Consequences, Risks and Resilience in Individuals, Families and Communities' (2010) 11 *Psychological Science in the Public Interest* 1.
26 Ibid.
27 Ibid.
28 J. C. Semenza *et al.*, 'Heat-Related Deaths during the July 1995 Heat-Wave in Chicago' (1996) 335 *New England Journal of Medicine* 84.
29 E. Klinenberg, 'Denaturalizing Disaster: A Social Autopsy of the 1995 Chicago Heat-Wave' (1999) 28 *Theory and Society* 239.
30 E. Klinenberg, *Heat-Wave: A Social Autopsy of Disaster in Chicago* (University of Chicago Press 2003).
31 Ibid.
32 M. Chambwera *et al.*, 'Economics of Adaptation' in C. B. Field, V. R. Barros, D. J. Dokken, K. J. Mach, M. D. Mastrandrea, T. E. Bilir, M. Chatterjee, K. L. Ebi,

Y. O. Estrada, R. C. Genova, B. Girma, E. S. Kissel, A. N. Levy, S. MacCracken, P. R. Mastrandrea and L. L. White (eds), *Climate Change 2014: Impacts, Adaptation and Vulnerability Part A: Global and Sectoral Aspects. Contribution of Working Group II to the Fifth Assessment Report of the Intergovernmental Panel on Climate Change* (Cambridge University Press 2014) 953.

33 P. Dandekar, *Shrinking and Sinking Deltas: Major Role of Dams in Delta Subsidence and Effective Sea Level Rise* (South Asia Network on Dams, Rivers and People 2014).

34 J. Syvitski *et al.*, 'Sinking Deltas due to Human Activities' (2009) 2 *Nature Geoscience* 681.

35 A. Brown *et al.*, 'Geomorphology of the Anthropocene: Time-Transgressive Discontinuities of Human-Induced Alluviation' (2013) 1 *Anthropocene* 3.

36 F. Pearce, *When the Rivers Run Dry: What Happens When Our Water Runs Out?* (Random House 2012).

37 P. P. Wong *et al.*, 'Coastal Systems and Low-Lying Areas' in Field *et al.* (eds), *Climate Change 2014*.

38 Syvitski *et al.*, 'Sinking Deltas'.

39 J. P. Ericson *et al.*, 'Effective Sea-Level Rise and Deltas: Causes of Change and Human Dimension Implications' (2006) 50 *Global and Planetary Change* 63.

40 J. Syvitski and S. Higgins, 'Going Under: The World's Sinking Deltas' (2012) 216 *New Scientist* 40.

41 L. W. Auerbach *et al.*, 'Flood Risk of Natural and Embanked Landscapes on the Ganges–Brahmaputra Tidal Delta Plain' (2015) 5 *Nature Climate Change* 153.

42 See, for example, Chapter 7, this volume.

43 IFAD, *Rural Poverty Report 2011* (2011).

44 W. A. Lewis, 'Economic Development with Unlimited Supplies of Labour' (1954) 20 *Manchester School of Economics and Social Studies* 139; L. A. Sjaastad, 'The Costs and Returns of Human Migration' in H. W. Richardson (ed.), *Regional Economics* (Springer 1970); J. R. Harris and M. P. Todaro, 'Migration, Unemployment and Development: A Two-Sector Analysis' (1970) 60 *American Economic Review* 126; M. P. Todaro, 'Internal Migration in Developing Countries: A Survey' in R. A. Easterlin (ed.), *Population and Economic Change in Developing Countries* (University of Chicago Press 1976).

45 O. Stark and D. E. Bloom, 'The New Economics of Labor Migration' (1985) 75 *American Economic Review* 173.

46 D. S. Massey *et al.*, 'Theories of International Migration: A Review and Appraisal (1993) 19(3) *Population and Development Review* 431.

47 H. S. Houthakker, 'An International Comparison of Household Expenditure Patterns, Commemorating the Centenary of Engel's Law' (1957) 25(4) *Econometrica, Journal of the Econometric Society* 532.

48 J. R. Porter *et al.*, 'Food Security and Food Production Systems' in Field *et al.*, *Climate Change 2014*.

49 E. W. Kimani-Murage, L. Schofield, F. Wekesah, S. Mohamed, B. Mberu, R. Ettarh, T. Egondi, C. Kyobutungi and A. Ezeh, 'Vulnerability to Food Insecurity in Urban Slums: Experiences from Nairobi, Kenya' (2014) 91(6) *Journal of Urban Health* 1098–1113.

50 L. Olsson *et al.*, 'Cross-Chapter Box on Heat Stress and Heat Waves' in Field *et al.*, *Climate Change 2014*.

51 S. C. Sherwood and M. Huber, 'An Adaptability Limit to Climate Change due to Heat Stress' (2010) 107 *Proceedings of the National Academy of Sciences* 9552.

52 K. K. Zander *et al.*, 'Heat Stress Causes Substantial Labour Productivity Loss in Australia' (2015) 5 *Nature Climate Change* 647; J. P. Dunne, R. J. Stouffer and J. G. John, 'Reductions in Labour Capacity from Heat Stress under Climate Warming' (2013) 3 *Nature Climate Change*.

53 H. L. Berry, K. Bowen and T. Kjellstrom, 'Climate Change and Mental Health: A Causal Pathways Framework' (2010) 55 *International Journal of Public Health* 123.

54 J. L. Gamble and J. J. Hess, 'Temperature and Violent Crime in Dallas, Texas: Relationships and Implications of Climate Change' (2012) 13 *Western Journal of Emergency Medicine* 239; C. A. Anderson, 'Climate Change and Violence' in D. J. Christie (ed.), *The Encyclopedia of Peace Psychology* (Wiley Online Library 2012); R. Agnew, 'Dire Forecast: A Theoretical Model of the Impact of Climate Change on Crime' (2012) 16 *Theorectical Criminology* 21.

55 B. Tawatsupa *et al.*, 'Heat Stress, Health and Well-Being: Findings from a Large National Cohort of Thai Adults' (2012) 2 *British Medical Journal Open*; S. Lock *et al.*, 'Secondary Stressors and Extreme Events and Disasters: A Systematic Review of Primary Research from 2010–2011' (2012) 4 *PLoS Currents*.

56 E. M. Fischer, K. W. Oleson and D. M. Lawrence, 'Contrasting Urban and Rural Heat Stress Responses to Climate Change' (2012) 39 *Geophysical Research Letters*.

57 A. Quisumbing, R. Meinzen-Dick, J. Njuki and N. Johnson (eds), *Gender, Agriculture and Assets: Learning from Eight Agricultural Development Interventions in Africa and South Asia* (IFPRI 2013).

58 V. Mueller, C. Gray and K. Kosec, 'Heat Stress Increases Long-Term Human Migration in Rural Pakistan' (2014) 4 *Nature Climate Change* 182.

59 Olsson *et al.*, 'Cross-Chapter Box'.

60 Merton, 'The Self-Fulfilling Prophecy' 195.

9 The human rights of climate-induced community relocation

Robin Bronen[1]

Complex governance issues must be resolved in order to facilitate relocation. No US or Alaskan government agency has the authority to relocate communities, no governmental organisation exists that can address the strategic planning needs of relocation and no funding is specifically designated for relocation. Determining which communities are most likely to encounter displacement will require a sophisticated assessment of a community's ecosystem vulnerability to climate change, as well as the vulnerability of its social, economic and political structures.

This chapter describes the steps that federal, state and tribal governments have taken to relocate Newtok, an Alaskan indigenous community, one of at least twelve communities that need to be relocated in Alaska due to climate change. The chapter also examines the human rights issues involved with climate-induced planned relocations. Refugee law and the UN's Guiding Principles on Internal Displacement do not outline the specific protections for people forced to relocate because of climate change threats. These protections must ensure that individual and collective human rights adhere before, during and after the relocation process. Newtok's relocation process provides an understanding of the complexity of institutional challenges and barriers related to community relocation and also offers an example of the tremendous resilience of indigenous populations seeking to maintain their culture and heritage.

Climate change

Climate change is most often associated with temperature changes in the earth's atmosphere. The warmest five-year period in the 136-year temperature record occurred between 2011 and 2015.[2] The latter year was the hottest ever recorded. In the northern polar regions, temperatures are rising at twice the global average.[3] The accelerated warming in the Arctic has tremendous implications not only in the Arctic but throughout the world.

These temperature increases impact the hydrosphere, cryosphere, atmosphere and biosphere. As a consequence, numerous and diverse climate-induced environmental changes are occurring and affecting the totality of the environment where humans live and work. Sea-level rise and thawing permafrost are two climate-induced environmental changes that, when combined with the loss of natural coastal barriers, such as sea ice, severely threaten coastal communities. Permafrost, permanently frozen soil that is the glue that makes land habitable in the Arctic, is thawing due to warming temperatures.[4]

Sea-level rise is accelerating and expected to worsen over the next century due to increased rates of ice sheet mass loss from Antarctica and Greenland.[5] The Greenland Ice Sheet experienced extensive melting in 2012 and 2015. In 2012, melting occurred over more than 96 per cent of the ice sheet; and in 2015, 50 per cent of the ice sheet was melting. Melt season duration in 2015 was as much as thirty–forty days longer than average in western, north-western and north-eastern Greenland.[6] Increased ocean temperatures, causing ocean water to expand and glaciers to melt, also contribute to sea-level rise.[7] Sea-level rise contributes to flooding, sea surges, erosion and salinisation of land and water.[8]

Warming temperatures also affect ocean ecosystems and cause a loss of Arctic sea ice, the natural barrier that protects coastal communities from sea surges, erosion and floods. Arctic sea ice is decreasing in thickness and extent. Record minimum levels of Arctic sea ice have been recorded since 2007.[9] Minimum sea ice extent in September 2015 was 29 per cent less than the average for 1981–2010.[10]

The decrease in extent of Arctic sea ice, coupled with warming temperatures, has caused a delay in freezing of the Bering and Chukchi seas.[11] Near-shore pack ice has historically provided a protective barrier to coastal communities.[12] Since the 1980s, the Arctic seas are remaining ice-free approximately three weeks longer in the autumn.[13] The delay in freezing of the Arctic seas has left many communities exposed to the autumnal storms that originate in the Pacific and occur primarily between August and early December.[14] The loss of Arctic sea ice, coupled with thawing permafrost, is causing severe erosion and storm surges along the northern and western Alaskan coast.

Relocation

The combination of repeated extreme weather events, ongoing and accelerating rates of environmental change, such as erosion, and the loss of protective coastal barriers is forcing coastal communities to relocate as a long-term adaptation strategy. Community relocation is required to protect residents from climate-induced ecological changes that cause extensive damage to infrastructure and repeatedly place people in danger.[15] Relocation is a process whereby a community's residents, housing and public infrastructure are reconstructed in another location.[16] In addition, relocation can include rebuilding livelihoods and social networks. Relocation is always an adaptation strategy of last resort, when no other strategies can protect populations in the places where they currently live.

Alaska

Newtok, a Yup'ik Eskimo village, is located near the Bering Sea in western Alaska. Approximately 320 residents reside in about 60 houses.[17] The Ninglick River borders Newtok to the south; to the east is the Newtok River.[18] A combination of increased temperatures, thawing permafrost and decreased Arctic sea ice is causing accelerating erosion, moving the Ninglick River closer to the village.[19] The State of Alaska spent about $1.5 million to control the erosion between 1983 and 1989.[20] Despite these efforts, in 2008 erosion associated with the movement of the Ninglick River was projected to reach the school, the largest structure in the community, by about 2017.[21]

Six extreme weather events between 1989 and 2006 exacerbated these gradual ecological changes. Five of these events precipitated Federal Emergency Management Agency (FEMA) disaster declarations.[22] FEMA declared three disasters between October 2004 and May 2006 alone.[23] These three storms accelerated the erosion and repeatedly 'flooded the village water supply, caused raw sewage to be spread throughout the community, displaced residents from homes, destroyed subsistence food storage, and shut down essential utilities'.[24] Public infrastructure that was significantly damaged or destroyed included the village landfill, barge ramp, sewage treatment facility and fuel storage facilities.[25] The only access to the community is by barge during the summer or by airplane. The barge landing, which allows for most delivery of supplies and heating fuel, no longer exists, creating a fuel crisis. Salt water is affecting the potable water.[26]

In 1994, the Newtok Traditional Council (henceforth 'the Council') analysed six potential relocation sites to start a relocation planning process. In September 1996, Newtok inhabitants voted – on the first of three occasions – to relocate to Nelson Island, nine miles south of Newtok.[27] The two subsequent votes occurred in May 2001 and August 2003. Newtok obtained title to its preferred relocation site, which was named Mertarvik, through a land-exchange agreement negotiated with the US Fish and Wildlife Service. Construction of pioneer infrastructure, including a multi-purpose evacuation centre and barge landing, began at the relocation site in 2009.[28]

State, federal and tribal government and non-governmental agencies have issued numerous reports documenting the socio-ecological crisis faced by Newtok residents and the habitability of the relocation site.[29] Between 2006 and 2016, more than two dozen reports were completed by federal and state government agencies to document the environmental changes threatening the health and well-being of community residents, to identify the steps federal, state and tribal government entities need to take during the relocation process and to plan for infrastructure development at the relocation site.[30]

The Council commissioned the *Newtok Background for Relocation Report*, which summarised the previous erosion studies, mapped the advancing Ninglick River to show the scope of erosion, documented the socio-ecological impacts of erosion on the village and developed a tentative timeline for the short-term and long-term relocation of residences.[31] The report also described the Council's evaluation of each potential village relocation site, including 'collocation' to one of four existing communities or relocation to one of six potential new sites in the region. In addition, it contained the results of the 2003 residents' survey, which asked Newtok residents to vote on relocation alternatives.[32] This report was instrumental to the community's relocation efforts because it provided background documentation to government agencies and officials to justify the village's relocation and to support the Council's requests for government assistance in this process.[33]

In addition, the US Army Corps of Engineers funded a report in 2008 that analysed five alternative responses to the social and ecological crisis facing Newtok village residents.[34] These alternatives included: taking no action; staying in place with erosion and flood control; collocation; relocation funded and orchestrated solely by the Corps of Engineers; and a collaborative relocation effort.[35] The report found that a coordinated relocation effort was in the best interests of Newtok residents, explaining:

> With no Federal and state action, relocation efforts will be piecemeal and uncoordinated and will increase ultimate costs many times over a coordinated, efficient relocation plan. Local efforts will take many years and the existing significant risk to health, life, and property will continue in Newtok. The disintegration of these people as a distinct tribe may result from splitting the community in two or more locations for many years as they relocate under their own efforts.[36]

The Corps also specifically rejected the collocation alternative, finding that '[c]ollocation would destroy the Newtok community identity'.[37] Furthermore, it issued several reports that evaluated the habitability of Newtok's relocation site and confirmed the Council's conclusion that Mertarvik is a suitable relocation site.[38]

The Newtok Planning Group

The Newtok Planning Group emerged in May 2006 from an ad hoc series of meetings. It is unique in Alaska because of its multi-disciplinary and multi-jurisdictional structure, and consists of about twenty-five state, federal and tribal government and non-governmental agencies that collaborate voluntarily to facilitate Newtok's relocation.[39] Since the Planning Group's inception, Newtok's tribal government has led the relocation effort. On 9 June 2011, the Council unanimously approved a set of guiding principles ('Maligtaquyarat') for the community's relocation to Mertarvik.[40] These are based on the Yup'ik way of life and include:

- Remain a distinct, unique community – our own community.
- Stay focused on our vision by taking small steps forward each day.

- Make decisions openly and as a community and look to elders for guidance.
- Build a healthy future for our youth.
- Our voice comes first – we have first and final say in making decisions and defining priorities.
- Share with and learn from our partners.
- No matter how long it takes, we will work together to provide support to our people in both Mertarvik and Newtok.
- Development should:

  - Reflect our cultural traditions.
  - Nurture our spiritual and physical well-being.
  - Respect and enhance the environment.
  - Be designed with local input from start to finish.
  - Be affordable for our people.
  - Hire community members first.
  - Use what we have first and use available funds wisely.

- Look for projects that build on our talents and strengthen our economy.[41]

These principles govern every aspect of the relocation process and they have been integrated into the strategic relocation master plan, which guides federal and state government participation in the relocation effort.[42]

Governance

The institutional and statutory barriers to relocation are enormous. With no designated relocation funding, each government agency must follow its own budgetary and funding prioritisation criteria to allocate funding for Newtok's relocation effort. The lack of a population base at the relocation site and the uncertainty of when and if people will be able to relocate because of the lack of any infrastructure has impacted Newtok's ability to receive state funding for capital expenditure at the relocation site. For example, Newtok's request for state funding for an airstrip – the only means of transportation to the relocation site – was initially given lower priority than similar requests from other communities who needed state funding to maintain and rebuild the infrastructure of established settlements.

Despite these challenges, the Newtok Planning Group has been exceptionally creative in exploiting existing funding sources to support the relocation effort and in coordinating different funding streams to meet cost-sharing eligibility requirements as well as increasing the available revenue. As an example, following a presidential disaster declaration in November 2013 after a storm impacted Newtok, funding from FEMA and the Alaska Division of Homeland Security and Emergency Management (DHS&EM) will focus on housing assistance. Newtok residents need homes if they are to move to their relocation site, Mertarvik.[43]

FEMA administers the Hazard Mitigation Grant Program (HMGP), which helps communities implement hazard mitigation measures following a presidentially declared disaster. In order for a local government (city or tribe) to qualify for HMGP funds, it must have a FEMA-approved Local Hazard Mitigation Plan (LHMP). Because Newtok had such a plan, the community was eligible to apply for an HMGP grant. The Council chose to pursue relocation of twelve structurally sound homes to Mertarvik.[44]

However, due to the lack of an institutional framework, the relocation process remains painfully slow, which places Newtok's residents at great risk as erosion continues to accelerate and threaten them. This lack of a governance framework hampers the ability of local, regional and national government agencies to respond. If climate-induced environmental change renders the places where people live uninhabitable and causes land to disappear, new governance institutions will need to be designed to determine whether people can be protected in place or require relocation.[45]

Recognising this institutional gap and the complex challenges of climate-induced population displacement, in its December 2013 report *Implementing the President's Action Plan: US Department of the Interior* the Bicameral Task Force on Climate Change recommended

> that the Administration devote special attention to the problems of communities that decide they have little choice but to relocate in the face of the impacts of climate change. Because the relocation of entire communities due to climate change is such an unprecedented need, there is no institutional framework within the US to relocate communities, and agencies lack technical, organizational, and financial means to do so.[46]

President Obama's Task Force on Climate Preparedness and Resilience (henceforth 'the Task Force') echoed this recommendation in November 2014 and affirmed that the federal government should take a lead role to establish a relocation institutional framework to respond to the complex challenges of climate-related population displacement.[47]

Creating an adaptive governance framework based in human rights

A relocation institutional framework needs to determine the appropriate role of federal, state, local and tribal governments and outline the decision-making process for relocations – who decides that relocation should take place and the steps communities must take to engage with government agencies to receive the technical assistance they will need to implement a relocation plan, including the building of critical infrastructure at the relocation site.[48] A relocation institutional framework must also outline the factors that will determine when and if relocations should occur.[49]

An adaptive governance relocation framework means that protection in the places where people live and work is always prioritised. Relocation of populations is always a last resort in response to climate change threats and should not be implemented until other adaptation strategies to protect communities have been implemented. Consequently, a relocation institutional framework should incorporate all available institutional mechanisms to protect people in place, such as sea walls and land use planning tools, *and* create new mechanisms to implement a relocation process so that national, state, local and tribal governments are able to refocus their efforts from protection in place to managed retreat and community relocation.[50]

Implementing an adaptive governance relocation framework requires multi-level and diverse governmental and non-governmental actors to engage in a collaborative process of knowledge production and problem-solving.[51] Adaptive capacity, an essential element of adaptive governance, is the ability to respond to socio-ecological disturbances and maintain resilience when responding to rapid ecological change.[52] Adaptive capacity in social systems refers to the ability of institutions to balance power among various interest groups and engage in an iterative learning process that will generate knowledge and prove flexible in solving problems. Networks of multiple and diverse organisations are critical for building adaptive capacity.[53]

Human rights protections must form the foundation of this adaptive governance framework. Four factors compel the creation of a specific human rights instrument to protect the rights of those living in communities that are no longer habitable due to climate-induced ecological change:

1   Nation-state governments have a duty to protect populations that reside within their jurisdiction.
2   Refugee law and the UN's Guiding Principles on Internal Displacement do not provide human rights protections for planned community relocations.
3   Relocation human rights guidelines must ensure the protection of collective rights because climate change impacts the habitability of entire communities whose residents will be forced to relocate permanently.
4   The human rights of host communities must also be protected.

Nation-state governments have a duty to protect their citizens

Nation-state governments have an obligation to protect vulnerable populations from climate-induced ecological change that threatens the civil, economic, social and cultural rights fundamental to the inherent dignity of individuals as well as collective society. A nation-state government's protection of human rights is a critical threshold for that nation state to claim sovereignty over its citizens and is also a minimum test for international legitimacy.[54] International law defines sovereignty as the legal identity of a state and signifies a nation-state government's capacity to make authoritative decisions about the people and resources within its territory.[55] The duty to protect is inherent in the concept of sovereignty and implies that the nation-state government has the primary responsibility for the protection of populations within its jurisdiction.[56]

The duty to protect is also considered a seminal principle for United Nations membership and for the attainment of international peace and security.[57] As recognised in international human rights conventions, nation-state governments have a primary duty to protect the human rights of their citizens if they are a party to such conventions.[58]

The duty to protect has three core principles.[59] Prevention – the most important of these principles – is defined as the responsibility to address the primary causes of crises that threaten populations. Second, the responsibility to react means that a nation-state government must respond appropriately to situations requiring humanitarian assistance. Third, a nation-state government must provide resources for reconstruction after a humanitarian crisis has occurred.[60]

International legal doctrine also specifically outlines the responsibilities of a nation-state government to protect internally displaced populations. The Inter-Agency Standing Committee (IASC) has defined the duties of a nation-state government to provide human rights protection to natural disaster victims.[61] In this context, protection means securing the physical safety of natural disaster victims and securing all of the human rights guaranteed in international human rights law.[62] The obligation also includes the responsibility to minimise damage caused by natural hazards.[63]

The Guiding Principles on Internal Displacement incorporate this sovereign responsibility to protect into a nation-state government's obligations to internally displaced populations. The responsibility includes the duty to provide safe access to housing 'at the minimum, regardless of the circumstances, and without discrimination'.[64] The Pinheiro Principles on Housing and Property Restitution echo the principle that nation states have an obligation to guarantee human rights protections to persons affected by internal displacement and emphasise the obligation to protect human rights related to housing and property restitution.[65]

The failure to protect is a human rights violation. The European Court of Human Rights found that government officials violated the right to life of community residents when they failed to implement land-planning and emergency relief policies after being alerted to the increasing risk of a large-scale mudslide. The Court also noted that the population had not been adequately informed about the risk.[66]

The duty to protect means that nation-state governments are responsible for implementing adaptation strategies. Communities will need a continuum of responses – from protection in place to community relocation – if they are to adapt to climate-induced ecological change. Disaster and hazard mitigation are critical components of this continuum in order to assess vulnerabilities and develop disaster mitigation strategies.[67] Socio-ecological indicators can also assess vulnerability and guide the design of adaptation strategies. A human rights framework is critical to the design and implementation of these adaptation strategies to ensure that nation-state governments focus on the protection of freedoms that are fundamental to collective society, and that relocation occurs only when there are no other feasible solutions to protect vulnerable populations.

Lack of capacity and resources can limit a government's ability to protect the economic, social and cultural rights of populations within its jurisdiction.[68] If human rights protections cannot be realised because of inadequate resources, then working for institutional capacity-building through expansion or reform may be a part of the international obligations generated by the recognition of these rights.

International cooperation is an essential component of the successful design and implementation of adaptation strategies. The UN Framework Convention on Climate Change clearly articulates the need for international cooperation in the development and implementation of adaptation strategies, including planned relocations, and specifically states that developed country parties shall 'assist the developing country Parties that are particularly vulnerable to the adverse effects of climate change in meeting costs of adaptation to those adverse effects'.[69]

Refugee law and the Guiding Principles on Internal Displacement fail to protect communities

Existing human rights instruments offer no protection to communities that need to relocate because of climate-induced environmental change. The 1951 UN Convention Relating to the Status of Refugees is the only global treaty that has created an international structure to manage forced human migration. The Convention provides for third-country resettlement, human rights protections and humanitarian assistance for those fleeing persecution or torture in their country of origin and crossing a nation-state border. The Convention initially applied only to those fleeing within Europe.[70] The 1967 Protocol Relating to the Status of Refugees removed both the temporal and geographic restrictions of the 1951 Convention, but it kept the primary elements of the refugee definition intact.[71]

To be considered a refugee pursuant to the post-Protocol 1951 UN Convention, a person must prove that they are unable or unwilling to return to their country of origin because they have been singled out by a government actor or an actor the government cannot control and persecuted on account of their race, religion, nationality, membership of a particular social group or political opinion. The definition does not include environmental causes for flight from a person's country of origin.[72]

Refugee law is based on the fundamental premise that the ordinary bonds between citizen and state have been broken and a person is outside of their country of origin because the nation-state government is unable or unwilling to protect them.[73] Refugees need international intervention to ensure there is safe refuge as they cannot turn to their own governments for protection because such nation states are often the source of their persecution.[74] As a consequence, the 1951 Convention relieves nation-state governments of their obligations to protect the human rights of their citizens and execute the necessary policies to enable populations who have fled to return.[75] Of course, this underlying premise of refugee law conflicts with nation states' obligation to guarantee human rights protections for all populations within their jurisdiction. In the context of climate-induced population displacement, communities should still be able to rely on national protection to resolve their humanitarian crisis.

Two non-binding international human rights documents that concern displacement are the UN's *Guiding Principles on Internal Displacement* and the IASC's *Operational Guidelines on the Protection of Persons in Situations of Natural Disasters*. Both of these outline the human rights protections for populations that are internally displaced, but neither adequately addresses the complex issues and human rights implications of climate-induced community relocation, for several reasons.

First, emergencies are clearly different from planned relocations. Neither the IASC's Operational Guidelines nor the Guiding Principles on Internal Displacement provide for the prospective needs of populations that are planning their permanent relocation, or provide any guidance on how such communities may sustain themselves and create the necessary infrastructure to provide for basic necessities without the assistance of humanitarian aid.[76] Most importantly, neither document clearly defines a mechanism for communities to make the decisions regarding the process of relocation. The IASC's Operational Guidelines state the need for informed consent and participation in decisions regarding the relocation process, but, as discussed below, these principles are different from the ability to make decisions about the relocation.[77]

The IASC's Operational Guidelines were developed to respond to situations when pre-planning is not possible.[78] They outline minimum core human rights obligations under the International Covenant on Economic, Social and Cultural Rights, such as the duty to provide food, shelter and health services, which a nation-state government must provide after a natural disaster has occurred.[79] However, they assume that humanitarian aid organisations will provide these basic necessities to populations displaced by natural disasters and do not describe how displaced populations may provide such necessities for themselves.

The UN's Guiding Principles on Internal Displacement also do not provide sufficient human rights protections for those facing climate-induced community relocation. This document is not a binding international treaty or convention, but the UN General Assembly has recognised it as 'an important international framework for the protection of internally displaced persons'.[80] Although the Guiding Principles include persons displaced by natural disasters, the primary focus of these guidelines is displacement caused by the state's inability or unwillingness to protect populations from political, religious, ethnic or otherwise discriminatory persecution or violence. In comparison, as stated above, those displaced by climate-induced ecological change should be able to continue to rely on state protection.

Second, both documents are based on the premise that populations may be able to return to their original homes. But climate-induced ecological change will cause *permanent* population displacement. There are enormous differences in policies and human rights protections between temporary and permanent population displacement.[81]

Relocation human rights guidelines must ensure the protection of collective rights

Climate-induced displacement will affect entire communities whose residents will collectively need protection from the threats caused by climate change. International human rights documents, such as the UN's *Declaration on the Rights of Indigenous Peoples*, recognise the rights of peoples collectively and that indigenous peoples have the collective right to the fundamental freedoms articulated in the *Universal Declaration of Human Rights* and international law. Like these documents, a human rights instrument that addresses climate-induced population displacement must ensure the protection of collective rights because climate change impacts the habitability of entire communities whose residents will be forced to relocate permanently. These rights include the collective right to relocate as a community, as well as the collective right to make decisions regarding where and how a community will relocate.

The human rights of host communities must also be protected

A human rights instrument that is developed to respond to climate-induced displacement must also ensure that human rights protections are extended to those who live in communities that provide sanctuary for those displaced by climate change. Host populations may experience shortages of water, sanitation, shelter and essential health services as a result of population increases. Schools may be overburdened if there is an influx of displaced students. Human rights protections for a host community will ensure that such a community benefits from the relocation and maintains or improves its standard of living, and that conflict or competition with the displaced population is averted.[82]

Guiding human rights principles

The *Peninsula Principles* – a human rights document drafted in 2012 to address the human rights principles that must pertain to the relocation of communities – creates a common language to guide the international, national and local humanitarian response.[83] It identifies the appropriate human rights standards to guide national government actions when climate-induced ecological change threatens community habitability and the lives of community residents.

Right to collective self-determination

The right to self-determination is the cornerstone of the human rights principles that need to guide community relocations. Both the International Covenant on Economic, Social and Cultural Rights and the International Covenant on Civil and Political Rights establish that 'all peoples have the right to self-determination', by virtue of which 'they freely determine their political status and freely pursue their economic, social and cultural development'. The inclusion of the right to self-determination in both treaties indicates that its importance spans all political, civil, economic, social and cultural rights.

The concept of self-determination has evolved since the creation of the United Nations in 1945, when the principle was initially interpreted to apply to the right of independence, non-interference and democracy of a nation-state in relation to other nation-state governments.[84] However, more recently, it has also included the development of self-government institutions in indigenous communities.[85]

The UN's Declaration on the Rights of Indigenous Peoples affirms that indigenous peoples possess collective rights that are indispensable for their existence and well-being, including the right to collective self-determination and the collective right to the lands, territories and natural resources they have traditionally occupied and used.[86] The collective right to self-determination ensures that indigenous communities can determine their own identity, belong to 'an indigenous community or nation, in accordance with the traditions and customs of the community or nation concerned' and make decisions about internal and local affairs.[87] The Declaration also provides that indigenous peoples should have the freedom to define and pursue their own economic, social and cultural development. Similarly, the UN's Convention for the Safeguarding of the Intangible Cultural Heritage also affirms the collective rights of communities to safeguard and respect their cultural heritage.[88]

In the context of climate-induced ecological change that threatens the habitability of entire communities, self-determination means that communities have the right to make decisions regarding adaptation strategies, which includes the right to make fundamental decisions about when, how and if relocation occurs.

Several existing international human rights documents include the right to participate in decision-making processes and the right to adequate and meaningful consultation as a means to ensure human rights protections. Informed consent and participation do not constitute effective self-determination, and they are insufficient to protect the human rights of those threatened by climate-induced ecological change. These principles, which form part of the World Bank's guidelines on involuntary resettlement, have not prevented the social fragmentation and impoverishment that have plagued involuntary resettlements caused by a World Bank-funded project.[89]

Insufficient attention has been paid to protecting communities' welfare and empowering them to make decisions regarding critical elements of their relocation, including site selection and community layout. These are the principal reasons why previous relocations have proved unsuccessful.[90] Success will be more likely if and when affected communities are able to participate in critical relocation and implementation decisions, such as identification of basic needs and settlement planning.[91] For these reasons, communities faced with climate-induced ecological threats must have the authority to decide whether to relocate or not. Collective self-determination ensures that communities are empowered to make all of the critical decisions affecting their relocation.[92]

Right to relocation

The right to relocate is a fundamental component of the right to self-determination when climate-induced ecological changes threaten the lives of people and cause degraded community habitability. The right to relocate, as with other human rights, is an entitlement when relocation is the only feasible solution to protect the human right to life as well as the right to the basic necessities inherent in living a dignified life.[93]

Several international legal instruments support the right to relocate, including the Universal Declaration of Human Rights and the Pinheiro Principles, both of which state that everyone has the right to freedom of movement and residence.[94] While this right has been interpreted to mean that no one shall be arbitrarily or unlawfully forced to remain within a certain territory, area or region and that no one shall be arbitrarily or unlawfully forced to leave a certain territory, area or region, it also includes the right to move when threatened by environmental events.[95] The human rights guidelines on how to respond to natural disasters interpret the right to life to mean that people affected by natural disasters should be allowed to relocate to other parts of the country.[96]

Right to non-discrimination

Relocation cannot be conducted in a discriminatory manner. All articles of non-discrimination articulated in the Guiding Principles on Internal Displacement are incorporated within the Peninsula Principles.

Right to basic necessities

Articles 14 and 23 of the UN's Declaration on the Rights of Indigenous Peoples affirm collective rights to the fundamental freedoms articulated in international human rights law and specifically the 'right to be actively involved in developing and determining health, housing and other economic and social programs affecting them and to administer such programs through their own institutions'. These fundamental freedoms include the collective right to basic necessities, which, at a minimum, means that relocated communities must have access to food and water, housing and adequate health. Sustainable development opportunities must also be incorporated into the relocation process. In this way, the relocation process will enhance the communities' resilience capacity by addressing socio-economic issues, such as lack of economic development, that are currently contributing to community vulnerability.

Rights to subsistence and food

Human rights doctrine explicitly states that the right to food and the right to be free from hunger are indispensable to human dignity and critically connected to other fundamental rights.[97] The right to food relates to an individual's lack of food, and to the economic or physical reasons why people do not have access to food.[98]

States have the primary responsibility to promote and protect people's right to food.[99] They have a duty to provide food '[w]henever an individual or group is unable, for reasons beyond their control, to enjoy the right to adequate food by the means at their disposal'. This obligation extends to persons who are victims of natural or other disasters.[100]

The right to subsistence, an element of the right to self-determination defined in both the International Covenant on Economic, Social and Cultural Rights and the International Covenant on Civil and Political Rights, is an essential human right that is connected to the right to food.[101] For indigenous peoples, the right to food is a collective right, and fundamentally connected to sovereignty and to rights to land and territories, health, subsistence, treaties, economic development and culture.[102] For these reasons, the community of Newtok has chosen its relocation site in order to maintain connection to traditional sites that are used for subsistence activities. Mertarvik is only twelve kilometres from Newtok, across the Ninglick River, so the community still has easy access to navigable waters leading to its traditional fishing grounds in the river and the Bering Sea.

Rights to work, economic development and improved standard of living

Human development goals that improve the economic and social conditions of residents who are required to relocate, including in the areas of education, employment, vocational training and retraining, housing, sanitation, health and social security, must be incorporated into community relocation planning.[103]

The Newtok tribal government is incorporating workforce development opportunities and improved living standards in its relocation efforts. Newtok residents are using recently acquired construction skills to build the necessary housing and infrastructure at the relocation site. In addition, the relocation site will have access to economic development opportunities for fishing and construction.

Right to water

Relocated communities must have sufficient water for their basic household needs, including drinking, cooking and hygiene. The human right to water is essential for leading a dignified life, indispensable to the realisation of all the human rights related to basic necessities, and fundamental for life and health.[104]

This right is not explicitly mentioned in the International Covenant on Economic, Social and Cultural Rights, but it is interpreted to be implicit in the right to an adequate standard of living and health.[105]

Access to water/degradation of water supply

Climate-induced ecological change will profoundly impact access to potable water. Extreme weather events, changes in precipitation and sea-level rise, causing saline intrusion, flooding and drought, will alter water supplies and could result in temporary disruptions to access to water while also reducing the size of the potable water supply. Long periods of drought will threaten the lives and health of those who depend on freshwater sources and rainwater catchment.[106]

In Alaska, climate change is impacting access to fresh water and water quality in many coastal communities. In Newtok, located on the Bering Sea in western Alaska, tundra ponds are the community's freshwater source. Saline intrusion due to sea surges and flooding has impacted the water quality of these ponds.[107]

Right to housing/property

Three human rights principles apply to community relocations and the right to housing: the right to replacement housing, the right to habitable housing and the right to choose the place of one's residence. The right to habitable housing means that the housing must provide adequate protection from weather hazards and that it is located away from hazardous zones. The human right to property, defined in the Universal Declaration of Human Rights, includes the right to landownership as well as housing.[108] The Pinheiro Principles specifically outline the human rights principles that must guide land, housing and property restitution, which is viewed as an essential remedy for displacement.[109] Although the principles are premised on the unlawful or arbitrary taking of housing, land or property, they outline a method for restitution that is highly relevant to those who lose their housing, land or property due to climate change.

Nation-state governments need to enact policies and laws to ensure that housing, land and property restitution procedures, institutions and mechanisms all fall within a legally sound, coherent and practical framework that should bring displacement to a permanent, sustainable and just end, and that they are fully compatible with international human rights, refugee and humanitarian law and related standards.[110] Principles that must be included within these laws include non-discrimination in housing restitution.[111] All displaced persons must also have the right to full and effective compensation as an integral component of the relocation process.[112]

Land is a critical issue for all people who need to relocate. The right to landownership restitution requires that specific arrangements are made to recognise claims to land title and ownership, especially for indigenous peoples who may not have formal land titles and may own land collectively.

Conclusion

Newtok's tribal government and the work of the Newtok Planning Group provide a model for other communities facing relocation as a consequence of climate change. The tribal government's role as a leader in the relocation process ensures that the community's culture and the collective and individual human rights of community residents are central to the relocation process. As climate change causes ever more extreme weather events and ongoing ecological change makes relocation an inevitability for ever more communities, human rights protections need to infuse the relocation process. This will enable relocated communities to protect their cultural cohesion even when they suffer enormous loss of land to which they are connected.

Notes

1   University of Alaska Fairbanks, Alaska Institute for Justice.
2   World Meteorological Organization (WMO), *State of the Climate Report 2015* (2015) http://public.wmo.int/en/media/press-release/state-of-climate-record-heat-and-weather-extremes accessed 25 October 2016.
3   M. O. Jeffries, J. Richter-Menge and J. E. Overland, *Arctic Report Card* (NOAA 2015).
4   J. E. Walsh *et al.*, 'Cryosphere and Hydrology' in *Arctic Climate Impact Assessment* (Cambridge University Press 2015).
5   R. J. Nicholls and A. Cazenave, 'Sea-Level Rise and Its Impact on Coastal Zones' (2010) 328 *Science* 1517.
6   Jeffries *et al.*, *Arctic Report Card*.
7   Nicholls and Cazenave, 'Sea-Level Rise'.
8   Intergovernmental Panel on Climate Change (IPCC), 'Summary for Policymakers' in C. B. Field *et al.* (eds), *Managing the Risks of Extreme Events and Disasters to Advance Climate Change Adaptation: A Special Report of Working Groups I and II of the Intergovernmental Panel on Climate Change* (Cambridge University Press 2012) 3–21.
9   Jeffries *et al.*, *Arctic Report Card*.
10 National Snow and Ice Data Center (NSIDC), 'Arctic Sea Ice News & Analysis' (2016) https://nsidc.org/arcticseaicenews/2016/03/ accessed 25 October 2016.
11 Walsh *et al.*, 'Cryosphere and Hydrology'; M. Shulski and G. Wendler, *The Climate of Alaska* (University of Alaska Press 2007).
12 Ibid.
13 G. Hufford and J. Partain, *Climate Change and Short-Term Forecasting for Alaskan Northern Coasts* (National Weather Service 2005).

14 Walsh *et al.*, 'Cryosphere and Hydrology'; Shulski and Wendler, *Climate of Alaska.*

15 R. Bronen, 'Climate-Induced Community Relocations: Creating an Adaptive Governance Framework Based in Human Rights Doctrine' (2011) 35(2) *NYU Review of Law and Social Change* 101.

16 K. J. Abhas, *Safer Homes, Stronger Communities: A Handbook for Reconstructing after Natural Disasters* (World Bank 2010)

17 S. Cox, *An Overview of Erosion, Flooding, and Relocation Efforts in the Native Village of Newtok* (Alaska Department of Commerce, Community and Economic Development 2007).

18 US Army Corps of Engineers (USACE), *Alaska Village Erosion Technical Assistance Program: An Examination of Erosion Issues in the Communities of Bethel, Dillingham, Kaktovik, Kivalina, Newtok, Shishmaref and Unalakleet* (2006).

19 Cox, *Overview of Erosion.*

20 US Army Corps of Engineers (USACE), 'Revised Environmental Assessment: Finding of No Significant Impact: Newtok Evacuation Center: Mertarvik, Nelson Island, Alaska' (2008) www.commerce.state.ak.us/dca/planning/pub/Newtok_Evacuation_Center_EA_&_FONSI_July_08.pdf accessed 25 October 2016.

21 Ibid.

22 Arctic Slope Consulting Group (ASCG), 'Village of Newtok, Local Hazards Mitigation Plan' (2008) www.commerce.state.ak.us/dca/planning/pub/Newtok_HMP.pdf accessed 25 October 2016.

23 Ibid.

24 USACE, 'Revised Environmental Assessment'.

25 Bronen, 'Climate-Induced Community Relocations'.

26 Cox, *Overview of Erosion.*

27 Ibid.

28 Bronen, 'Climate-Induced Community Relocations'.

29 Ibid.

30 Ibid.

31 Ibid.

32 Ibid.

33 Cox, *Overview of Erosion.*

34 US Army Corps of Engineers (USACE), 'Section 117 Project Fact Sheet' (2008) www.commerce.state.ak.us/dca/planning/pub/Newtok_Sec_117.pdf accessed 25 October 2016.

35 Ibid.

36 Ibid.

37 Ibid.

38 USACE, 'Revised Environmental Assessment'.

39 Bronen, 'Climate-Induced Community Relocations'.

40 Agnew:Beck Consulting, *Strategic Management Plan: Newtok to Mertarvik* (2012).

41 Ibid.

42 Ibid.

43 Alaska Division of Community and Regional Affairs (DCRA), 'Newtok Planning Group Mertarvik Housing' (n.d.) www.commerce.alaska.gov/web/dcra/Planning LandManagement//NewtokPlanningGroup/MertarvikHousing.aspx accessed 25 October 2016.

44 Ibid.

45 Bronen, 'Climate-Induced Community Relocations'; R. Bronen and F. S. Chapin, 'Adaptive Governance and Institutional Strategies for Climate-Induced Community Relocations in Alaska' (2013) *Proceedings of the National Academy of Sciences.*

46 United States Congress Bicameral Task Force on Climate Change, *Implementing the President's Action Plan: US Department of the Interior* (2013).

47 White House, *President's State, Local and Tribal Leaders' Task Force on Climate Preparedness and Resilience, Recommendations to the President* (2014).

48 Bronen, 'Climate-Induced Community Relocations'.

49 R. Bronen, 'Climate-Induced Community Relocations: Using Integrated Social-Ecological Assessments to Foster Adaptation and Resilience' (2015) 20(3) *Ecology and Society* 36.

50 Bronen, 'Climate-Induced Community Relocations'; Bronen and Chapin, 'Adaptive Governance'.

51 Bronen, 'Using Integrated Social-Ecological Assessments'.

52 D. Armitage and R. Plummer, 'Adapting and Transforming: Governance for Navigating Change' in D. Armitage and R. Plummer (eds), *Adaptive Capacity and Environmental Governance* (Springer 2010).

53 Bronen, 'Using Integrated Social-Ecological Assessments'.

54 J. C. Hathaway, 'Reconceiving Refugee Law as Human Rights Protection' (1991) 23 *Journal of Refugee Studies* 113; International Commission on Intervention and State Sovereignty (ICISS), *Responsibility to Protect* (International Development Research Centre 2001).

55 *Montevideo Convention on the Rights and Duties of States* (adopted 13 July 1934, entered into force 26 December 1934).

56 ICISS, *Responsibility to Protect*.

57 Ibid.

58 Ibid.

59 Ibid.

60 Ibid.

61 Inter-Agency Standing Committee (IASC), *IASC Operational Guidelines on the Protection of Persons in Situations of Natural Disasters* (Brookings–Bern Project on Internal Displacement 2011).

62 UN Economic and Social Council, *Specific Groups and Individuals: Mass Exoduses and Displaced Persons, Report of the Representative of the Secretary-General on the Human Rights of Internally Displaced Persons, Walter Kälin* (2006) E/CN.4/2006/71.

63 Ibid. paras. 4–8.

64 United Nations, Office of the High Commissioner for Human Rights (UN OHCHR), *Guiding Principles on Internal Displacement* (2008) E/CN.4/1998/53/Add.2.

65 UN Economic and Social Council, *Final Report of the Special Rapporteur, Paulo Sérgio Pinheiro: Principles on Housing and Property Restitution for Refugees and Displaced Persons* (2005) E/CN.4/Sub.2/2005/17.

66 *Budayeva and Others v. Russian Federation* (European Court of Human Rights 20 March 2008).

67 Bronen, 'Climate-Induced Community Relocations'; Bronen and Chapin, 'Adaptive Governance'.

68 R. Zetter, 'Protecting People Displaced by Climate Change: Some Conceptual Challenges' in J. McAdam (ed.), *Climate Change and Displacement: Multi-Disciplinary Perspectives* (Hart 2010).

69 United Nations, *Framework Convention on Climate Change* (UNFCCC) (concluded 9 May 1992, entered into force 21 March 1994) Article 4(1)(b).

70 United Nations, *Convention Relating to the Status of Refugees* (adopted 28 July 1951, entered into force 22 April 1954) 189 UNTS 137.

71 United Nations, *Protocol Relating to the Status of Refugees* (adopted 31 January 1967, entered into force 4 October 1967) 606 UNTS 267.

72 United Nations, *Convention*.

73 Hathaway, 'Reconceiving Refugee Law'.

74 Ibid.

75 Ibid.

76   IASC, *Operational Guidelines*.
77   Ibid.
78   Ibid.
79   United Nations, *International Covenant on Economic, Social and Cultural Rights* (adopted 16 December 1966, entered into force 3 January 1976) 993 UNTS 3.
80   UN General Assembly, Resolution 60/1 (2005).
81   Bronen, 'Climate-Induced Community Relocations'.
82   Abhas, *Safer Homes, Stronger Communities*.
83   Displacement Solutions, *The Peninsula Principles on Climate Displacement within States* (2013) http://displacementsolutions.org/wp-content/uploads/FINAL-Peninsula-Principles-FINAL.pdf accessed 25 October 2016. See also Chapter 6, this volume.
84   E. G. Broderstad and J. Dahl, 'Political Systems' in *Arctic Human Development Report* (Stefansson Arctic Institute 2004) 85–99; UN Committee on Economic, Social and Cultural Rights, Fact Sheet No. 16 (1945) 4.
85   Ibid.
86   UN General Assembly, *Universal Declaration on the Rights of Indigenous Peoples* (2007) Article 1.
87   Ibid. Articles 9 and 33.
88   UN General Assembly, *Convention for the Safeguarding of the Intangible Cultural Heritage* (2006) Article 1.
89   A. O. Smith, 'Introduction' in A. O. Smith (ed.), *Development and Dispossession: The Crisis of Forced Displacement and Resettlement* (Santa Fe School for Advanced Research Press 2009).
90   Abhas, *Safer Homes, Stronger Communities*.
91   Ibid.
92   See, for example, Chapter 7, this volume.
93   S. Moyn, *The Last Utopia: Human Rights in History* (Harvard University Press 2010).
94   UN, *Universal Declaration*; UN, *Pinheiro Principles*.
95   Ibid.
96   IASC, *Operational Guidelines*.
97   UN Committee on Economic, Social and Cultural Rights, *General Comment No. 12: The Right to Adequate Food* (1999) E/C.12/1995/5 para. 1.
98   Ibid. paras. 4–5.
99   UN Human Rights Council, *The Right to Food* (2011) A/HRC/RES/16/27 para. 11.
100   UN Committee on Economic, Social and Cultural Rights, *General Comment No. 12* para. 12.
101   UN, *International Covenant*.
102   United Nations, Office of the High Commissioner for Human Rights (OHCHR), *Consultation on the Relationship between Climate Change and Human Rights* (2008) 4.
103   UN, *Universal Declaration* Article 21.
104   United Nations, Office of the High Commissioner for Human Rights (OHCHR), *Consultation on Human Rights and Access to Safe Drinking Water and Sanitation* (2007) 4.
105   UN Committee on Economic, Social and Cultural Rights, *General Comment No. 14: The Right to Water* (2002) E/C.12/2002/11; OHCHR, *Consultation on Safe Drinking Water and Sanitation* 7.
106   Submission of the Maldives to United Nations, Office of the High Commissioner for Human Rights (OHCHR), *Human Rights and Climate Change* (2008) Resolution 7/23; Climate Change Portal of the Office of the President of Kiribati, *Climate Change in Kiribati* (2017) www.climate.gov.ki/accessed 12 January 2017.
107   USACE, 'Section 117 Project Fact Sheet'.

108   IASC, *Operational Guidelines.*
109   UN, *Pinheiro Principles.*
110   Ibid.
111   Ibid.
112   S. Leckie, 'Climate-Related Disasters and Displacement: Homes for Lost Homes, Lands for Lost Lands' in J. M. Guzmán *et al.* (eds), *Population Dynamics and Climate Change* (UNFPA 2009).

10 Land matters

Challenges to planned relocation as a durable solution to environmentally induced displacement in Kenya

Jeanette Schade[1]

Introduction[2]

Planned relocation as an adaptive measure to deal with forced migration in the context of environmental and climate change is increasingly gaining acceptance amongst international actors. In 2010, the outcome of the COP16 of the UN Framework Convention on Climate Change (UNFCCC) in Cancún invited all parties 'to enhance understanding, coordination and cooperation with regard to climate change induced displacement, migration and planned relocation'.[3] Five years later, in March 2015, planned relocation gained further momentum when it was incorporated as a measure to achieve durable solutions in the UN's new agenda for disaster risk reduction (DRR), the so-called *Sendai Framework for Disaster Risk Reduction 2015–2030*.[4] In the run-up to the Paris summit, COP21, several documents dealing with planned relocation were published. The UN High Commissioner for Refugees (UNHCR), together with the Brookings Institution and Georgetown University, published the 'Guidance on Protecting People from Disasters and Environmental Change through Planned Relocation'.[5] The Advisory Group on Climate Change and Human Mobility (AGCCHM) lobbied extensively for 'human mobility', encompassing planned relocation, to be integrated into the Paris Agreement of COP21.[6] And a group of concerned social scientists and experts launched critical recommendations on planned relocation in the context of climate policies.[7] Planned resettlement was again emphasised as a form of preferable and sustainable long-term assistance (as opposed to short-term relief) by the UN Secretary-General in his report for the World Humanitarian Summit, which took place in May 2016.[8]

Planned relocation in the context of natural disasters and climate change can be both a preventive measure to avoid disaster displacement and a response if it has already occurred. However, planned relocation can also be a second-order measure and consequence of climate policies and mitigation and adaptation interventions alike. To this extent, it intersects with the broader field of development-based and conservation-based evictions, where measures to remove people from project zones are usually called 'involuntary resettlement'.[9] In fact, it is reasonable to assume that whatever the cause for planned relocation might be, applied frameworks should offer analogous protections, and implementation should follow similar procedures. Though considerable progress has been made at the global level to develop appropriate standards and safeguards, the question remains how this translates into the realities of national-level policies and practices.

This chapter elaborates on the prospects for planned relocation in Kenya by taking into consideration historical and current experiences and available regulations. Generally, planned relocation is known to cause severe livelihood stress with a high risk of infringing human rights. In fact, forced eviction constitutes a 'gross violation of human rights'[10] if not carried out 'solely for the purpose of promoting the general welfare in a democratic society'[11] and 'in conformity with the provisions of the International Covenants on Human Rights'.[12] At first glance, the Kenyan case looks as if planned relocation might be the right thing to do. The environmental challenges described in the next section seemingly justify placing it in the basket of policy options for Kenya, and indeed Kenya in recent years has made considerable progress in reforming, if not developing, its regulatory framework for humanitarian action, including planned relocation. Kenya is further party to relevant human rights treaties and humanitarian accords that offer normative guidance for such a regulatory framework. It has, inter alia, ratified the two international human rights covenants (both in 1972), the African Charter on Human and Peoples' Rights (Banjul Charter; in 1992), the 1951 Convention Relating to the Status of Refugees (in 1966) and its 1967 Protocol (in 1981), the African Union (AU) Convention Governing the Specific Aspects of Refugee Problems in Africa (in 1992), and the Pact on Security, Stability and Development in the Great Lakes Region and its Protocol on the Protection and Assistance to Internally Displaced Persons (Great Lakes Protocol; acceded to both in 2006). It is, however, not a party to the AU Convention for the Protection and Assistance of Internally Displaced Persons in Africa (Kampala Convention; entered into force in 2012).

This promising point of departure should, however, be put into perspective by looking at Kenya's internal displacement problem more generally, and at the historical and current experiences of Kenya with state-sponsored resettlement programmes. Indeed, the challenges of the past seem to mirror the challenges that lie ahead, with land issues being both at the core of various problems and key to long-term solutions. The remainder of this chapter will therefore deal with both the humanitarian and the land policy aspects of developing an appropriate regulatory framework for planned relocation. In brief, the initiated reform process is not yet finalised; and what has been achieved so far in the humanitarian field is not yet harmonised with the other reform process: the reform of land regulations.

Environmental change, land and displacement in Kenya

The impact of climate and environmental change in Kenya on the lives and livelihoods of people is evident. According to the Emergency Events Database (EM-DAT), since 1964 Kenya has suffered a total of 101 natural disasters (mainly droughts, floods and related epidemics), of which the great majority (72) have occurred since the turn of the millennium.[13]

Evidence of the extent to which these events relate to patterns of forced migration and displacement is difficult to obtain and usually anecdotal.[14] The EM-DAT category of 'affected persons' has a broad meaning, reaching far beyond internally displaced persons (IDPs), but systematic data collection on IDPs in Kenya is non-existent.[15] The following overview on the impacts of natural disasters on human beings therefore relies on the EM-DAT category. The focus is on droughts and wet events (floods and mudslides), which regularly occur in specific parts of the country, though some counties – such as Tana River – experience both, and a few droughts have even affected the entire country (1980/81, 1938/39, 1896–1900).[16]

As regards droughts, EM-DAT records show that 10 of the 14 events since 1964 have occurred during the past 25 years. With a share of 83 per cent of the total number of affected persons, droughts have the greatest impact on the Kenyan population. The consecutive droughts from 2008 to 2011 alone affected close to 12 million people (2008: 3.8 million; 2010: 4.3 million; 2011: 3.75 million). In an overwhelmingly agricultural society, consecutive droughts pose a major challenge to livelihood recovery and, hence, increase the proclivity to migrate or, as Kenya's arid and semi-arid areas are mainly affected, trigger pastoralist dropout which feeds into sedentarisation and urbanisation trends.[17] More than 83 per cent of the Kenyan landmass is classified as arid or semi-arid land (ASAL), located mainly in the northern parts of the country, and it hosts about 20 per cent of the population.[18] Counties that are prone to drought include Baringo, Laikipia, Turkana, Samburu, Narok and

Table 10.1 Number of natural disasters and affected persons in Kenya, 1964–January 2016

Disaster type	Occurrence	Total deaths	Affected	Homeless	Total affected
Epidemic	32	4,856	6,881,995	0	6,881,995
Drought	14	196	48,800,000	0	48,800,000
Earthquake	2	1	0	0	0
Flood	48	1,350	2,969,894	6,200	2,976,123
Landslide	4	56	0	0	26
Storm	1	50	0	0	0
Total	**101**	**6,509**	**58,651,889**	**6,200**	**58,661,603**

Source: CRED (2016)[19]

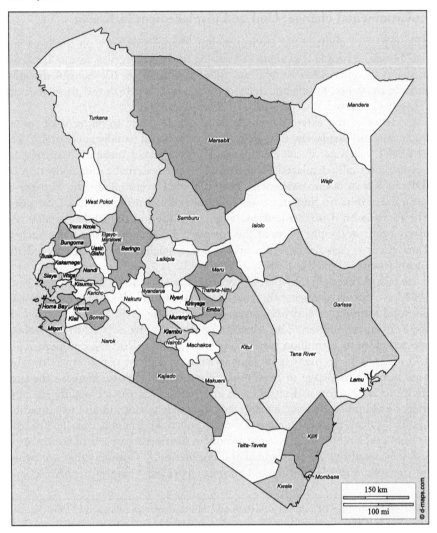

Figure 10.1 Map of Kenyan counties, replacing districts as per constitutional reforms
        of 2010
Source: http://d-maps.com/carte.php?&num_car=35033&lang=en accessed 18 December
2016

Kajiado (previously parts of the Rift Valley province), Marsabit and Isiolo
(previously parts of the Eastern province), Mandera, Garissa and Wajir
(previously parts of the North Eastern province), and Tana River, Kilifi,
Kwale and Taita-Taveta (previously parts of the Coast province).[20]

As regards wet events, the EM-DAT database records close to 50 floods in
Kenya since 1964, of which 34 have been riverine floods affecting close to two
million people in total.[21] The main counties affected are those at the shores

of Lake Victoria (mainly the former province of Nyanza and Busia), and Tana River. Another major challenge for certain regions in Kenya are landslides, which mainly affect Muranga County (in central Kenya) and Kakamega County (in western Kenya),[22] but also occur in slum areas of major cities. Finally, though evidence of current sea-level rise is quite weak,[23] it is estimated that levels will rise by 1–2 millimetres per year over the next hundred years.[24] If this comes to pass, it will threaten, inter alia, parts of Mombasa city with submergence.[25]

Though we lack a reliable census of people who have been displaced by natural disasters and still need assistance to re-establish their livelihoods, and reliable assessments and projections of how many people are at risk of displacement, the above summary may be sufficient evidence to justify exploration of planned relocation as a possible long-term DRR solution in Kenya. The need for resettlement land is, however, not confined to the accommodation of IDPs generated by natural disasters and climate change. Internal displacement may arise through other causes, particularly violence during general elections, the increasing insecurity in the north due to the spread of small arms and commercialisation of cattle rustling, development- and conservation-based forced evictions, land disputes and squatter displacement.[26] Everyone displaced by such causes may be in need of shelter. Though reliable figures on the total number of IDPs in Kenya are unavailable, the challenge is likely to be huge. At the peak of displacement in 2008, experts estimated that Kenya had about a million IDPs,[27] including a large number of so-called 'integrated IDPs', who cannot be counted accurately because they have never sought official assistance. Instead, they have turned to relatives for refuge and support.

Displacement due to political conflict has reached unprecedented levels since the introduction of the multi-party system. An estimated 300,000 people were displaced during the general election in 1992, 150,000 in 1997, and over 660,000 in 2007.[28] Some experts regard political violence in the fertile areas of Kenya to have an environmental angle, because it has coincided with a shrinking land per person figure due to rapid population growth: 'by the time violence erupted, the availability of good agricultural land … [had] diminished … from an average of 1.66 ha per person in 1969 to 1.02 in 1979, and 0.63 in 1989.'[29] Large-scale development projects and the demarcation of protected areas have also reduced access to land for agricultural purposes (including pastoralism). The former have generated an unknown number of evictees and the latter far more than 10,000 IDPs.[30]

The ongoing problem of IDPs in Kenya suggests that planned relocation cannot be discussed solely as a response to environmental displacement but must also be considered as a long-term solution to the IDP issue more generally. Furthermore, since IDPs frequently move to environmentally risk-prone sites for want of better alternatives, there may be great overlaps, and many IDPs may suffer repeated displacement, including for environmental reasons.

This brief overview indicates that displacement and planned relocation as a potential solution are inextricably linked to the question of land. First, climate and environmental change triggers and accelerates the loss of land due to sea-level rise, coastal erosion, landslides and other forms of land degradation, and, hence, reduces the availability of land in sufficient quantity and quality for settlement and the maintenance of land-based forms of livelihood. Second, planned relocation as a state-sponsored response to displacement and as a preventive measure to the risk thereof creates additional demand for land. Planned relocation thus finds itself in stiff competition with other proposals for land-use change, such as development and conservation projects (including mitigation and adaptation measures), which in themselves may create more IDPs. Moreover, urbanisation, both planned and unplanned, is eating into available land. At independence, only 8 per cent of the Kenyan population lived in urban areas;[31] in 2009, it was 21 per cent.[32] Third, the ruthless struggle for land is one of the major reasons for displacement in Kenya; hence, the issue of land is both a spatial and a political obstacle to successful relocation. This suggests that a holistic approach to planned relocation is needed – an approach that considers the humanitarian as well as the land-related aspects of resettlement.

Before exploring Kenya's current efforts and its prospects for achieving such a holistic policy, the next section will present a more detailed analysis of resettlement in Kenya thus far.

State-sponsored resettlement in Kenya

The history of state-sponsored relocation in Kenya is far from impressive. The country's first experience of 'resettlement' came when the British authorities established native reserves for the major tribes – the so-called Native Trust Land Areas – in 1904.[33] The reserves' boundaries did not necessarily coincide with what the various ethnic groups (43 in total)[34] called their ancestral lands; nor was every tribe and sub-tribe awarded its own reserve. In total, it is estimated that Kenyan tribes lost about 5 million hectares of land to white settlers during the period of British rule (1895–1963).[35] This land grab was accompanied by forced labour schemes, which comprised another cause of forced relocation during colonialism. As the 'White Highlands' were originally populated by non-farming pastoral communities, the colonial authorities after the First World War resorted to coercive policies for recruiting labour from the overpopulated reserves in the Central, Nyanza and Western provinces, which resulted in mass migration of Kikuyu, Abagusii, Luhya and Luo, who then lived as 'squatter labourers' on the plantations.[36]

Resettlement schemes after independence in 1963 were originally meant to return land to the Kenyans, including the landless and those with little access to land. However, they resulted in the concentration of the most fertile lands in the hands of specific ethnic groups and, indeed, a few specific families.[37] The most famous project, the One Million Acre Scheme (1962–1967), offered foreign funding for Africans to purchase a total of 1 million acres out of the 7.5 million acres that were then held by European settlers. But the original intentions of the scheme were thwarted by implementing officers and their superiors, leaving the original inhabitants landless or with unproductive land.[38] The area of the Lugari Settlement Scheme in the Western province was cleared of squatters and farm workers originating from Central province so the land could be distributed amongst members of the Luhya community. In the Aberdares, the government evicted members of every ethnic group other than Kikuyu in order that the latter could be resettled there. Moreover, irregularities in the purchase of (re)settlement land were reported in the Sitatunga, Maridadi and Liyavo Settlement Schemes in Trans Nzoia. Settlement schemes along the coast favoured 'up-country communities'. In Lamu, for example, the scheme benefited only 15–20 per cent of the coastal communities, yet within a decade (1969–1979) contributed to a 20 per cent increase in the Kikuyu population.[39] Indeed, all of the post-colonial settlement schemes involved population movements of certain ethnic groups into fertile and economic attractive areas, and the consequent displacement of other groups. They were all constrained by both racialisation and class thinking. The elites of various tribes competed with each other to grab resettlement land at the cost of those who were poor and landless, regardless of the latter's ethnicity.[40] Finally, according to witnesses before the Truth, Reconciliation and Justice Commission (TRJC), supposed resettlement land in Kericho was actually given to multinational companies that had cultivated tea in the area since the 1920s.[41]

The unequal treatment of IDPs after independence and the unsolved issue of land alienation more generally in both colonial and post-colonial times have continued to be major sources of conflict, and have led to the creation of new IDPs throughout the history of modern Kenya. As Karanja puts it, '[t]he discriminate resettlement of some colonial displaced people and not others has led to a feeling of dispossession and new displacements where some colonial displacement victims have become perpetrators and the beneficiaries of resettlement have become new victims of displacement'.[42] Providing humanitarian assistance to the IDPs who have been created by this political violence – and especially finding a long-term solution to their plight – has always been a difficult and tenuous issue. Efforts at independence to draw administrative and constituency boundaries between 'native lands' fostered ideas of ethnic homogeneity within such borders. This was combined with a vow to reclaim ancestral lands from so-called 'migrants', 'outsiders' and 'foreigners' – all terms for black Kenyans who reside in areas that are not regarded as their tribes' ancestral lands. As political parties in Kenya tend to be structured along ethnic lines, such sentiments have been voiced regularly during elections to shape the 'electoral demography' and hence the election results.[43] Local administrations and communities – strongly involved in the forcible eviction of their neighbours – do not necessarily welcome returnees, and security threats remain.

The most recent large-scale Kenyan resettlement scheme is Operation Rudi Nyumbani (Operation Return Home), implemented in the aftermath of the post-election violence of 2007/8. The related displacement was unprecedented and the challenges were huge. It is estimated that 1,133 lives were lost, 78,254 homes were destroyed, some 663,921 people were displaced, of whom about 350,000 sought refuge in 118 camps while the remainder (around 47 per cent) became integrated IDPs, and 640 households fled to Uganda.[44] Not surprisingly, the central government was overwhelmed by the task it faced and funds for the immediate response were woefully insufficient. In consequence, the evictees' plight was exacerbated by human rights failures in the context of emergency assistance, such as a lack of adequate access to clean water, food, health, education and so on.[45]

The government's main priority when it initiated Operation Rudi Nyumbani in May 2008 was to facilitate return (not permanent relocation) in order to dissolve all of the IDP camps, and hence all of their associated problems. Every registered IDP was eligible for an ex gratia payment of 10,000 KES, and those who were able to demonstrate that their homes had been destroyed were entitled to a further 25,000 KES for reconstruction.[46] However, the scheme was widely criticised,[47] and at the end of 2010 the Kenyan parliament established the Parliamentary Select Committee on the Resettlement of IDPs (PSC) to evaluate the government's programme.[48] The committee's analysis echoed the criticism that previous schemes had received:[49]

- It was premature, because the underlying tensions that had caused the violence had not been resolved and the government did not take due account of the prevailing insecurity at the places of origin.
- The scheme privileged home-owners and neglected those who had never owned land and/or a house (the landless poor, but also many traders).
- Most of the money was spent in the Western, Central and Rift Valley provinces, with little attention paid to IDPs in the north of Kenya.
- Encamped IDPs who refused to return to their places of origin because of fear or because they had nowhere to go were threatened with ultimatums as the dissolution of the already poor camps began.[50]
- Programmes and funding to replace lost assets and re-establish livelihoods were inadequate, while the lack of access to local labour markets prevented many IDPs from regaining their previous standard of living. Hence, they were pushed into aid dependency, beggary or prostitution, or suffered family separation because of the necessity to search for job opportunities elsewhere.
- Officials and camp chairpersons manipulated IDP registries to benefit non-IDPs, such as political friends and other cronies. Of course, this widespread corruption disadvantaged genuine IDPs.

After their forced evictions from the camps, many of the landless IDPs pooled their 10,000 KES payments to purchase land jointly. However, this merely led to the proliferation of new overcrowded camps, because the money was insufficient to secure an adequate balance of land per person. In total, these 'self-managed', congested camps hosted about 9,571 households, who lived without access to sanitation, water, electricity, work or security. The government had to do something, so in late 2008 it decided to purchase land – 2.25 acres per household – and start the task of permanently resettling these IDPs in an orderly manner. Although considerable funds were allocated to this scheme (close to 3 billion KES for the financial years 2009/10–2010/11), the process proved incredibly slow due to protracted land transfer negotiations. Thus, by May 2012, of the required 27,000 acres, only about 8,800 had been purchased, and only about 24 per cent of the households had been resettled.[51] The resettlement programme was still incomplete four years later, so in February 2016 the government was finally forced to announce compensation payments along with a schedule for closure of the remaining camps.[52] Furthermore, as with earlier resettlement schemes, the project was marred by endemic corruption and the alienation of land earmarked for the resettlement of IDPs. This time, however, there were at least some criminal prosecutions.

Finally, it should be noted that Operation Rudi Nyumbani did not attempt to help any IDPs who had been forced to flee amid earlier outbreaks of violence (particularly in 1992 and 1997) and had not yet found permanent homes. Moreover, a survey of several camps in Uasin Gishu revealed that about 85 per cent of the IDPs created by the 2007/8 violence had also been displaced in 1992 and 1997. This indicates that no long-term solution has been found, because the underlying causes of violence – particularly those relating to land issues – have not yet been addressed.[53]

Developing a framework to assist and resettle IDPs: the humanitarian perspective

At the time of the political violence in 2007/8 and Operation Rudi Nyumbani, there was no legal scheme in place to protect Kenya's IDPs.[54] Unfortunately, few politicians are interested in these people as they have typically lost their documents and hence their voting power. Furthermore, the violence that led to their displacement was often incited by those in power. Hence, if assisting IDPs is a low priority, prosecuting those who are responsible for their predicament is even lower. For these reasons, IDPs comprise a very weak lobby in Kenya, which helps to explain why policy-makers were able to turn a blind eye to their plight for so many years.[55]

However, the violent events of 2007/8 may have been a turning point. This time, the displacement was so acute that international actors and Kenyan civil society felt compelled to act. In 2008, over 30 agencies, headed by the UNHCR, combined to form an IDP Protection Cluster, which coordinated an immediate response. The following year, this evolved into the Protection Working Group for Internal Displacement (PWGID), co-chaired by the former Ministry of Justice (now the Department of Justice) and the Kenya National Commission on Human Rights (KNCHR), which held discussions on how to improve Kenya's capacity to assist IDPs.[56] A sub-group of the PWGID, under the leadership of Refugee Consortium Kenya (RCK), was entrusted with the task of developing a framework for IDP protection.[57] In 2010, the PWGID drafted an IDP policy and subsequently a draft bill which was then revised by the PSC. In December 2012, the Kenyan parliament finally passed the Act on the Prevention, Protection and Assistance to Internally Displaced Persons and Affected Communities (the IDP Act).

This Act (para. 3) domesticates the UN's Guiding Principles on Internal Displacement and the 2006 Great Lakes Protocol. It takes a holistic approach and addresses all types of displacement, be it due to political violence, natural disasters or development and conservation projects. It sets out a rights-based and participatory approach (paras. 4 and 8(3)) and highlights the need to pay special attention to communities 'with a special dependency on and attachment to their lands' (para. 8(1)). Furthermore, the government is now obliged to provide affected populations with 'durable solutions' (paras. 1–3). Part II of the Act stipulates that such durable solutions – which encompass return, local integration and resettlement elsewhere within Kenya – must include at least (para. 9(2)):

(a)   long-term safety and security;
(b)   full restoration and enjoyment of the freedom of movement;
(c)   enjoyment of an adequate standard of living without discrimination;
(d)   access to employment and livelihoods;
(e)   access to effective mechanisms that restore housing, land and property;
(f)   access to documentation;
(g)   family reunification and the establishment of the fate and whereabouts of missing relatives;
(h)   equal participation in public affairs; and
(i)   access to justice without discrimination.

Development-based evictions and resettlement are addressed in Part V of the Act. It covers situations in which the government wishes to utilise vacant land for development or conservation purposes. The Act stipulates that the government 'shall abstain' from displacement and relocation in such circumstances, except in cases of 'overriding public interest' where 'no feasible alternative' exists. If the government still argues that displacement and planned relocation are unavoidable, it must seek the 'free and informed consent' of the affected persons, hold 'public hearings' about and ensure 'effective participation' in the planning and managing processes, and guarantee access to 'effective remedies' before proceeding any further with its plans. Furthermore, the government must ensure that the displacement is 'respectful of human rights', including 'protection of community land' and 'special needs' of vulnerable groups (Part V, para. 4).

Overall, the provisions of the IDP Act constitute an enormous improvement compared to previous attempts to deal with IDPs. The stipulated conditions for durable solutions address all of the shortcomings of earlier resettlement schemes (as identified in the previous section). The IDP Act does not, however, provide details of compensation and how to determine it, even though adequate compensation is often key to successful livelihood restoration. Experts have further criticised the government for failing to adopt an IDP policy, which is necessary to operationalise the Act, to define the responsibilities of different levels of government, and to coordinate their activities. They have also called for ratification of the African Union's regional Kampala Convention on internal displacement.

Beyond the IDP Act, planned relocation within Kenya, or more precisely 'resettlement', is considered in other policy development processes, which are equally relevant to approaching relocation in an integrated manner. In 2008, the then Ministry of State for Special Planning (MOSSP), which was heading Operation Rudi Nyumbani, was mandated (Presidential Circular 1/2008) to formulate and coordinate a comprehensive disaster management policy. Identified policy tasks included, inter alia, resettlement of IDPs and refugees, and climate change adaptation.[58] However, no policy for disaster management has so far been approved. Likewise, as regards urban settings, where the majority of poor and vulnerable people live, an urban development policy has been drafted. It explicitly provides for relocation of households from hazard-prone areas, 'such as flood plains, steep slopes, and fault lines, thereby exposing residents to various risks'.[59] As with the Final Draft National Policy for Disaster Management (DNPDM), the Draft National Urban Development Policy (DNUDP) is still pending. Finally, and most importantly, resettlement is a major task running through various regulations concerning land, which will be the focus of the next section.

Developing a framework to assist and resettle IDPs: the land policy perspective

Land is both a challenge and the key to successful relocation, and even more so land legislation. The latter has been a core reason for displacement and landlessness, for settlement in high-risk zones and for encroachment into protected areas in Kenya. Post-independence land regulations gave little power to local communities, and even less to minorities, which led to irregular and illegal allocations of land and subsequent evictions of occupants.[60] At the turn of the millennium, a political process was set in motion that aimed to highlight and resolve injustices related to land issues, such as election violence, irregular allocation of land, and biases of and gaps in land legislation. Several commissions were established, including the Committee on Land Clashes (1999), the Commission of Inquiry into the Land Law System of Kenya (1999), the Constitution of Kenya Review Commission (2000), the Commission of Inquiry into the Illegal/Irregular Allocation of Public Land

(2003) and the Truth, Justice and Reconciliation Commission (2008). Also, the Commission of Inquiry on Post-Election Violence (2008) had a strong focus on land injustice.

A national land policy formulation process started in 2004 and resulted in the consolidation of the recommendations of many of the aforementioned commissions into Sessional Paper No. 3 (2009), the new National Land Policy (NLP).[61] This document, which was strongly informed by the 2007/8 election violence, was an attempt to solve the inherited burden of land injustice and hence displacement. Equally, it sought to shape land regulations in a way that took into account the importance of land for durable solutions, including planned relocation.

The new Constitution of 2010 then included a chapter on 'Land and Environment' (Chapter V), which, to a large extent, reflects the spirit of the NLP and, inter alia, replaced the previous categories of government and trust land with the new categories of public and community land (in addition to private land). One major discrepancy, however, is that while the NLP postulates a single piece of framework legislation for all categories of land, the Constitution stipulates a separate one for community land. The latter constitutes the majority of Kenyan territory, and it is also the most emotive category of land. The constitutional schedule stipulated a maximum of five years – three years more than for other land-related law – to enact legislation on community land. Nevertheless, this generous constitutional deadline was exceeded by a year, as the Community Land Act (No. 27 of 2016) was not adopted until August 2016. By contrast, the other core land acts – the Land Act (CAP 280), the Land Registry Act (CAP 300) and the National Land Commission Act (CAP 5D) – were adopted in line with the original schedule, in 2012.[62] The pending enactment of the Community Land Act over such a long period created a legal limbo and allowed the conversion of community land into other types of land tenure, particularly private land, to continue.[63]

Furthermore, the Community Land Bill's provisions on benefit-sharing were similarly delayed, as was the case with other benefit-sharing bills. Benefit-sharing is an important entry point to mitigate the need for planned relocation in the first place and to negotiate more favourable terms if it is unavoidable, as it gives communities more power to decide on and take advantage of development interventions. Indeed, Article 69 of the Constitution stipulates that the state shall 'ensure sustainable exploitation, utilisation, management and conservation of the environment and natural resources, and ensure the equitable sharing of the accruing benefits' (Article 69(1)(a); similarly, paras. 97–100 of the NLP). The benefit-sharing rules of the Community Land Act (Article 36) are unfortunately limited in coverage, because they do not apply to communities that live on other categories of land. Furthermore, the Act does not define, for example, the payable royalties; rather, it leaves agreement outcomes to a 'free, open consultative process' ('prior' is not mentioned) between communities and investors (Articles 36(1) and (2)).[64] Another recently adopted law, the Mining Act (No. 12 of 2016), partly resolves these flaws as it defines revenue shares (Article 183(5)) and is applicable to mineral resources (but not other natural resources) on all categories of land.[65] However, the Act does not address (democratic) procedures of how to determine and control the usage of such revenues in order to avoid maladministration. Instead of that this task is delegated the Cabinet Secretary (Articles 223 and 224), notwithstanding that an excelent proposal is already included in Part IV of the still-pending Natural Resource (Benefit-Sharing) Bill (2014). In sum, the new laws potentially empower communities and thus decrease the vulnerability that arises from development-based evictions and involuntary resettlement. However, the legislation is fragmented, incomplete and riddled with loopholes, which could weaken the positive empowerment aspects.

In contrast, means to secure land for resettlement purposes are reasonably well developed. Generally, the Kenyan state retains the right to allocate land for public purpose, including by means of compulsory acquisition. The Land Act of 2012 stipulates that 'public purpose' includes, inter alia, the settlement of squatters and IDPs (Article 2; see also Articles 160(2)(d) and 160(2)(e)(i)), which is crucial if repeated displacement is to be avoided in the future. The National Land Commission (NLC), established by Article 67 of the new Constitution, is mandated to provide 'access to land for shelter and livelihood' for such purposes (Article 134), and to exercise power over the regularisation of existing informal settlements erected on public and community land (Article 160(2)(e)). This is also meant to facilitate investment into upgrading and developing such settlements (Article 135(3)). Land regulation is further advanced in respect to the provision of compensation entitlements. If land is alienated (for any public purpose), the NLC has a key role to play in determining compensation entitlements (Article 112). This includes assessing eligibility for compensation of people who occupy land without title deeds (Article 155(4)). Adequate compensation is a crucial factor if evictees are to re-establish their livelihoods successfully.

However, the Land Act – along with the IDP Act, the DNPDM and the DNUDP – lacks detailed regulations on how to operationalise the implementation of planned relocations in various contexts. The IDP Act, for example, highlights livelihood restoration as one of its core principles but does not even mention compensation (although the UN's Guiding Principles on Internal Displacement and the Great Lakes Protocol do) – not even in its section on development-based evictions. The Land Act sets forward principles of compensation for the alienation of land, which are progressive in that they protect the rights of people without proper title deeds, but likewise does not define adequate compensation. Unfortunately, the legislation that was supposed to address this gap – the Eviction and Resettlement Procedures Bill (ERP Bill) – was still stalled due to political deadlock at the time of writing (late 2016).

In 2009, the NLP demanded the development of eviction and resettlement guidance. A multi-stakeholder task force chaired by the then Ministry of Lands was established and produced – in a consultative process with civil society actors – an internal framework document: the Eviction and

Resettlement Guidelines. However, these guidelines were regarded as too weak to serve as a powerful tool, and a draft bill was produced instead.[66] This first ERP Bill was introduced to parliament in 2012, but the approval process was interrupted by the 2012/13 elections. Thereafter, the bill was renegotiated alongside the Community Land Bill by a task force within the new Ministry of Land, Housing and Urban Development. The resulting 2013 draft bill was then reviewed by the Commission for the Implementation of the Constitution (CIC).[67] Confusingly, the NLC then decided to develop its own set of regulations, which led to a rival draft bill in the same year.[68] However, neither of these draft bills was introduced to parliament. Rather, in 2014, the CIC recommended addressing eviction procedures and resettlement procedures in separate bills, with the latter dealing only with victims of armed conflict, general violence and natural and human-made disasters, not with squatters.[69] Finally, in August 2015, eviction procedures were introduced to parliament, not as a stand-alone bill but as a section of the Land Laws (Amendment) Bill, 2015 (Article 105) to amend Article 152 of the Land Act. The aim of the amendment was to strengthen the authorities' power to carry out evictions smoothly. In contrast, no efforts were made to develop parallel regulations for relocation measures. If resettlement procedures continue to lack regulatory guidance, the quality of planned relocation and hence the prospects for successful resettlement will likely remain poor.

Outlook

In sum, achieving a robust framework for planned relocation in Kenya, in response to climate change and natural disasters or for other purposes, still faces considerable challenges. The recently completed reforms in the regulation of community land are an important step forward. However, the half-hearted reform of other land sector laws, particularly those relating to adequate procedures for resettlement and benefit-sharing, means that the obstacles to establishing planned relocation as a truly durable solution remain. The political obstacles in implementing fair land regulations, including adequate resettlement procedures and benefit-sharing systems, epitomise the Kenyan struggles over land on a different level than election violence. In fact, the current government has sought to curtail the NLC's mandate on these issues by using the Land Laws (Amendment) Bill to reverse many recent land reforms.[70] This reflects competing ideologies over whether land should be at the easy disposal of national development plans and hence privileged investors, or whether land policies should also address the ongoing problems of IDPs and historical land injustice. This leads to a final important point.

Putting into effect effective programmes of planned relocation is also a matter of finance and tenacity. By 2012, the government had allegedly spent around 6 billion KES on Operation Rudi Nyumbani for the resettlement of about 350,000 IDPs, including the provision of ex gratia support (that is, around 17,150 KES per person). In contrast, a company-led process of involuntary resettlement of about 2,000 people under the supervision of international lenders in Olkaria was calculated at close to 600 million KES (300,000 KES per person).[71] The Olkaria resettlement was a flagship project to accommodate lenders' standards, and far from typical in Kenya. But even in this case the transfer of title deeds to the affected population has been pending since 2012 due to disputes over landownership and lengthy land transfer negotiations, and the scheme was repeatedly marred by corruption and exclusion.[72]

Notes

1 Center on Migration, Citizenship and Development, Bielefeld University.
2 This contribution is based on the insights gained during the author's research for the MECLEP project 'Migration, Environment and Climate Change: Evidence for Policy' www.iom.int/meclep accessed 9 June 2016, and the ClimAccount project 'Human Rights Accountability of the EU and Austria for Climate Policies in Third Countries and Their Possible Effects on Migration' http://bim.lbg.ac.at/en/climaccount-human-rights-accountability-eu-and-austria-climate-policies-third-countries-and-their-possible-effects-migration accessed 9 June 2016.
3 United Nations, *The Cancun Agreements: Outcome of the Work of the Ad Hoc Working Group on Long-Term Cooperative Action under the Convention* (2011) FCCC/CP/2010/7/Add.1 Section 14(f).
4 United Nations, *Sendai Framework for Disaster Risk Reduction 2015–2030* (2015) A/CONF.224/CRP.1.
5 Brookings Institution, Georgetown University and UNHCR, 'Guidance on Protecting People from Disasters and Environmental Change through Planned Relocation' (2015) www.brookings.edu/research/planned-relocations-disasters-and-climate-change accessed 4 January 2017.
6 Advisory Group on Climate Change and Human Mobility (AGCCHM), 'Human Mobility in the Context of Climate Change UNFCCC-Paris COP-21: Recommendations from the Advisory Group on Climate Change and Human Mobility' (2015) www.internal-displacement.org/assets/publications/2015/201511-human-mobility-in-the-context-of-climate-change-unfccc-Paris-COP21.pdf accessed 25 October 2016.
7 J. Schade *et al.*, 'Climate Change and Climate Policy Induced Relocations: A Challenge for Social Justice – Recommendations of the Bielefeld Consultation' (2015) Migration, Environment and Climate Change Policy Brief Series 1(10) http://publications.iom.int/system/files/pdf/policy_brief_series_issue10_0.pdf accessed 9 June 2016. For results see United Nations, Decisions adopted by the Conference of the Parties (2015) FCCC/CP/2015/10/Add.1 Section 49.
8 UN General Assembly, 'One Humanity: Shared Responsibility. Report of the Secretary-General for the World Humanitarian Summit' (2016) A/70/709, see 34 and 54.
9 Term established by the World Bank and used by many other development banks.
10 United Nations, Office of the High Commissioner for Human Rights (OHCHR), 'Forced Evictions: Commission on Human Rights Resolution 1993/77' (1993) para. 1 http://ap.ohchr.org/Documents/E/CHR/resolutions/E-CN_4-RES-1993-77.doc accessed 25 October 2016.
11 United Nations, *International Covenant on Economic, Social and Cultural Rights* (adopted 16 December 1966, entered into force 3 January 1976) 993 UNTS 3 Article 4.
12 UN Committee on Economic, Social and Cultural Rights, *General Comment No. 7: The Right to Adequate Housing (Art.11.1): Forced Evictions* (1997) E/1998/22 para. 3.

13 CRED, EM-Database (2016) www.emdat.be/database accessed 9 June 2016.
14 An overview is available in D. Nyaoro, J. Schade and K. Schmidt, 'Assessing the Evidence. Migration, Environment and Climate Change in Kenya' (International Organization for Migration (2016) https://publications.iom.int/books/assessing-evidence-migration-environment-and-climate-change-kenya accessed 10 February 2017.
15 Internal Displacement Monitoring Centre (IDMC), 'Kenya: Too Early to Turn the Page on IDPs, More Work Is Needed' (2014) 1 www.internal-displacement.org/sub-saharan-africa/kenya/2014/kenya-too-early-to-turn-the-page-on-idps-more-work-is-needed accessed 9 June 2016.
16 UN Development Programme (UNDP), 'Kenya Natural Disaster Profile' (n.d.) retrieved from the Global Risk Information Platform (GRIP) www.gripweb.org/gripweb/sites/default/files/disaster_risk_profiles/Preliminary%20Natural%20Hazard%20Risk%20Profile%20of%20Kenya.pdf accessed 25 October 2016.
17 According to Kamungi, pastoralist displacement 'refers to relocation to another part of the land rather than moving into camps. [It] is marked by the absence of people in an area … However, they are indeed IDPs because when they lose their cattle to rustling, and insecurity compels them to leave watering points, they move to a more hostile environment with fewer survival alternatives. Restocking of herds is difficult due to drought and excessive pressure on the land in safer areas, hence impoverishment' (P. M. Kamungi, 'The Current Situation of IDPs in Kenya' (Jesuit Refugee Service 2001) 17–19 http://jrs.net/Assets/Publications/File/ken-idp.pdf accessed 25 October 2016). On sedentarisation in Turkana, see, for example, A. Catley, J. Lind and I. Scoones, *Pastoralism and Development in Africa: Dynamic Change at the Margins* (Routledge 2013).
18 Kenya National Bureau of Statistics (KNBS), 'Kenya Population and Housing Census 2009: Counting Our People for the Implementation of Vision 2030: Volume IC: Population Distribution by Age, Sex and Administrative Units' (2010) www.knbs.or.ke/index.php?option=com_phocadownload&view=category&download=584:volume-1c-population-distribution-by-age-sex-and-administrative-units&id=109:population-and-housing-census-2009&Itemid=599 accessed 25 October 2016.
19 CRED, EM-Database.
20 United Nations Environment Programme (UNEP), 'Kenya: Atlas of Our Changing Environment' (2009) www.unep.org/pdf/Kenya_Atlas_Full_EN_72dpi.pdf accessed 25 October 2016. Note that the new Constitution of 2010 has abolished the provinces as administrative units.
21 CRED, EM-Database.
22 W. M. Ngecu, C. M. Nyamai and G. Erima, 'The Extent and Significance of Mass-Movements in Eastern Africa: Case Studies of Some Major Landslides in Uganda and Kenya' (2004) 46(8) *Environmental Geology* 1123; B. K. Rop, 'Landslide Disaster Vulnerability in Western Kenya and Mitigation Options: A Synopsis of Evidence and Issues of Kuvasali Landslide' (2011) 5(1) *Journal of Environmental Science and Engineering* 110.
23 S. B. Mahongo, 'The Changing Global Climate and Its Implication in Sea Level Trends in Tanzania and the Western Indian Ocean Region' (2009) 8(2) *Western Indian Ocean Journal of Marine Science* 147.
24 C. B. Awuor, V. A. Orindi and A. Ochieng Adwera, 'Climate Change and Coastal Cities: The Case of Mombasa, Kenya' (2008) 20(1) *Environment and Urbanization* 231.
25 Government of Kenya (GOK), *National Disaster Management Policy of Kenya: Final Draft* (2010) http://de.scribd.com/doc/136662332/National-Disaster-Management-Policy-of-Kenya-Final-Draft-Oct-2010#scribd accessed 25 October 2016.
26 Kamungi, 'Current Situation' 17–19.
27 P. M. Kamungi, 'The Politics of Displacement in Multiparty Kenya' (2009) 27(3) *Journal of Contemporary African Studies* 345, 355.

28 P. M. Kamungi, 'Municipalities and IDPs Outside of Camps: The Case of Kenya's "Integrated" Displaced Persons' (2013) 3 www.brookings.edu/~/media/research/ files/reports/2013/05/kenya-displacement/idp-municipal-authorities-kenya-may-2013-final.pdf accessed 25 October 2016. During the 2002 general election 'only' 20,000 people were displaced. This comparatively low figure was associated with the campaign of the National Rainbow Coalition (NARC), which united rival ethnic groups around a common agenda for constitutional reform, the implementation of the Ndung'u recommendations on land, IDP resettlement and, last but not least, the removal of the long-term and increasingly dictatorial president, Daniel arap Moi, from office (Kamungi, 'Politics of Displacement' 352f).

29 C. H. Kahl, 'Population Growth, Environmental Degradation, and State-Sponsored Violence: The Case of Kenya, 1991–93' (1998) 23(2) *International Security* 105.

30 The estimate on forest evictees is based on figures in the report of the Parliamentary Select Committee on the Resettlement of Internally Displaced Persons (PSC), which was tasked with evaluating Operation Rudi Nyumbani and the IDP problem more generally. According to the PSC, there were 2,954 IDPs in the Embobut forest and about 2,459 displaced households in the Mau forest evicted as a result of government measures (PSC, 'Report of the Parliamentary Select Committee on the Resettlement of Internally Displaced Persons' (2012) 41–42 www.knchr.org/portals/0/reports/psc_final_idps_report_2012-2.pdf accessed 25 October 2016).

31 I. N. Okeke, 'Towards a New Growth Path in Africa: A Study of National Urban Policy Responses to Urbanisation' (2014) South African Cities Network Working Paper 20 http://sacitiesnetwork.co.za/wp-content/uploads/2014/09/2014-08_sacn_ national_urban_policy_in_africa_working_paper.pdf accessed 25 October 2016.

32 KNBS, 'Kenya Population and Housing Census 2009'.

33 M. Rutten and S. Owuor, 'Weapons of Mass Destruction: Land, Ethnicity and the 2007 Elections in Kenya' (2009) 27(3) *Journal of Contemporary African Studies* 308. Kenya's colonial history is complex. In 1885, the Germans claimed land in Kenya, although the country had previously been colonised by the Sultan of Zanzibar. At the Berlin Conference of 1885, the Germans and the British agreed on separate spheres of influence, but in 1890 the Germans (in another land deal) handed over their coastal protectorate to the British, who in 1895, proclaimed their East African Protectorate (which in 1902 was extended to Uganda). The British started a policy to resettle Africans on 'native reserves' in 1904, but the history of these reserves is equally complex, and regulations lagged behind political practice. The Crown Land Ordinance of 2015 acknowledged the existence of native reserves by allowing for 'native rights' on land, but demarcation of native lands started only in 1926. Moreover, in 1921, a Kenyan High Court ruling had denied Africans any right to land, declaring them 'tenants' of the Crown who could be removed from their habitats at any time. This situation was mitigated by the Native Lands Trust Ordinance of 1930, which provided Africans with a permanent right to these lands, but this was amended in 1933 to allow for the eviction of Africans from reserves for the purpose of mineral extraction by Europeans. See P. Veit, 'History of Land Conflicts in Kenya' (2008) www.focusonland.com/download/52076c59cca75 accessed 25 October 2016; and E. W. Smith, 'Land in Kenya' (1936) 35(140) *Journal of the Royal African Society* 246.

34 G. T. Kurian, *Encyclopaedia of the Third World* (4th edn, Facts on File 1992) Volume III, 970.

35 B. Berman and J. Lonsdale, *Unhappy Valley: Conflict in Kenya & Africa* (Ohio University Press 1992) 38. There have been different phases of eviction and annexation of land. For example, on the coast, the British leased a ten-mile strip (Mwambao) to the Sultan of Zanzibar in 1895, a lease that was largely transformed into individual freeholds for the Arab elite (many of them slave traders) during an

adjudication process in 1908. In the central highlands (the 'White Highlands'), most of the land was expropriated between 1899 to 1915. In Trans Nzoia, appropriation by white settlers mainly took place between 1913 and 1938. And international companies and missionaries acquired land (often with military support from the colonial authorities) in many other 'non-scheduled' areas over time, particularly in the Rift Valley (and especially Kericho) (Truth, Justice and Reconciliation Commission (TJRC), 'Report of the Truth, Justice and Reconciliation Commission' (2013) Volume IIB, 104–193 http://digitalcommons.law.seattleu.edu/tjrc accessed 25 October 2016).

36 Kahl, 'Population Growth' 80. Official compulsory labour for railway construction was introduced in 1920. However, the colonial authorities – beyond seeking labour for governmental tasks – applied additional coercive policies to secure a labour force for white settlers, including for British veterans of the First World War, who were encouraged to purchase (cheaply) and cultivate land in Kenya. These policies included, inter alia, the application of the *kipande* (passport) system from 1919. The system was used to restrict the movement of individuals and groups between the reserves and to channel them to areas where labour was in short supply. Labour migration to the farms was further triggered by imposing and increasing taxes on Africans. These had to be paid in British currency, which could be earned only through employment in the service of the British, which 'for most Africans already quarantined in the reserves was labour on European farms' (see TJRC, 'Report' Volume IIA, 186; A. Clayton and D. C. Savage, *Government and Labour in Kenya, 1895–1963* (Cass 1974) 108–163). This marked a change from before the war, when the colonial government had encouraged peasant production in the White Highlands because of the weakness of the settler export sector, which by then had already contributed to the displacement of the Maasai pastoralists by Kikuyu farmers (see J. Lonsdale and B. Berman, 'Coping with the Contradictions: The Development of the Colonial State in Kenya, 1895–1914' (1979) 20(4) *Journal of African History* 501, 504).

37 C. Leo, 'The Failure of the "Progressive Farmer" in Kenya's Million-Acre Settlement Scheme' (1978) 16(4) *Journal of Modern African Studies* 622; TJRC, 'Report' Volume IIB, 213–216.

38 Ibid. 225.

39 Ibid. 245.

40 Kamungi, 'Politics of Displacement' 349. The 'landed gentry' from various ethnic backgrounds owned up to 43 per cent of all registered land.

41 TJRC, 'Report' Volume IIB, 193.

42 S. K. Karanja, 'Land Restitution in the Emerging Kenyan Transitional Justice Process' (2010) 28 *Nordic Journal of Human Rights* 182.

43 Kamungi, 'Politics of Displacement' 350–354. The widespread violence that occurred after the 2007 general election was widely attributed to the surprising result (ibid. 354).

44 PSC, 'Report' 1. In this context, the current President of Kenya, Uhuru Muigai Kenyatta, was accused of five counts of crimes against humanity before the International Criminal Court, but the prosecutors withdrew the charges in December 2014 due to insufficient evidence (ICC-01/09–02/11). See https://www.icc-cpi.int/kenya/kenyatta, accessed 25 October 2016.

45 C. Ikobe and E. O. Abuya, 'Wasted Lives: Internally Displaced Persons Living in Camps in Kenya' (2010) 1(2) *Journal of International Humanitarian Legal Studies* 233.

46 PSC, 'Report' 8.

47 O. A. Adeagbo and J. M. Iyi, 'Post-Election Crisis in Kenya and Internally Displaced Persons: A Critical Appraisal' (2011) 4(2) *Journal of Politics and Law* 174; Kamungi, 'Politics of Displacement'; Kamungi, 'Municipalities and IDPs'; L.

Kiama and F. Koome, 'Internal Displacement in Kenya: The Quest for Durable Solutions' (2014) 45 *Forced Migration Review* 92; J. Klopp and P. M. Kamungi, 'Failure to Protect: Lessons from Kenya's IDP Network' (2007) 28 *Forced Migration Review* 52; J. Klopp and N. M. Sheekh, 'Can the Guiding Principles Make a Difference in Kenya?' (2008) Special Issue *Forced Migration Review* 19.

48 PSC, 'Report' vi.

49 Ikobe and Abuya, 'Wasted Lives'; Kamungi, 'Current Situation'; Kamungi, 'Politics of Displacement; Kamungi, 'Municipalities and IDPs'.

50 As the government ordered the dissolution of the camps, the partners in the UN cluster had to withdraw their assistance, and reportedly made few protests.

51 PSC, 'Report' 7f.

52 DPPS, 'Govt Gives IDPs Sh1bn, Orders Camps Closed' (4 February 2016) *Daily Nation* www.nation.co.ke/news/politics/Govt-gives-IDPs-Sh1bn-closes-camps/-/1064/ 3062636/-/3q74fl/-/index.html accessed 25 October 2016, 7f. Not one of the 37 online comments on this article support the government's action, however. The comments mention ongoing lack of assistance for families and suggest that most of the money was diverted into private pockets.

53 D. M. Kungu, 'The Dilemma of Integration: Internally Displaced Persons in Uasigishu County, Kenya' (2015) 11(16) *European Scientific Journal* 221.

54 Ikobe and Abuya, 'Wasted Lives' 268.

55 Kiama and Koome, 'Internal Displacement' 92–94.

56 Internal Displacement Monitoring Centre (IDMC), 'A Review of the Normative Framework in Kenya Relating to the Protection of IDPs – in the Context of the Kampala Convention and Other Supranational Frameworks' (2015) www.internal-displacement.org/assets/publications/2015/20150827-af-kenya-review-of-normative-framework-relating-to-protection-of-idps-en.pdf accessed 20 April 2016, 43.

57 Kiama and Koome, 'Internal Displacement' 93.

58 International Federation of Red Cross and Red Crescent Societies (IFRC), 'Background Report Law and Regulation for the Reduction of Risk from Natural Disasters in Kenya: A National Law Desk Survey' (2012) 31, 43 http://drr-law.org/ resources/Kenya-Desk-Survey.pdf accessed 25 October 2016.

59 Kenyan Ministry of Environment and Mineral Resources, *National Environmental Policy: Revised Draft #4* (2012) http://theredddesk.org/sites/default/files/national-environment-policy-may-2012_1.pdf accessed 25 October 2016.

60 Kenyan Ministry of Lands, 'Sessional Paper No. 3 of 2009 on National Land Policy' (2009) para. 46.

61 Ibid.

62 The drafting of the Land Act and the Land Registry Act has been criticised by experts and civil society organisations alike for its hastiness, lack of adequate parliamentary and public discussion, and consequent inconsistencies between land laws and mandates of the implementing institutions (A. Manji, 'The Politics of Land Reform in Kenya 2012' (2014) 57(1) *African Studies Review* 115).

63 C. N. Musembi and P. Kameri-Mbote, 'Mobility, Marginality and Tenure Transformation in Kenya: Explorations of Community Property Rights in Law and Practice' (2013) 17(1) *Nomadic Peoples* 23.

64 The Community Land Act pre-defines relevant subjects of such negotiations such as royalties, impact assessments and mitigation measures (Article 36(2)). Article 36(3) further stipulates procedures for community approval of such agreements. However, power imbalances between communities and investors in many cases might favour the latter.

65 The defined shares are 70 per cent for the national and 20 per cent for the county government, and 10 per cent for the affected communities (Mining Act, Article 183(5)). As to mineral rights over community land, the Act emphasises that

agreements 'should be sought prior' to any activities (Article 128(1)) but does not allow for renegotiation of agreements in the course of project development by emphasising that 'such consent shall be valid for as long as the mineral right subsists' (Article 128(3)). These agreements thus have no capacity for adjustment due to unforeseen circumstances.

66 Hakijamii, 'Draft Eviction and Resettlement Guidelines and Draft Bill, 2012: An Abridged Version' (2012) 4 www.escr-net.org/sites/default/files/Final%20evictions%20booklet.pdf accessed 25 October 2016.

67 Interview with the National Land Commission conducted by Jeanette Schade and Jane Hofbauer in Nairobi, Kenya (25 March 2015). At the time of the interview, this review process was still ongoing.

68 The Land Act of 2012 is not clear which body is expected to develop which type of regulation/law. On the one hand, it allows both the NLC and the Cabinet (and hence the lead ministry) to develop 'procedures to be followed with respect to the making of any claim for compensation and the payment of any compensation under this Act' (Article 160(1)(d)). On the other, it gives power to the NLC to make regulations 'to provide for the settlement of the internally displaced persons' (Article 160(2)(d)) and 'to establish appropriate mechanisms for their [squatters'] removal from unsuitable land and their settlement' (Article 160(2)(e)(i)). This may have contributed to the battles between the NLC and the Cabinet over mandates and powers.

69 Commission for the Implementation of the Constitution (CIC), 'CIC Matrix on the Eviction and Resettlement Bill, 2014' (n.d.).

70 J. Schade, 'Land Matters: The Role of Land Policies and Laws for Environmental Migration in Kenya' (2016) Migration, Environment and Climate Change Policy Brief Series 2(1) https://publications.iom.int/books/migration-environment-and-climate-change-policy-brief-series-issue-1-vol-2-january-2016 accessed 25 October 2016.

71 GIBB Africa, 'Olkaria IV (Domes) Geothermal Project in Naivasha District: Resettlement Action Plan for Olkaria IV Power Station' (2012) 12–1 www-wds.worldbank.org/external/default/WDSContentServer/WDSP/IB/2012/07/27/000333037_20120727015202/Rendered/PDF/RP8830v110P1030IA0IV0RAP0JULY002012.pdf accessed 25 October 2016.

72 J. Schade, 'Kenya Case Study Report: ClimAccount – Human Rights Accountability of the EU and Austria for Climate Policies in Third Countries and Their Possible Effects on Migration' (forthcoming) COMCAD Working Paper.

11 Politicising climate change adaptation

Negotiating environmental migration in the European Union and the Pacific

Silja Klepp and Johannes Herbeck[1]

Introduction

Environmental and climate change are increasingly discussed with regard to their potential impact on human migration.[2] In those debates, a multitude of different approaches and levels of causality, of figures and notions, and of connections to wider contexts and policy fields can be observed. In this chapter, we contrast debates situated in the European Union (EU) with those in various political fora in the Pacific region. In doing so, we observe that in Europe connections between climate change and migration are framed mainly in humanitarian terms, delegating 'palliative' solutions either to the aid sector or, in some cases, to foreign or security actors. In contrast, discussions in the Pacific address more fundamental questions – for example, when connections are made with climate justice and new forms of global/environmental citizenship, or when colonial boundaries are called into question.

We regard the local reception, regional negotiation processes and interpretation of climate change discourses as crucial for understanding the anthropology of climate change – an aspect that has been widely neglected in the anthropological study of climate change, according to Rudiak-Gould (2011).[3] Our chapter introduces the concept of a *legal anthropology of emergence*, an approach that draws on the 'sociology of emergence' developed by de Sousa Santos and Rodríguez-Garavito (2005).[4] This approach connects the concept of legal pluralism[5] and emergence debates in anthropology[6] with post-colonial perspectives.[7] A legal anthropology of emergence makes visible bottom-up processes in law and decision-making, including the way that informal actors negotiate rights and resources in transnational law-setting processes. In this chapter, we use this approach to analyse debates on environmental migration in two different geographic and institutional settings: the European Union and the Pacific region. We thereby contrast the top-down, bureaucratic approach taken in EU policy with the more process-oriented approach one finds in the Pacific. This decentred view on global law-setting processes *re*-centres the respective negotiations on migration strategies and new rights in the Global South. It offers insights into the increasingly complex decision-making processes and development of policies and laws in the context of global climate change.

Specifically, we show how concerns about climate change and its impact on migration patterns are tethered to controversies about social, political, economic and ecological inequalities in North–South relations. Studies on the social impacts of climate change point to developments that might exacerbate differences between industrialised and developing nations.[8] In the context of international climate change debates, the differentiated impacts of climate change and the clear distribution of responsibilities for greenhouse gas emissions are especially significant for their conflict potential. The historically high emissions of industrialised countries and commensurate responsibilities for observable and expected changes in global climate have been subsumed under the notion of 'shared but differentiated responsibilities'. This has not, however, resulted in far-reaching political concessions towards the developing world.[9] Rather, global power structures themselves have complicated negotiations about 'fair' goals of climate politics and about compensatory payments for adaptation measures.[10] The 'multidimensional inequalities'[11] in the context of global climate change are adversely affecting developing countries, such as the Republic of Kiribati, an island nation in the central tropical Pacific. With very low per capita emissions, Kiribati bears little responsibility for anthropogenic climate change, yet it is heavily impacted by actual and expected environmental changes.[12]

The potential conflict during climate justice debates is especially apparent in discourses that draw connections between climate change and migration. Countries like Kiribati are often perceived as the first victims of climate change,[13] and although this perception is sometimes contested, they nevertheless have to anticipate a future in which their territory becomes uninhabitable. Such countries claim global and regional solidarity to assist them in their search for adequate long-term options for potential climate migrants. These negotiation processes on climate justice and environmental migration, which involve government officials, non-governmental organisations (NGOs) and other members of civil society, such as church representatives, are an important arena in which battles for ecological and post-colonial justice are fought and the recognition of new rights is claimed.

Starting from a critical discussion of current arguments and concepts on the environment–migration nexus in existing research, this chapter analyses how the issue is discussed in two 'multi-sited arenas of negotiation'[14] – namely, the European Union and Kiribati. They show 'the importance of looking at the chains of interactions connecting transnational, national and local actors ... along with the power relations that structure these interactions and are reproduced or changed by them'.[15] The first section shows how the position papers and communications of different EU institutions frame the migration effects of climate change as a developmental and humanitarian issue, thus impeding any politicisation of the discourse and preventing its explicit connection to climate justice debates. The second section analyses the debate on climate change and migration in the Pacific region. Our aim is to contrast these two different arenas of negotiation without claiming a direct comparability of the two cases. We are especially aware of the different actors in the two arenas, which strongly determine contrasting positions.

Critical perspectives towards environmental migration

The origin of the contemporary policy discourse on human mobility in relation to environmental change is often traced to the United Nations Environment Programme of the mid-1980s.[16] By the early 1990s, the Intergovernmental Panel on Climate Change (IPCC) was describing climate change-induced migration as possibly 'the most threatening short-term effect of climate change on human settlements'.[17] More recently, different strands of debate have emerged, such as those concerning the possible classification of different types of environmental migrants,[18] the expected extent of the phenomenon[19] and the situation in international law.[20]

Many of the individual strands of the discussion have themselves been controversial. More fundamentally, many scholars have asked *how* environmental changes affect migration events, while others have questioned whether it is even reasonable to use *the environment* to explain migration. This latter criticism has been central to the discussion about migration and environmental change since its inception, and appears prominently, for example, in a much-cited study commissioned by the United Nations High Commissioner for Refugees (UNHCR), which states that the term 'environmental refugees' is 'unhelpful and unsound intellectually, and unnecessary in practical terms'.[21] The same study argues that reducing migration decisions to environmental factors neglects the interaction between various cultural, political and social factors, which together form the basis of migration decisions. It is therefore neither possible nor productive to consider these dimensions in isolation from each other.

In our view, the basic rationale for the evident dichotomisation of environment and society in the presentation of environmental change as a push factor in migration is doubtful.[22] The rhetoric of climate-induced flight, often in conjunction with violent conflict, abbreviates or masks the structural, political and social 'root causes' of both environmental degradation and migration. Hartmann (2010) describes a 'degradation narrative' that forms the basis of respective scenarios, and serves colonial stereotypes of destructive cultivation practices, population explosions and downstream conflict and migration scenarios.[23]

Even if clear differences exist within the scientific discourse on the environment–migration nexus, the debate tends to overemphasise environmental pressures' influence on migration decisions and thereby undermines recent progress in theorising migration as a multi-causal relationship between individual ranges of action and structural factors.[24] This relationship has been discussed, for example, in the 'autonomy of migration' approach,[25] which understands migration as a social movement or creative strength within a global economic system. Such thinking has been integrated only slowly into the environment–migration nexus, which has hitherto often downplayed presented structural (environmental) conditions and often conceptualises migration as inevitable and independent of migrant agency.

Authors such as Gupta, Hartmann, and Herbeck and Flitner[26] even argue that discussions about migration as a consequence of climate change form a significant part of a broader securitisation discourse, which depicts climate change as an increasing threat to national security.

In view of the threat scenarios that are built up in this context,[27] the question of what might be gained through the creation of a new refugee category in international human rights law for the protection of environmental migrants is difficult to answer. McAdam (2011) suggests that instead of a new international instrument, regional solutions and soft-law declarations such as the Niue Declaration on Climate Change 2009 might be more appropriate for the various and complex realities of environmental migrants.[28] A potential protection status is often viewed critically in the face of the Global North's actual treatment of refugees.[29]

The European Union and environmental migration

Even though the European Union has treated the topic of environmental or climate migration as no more than a 'niche concern' to date,[30] over recent years the debate has cropped up in various political processes and institutions in the EU, such as the Global Approach to Migration and Mobility and a number of EU development cooperation programmes. In order to understand them properly, these political processes must be viewed within the general trajectory of the EU's migration policies, which place a strong emphasis on effectively controlling immigration and 'managing' 'legal' migration. In the course of the greater standardisation of justice and domestic policy in EU states through the 2010 Stockholm Programme,[31] and the related harmonisation of European migration and asylum rights, the decision-making processes at the EU level have gained increased relevance for EU states.[32]

The Global Approach to Migration and Mobility (GAMM) is the central approach that is used to harmonise migration policy. In the GAMM, the European Commission names several basic objectives, including the organisation and alleviation of legal migration and mobility, the containment of irregular migration and human smuggling, the promotion of international protection for refugees and a corresponding strengthening of the external dimensions of European asylum policy, as well as the increased use of migration for global development.[33] Many of the policies that are necessary to achieve these goals require extra-territorial measures, which third countries must be persuaded to implement.[34] Although far from universally accepted, the European Commission's 'holistic' migration policy and the related 'Root Cause Approach' towards the prevention of unwanted migration in potential regions of origin have been subject to important critical evaluation,[35] especially with regard to their circumvention of refugee rights.

Where does the environmental migration debate come into play? The 'swelling' of refugee and migration movements is perceived to have the potential to overburden the Union's capacity. Two contrasting reactions to such projections follow. First, they may increase recognition of environmental changes as a cause for migration. The current debate could create a window of opportunity during which the rights of migrants are strengthened and European states come to acknowledge their historical responsibility for climate change.[36] More pessimistically, the debate could become another building block in the wall around Fortress Europe.

In what follows, we retrace the growing interest in the environment–migration nexus in the EU's political processes and identify four such processes in which references to the nexus are found.

Individual initiatives of parliamentarians and NGOs

The first efforts to feed environmental or climate migration into EU legislation began in the early 2000s, when British MEP Jean Lambert began to lobby the European Parliament to recognise climate change as a legitimate cause for flight and migration. In a 2002 report, she describes in detail the debate about environmental migration and clearly advocates for an official protection status of 'environmental refugees'.[37] In 2008, the Green party grouping in the European Parliament reaffirmed these demands, insisting on the creation of a high-profile working group on the protection of the rights of possible displaced persons.[38] Three years later, the Belgian NGO Pimpampoentje Climate and the Peace Action Group launched an initiative that urged the European Parliament to acknowledge the category of 'climate refugee'.[39]

A commitment to humanitarian concerns was central to each of these initiatives, and all sought legal recognition of the rights of potentially displaced persons. More stringent demands have also been advanced, such as more consequent emission reductions and a strengthening of adaptation measures in affected regions, but the main focus in this area of policy development has been on the creation of a new 'climate refugees' protection category.

The Global Approach to Migration and Mobility

At a meeting in December 2005, the European Council adopted a submission of the European Commission for a Global Approach to Migration and Mobility (GAMM). The GAMM mainly aims to establish partnerships with African Mediterranean neighbours for a joint 'management' of migration. The main focus is a jointly implemented policy to control 'illegal' migrations and to utilise the positive effects of 'legal' migration.[40] This extra-territorial migration control and the underlying approach of migration management have both generated criticism, particularly with regard to refugees' and migrants' rights.[41]

The debate about environmental and climate migration has only gradually gained entry into the GAMM. In the Stockholm Programme of 2010, the European Council demanded a more detailed exploration of the connection between climate change, migration and development, and challenged the Commission 'to present an analysis of the effects of climate change on international migration, including its potential effects on immigration to the Union'.[42] In an announcement, the Commission confirmed that environmental migration is part of the GAMM.[43] An accompanying working paper describes the possible 'destabilising effects' of migration on freedom and stability in affected countries and emphasises the challenges for EU development aid.[44]

In line with the increasing convergence of the Union's migration and development policies through the GAMM, the nexus between environmental change and migration is associated with questions of development cooperation and extra-territorial adaptation, as is obvious in a 2013 strategy paper from the DG Home Affairs.[45] In this framing, the problem is delegated to the local or regional level of affected countries, and affected persons are to be supported in the continuation of their local life strategies, particularly through development cooperation measures, without creating a connection to any admission scenarios for potential migrants.[46]

European development cooperation

Traces of the discourse can also be found in policy processes in the context of European development cooperation. In 2003, the Commission contemplated a possible increase in migration movements, particularly in the context of sea-level rise, and identified the corresponding hotspots in countries in South and South East Asia and sub-Saharan Africa.[47] To date, the debate has resurfaced in various documents, but there have been few concrete proposals. For instance, the measures in the 'Cooperation with Third Countries in the Areas of Migration and Asylum' programme are extremely vague.[48]

A study published in 2011 and financed by the Commission is more illuminating, although the Commission has not yet officially adopted its recommendations. The conclusion states:

> For the near term, palliative actions such as humanitarian assistance and small-scale relocation seem much more likely than long-term preventive and adaptive action ... The time horizon of major policy change suggests that crises will be dealt with as they arise.[49]

Environmental and climate migration is assigned to the sphere of local humanitarian assistance in emergencies, which is, significantly, described as a 'palliative' measure, without addressing the root causes of the problem.

Security implications of climate change

> The EU is ... strengthening its analysis and early warning systems and integrating climate change into existing tools such as conflict prevention mechanisms and security sector reform. The effects of climate change on migratory flows should also be considered in the broader EU reflection on security, development and migration policies.[50]

Apparently, a wide range of fields converge within the debate around environmental migration; in connection with security questions, this results in a questionable potential capacity for security policies. And, in fact, EU contributions to the debate mainly return to the initiatives from 'foreign and security policy actors' within the executive EU institutions.[51] When comparing the EU to the United Nations and Germany, Herbeck and Flitner conclude that the 'securitisation' of climate change is strongest in the former, since 'decidedly military perspectives in the struggle with climate change have been sanctioned from the highest levels'.[52] The impact on migration events is conceived as one of many ways in which climate change is likely to have a destabilising effect on the world and thus endanger the security of individual member states, as well as the Union as a whole.[53]

In two consecutive reports, the Commission claimed that the EU should not restrict its response to climate change to the classical international climate policy, but should also include foreign and security policy measures along with European security and defence policy.[54] However, the details of such a policy are unclear. One obvious focus is the construction of early warning and monitoring systems, which could deliver satellite-based information about developing crisis situations, environmental degradation and potential migrations. The subsequent report from the EU High Representative supported these findings on the whole and also provided interesting insights into the perceived geographic priorities of security risks.[55] While the first report retains a global perspective, the follow-up report concentrates on Africa (in particular the Sahel region, as well as countries in West and East Africa), the Maghreb and the Near East, as well as Central Asia. The Mediterranean is constructed as a central hotspot for the expected tendency towards destabilisation, with corresponding, though unspoken, implications for European migration policy.

In summary, the analysis of various discussion strands within the institutions of the European Union show that it is neither clear where the subject of 'environmental migration' will be embedded within future European policy nor which concrete measures will be taken. However, the issue can clearly be connected to the European migration policy's tendency to externalisation and to wider discourses around migration management.

The political environment in which EU discourses around environmental migration evolve, and the dominance of development or security actors, seems well suited to the EU's theoretical abridgement in the neoclassical push–pull model of migration,[56] and therefore plays into a continuation of a preventive course in European migration policy, including extra-territorial measures against migration, as well as technocratic management approaches. The transfer of the issue into a developmental and humanitarian framework outsources the problems both geographically and politically, and prevents the discourse from becoming inherently politicised.

An alternative view of climate change and migration

From the perspective of international law and from a European perspective, the treatment of climate and environmental migrants appears to be characterised by ad hoc solutions and the individual approaches of nation states, rather than by the development of a global solution. In recent years, the Nansen Initiative has tried to close this blind spot in international law by advocating for an international protection regime for cross-border displacement due to disasters. An initiative of two states (Switzerland and Norway), this underlines that if regulations for migrants' rights are to be established, this will occur only through bottom-up processes that take place in Europe as well as other regions. This tendency raises interesting questions, the analysis of which in this chapter leans on the theoretical perspective of legal pluralism[57] in combination with aspects of the sociology of emergence advanced by de Sousa Santos and Rodríguez-Garavito, who highlight the bottom-up processes in justice building.[58]

Our own theoretical perspective underlines the sources of justice that actors use and develop in the context of climate change, and the ways in which these are used and interpreted on the ground. We examine the ways in which universal concepts, such as human rights, cultural rights and environmental rights, but also political ideas with post-colonial influences, appear in debates around environmental migration and climate justice. How might these concepts be used, modified and developed in the different fora of debate around new rights and resources for environmental migrants?[59] How far does the language of justice work not only as a neutral medium in societal debates but also as a 'technology of power',[60] which is important to apply at the right moment during conflicts?

New knowledge in the area of climate change raises new ethical considerations, where responsibility can only indirectly be related to legal traditions or to general human experiences and values.[61] These new ethical considerations have a particular seriousness, reflected in their wide geographical reach, their complexity and their uncertainty. The protection of interests and the balance of responses between current and future generations is one of the challenges we face in this regard.[62]

Given our central concern with social and legal decision-making processes, our theoretical perspective is process-oriented and takes into account various actors, levels and legal sources. A central aim is to describe legal changes within legal institutions and not simply use conventional ethnographic methods. The approach taken here includes examining interpretations of climate change discourses on the ground and the translation of these inter-pretations into norms, demands and, finally, rights. By concentrating on emerging developments in policy and rights development in the context of environmentally induced migration in the Global South, the present perspec-tive avoids the often-criticised victimising perspective on Pacific islands and climate change adaptation,[63] focusing instead on the agency of the Pacific peoples who are fighting for their futures. This is demonstrated by the example of the Republic of Kiribati, which – as noted above – is expected to be heavily affected by climate change[64] and has a strongly developed response to the challenges it faces in relation to climate change and its potential effects on migration.

New rights and resources for environmental migrants in the Pacific region

The expected environmental changes and anticipated results of anthro-pogenic climate change currently lead to intensive debates around migration and resettlement in the Pacific region. Some of the expected environmental changes are already occurring, including stronger storm tides, coastal erosion and salinisation of freshwater stores and agricultural land.[65] There is also a significant and observable increase in the number of floods,[66] and sea level is expected to rise by 124 centimetres by 2100[67] (although some researchers are predicting a 200-centimetre rise).[68] Predictions about the extent to which these developments will affect Kiribati and over what sort of time scale are tentative and extremely variable.[69] With an increasing number of climate adaptation projects being carried out in the region, the work of so-called knowledge brokers[70] has also gained significance. Nearly all of the institutions that carry out these projects, such as church groups, NGOs and govern-mental organisations, employ consultants who enjoy considerable influence. These knowledge brokers explain climate change and its impacts, and thus mediate between the different actors and the project work.

The Republic of Kiribati is an island state in the central Pacific, comprising 32 atolls with a population of approximately 110,000. Globally, on the basis of predictions based on climate research, Kiribati has developed the most concrete international migration strategies so far, and it engages in various negotiations to realise them. The government of Kiribati is planning the long-term evacuation of all its citizens, the I-Kiribati. This evacuation has already begun, and is due to be carried out 'with dignity' and self-determination, in spite of the potential loss of citizenship. The motto and strategy of the government – 'migrate with dignity' – has been mentioned in many interna-tional as well as regional negotiations. Besides many legal and political ques-tions, conflicts around migration and resettlement projects for the residents of Kiribati remain open, including those concerning sovereignty and the future of the Exclusive Economic Zone (EEZ).[71] In the search for solutions for affected migrants in the region, legal and political proposals are under discussion, and various state and non-state actors are participating. In order to cover the current and future needs of 'environmental' and 'climate' migrants, several legal fields are drawn on, such as human or indigenous rights, but also aspects of *soft law*, such as humanitarian appeals and declarations. Furthermore, various political instruments, such as the creation of adaptation and refugee funds, or regional programmes for labour migration, are being negotiated.

One of the authors studied this regional Pacific negotiation process and the possibilities and limits of various strategies and alliances during four months of field research in Vanuatu, Kiribati and New Zealand in 2010 and 2011, and over a similar period of time in Fiji and Kiribati in 2015. The research was based mostly on interviews and discussions with government officials in these countries and their co-workers in international organisations and NGOs, as well as other actors working in the area of international cooperation. The following section will present the negotiation processes around new rights and resources for environmental migrants which are advanced by the government of Kiribati as well as their supporters, including several NGOs. It is apparent that the debates in the region and the potential launch of new migration and adaptation strategies are inseparably connected to ideas about global climate justice, discourses around unequal North–South relationships, and coping with the colonial heritage.

The Pacific region as arena of negotiation

Contrary to global politics and solutions for environmental migrants that have hitherto focused mainly on the Nansen Initiative, today most transnational and regional alliances are looking for rules and compensation in the area of climate change, development and migration. In the Pacific region, these organisations include the Alliance of Small Island States (AOSIS) and the Small Island Developing States (SIDS). Here, the Malé Declaration on Global Warming and Sea Level Rise, which was drafted in 1989 and relaunched in 2007 by the SIDS as the Malé Declaration on the Human Dimension of Global Climate Change,[72] is one important example. The Malé Declaration demands solidarity from industrial countries and engagement in the admission of refugees within the framework of the climate change, migration and justice debate. The SIDS and the AOSIS both emphasise that their member states have made very few contributions to the climate change crisis, but are now strongly affected by the consequences. They demand the provision of effective tools that will allow them to cope with the effects of climate change and make their own decisions on the basis of self-determination. The government of Kiribati is very active in these forums.

On the grounds of climate justice, financial transfers and resources are being set aside for countries, such as Kiribati, that are expected to be significantly affected by climate change.[73] Since the Kiribati Adaptation Project (KAP) started implementing infrastructure and awareness-raising programmes on adaptation to climate change, the Global Environment Facility (GEF) and other international organisations and donors have financed Kiribati. Precisely in the area of soft law instruments, described by Francis Snyder as 'those rules of conduct which, in principle, have no legally binding force but which nevertheless may have practical effect',[74] our research perspective found a growing number of instruments in the discussed area whose results cannot always be directly found in securitised rights, but which can have broad effects indirectly. Repeated appearances by the President and his cabinet have made Kiribati something of a 'climate change poster child'[75] in the world's public consciousness. Above all, since 2003, President Anote Tong has presented numerous appeals to the global community – in the spirit of climate justice – to reduce greenhouse gas emissions and take responsibility for the fate of his country (a 'victim of climate change') and the environmental migrants of Kiribati.[76] In addition to these broad demands for the development of new rights and the provision of adequate resources for climate migrants, Tong has appealed directly to neighbouring Pacific countries, such as Australia and New Zealand. The citizens of Kiribati, as well as Tong's government, have refused to accept humanitarian refugee status as a basis for their future, calling instead for migration programmes.[77] Tong advocates long-term planning, 'so that when people migrate, they will migrate on merit and with dignity'.[78]

At the behest of Pacific island states, since 2002 New Zealand has created a yearly labour migration quota – named the Pacific Access Category – for the island states of Kiribati, Tuvalu and Tonga. This allows seventy-five migrants from Kiribati to move to New Zealand with their immediate families every year.[79] Furthermore, work programmes have been created, mainly in the field of harvesting operations (Recognised Seasonal Employment – RSE), which allow seasonal I-Kiribati workers to travel to New Zealand. In contrast to the situation in Europe, this form of circular migration – in which workers travel to New Zealand seasonally to work in agricultural harvesting and packaging before returning to their home countries – often includes the possibility of future permanent settlement in New Zealand.[80]

Australia has responded to Kiribati's appeals more hesitantly than New Zealand.[81] In 2014, the Seasonal Worker Programme (SWP) with Australia (which is similar to the RSE and has been in existence since 2009) encompassed only 9 I-Kiribati fruit pickers, compared to 110 I-Kiribati RSE workers in New Zealand in the same year.[82] Further agreements and programmes are planned, such as a work programme in Croatia in the field of tourism, and another in Canada in the service sector.[83] However, these have yet to be finalised, and ministry sources refused to speculate on when they might come into effect.

Kiribati describes these migration programmes as 'climate change adaptation strategies',[84] but the host countries explicitly refuse to acknowledge a link between them and environmental migration and/or climate change adaptation.

For instance, for many years, the home page of New Zealand's Department of Foreign Affairs explicitly denied that any admissions were made on the basis of climate change.[85] Nevertheless, such official denials highlight the dynamic nature of the debates around climate migration and the hosting of 'climate migrants' in the Pacific, even though no official agreements with New Zealand and Australia under the 'climate migration' label have yet been reached.

During the UNFCCC negotiations in Copenhagen in 2009, representatives of the Republic of Fiji announced that the island state would be willing to host individual citizens and indeed whole communities from Kiribati.[86] One advantage here could be the protection of some of Kiribati's cultural dimensions, even outside the state's borders, through communal resettlement. The importance of settling in areas of similar climate and standard of living has been repeatedly highlighted by the I-Kiribati. It could further protect the cultural rights of the I-Kiribati. The government of Fiji gained power in 2006 through a military coup, and it hopes to gain more regional and international recognition by playing a leading role in efforts to find regional solutions for environmental migrants and through its offer to Kiribati.[87] In 2012, negotiations began for the acquisition of 2,000 hectares of freehold land owned by the Church of England on Vanua Levu, Fiji's second-largest island; these negotiations were concluded two years later. In May 2015, one of the authors visited the site, which is quite close to the town of Savusavu, and discussed its acquisition with the Kiribati High Commissioner in Fiji, who facilitated the deal, and several I-Kiribati government officials and parliamentarians. The aim is to use the land for 'food security, in order to grow fruits and vegetables and raise animals, which will be exported to Kiribati'.[88] The High Commissioner also stressed that the government of Fiji was closely consulted on the land acquisition. All of the officials agreed that the site may well be used for resettlement from Kiribati in the future.

In its negotiations with the Fijian government, Kiribati's strategy partially connects to historical migration movements as well as post-colonial-influenced discourses in Oceania. The leading post-colonial thinker in the Pacific, Epi Hau'ofa, has conceptualised pre-colonial Oceania as a meeting space for skilled seamen, a 'sea of islands',[89] where the islanders' freedom of movement was not circumscribed by national borders. It was only during the colonial period that active travel and resettlement activities (often resulting from intermarriage) were impeded by the colonial powers. Until today, this has shaped an image of Oceania as a collection of isolated, vulnerable and distant island states, the 'islands in a far sea'. However, according to Hau'ofa, since the 1990s a new, post-colonial self-image of Oceania has developed which views the ocean as a pathway between islands and calls into question the colonial powers' border demarcations between nation states.[90]

Kempf underlines the potential usefulness of Hau'ofa's concept in the face of strong consequences of anthropogenic climate change for the islands of the Pacific. In connection to Lazrus (2009),[91] he emphasises the necessity of recognising and using the special skills, experiences and networks of Oceania's citizens in the field of adaptation to climate change.[92] Much too often, top-down approaches have predominated in Pacific climate change adaptation projects, in disregard of cultural and regional factors. Consequently, self-created goals are frequently displaced, while the threat increases.

Against the backdrop of climate change, the possibilities of an increasingly fragmented juridical landscape are being utilised today. The central actors, in particular the government of Kiribati, but also advisers, transnational networks and NGOs, appear as so-called knowledge brokers and advocates of interest. They relate to concepts of order that have a global reach, such as human rights, and they argue on moral grounds. These 'universals', which build the core of modern humanistic and humanitarian projects,[93] become ever more crucial as demands for climate justice in the context of debates around climate change strengthen. Our April 2011 interviews reveal the prevalence of the discourse around climate justice in Kiribati. For instance, Kaia Miller, an employee of the Ministry of the Environment, declared: 'The head of the unit, the minister, actually said that … "Australia should buy us this and that, because climate change is all their fault."'[94] Here, ascribing responsibility for climate change and its consequences is strongly connected to financial and judicial demands. The realisation of these demands and agreements, beyond financial aid through adaptation projects, is still far from guaranteed.

Conclusion: decentring and politicising climate change

In both of the arenas described in this chapter, basic differences have emerged in the debate around environmental and climate migration. Aside from isolated attempts by individuals and organisations, the EU addresses the subject under specific guidelines: the phenomenon is conceptualised primarily as a deficit in adaptation in the affected regions. Therefore, on the one hand, it is understood as a subject of development policy, while on the other, it is largely outsourced from the sovereign territory of the European Union. Though the EU's co-responsibility for the problems that are arising from global climate change is not fundamentally disputed, according to the EU's position, these problems should be addressed within the affected regions. The restrictive European asylum and migration policy remains unaffected by possible new pleas and funding, such as concrete scenarios for hosting refugees or an inclusive Mediterranean policy.

The debates in Kiribati, on the other hand, show that current and anticipated migration movements raise far-reaching questions. Here, the debate has not been caught up in the abbreviations of developmental and security policies, but rather concerns itself with concrete questions relating to climate justice, and includes decidedly concrete migration-'friendly' perspectives and a basic questioning of nation-state border demarcations. At the same time, some of the negotiated labour programmes in Oceania can be connected easily to discourses around the 'usefulness' of migration for the regions of origin in the Global South and particularly the economies of OECD countries.[95]

It remains to be seen whether and how regional answers and solutions for climate migrants – as currently advocated in the Pacific region – offer the best migration opportunities. The debates suggested above repeatedly highlight the originally global character of the subject of anthropogenic climate change and its social repercussions.[96] Altogether, current negotiation processes recognise a shift, visible, for example, in some fora of negotiation, such as the AOSIS and the SIDS, and in bilateral relations with Fiji. Kiribati has gained influence on the global stage and, rather than accepting the role of 'victim of climate change', the government has achieved positive results through negotiated migration programmes. For instance, the new resources of the Global Environment Facility and the remittances from labour programmes are already benefiting the I-Kiribati.

In the future, it will surely be necessary for Kiribati and other Pacific islands to review a number of migration and adaptation strategies in order to find long-term alternatives for various individuals and communities.[97] Not all of the pursued strategies are emancipatory, as is clear in the current circular labour programmes that Kiribati is negotiating with New Zealand and Australia.

Considering the view of EU countries and institutions, which have a tendency to frame the subject of climate change and future migration through development and security policies, as well as Kiribati's efforts, it is important to address sensitive questions of power and to consider the different perspectives and interpretations of climate change. Climate justice must be turned into an important argument. This is applicable in the debates and research around climate change and migration, and is frequently mentioned in discussions on and studies into adaptation to anthropogenic climate change. In the context of climate change and frequent reliance on expert views, structural and economic aspects often seem non-political and supposedly objective and thereby appear non-negotiable. With the help of a post-colonial, decentralising perspective, these aspects must be taken into account, made visible and re-politicised. Therefore, *decentring climate change* means turning our attention to legal and decision-making processes in the context of climate change, attending to assumptions from the Global South and actors who are not experts. In addition, the analysis should not be reduced to political and ethical questions. Instead, the conceptualisation of the research field should experience a decentring and widening in the context of climate change if we are to address the complex subject of environmental migration fairly.[98] The attempts within the European debate to avoid the immanent aspects of climate justice by framing it as a development topic, and the tendency of industrialised countries to refuse to accept responsibility for the social consequences of climate change, should become clear through this research. New options for action and manoeuvring space for accountable and solidary migration and climate policies could open up in this way.

Notes

1 S.Klepp is Professor at Kiel University. J. Herbeck is Researcher at University of Bremen.
2 E. Piguet, 'From "Primitive Migration" to "Climate Refugees": The Curious Fate of the Natural Environment in Migration Studies' (2013) 103 *Annals of the Association of American Geographers* 148–162; G. White, *Climate Change and Migration: Security and Borders in a Warming World* (Oxford University Press 2011); A. Baldwin, 'Pluralising Climate Change and Migration: An Argument in Favour of Open Futures' (2014) 8(8) *Geography Compass* 516–528.
3 P. Rudiak-Gould, 'Climate Change and Anthropology: The Importance of Reception Studies' (2011) 27 *Anthropology Today* 9–12.
4 B. de Sousa Santos and C. A. Rodríguez-Garavito, *Law and Globalization from Below: Towards a Cosmopolitan Legality* (Cambridge University Press 2005).
5 S. E. Merry, 'Legal Pluralism' (1988) 22(5) *Law and Society Review* 869–896.
6 M. M. J. Fischer, 'Technoscientific Infrastructures and Emergent Forms of Life: A Commentary' (2005) 107 *American Anthropologist* 55–61; B. Maurer, 'Introduction to "Ethnographic Emergences"' (2005) 107 *American Anthropologist* 1–4.
7 E. Hau'ofa, 'Our Sea of Islands' in V. Naidu and E. Waddell (eds), *A New Oceania: Rediscovering Our Sea of Islands* (University of the South Pacific 1993) 2–17; W. Kempf, 'A Sea of Environmental Refugees? Oceania in an Age of Climate Change' in E. Hermann, K. Klenke and M. Dickhardt (eds), *Form, Macht, Differenz: Motive und Felder ethnologischen Forschens* (Universitätsverlag Göttingen 2009) 191–205.
8 OECD, *Integrating Climate Change Adaptation into Development Co-operation* (2009).
9 K. Dietz, 'Prima Klima in den Nord–Süd-Beziehungen? Die Antinomien globaler Klimapolitik: Diskurse, Politiken und Prozesse' in H.-J. Burchardt (ed.), *Nord–Süd-Beziehungen im Umbruch: Neue Perspektiven auf Staat und Demokratie in der Weltpolitik* (Campus Verlag 2009) 189.
10 B. C. Parks and J. T. Roberts, 'Climate Change, Social Theory and Justice' (2010) 27 *Theory, Culture and Society* 134–166.
11 Dietz, 'Prima Klima'.
12 N. Mimura *et al.*, 'Small Islands' in M. L. Parry *et al.* (eds), *Climate Change 2007: Working Group II: Impacts, Adaptation and Vulnerability* (Cambridge University Press 2007) 687ff.
13 C. Farbotko, 'Skilful Seafarers, Oceanic Drifters or Climate Refugees? Pacific People, News Value and the Climate Refugee Crisis' in K. Moore, B. Gross and T. Threatgold (eds), *Migrations and the Media* (Peter Lang Publishing 2012) 119–142.
14 F. von Benda-Beckmann, K. von Benda-Beckmann and A. Griffiths, 'Mobile People, Mobile Law: An Introduction' in F. von Benda-Beckmann, K. von Benda-Beckmann and A. Griffiths (eds), *Mobile People, Mobile Law: Expanding Legal Relations in a Contracting World* (Ashgate 2005) 9.
15 Ibid.
16 E. El-Hinnawi, *Environmental Refugees* (United Nations Environment Programme 1985); D. C. Bates, 'Environmental Refugees? Classifying Human

Migrations Caused by Environmental Change' (2002) 23 *Population and Environment* 465–477.

17 C. Rouviere *et al.*, 'Human Settlement; the Energy, Transport and Industrial Sectors; Human Health; Air Quality; and Changes in Ultraviolet-B Radiation' in W. J. M. Tegart, G. W. Sheldon and D. C. Griffiths (eds), *Climate Change: Working Group II: Impacts Assessment of Climate Change* (Australian Government Publishing Service 1990) 5–9.

18 Bates, 'Environmental Refugees?'; F. Biermann, 'Umweltflüchtlinge: Ursachen und Lösungsansätze' (2001) 12 *Aus Politik und Zeitgeschichte* 24–29; C. Jakobeit and C. Methmann, *Klimaflüchtlinge: Die verleugnete Katastrophe* (Greenpeace e.V. 2007).

19 Christian Aid, *Human Tide: The Real Migration Crisis* (2007); N. Myers, 'Environmental Refugees' (1997) 19 *Population and Environment* 167–182; N. Myers, 'Environmental Refugees: A Growing Phenomenon of the 21st Century' (2002) 357 *Philosophical Transactions of the Royal Society of London: Biological Sciences* 609–613.

20 B. Docherty and T. Giannini, 'Confronting a Rising Tide: A Proposal for a Convention on Climate Change Refugees' (2009) 33 *Harvard Environmental Law Review* 349–403.

21 R. Black, 'Environmental Refugees: Myth or Reality?' (2001) UNHCR Working Paper on New Issues in Refugee Research No. 341.

22 See, for example, C. T. M. Nicholson, 'Is the "Environmental Migration" Nexus an Analytically Meaningful Subject for Research?' (Center on Migration, Citizenship and Development 2011).

23 B. Hartmann, 'Rethinking Climate Refugees and Climate Conflict: Rhetoric, Reality and the Politics of Policy Discourse' (2010) 22 *Journal of International Development* 233–246.

24 Piguet, 'From "Primitive Migration" to "Climate Refugees"'.

25 R. Andrijasevic *et al.*, 'Turbulente Ränder: Konturen eines neuen Migrationsregimes im Südosten Europas' (2005) 35 *PROKLA: Zeitschrift für kritische Sozialwissenschaft* 345–362; S. Mezzadra, 'The Right to Escape' (2004) 4 *Ephemera: Theory and Politics in Organization* 267–275; S. Mezzadra, 'Kapitalismus, Migrationen, soziale Kämpfe: Vorbemerkungen zu einer Theorie der Autonomie der Migration' in M. Pieper *et al.* (eds), *Empire und die biopolitische Wende: Die internationale Diskussion im Anschluss an Hardt und Negri* (Campus 2007) 179–193; Y. Moulier Boutang, 'Europa, Autonomie der Migration, Biopolitik' in Pieper *et al.* (eds), *Empire und die biopolitische Wende* 169–178; V. Tsianos, *Imperceptible Politics: Rethinking Radical Politics of Migration and Precarity Today* (Department Sozialwissenschaften, Universität Hamburg 2007).

26 D. Gupta, 'Climate of Fear: Environment, Migration and Security' in F. Dodds, A. Highham and R. Sherman (eds), *Climate Change and Energy Insecurity* (Earthscan 2009) 71–79; Hartmann, 'Rethinking Climate Refugees and Climate Conflict'; J. Herbeck and M. Flitner, '"A New Enemy Out There"? Der Klimawandel als Sicherheitsproblem' (2010) 65 *Geographica Helvetica* 198–206.

27 See S. Chaturvedi and T. Doyle, 'Geopolitics of Climate Change and Australia's "Re-engagement" with Asia: Discourses of Fear and Cartographic Anxieties' (2010) 45 *Australian Journal of Political Science* 95–115.

28 J. McAdam, 'Swimming against the Tide: Why a Climate Change Displacement Treaty Is Not the Answer' (2011) 23(1) *International Journal of Refugee Law* 2–27.

29 See S. Klepp, *Europa zwischen Grenzkontrolle und Flüchtlingsschutz: Eine Ethnographie der Seegrenze auf dem Mittelmeer* (Transcript Verlag 2011); A. Oels, 'Saving "Climate Refugees" as Bare Life? A Theory-Based Critique of Refugee Status for Climate-Induced Migrants' in *Papers Prepared for the ESF-ZiF-Bielefeld Conference*

on 'Environmental Degradation and Conflict: From Vulnerabilities to Capabilities' (Center for Interdisciplinary Research 2010).

30 W. Somerville, *Environmental Migration Governance: Debate in the European Union* (Foresight 2011) 14.

31 European Council, 'The Stockholm Programme: An Open and Secure Europe Serving and Protecting Citizens (2010/C 115/01)' (2010) 53 *Official Journal of the European Union*.

32 Andrijasevic *et al.* ('Turbulente Ränder' 348) state that this Europeanisation of migration and asylum policy is connected not only to an increased harmonisation within the EU and an expansion of the appropriate policies beyond EU territory but also to a 'transformation in the political method', and even to a growing lack of formality in political decision-making processes and practices.

33 European Commission, 'Communication from the European Commission to the European Parliament, the Council, the European Economic and Social Committee and the Committee of the Regions: The Global Approach to Migration and Mobility' (2011) COM (2011) 743 final 7.

34 White, *Climate Change and Migration*.

35 M. Gassner, *Prävention irregulärer Migration im integrierten Gesamtansatz zur Migrationsfrage: Entwicklungszusammenarbeit im Dienst der europäischen Migrationspolitik am Beispiel Marokko* (Diplomarbeit, Philologisch-Kulturwissenschaftliche Fakultät, Universität Wien 2010); J. Hyndman and A. Mountz, 'Another Brick in the Wall? Neo-Refoulement and the Externalization of Asylum by Australia and Europe' (2008) 43 *Government and Opposition* 249–269; S. Lavenex and E. M. Uçarer, 'The External Dimension of Europeanization' (2004) 39 *Cooperation and Conflict* 417–443.

36 See, for example, N. de Moor and A. Cliquet, 'Environmental Displacement: A New Challenge for European Migration Policy' (2009) paper prepared for the 'Protecting People in Conflict and Crisis: Responding to the Challenges of a Changing World' conference, Refugee Studies Centre, University of Oxford; V. Kolmannskog and F. Myrstad, 'Environmental Displacement in European Asylum Law' (2009) 11 *European Journal of Migration and Law* 313–326; T. Schmedding, *Environmental Migration: A Global Issue under European Union Leadership?* (Centre international de formation européenne, Institut européen des hautes études internationales, Academy of Nice 2011); L. Westra, *Environmental Justice and the Rights of Ecological Refugees* (Earthscan 2009).

37 J. Lambert, *Refugees and the Environment: The Forgotten Element of Sustainability* (The Greens/European Free Alliance in the European Parliament 2002) 5.

38 Greens/EFA Group, *Declaration on Climate Migration* (2008), adopted at the conference on 'Climate Migrations', European Parliament, Brussels, 11 June 2008.

39 Committee on Petitions of the European Parliament, 'Notice to Members on Petition 1312/2009 by Andy Vermaut (Belgian) on Behalf of the Pimpampoentje (Ladybird) Climate and Peace Action Group, on Legal Recognition by the European Union of Climate Refugees' (2011).

40 Council of the European Union, 'Presidency Conclusions of the Brussels European Council, 15/16 December 2005' (2006) 15914/1/05. REV 1.

41 F. Georgi, 'Kritik des Migrationsmanagements: Historische Einordnung eines politischen Projekts' (2009) *Juridikum: Zeitschrift für Politik / Recht / Gesellschaft* 81–84; S. Klepp, 'A Contested Asylum System: The European Union between Refugee Protection and Border Control in the Mediterranean Sea' (2010) 12 *European Journal of Migration and Law* 1–21.

42 European Council, 'The Stockholm Programme' 29.

43 European Commission, 'Global Approach to Migration and Mobility'.

44 European Commission, 'Migration and Development: Commission Staff Working Paper' (2011) SEC (2011) 1353 final.

45 European Commission, 'Climate Change, Environmental Degradation, and Migration' (2013) SWD (2013) 138 final.

46 G. Bettini, 'Climate Barbarians at the Gate? A Critique of Apocalyptic Narratives on Climate Refugees' (2013) 45 *Geoforum* 63–72.

47 European Commission, 'Communication from the Commission to the Council and the European Parliament: Climate Change in the Context of Development Cooperation' (2003) COM (2003) 85 final.

48 EU Directorate-General on Development and Cooperation, 'Thematic Programme "Cooperation with Third Countries in the Areas of Migration and Asylum": 2011–2013 Multi-Annual Strategy Paper' (European Commission 2010) 217f.

49 K. Newland, *Climate Change and Migration Dynamics: Improving US and EU Immigration Systems* (Migration Policy Institute 2011) 9f.

50 European Commission, 'Adapting to Climate Change: Towards a European Framework for Action' (2009) COM (2009) 147 final.

51 Somerville, *Environmental Migration Governance* 14.

52 Herbeck and Flitner, '"A New Enemy Out There?"' 202.

53 EU High Representative and the European Commission, 'Climate Change and International Security: Paper from the High Representative and the European Commission to the European Council' (2008) S113/08 4.

54 Ibid. 2.

55 EU High Representative, 'Climate Change and Security: Recommendations of the High Representative on Follow-Up to the High Representative and Commission Report on Climate Change and International Security' (2008) S412/08.

56 Gassner, *Prävention irregulärer Migration*.

57 Merry, 'Legal Pluralism'.

58 de Sousa Santos and Rodríguez-Garavito, *Law and Globalization from Below*.

59 See also S. E. Merry, 'Legal Pluralism and Transnational Culture: The Ka Ho'O-kolokolonui Kanaka Maoli Tribunal, Hawai'i, 1993' in R. A. Wilson (ed.), *Human Rights, Culture and Context* (Pluto Press 1997).

60 S. Buckel, R. Christensen and A. Fischer-Lescano, 'Einleitung: Neue Theoriepraxis des Rechts' in S. Buckel, R. Christensen and A. Fischer-Lescano (eds), *Neue Theorien des Rechts* (UTB, Lucius & Lucius 2009) xv.

61 See also J. S. Collier and A. Lakoff, 'On Regimes of Living' in A. Ong and S. J. Collier (eds), *Global Assemblages: Technology, Politics, and Ethics as Anthropological Problems* (Blackwell 2005) 22–40.

62 R. Hillerbrand, *Technik, Ökologie und Ethik* (Mentis Verlag 2006).

63 Farbotko, 'Skilful Seafarers'; J. Barnett and J. Campbell, *Climate Change and Small Island States: Power, Knowledge and the South Pacific* (Earthscan 2010).

64 L. A. Nurse *et al.*, 'Small Islands' in V. R. Barros *et al.* (eds), *Climate Change 2014: Working Group II: Impacts, Adaptation and Vulnerability. Part B: Regional Aspects* (Cambridge University Press 2014); S. Rahmstorf, 'New View on Sea Level Rise' (2010) 4 *Nature Reports Climate Change* 44–45; N. Mimura *et al.*, 'Small Islands'.

65 Nurse *et al.*, 'Small Islands'.

66 Mimura *et al.*, 'Small Islands'.

67 Rahmstorf, 'New View on Sea Level Rise' 44–45.

68 A. Grinsted, J. C. Moore and S. Jevrejeva, 'Reconstructing Sea Level from Paleo and Projected Temperatures 200 to 2100 AD' (2010) 34 *Climate Dynamics* 461–472.

69 D. Storey and S. Hunter, 'Kiribati: An Environmental "Perfect Storm"' (2010) 41 *Australian Geographer* 172.

70 S. E. Merry, 'Transnational Human Rights and Local Activism: Mapping the Middle' (2006) 108 *American Anthropologist* 40.

71 According to the United Nations' Convention on Sea Rights (1982), the Exclusive Economic Zone stretches 200 nautical miles (370 kilometres) out to sea. In this area, the coastal state can exercise certain sovereign rights and jurisdictions, above all the right to the economic exploitation of fishing rights. See also M. Esteban and L. Yamamoto, 'Vanishing Island States and Sovereignty' (2010) 53 *Ocean and Coastal Management* 1–9.

72 Alliance of Small Island States, *Malé' Declaration on the Human Dimension of Global Climate Change* (2007) www.ciel.org/Publications/Male_Declaration_Nov07.pdf accessed 25 October 2016.

73 T. Tanner and J. Allouche, 'Towards a New Political Economy of Climate Change and Development' (2011) 42 *IDS Bulletin* 4.

74 F. M. Zerilli, 'The Rule of Soft Law: An Introduction' (2010) 56 *Focaal* 7.

75 This expression was repeatedly used in conversations with the workers of International Collaboration during the research period in Kiribati in the spring of 2011.

76 BBC, 'The President's Dilemma: Should Kiribati's President Anote Give In to Climate Change?' (2009) produced by the International Fund for Agricultural Development (IFAD), shown in *Life on the Edge*.

77 Interview with Scott Leckie, director of the NGO Displacement Solutions on 4 April 2011 in Melbourne, Australia. Displacement Solutions advises the governments of Kiribati and Papua New Guinea on questions relating to migration due to climate change.

78 M. Risse, 'The Right to Relocation: Disappearing Island Nations and Common Ownership of the Earth' (2009) 23 *Ethics and International Affairs* 281.

79 Immigration New Zealand, 'Pacific Access Category' www.immigration.govt.nz/migrant/stream/live/pacificaccess/ accessed 25 October 2016.

80 Interview with Ken Graham, Member of Parliament in New Zealand, Green Party, on 18 May 2011 in Wellington, New Zealand.

81 Ibid.

82 Interview with Baatetake Tatoa, section head in Kiribati's Ministry of Labour, on 18 May 2015 in Bairiki, South Tarawa, Kiribati.

83 Interview with several of Kiribati's Ministry of Labour workers on 20 April 2011 in Bairiki.

84 Interview with Baatetake Tatoa on 20 April 2011 in Bairiki. For further discussion of labour mobility options in the Pacific, see Chapter 13, this volume.

85 S. Pillwein, *Climate Refugees: Klimawandel und Migration am Beispiel des Inselstaates Tuvalu im Pazifik* (Diplomica Verlag 2013) 54.

86 R. Bedford and C. Bedford, 'International Migration and Climate Change: A Post-Copenhagen Perspective on Options for Kiribati and Tuvalu' in B. Burson (ed.), *Climate Change and Migration: South Pacific Perspectives* (Institute of Policy Studies 2010) 90.

87 Interview with Scott Leckie.

88 Interview with Reteta Rimon, High Commissioner of Kiribati in Fiji, on 6 May 2015 in Suva, Fiji.

89 Hau'ofa, 'Our Sea of Islands'.

90 Kempf, 'A Sea of Environmental Refugees?' 194.

91 H. Lazrus, 'The Governance of Vulnerability: Climate Change and Agency in Tuvalu, South Pacific' in S. Crate and M. Nuttal (eds), *Anthropology and Climate Change: From Encounters to Actions* (Left Coast Press 2009) 240–249.

92 Kempf, 'A Sea of Environmental Refugees?' 195.

93 A. L. Tsing, *Friction: An Ethnography of Global Connection* (Princeton University Press 2005) 7.

94 Interview with Kaia Miller (pseudonym), employee of Kiribati's Ministry of the Environment, on 14 April 2011 in her office.

95 R. Felli and N. Castree, 'Neoliberalising Adaptation to Environmental Change: Foresight or Foreclosure?' (2012) 44 *Environment and Planning A* 1–4.
96 P. Boncour and B. Burson, 'Climate Change and Migration in the South Pacific Region: Policy Perspectives' in Burson (ed.), *Climate Change and Migration* 19.
97 Bedford and Bedford, 'International Migration and Climate Change' 93.
98 Baldwin, 'Pluralising Climate Change and Migration'; S. Klepp and J. Herbeck, 'The Politics of Environmental Migration and Climate Justice in the Pacific Region' (2016) 7 *Journal of Human Rights and the Environment* 54–73.

12 Climate and community

The human rights, livelihood and migration impacts of climate change

Brooke A. Ackerly, Mujibul Anam, Jonathan Gilligan and Steven Goodbred[1]

Introduction

Climate change is a global problem. However, between the global forces of climate change and the individual challenges of meeting basic needs, communities are the context in which people experience the effects of climate change and seek to adapt to its impact on their livelihoods. Such adaptation may include permanent migration, and this has certainly been one of the foci of international relations and security politics related to climate change. Of course, such migration will have human rights consequences; and there are also human rights causes of some of this migration, particularly as parts of the planet where people have made their homes and livelihoods become uninhabitable. Of equal importance are the problems related to climate change effects that do not cause mass migration but also have human rights causes and consequences. In this chapter, we use a study in rural Bangladesh to demonstrate the import of the human rights considerations of this second, community-level, impact of climate change on human rights.

Climate change poses new sources of threats to the most basic of human rights concerns. As Kyung-wha Kang, UN Deputy High Commissioner for Human Rights, said in 2008: 'Global warming and extreme weather conditions may have calamitous consequences for the human rights of millions of people ... [U]ltimately, climate change may affect the very right to life.'[2] Food, water, health, housing and life are basic individual human rights that are all threatened by the anticipated impacts of climate change.[3]

Even while climate scientists dispute the specifics of the relationship between environmental change and anthropogenic climate change, there is no disputing that Bangladesh is on the 'front line' of climate change impacts. Moreover, because Bangladesh is currently experiencing environmental conditions that scientists argue will become increasingly prevalent with climate change, studying the impacts of certain environmental changes on the people of Bangladesh should provide a better understanding of the potential social, political and economic impacts of climate change.

Migration plays a part in these impacts, but as we will show, its role is interwoven throughout a range of social, political and economic impacts of changing environmental conditions. As a way of diversifying sources of livelihood, migration has become a part of the changes in political economy and livelihoods. Thus, to understand the relationships among climate change and migration, we need to understand the ways in which environmental change affects communities. Specifically, we need to understand the dynamics between the built and natural environments and the political economies these sustain.[4] Community-level political economies affect the sources of income and livelihood available in distressed environmental conditions, and therefore influence how well the people who live there can adapt to changing environmental conditions. To anticipate the argument of the paper, slow-onset environmental changes and disastrous (rapid-onset) environmental events have become features of the underlying political economies of these communities. These complex dynamics (and indirectly environmental changes) are pushing Bangladeshis to incorporate migration strategies into their livelihood strategies, affecting how they do so, and impacting the human rights consequences of these dynamics.

In this chapter, we first outline the methods of a multi-site, cross-community transdisciplinary study of the effects of slow- and rapid-onset environmental changes that are similar to those anticipated to be more common and more widespread with climate change. Second, we discuss those findings that are related to one particularly pernicious – and anticipated to be widespread – consequence of environmental and climate change: threats to populations living at sea level. Finally, we argue that the human rights impacts of these environmental changes are integrated throughout the political economy. Thus, addressing the human rights impacts of climate change entails addressing not only environmental change but also the way in which inequalities in the power to influence the local political economy affect human rights consequences of that change.

Transdisciplinary methods

So much of what we anticipate to be the migration and human rights impact of climate change depends on how we understand its effects on the physical environment in dynamic relationship with the local social, economic, political and engineered environment. Therefore, our research is transdisciplinary – across the social and physical sciences – and focuses on identifying the dynamics among these forces rather than on the consequences of these dynamics at a particular moment in time and in a particular place. Based on our preliminary research, we identified a particular place and time when these dynamics were likely to be in evidence.

Site selection: meso-level and transdisciplinary observations

Although we could have organised our study around any number of environmental changes that we expect climate change to accelerate or exacerbate, we focus on those that are relevant to low-lying populations.

South-western Bangladesh is a globally relevant site for studying the localised ways in which certain global trends are experienced because it is a site of enduring poverty, of environmental stresses that are similar to those anticipated from future climate change, of the influence of the global export market for shrimp (which might be considered both an adaptive response to environmental stress and an activity that degrades the environment), of saline ground and surface water (which may become more prevalent with climate change) and of vulnerability to seasonal flooding and cyclone events (which may become more severe with climate change).[5]

During the decade of advancement towards the Millennium Development Goals, the south west of Bangladesh did not see the improvements that other regions enjoyed. Moreover, even the successes that Bangladesh claims in advancing towards those goals are contested when national averages are disaggregated to reveal severe deficiencies at the seasonal, regional and local levels.[6] Additionally, when the impacts of climate change are discussed globally, the inhabitants of Bangladesh's low-lying river delta are often identified as the community that is most at risk. In these two ways, south-west Bangladesh is already an important area on the global stage.

In the 1960s and 1970s, following recommendations from the United Nations, and with funding provided by the United States Agency for International Development (USAID) and the Asian Development Bank (ADB), the Bangladeshi government built embankments around the river islands. While each island's boundaries were originally defined by the river's hydrology and sediment deposits over the long geological history of the delta, these islands – or 'polders' as they are called locally – are now defined by the embankments, which were constructed to protect the land from saline inundation during the dry season and from storm surges generated by tropical cyclones.

The findings presented here come from integrated social and physical science research across thirteen communities who live on one small (less than sixty-two square kilometres) diamond-shaped island in south-western Bangladesh (identified as 'Polder 32'). Much of the variation in political, economic and social experience that is found across the region is similarly evident on this island. For instance, there are differences in changes in land use related to shrimping and political activity related to resisting shrimping. There is also variability in the national response to the impacts of low-mortality, high-damage cyclones and the impact the storms and recovery efforts have had on local economies. Most graphically, satellite imagery of our region of study before and after a major storm (Cyclone Aila, May 2009) led us to focus our initial study on a district where some communities were left exposed to inundation from tidal waters for more than a year after Aila struck.

The area of study sits just north of the Sunderbans, the largest mangrove forest in the world. This UNESCO World Heritage Site encompasses parts of Bangladesh and the Indian state of West Bengal. It contains valuable natural resources that communities who live adjacent to the Sunderbans have relied on for years, including crabs, honey, fish, wood and golpata palm, which the locals use for their roofs. Access to these resources is generally controlled through permits, although unregulated use continues and is often highly organised.

Social methods

The social dimensions rely on qualitative data collected before the monsoon season in 2012 and 2013. This time of year was selected because employment opportunities are low, so the opportunity cost to a villager of participating in our research was similarly low. Using multiple qualitative methods, participants were asked to share their observations about changes in rivers, embankments and forms of employment over the course of their lifetime, but their responses generally focused on the preceding decade.

The boundaries of each community were determined using a grounded approach. In a qualitative method called the 'village transect walk', at each site researchers walked throughout the community, asking villagers to identify landmarks, boundaries, neighbourhoods, fields, water sources, the informal adjudicatory authority (shalish), schools and other features.[7]

We used three other qualitative methods that were designed to provide us with a rich understanding of the community dynamics. Key informants were defined broadly as those with particular knowledge of a certain aspect of village life, including each form of livelihood that community members practised. Migrants, day labourers and the unemployed were key informants about their own experiences. Participatory rapid appraisal methods were used to create a village map, a seasonal calendar of employment and a calendar of migration for each village. We supplemented these methods with targeted focus group discussions, usually topically oriented. In each community these included at least one women's focus group.

Triangulation across this range of qualitative data enabled us to develop an understanding of the social, economic, political and environmental dynamics of a village from the villagers' own perspectives.

Physical methods

Two scientific claims are present in the background of this chapter. The first (as discussed earlier) is that the environmental conditions in present-day south-western Bangladesh are likely to become more prevalent with ongoing climate change. The second is that climate change affects people's living conditions. So, for example, while there is a general view that sea levels are rising with climate change, we need to know what this means for the dynamics of the whole environment, not just for the absolute eustatic level of the oceans.

To appreciate this perspective, it is important to note that the deltaic environment of south-western Bangladesh is dynamic and self-organised.[8] It is perpetually changing due to the supply of water and sediment from the rivers, the energy of tides and storms, and the strong overprint of the regional monsoon climate's seasonal and annual variability. Thus, perturbations of this strongly interconnected system, whether by humans or nature, lead to a cascade of interrelated adjustments to the network of islands and channels. Typically, the magnitude of such responses scales to that of the perturbation, whereby alterations over larger areas or longer periods of time, or even an aggregation of small-scale changes, will have a correspondingly greater effect on the natural system.

We studied these interacting physical processes, and their relation to human activities, using multiple field methods and remote sensing approaches. In the field, we deployed instruments that collected continuous measurements of water level, temperature, salinity and sediment concentrations. We monitored these attributes in the tidal channels and on the mangrove and poldered landscapes in order to understand how water and sediment are transported through the tidal channels and onto the land, where they help sustain its elevation against rising sea levels. To place this recent snapshot of the physical environment in its proper perspective, we also collected sediment cores that reveal the longer-term decadal–millennial-scale behaviour of the natural landscape. Furthermore, our ground-based observations regarding channel erosion, infilling and changing land cover are supported by spatiotemporal analysis of agricultural land use and coastal processes from a compilation of Landsat (satellite) scenes.[9]

Findings

The dynamics between humans and their environment in coastal Bangladesh are nested among interacting global, regional and local forces, some of which are human-led, some of which are environment-led, some of which are events, some of which are trends. Our study revealed many. We focus on those dynamics that are related to the physical condition of the local landscape relative to local water levels in part because this dynamic is so dominant in shaping the livelihoods of those in the region and in part because, with climate change, this dynamic is expected to become more widespread and to affect previously unaffected areas. Moreover, the migration-related dimensions of these dynamics shed light on the complexity of the human rights implications of climate change.

In presenting our findings, we also make reference to scholarship that suggests that our findings are relevant beyond our particular area of study. The import of our research for human rights, livelihoods and migration lies not in the findings that relate to the consequences of these dynamics for specific people but rather in the generalisable findings about the dynamics themselves.

Slow-onset changes in a dynamic landscape

Multiple forces are affecting the height of the local landscape relative to water levels in adjacent rivers or channels. Without polders, this depends on how much sediment is carried by the rivers, and the ways in which the rivers and tides determine where these sediments accumulate or decline. Outside the polders, high tide levels, due to a complex set of river dynamics and the polder system itself, prevent water from diffusing across the natural landscape.[10] Inside the polders, land levels are falling relative to the rivers due to the subsidence and sediment starvation of land inside the embankments.[11]

Poldering changes the dynamics of tides in the rivers and tidal channels, and also changes the erosion, transportation and deposition of sediment. In the natural landscape, the twice-daily inundation by tides deposits fresh sediment and builds the land up as sea level rises or the underlying land subsides. As evidence of this, with no embankments, the land of the Sunderbans is as much as 1.5 metres higher above sea level than many polders that have been embanked. Seasonal inundation is prevented by permanent embankments. The landscape cannot adjust to subsidence or to rising sea levels without the annual supply of sediment, so it may become more vulnerable to catastrophic flooding, should the embankments breach (as happened in 2009). In the course of this century, sea-level rise is expected to exceed the capacity of the natural sediment supply, creating conditions of low land relative to water levels even in unpoldered areas. Human-made sources can contribute to this process in other ways as well. For example, India's planned diversion of the Ganges River is expected to reduce the natural sediment supply substantially, which will increase the threat to the sustainability of the coastal lands.

Outside and between the polders, south-western Bangladesh has been experiencing ongoing river migration and saltwater intrusion. Hence, some present-day agricultural fields used to be within the river channel, whereas others have suffered river erosion and encroachment. These changes have taken place within the lifetimes of young people and are confirmed by satellite imagery.[12]

Rapid-onset changes in a dynamic landscape

In addition to the steady dynamics of change over time, Bangladesh experiences frequent cyclonic storms. On average, severe cyclones strike the coast once every three years. The communities we studied felt the impact of Cyclone Sidr (2007) and were severely affected by Cyclone Aila (2009). Breaches in the external embankments allowed in river water and the force of the storm and subsequent tidal flows eroded internal embankments too. Because the embankments were erected decades ago, the land within them had subsided; without fresh sediment from seasonal flooding over those decades, it was significantly lower than the river or channel, particularly at high tide. Hence, people could resume neither agriculture nor aquaculture until the embankments were rebuilt. Satellite imagery reveals that land was intertidal in some of the communities affected by Aila, so it continued to be inundated with tidal water for up to ten hours a day more than two years after the storm.

The disaster response to Aila was not immediate, but once it began it included a range of construction projects: embankment reconstruction; road reconstruction; new homes; and a planned community comprising families relocated from a portion of the interior of the polder that would not be restored. All of these construction projects required day labour, much of which was provided by women. This became an important element in many families' livelihood strategies. As we will see in the next section, the availability of day labour is an important aspect of human–environment coupling in disaster-prone areas.

Changing political economy

While migration is part of a complicated story of the effects of environmental change on human rights, it is not a singular part. There are eight main trends in the changing political economy of Polder 32 that manifest differently across the communities.[13] This section will describe these trends and their dynamic relationships with each other, the environmental conditions, and certain dynamics in the broader political economy. They are:

- declining reliance on rice cultivation;
- livelihoods drawn from the Sunderbans and protein sources from household river fishing;
- increasing reliance on seasonal migration;
- local day labour in construction;
- long-term migration to urban settings, usually for factory work;
- cash crops (in the northern communities);
- shrimp cultivation (in the southern communities); and
- seasonal high-yield fishing (for one southern community).

These trends – which feature declines in certain opportunities and increasing reliance on other opportunities – are related to each other and to the environmental factors discussed above, including slow and sudden environmental changes, the availability of external resources, and the construction and management of the embankments. Although we focus on those relating to changing land use and migration in order to highlight the relationship between the changing environment and migration and human rights, the other dynamics are also important to human rights and migration because they influence livelihood opportunities throughout the year. Again, as we stated in our discussion of site selection, the country and region have been experiencing human–environmental coupling over recent years. We used qualitative data and analysis to understand the dynamics of this coupling.

Under normal conditions, the difference between the height of the land and the height of the rivers is such that people can control the flow of water onto the land with sluice gates. When opened at high tide, these allow water to run onto the land; when opened at low tide, they let water run off the land. Note that the tidal amplitude in much of the region – and around Polder 32 – is between 2.5 and 4.5 metres, depending on the season, lunar cycle, storm conditions and specific location within the channel network.

This difference has generated opportunities to expand agriculture or aquaculture. Initially, the embankment system allowed the estuarine islands to become 'green revolution' farmland. Rainwater accumulated in ponds and internal canals (created by closing off small channels that had formerly allowed tidal water to move on and off the landscape) during the monsoon season, and this was then used for drinking and irrigation throughout the year.

Declining reliance on rice cultivation

As in many parts of south-western Bangladesh, the groundwater in Polder 32 is naturally saline and thus cannot be used to irrigate rice. Conceivably, shrimp farming has the potential to provide livelihood activities during the dry season, when rice cultivation is impossible. However, in Polder 32, the seasonal experiment with shrimping and rice cultivation did not work as rice yields declined.

Increased shrimp cultivation

Thus, the embankment system created opportunities for conflict over both control of and responsibility for maintaining the embankments and sluice gates, and consequently over which portions of the polder had access to large stores of fresh water for rice irrigation (and, more recently, irrigation of cash crops; see below) and which aquaculture ponds had access to brackish water. In the late 1980s, the south converted to shrimp cultivation after a storm damaged the embankment and local landowners, afraid that their land might be washed away, invited shrimp industry leaders to lease their land in exchange for repair of the embankment. In the north, other outsiders sought to convert land adjacent to a large interior canal to shrimping. This created shrimp-dependent economies in both the north and the south for a time. However, labourers and landowning elites eventually formed an alliance to end leasing for shrimping in the north. Thus, at the time of our research, the north-east communities had cash crop economies and no shrimping.

Shrimping and rice cultivation affect different populations in different ways. For some, shrimp production is lucrative, generating higher incomes than rice production (although it is unclear how it compares with cash crop cultivation). Outsiders have often used threats of physical violence or other forms of intimidation to secure the leases for shrimp production, and the landowners rarely receive the promised returns. In consequence, some land-owners have attempted to establish their own shrimp farms with the goal of securing all of the returns for themselves. Disputes around entitlement to land use have not been conflict free, but we have a duty to protect our respondents' interests, so we do not include details here. In short, relative political power has influenced how such disputes have been adjudicated.

Furthermore, shrimp production changed the political economy in ways that exacerbated inequalities among poor people. Shrimp aquaculture is much less labour intensive than either rice or cash crop cultivation. Additionally, one important shrimp cultivation job is guarding the shrimp ponds from theft. Concerned about the reluctance of shrimp guards to accuse their fellow villagers, family members or local elites, the shrimp farmers (particularly industrial-scale shrimp farmers) hired people from outside the local community. Thus, low-wage workers were brought in to do the low-wage labour of shrimp farming, displacing locals who would have worked on the same fields if they had been designated for rice or cash crop cultivation. Furthermore, the shrimp industry has a supply chain that does not favour those doing most of the work. Some people earn wages that are comparable to day wages in other sectors – 200–250 taka (about US$3US) per day. However, at the bottom of the supply chain, those who collect and sell shrimp fry generally sell them to middlemen on a per-shrimp basis and earn less than the typical day wage. In short, the shrimp industry provides low-wage employment for some poor people (though mostly not for locals) and forces others to find other sources of work.

The introduction of shrimp farming caused other shifts in the local political economy that have reduced the options available to those who face a family crisis, such as ill health or a work injury. In a rice economy, people tend to have savings in the form of stores of rice which can be exchanged between households. By contrast, most shrimp farmers make an upfront investment with which they purchase inputs (shrimp fry) from a middleman who then buys the back the fully grown shrimp at a price that was fixed at the time of the loan. Because of this lending structure, some small landowners convert to shrimp farming after a personal event causes them to borrow money. In this system, the shrimp dealer loans money on the promise of shrimp production, while the need to pay back the loan with interest ties the new shrimp farmer to his lender–dealer.

Increasing reliance on seasonal migration, local day labour in construction, long-term migration

Displaced people may shift to wage labour in the local fishing economy, migrate for seasonal agricultural work or migrate to work in shrimp processing or garment factories for a few years. Some of these opportunities existed prior to the growth in shrimping. Both kinds of factory work have been supported by growth in these export sectors near the cities.

Shrimping impacts the political economy in additional ways that are not directly connected to the supply chain for shrimp, but rather to the growing trend of seasonal migration. Where rice fields have been converted to shrimp and cash crops, local rice is less available. Families with some savings send a husband for seasonal employment in rice cultivation in other parts of Bangladesh, including Gopalgonj, Dumuria and Norail, for which they are paid in rice. These husbands enable their families to have rice even though they cannot cultivate rice or earn enough money to buy rice at home.

While Cyclone Aila further reduced the range of livelihood options in the region by reducing the availability of day labour in shrimping and agriculture in all but a few communities in the north-east (which were able to return to cash crop production in one season), through an indirect effect the cyclone increased the possibility of seasonal migration – and thus a potential new source of income – for poorer families. There are two costs of seasonal migration: the transportation cost and the cost of sustaining the family in the absence of the migrated worker. A family cannot even consider sending a husband to labour without savings to cover both.

As we saw in the previous section, post-Aila construction projects introduced new day labour opportunities, especially for women. The availability of local work for women facilitated seasonal migration for their husbands, even among families with limited savings. With a wife earning a day wage that was sufficient to feed the family, some families with no savings were able to send their husbands or sons to seasonal agricultural employment. They generally returned with payments in the form of rice. Although the jobs created by post-disaster construction and foreign aid more generally are often much needed, such employment opportunities can be parasitic and/or exacerbate community power dynamics.

The human rights effects of slow-onset and rapid-onset environmental change are mediated by the dynamics of the political and economic rights and their consequences for local employment opportunities. Opportunities for employment through migration form part of these dynamics. Therefore, as we argue in the next section, it is just as important to consider the ways in which human rights *conditions* affect the impact of environmental change on people as it is to consider the ways in which environmental change affects human rights.

Implications: human rights, livelihoods and migration effects

In this chapter, we have focused on the dynamics of environmental and economic change in a region that is currently experiencing environmental conditions that will likely become more widespread in the future. We have provided evidence that there is a firm basis for using a human rights lens for thinking about the injustices caused by climate change. Rising sea levels threaten homesteads and livelihoods; storms threaten homes and lives. However, our discussion also shows that the 'threat' to human rights comes not from particular changes or events, but rather from the dynamics in the political economy that affect the extent to which people can survive such threats. In this conclusion, we highlight the implications of these findings: that while certain rights – to food, water, health, housing and life – are threatened by the anticipated impacts of climate change, a continuing absence of democratic and economic rights will exacerbate those threats. We begin by focusing on food, water, health, housing and life, and the role of migration in relation to these, which our data support. We further argue that the human rights implications of climate change are more fully understood if we consider the context of enjoyment of rights.[14]

Some of the effects of environmental change on human rights are direct, such as when Cyclone Aila caused loss of life, livestock, livelihoods, homes and drinking water. However, the indirect effects and complex interactions among environmental, social, economic and political conditions, as well as the ways in which power inequalities may be exploited (for example, to effect one's will over land use within a polder), can be even more pernicious. If we focus solely on migration's immediate human rights-related causes, then we miss the more pernicious human rights violations. In the context of mass migration, political inequalities may migrate with communities or affect the distribution of the range of options for community members.

Likewise, we have seen migration function as a way of dealing with environmental change and opportunities for migration facilitated by the political response of construction to environmental disaster. These are also indirect, as when Cyclone Aila destroyed embankments, which created opportunities for local employment, which in turn allowed husbands to migrate for seasonal agricultural work, for which they were paid in rice, so they could feed their families despite the transformation in the local economy from rice farming to shrimping (in the south) or cash crops (in the north) and regardless of fluctuations in the price of staples.[15]

In light of the direct and indirect effects of environmental change on human rights and migration, the latter is not only an indicator of human rights violations but also a means of dealing with these violations. This poses difficult challenges for how we study changes in patterns of migration due to slow-onset and rapid-onset environmental change.

In south-western Bangladesh, embankments themselves have no political power, but they can enhance landowners' and the political elite's power to control the range of employment opportunities in their communities, depending on how they are designed and used. By altering the physical landscape, embankments also alter the social, economic and political landscapes by defining the spaces in which people live, travel, farm and fish. By supporting embankment-based climate change mitigation and economic development, the government of Bangladesh and the country's international donors are creating economic opportunities and investing in environmental protection. However, the benefits of these are distributed through existing power structures, such that they might ameliorate or exacerbate existing economic and political power inequalities surrounding the construction, maintenance and control of the embankments.

Both elites and villagers within our study communities believe that the decision-making related to the construction and use of the embankments is controlled by political elites locally and nationally and by economic elites locally and in the shrimp industry. A range of actors influence these dynamics. Outside of the community are government officials, foreign donors and lenders, the members of an economic elite who lease shrimp ponds and employ workers in factories or in large-scale agriculture, and the courts that adjudicate on land titles. Inside the community, there are local government leaders, water committees, informal adjudicatory bodies, money lenders and other middlemen, and landowners.

The point for human rights considerations is to recognise that the embankments, combined with the complex dynamics of social, economic, environmental and political forces, create or exacerbate potentially exploitable inequalities. By considering the indirect human rights effects of environmental change, we highlight that the threats to human rights are not only threats to individual rights to life, health, food, water and housing, but also threats to democratic political equality. In this study, we have seen that the underlying political economies, more than slow-onset environmental changes or disastrous environmental events, are threatening Bangladeshis' human rights and pushing Bangladeshis to incorporate migration strategies into their livelihood strategies. This means that in order for climate adaptation and mitigation strategies to benefit local populations, they must consider their impacts on local political economies, and particularly on the advantages and disadvantages *within those local populations*, as well as across the nation. How these plans are implemented and to whom their management is accountable will have significant impacts on local livelihoods, perceptions of political security and migration.

Whereas sea-level rise over the past half-century has been sufficiently slow to allow sediment deposition on unpoldered lands to keep up, global warming is expected to accelerate sea-level rise to unprecedented rates, such that large areas are likely to be inundated, regardless of local land-use practices. This change implies that in many places the socio-ecological dynamics over the coming century are likely to be very different from those of today.

As sea-level rise accelerates, embankments may be insufficient to preserve many of the coastal islands, and entire populations may be displaced. The inequalities in these communities will be one of the challenges to their resettlement. A much greater fraction of Bangladesh's population lives further inland, where we expect the dynamics we describe here to play out with greater intensity in the future. The interplay between environmental change and the changing social, political and economic context of affected communities will vary from place to place and over time, but the importance of this interplay will remain crucial to understanding the impacts of and responses to environmental change and their human rights implications.

The environmental changes witnessed in south-western Bangladesh – erosion of land, infilling of waterways and increasing threat of flooding and saline inundation from the coast, floods and cyclones – are just some of the conditions that are expected to increase with climate change. By focusing on the dynamics of the indirect causes of human rights implications of these changes and of their relationship to other social, economic and political dynamics that are not explicitly related to climate change, we can see the importance of addressing climate change as a matter of development and justice and not considering these as discrete areas of expertise or policy design. Climate change policy that does not take into account the justness of the development plans it includes will exacerbate the human rights-violating consequences of climate change, not ameliorate them. Migration will be part of this story, but not an unmediated solution to the problems associated with climate change.

Notes

1 This chapter shares insights published in Bangladesh: B. Ackerly, M. Anam and J. Gilligan, 'Environment, Migration and Adaptation: Evidence and Politics of Climate Change in Bangladesh' in B. Mallick and B. Etzold (eds), *Environment, Migration and Adaptation: Evidence and Politics of Climate Change in Bangladesh* (AHDPH 2015).
2 Human Rights and Equal Opportunity Commission (HREOC) *Background Paper: Human Rights and Climate Change* (2008) 1.
3 UN General Assembly, 'Agenda Item 2' (2009) A/HRC/10/61 HRC.
4 This research is part of ISEE Bangladesh (www.vanderbilt.edu/ISEEBangladesh), a multi-disciplinary, multi-university (Vanderbilt, Columbia, Dhaka, Khulna and Jahangirnagar) project studying community and regional resilience to environmental change in the context of coastal Bangladesh. The partnership is funded by the US Office of Naval Research (Vanderbilt IRB approval 120454). The study includes the study of the sedimentology, hydrology, sociology, economics and politics in historical perspective from qualitative and quantitative sources. Additional data collection and analysis are still ongoing. Other persons whose efforts significantly contributed to the data analysed in this article include Leslie Wallace Auerbach (physical), John Ayers (physical), Sayed Md Saikh Imtiaz (social field research), Bishawjit Mallick (social) and Anna Carella (social). Preliminary research by Bina D'Costa and Gouranga Nandy was essential for site selection.
5 See, for example, H. Murakami, M. Sugi and A. Kitoh, 'Future Changes in Tropical Cyclone Activity in the North Indian Ocean Projected by the New High-Resolution MRI-AGCM' in M. Mohapatra *et al.* (eds) *Monitoring and Prediction of Tropical Cyclones in the Indian Ocean and Climate Change* (Springer 2014) 253–271.
6 L. Benneyworth *et al.*, 'Drinking Water Insecurity: Water Quality and Access in Coastal South-Western Bangladesh' (2016) 26(5–6) *International Journal of Environmental Health Research* 1; T. Gunda, L. Benneyworth and E. Burchfield, 'Exploring Water Indices and Associated Parameters: A Case Study Approach' (2015) 17(1) *Water Policy* 98.
7 Generally, the meso level is between large-scale macro forces, such as economics, politics and social norms, and the micro scale of individual economic, political and social interactions. For the purposes of this study, the meso level is synonymous with community, which we define as indicated in the text through those sharing geographic, political and social institutions and activities. We will argue that, despite formal entitlements in law, human rights may or may not be enjoyed in communities. See B. A. Ackerly, 'Human Rights Enjoyment in Theory and Activism' (2011) 12(2) *Human Rights Review*; B. A. Ackerly and J. M. Cruz, 'Hearing the Voice of the People: Human Rights as if People Mattered' (2011) 33(1) *New Political Science*; B. A. Ackerly, J. Gilligan and S. Goodbred, 'From

Coastal Bangladesh: Climate Change, Migration and the Importance of Community Level Analysis for Using Human Rights to Guide "New" Legal Frameworks' (2012) paper prepared for COST Action programme IS1101.

8 H. Brammer, 'After the Bangladesh Flood Action Plan: Looking to the Future' (2010) 9(1) *Environmental Hazards*; H. Brammer, 'Bangladesh's Dynamic Coastal Regions and Sea-Level Rise' (2014) 1 *Climate Risk Management*.

9 http://landsat.usgs.gov accessed 25 October 2016.

10 J. Pethick and J. D. Orford, 'Rapid Rise in Effective Sea-Level in Southwest Bangladesh: Its Causes and Contemporary Rates' (2013) 111 *Global and Planetary Change*.

11 L. W. Auerbach *et al.*, 'Flood Risk of Natural and Embanked Landscapes on the Ganges–Brahmaputra Tidal Delta Plain' (2015) 5 *Nature Climate Change*.

12 Ibid. Details in supplementary data (C. Wilson, S. Goodbred, C. Small, J. Gilligan and S. Sams, 'Widespread Infilling of Tidal Channels and Navigable Waterways in Human-Modified Delta Plain of Southwest Bangladesh', submitted to *PNAS Sustainability Science*).

13 Our observations are consistent with a longitudinal study of land use in one village (A. M. S. Ali, 'Rice to Shrimp: Land Use/Land Cover Changes and Soil Degradation in Southwestern Bangladesh' (2006) 23(4) *Land Use Policy*) and a comparative study of disaster and migration in two villages (C. L. Gray and V. Mueller, 'Natural Disasters and Population Mobility in Bangladesh' (2012) 109(16) *Proceedings of the National Academy of Sciences*). Studies by NGOs seek to explore the complexity of these dynamics and their impact on rights (Environmental Justice Foundation (EJF), *A Nation under Threat: The Impacts of Climate Change on Human Rights and Forced Migration in Bangladesh* (2012)). Due to the combination of physical and social data, we are able to provide insights into these dynamics as they relate to each other.

14 S. Caney, 'Human Rights, Responsibilities, and Climate Change' in C. R. Beitz and R. E. Goodin (eds), *Global Basic Rights* (Oxford University Press 2009); Environmental Justice Foundation (EJF), *Climate Change Migration Human Rights* (2011). For a review of UN human rights resolutions and reports related to the environment and human rights, see United Nations Mandate on Human Rights and the Environment (John H. Knox, UN Special Rapporteur), 'UN Documents' (n.d.) http://srenvironment.org/un-documents accessed 25 October 2016.

15 On the rights-based dimensions of changes in the global food economy, see B. A. Ackerly, *Just Responsibility: A Human Rights Theory of Global Justice* (Oxford University Press forthcoming).

13 Labour mobility options as adaptation strategies to environmental changes?

Elisa Fornalé[1]

Introduction

The international community has devoted substantial effort to understanding the concrete impact of environmental degradation (defined as slow-onset environmental degradation, such as rising sea levels, increased salinisation, desertification and soil or coastal erosion) on human mobility and to fostering research to identify migration, in particular labour mobility, as a positive adaptation strategy.[2] For example, the latest report of the Intergovernmental Panel on Climate Change (IPCC) focuses on human mobility, noting that:

> climate change is projected to increase the displacement of people throughout this century. The risk of displacement increases when populations who lack the resources to migrate experience higher exposure to extreme weather events, in both rural and urban areas, particularly in low-income developing countries. Changes in migration patterns can be responses to both extreme weather events and longer-term climate variability and change, and migration can also be an effective adaptation strategy.[3]

In line with this statement, a major achievement of the 2012 Conference of the Parties (COP18) to the UN Framework Convention on Climate Change (UNFCCC) was the adoption of paragraph 7(a)(vi) of the draft decision, which links migration and the emerging issue of 'loss and damage' by acknowledging the need for further research and work towards 'enhancing the understanding of … [h]ow impacts of climate change are affecting patterns of migration, displacement and human mobility'.[4] More recently, the adoption of the Paris Agreement in December 2015 established a new mechanism – the Task Force on Displacement – with the aim to 'develop recommendations for integrated approaches to avert, minimise and address displacement related to the adverse impacts of climate change'.[5] Over the course of the next two years, this Task Force will elaborate and identify innovative measures to address the impact of climate change, in particular human mobility from affected countries.

Equally, the outcomes of the Nansen Initiative's[6] consultations in the Pacific, Central America and the Greater Horn of Africa focused on the migration–environment nexus and reflect the scientific consensus regarding its reality, urgency and significance.[7] The Nansen Initiative's Protection Agenda, adopted in October 2015, highlights significant legal gaps related to cross-border displacement in the context of disasters linked to natural hazards, including critical issues such as 'admission, access to basic services during temporary or permanent stay, and conditions for return'.[8]

The European Commission has further situated the discussion within the context of migration law, as well as international law, suggesting that 'facilitating well-managed mobility and labour mobility from environmentally degraded areas can represent an effective strategy to reduce environmentally induced displacement'.[9] Likewise, the Advisory Group on Climate Change and Human Mobility (hereinafter the Advisory Group) has noted that 'voluntary migration, whether circular, temporary, or permanent, can be a potentially positive form of adaptation to climate change'.[10] Although it is a global problem, the impact of climate change on human mobility will not be uniform within countries, and therefore it may be relevant to explore and identify different 'entry points' with a view to formulating appropriate and flexible strategies.[11]

In this regard, this chapter examines the potential of existing mobility options for reducing the vulnerability of affected communities by strengthening the nexus between human mobility regimes and climate change-related policies. In the past decade, a growing body of literature[12] has contributed to a broader conceptualisation of mobility by welcoming the idea that migration can be a legitimate 'adaptation strategy'.[13] In this context, the emerging debate on the environment–migration nexus relies on economic development and labour markets to foster resilience.[14] Drawing on this approach, the chapter analyses the potential of existing avenues and tools that are available to facilitate mobility. The focus of the analysis will be on a case study of the Pacific Island Countries and the negotiations that have taken place in the context of trade-related measures to expand labour mobility channels. It is crucial to explore the added value that the progressive liberalisation of the temporary movement of natural persons as service suppliers may have for affected nations as a measure that can be used to complement traditional avenues of migration policy.

Environmental degradation and mobility strategies

Slow-onset environmental degradation may generate diverse migratory outcomes: in some cases forced migration may occur for survival, whereas in others voluntary migration may be an efficient adaptation strategy.[15] In particular, the estimates of actual and expected flows as a result of slow-onset environmental changes suggest that the pressure towards labour mobility across countries will increase.[16]

It is undisputed that individuals who are displaced across international borders as a result of environmental changes are especially vulnerable to human and economic losses and impacts,[17] as well as to numerous protection and institutional gaps that arise because they do not have access to the same legal protection as other vulnerable groups.[18] The Advisory Group identifies human mobility as a 'positive coping and survival strategy' and recognises its potential to improve the 'adaptive capacity' of affected communities by developing 'context-specific solutions'.[19] Thus, facilitating and increasing labour mobility options can complement and support unilateral initiatives developed by states, either on their own or as a group.[20]

In this regard, Bettini *et al.* (2016) highlight how the emerging discourse on 'migration as adaptation' is helping to reorient the development of 'individualised' adaptation processes.[21] In their analysis, they argue that the relationship between climate change and migration has the potential to contribute to shifting rights, duties and state responsibility regarding economic development and delegating responsibility to the labour market, but they raise concern that this can "represent a step backwards of the possibility of posing the question of justice".[22] In this new context, they describe how the discourse around individual agency highlights that migrants may increase their resilience by securing access to the labour market. Conversely, the role of the state and the international community is 'to govern the movement of labour migrants in order for them to undertake adaptation measures and secure themselves'.[23] In other words, the current debate provides an interpretation of 'migration as adaptation' that will no longer identify migrants as victims of environmental degradation but as 'agents of adaptation'.[24] Such an interpretation can help understanding of how existing mobility regimes become strategic in their adaptation process.[25]

To complement this analysis, the aim of this chapter is therefore to explore the possible implications of conceiving migrants as a form of 'mobile labour power'[26] and how existing instruments can be reconfigured to ensure that mobility regimes positively foster resilience and so indirectly protect human rights.[27]

Human mobility and adaptation in the Pacific

As part of this debate, the Pacific Island Countries (PICs)[28] are becoming aware that they need to explore sustainable solutions to deal with issues linked with environmental degradation, such as increased unemployment.[29] This is the case, for instance, for Kiribati and Tuvalu, which are particularly 'affected by climate change, and which cannot rely on domestic industries'.[30] Eberhard (2012) has emphasised that migration strategies have been widely and traditionally used by the citizens of low-lying states and that, rather than focusing on statelessness, the contemporary debate needs to focus on how to remove obstacles for the legal admission of citizens of affected states to countries of destination, and how to secure their acceptance and integration within these countries.[31]

Moreover, the implementation of different migration schemes may play a relevant role in preventing forced displacement and promoting voluntary movement from at-risk areas.[32] As discussed further in this chapter, there is now a pluralised normative framework of labour mobility negotiations in the Pacific. The PICs are implementing and negotiating labour migratory instruments at the bilateral, regional and multilateral levels, and the following analysis will discuss the relevance of these instruments for individual countries.[33] As Kagan (2015) stated recently:

> not all Pacific island countries are created equal when it comes to employment creation. Some countries have natural resources that can drive respectable employment growth. Some have the right climate and conditions to attract tourists, even within a niche tourism market. Others have colonial connections that ensure some level of migration or trade with Australia, New Zealand and the US.[34]

In addition, some countries, such as Kiribati, recognise the need to enhance growth in entrepreneurial development of human capital to ensure that their citizens have the appropriate skills to contribute to the economy of their potential country of destination.[35] The lack of adequate investment in skills development or qualifications may also affect the equal access of Pacific islanders to different countries and labour markets.[36]

Overview of existing labour mobility programmes

Contemporary cross-border migration exhibits three main trends: migration from PICs to countries of the Pacific Rim (e.g. New Zealand and Australia); migratory flows between New Zealand and Australia; and intra-regional mobility between PICs.[37] Migration has played a particular role throughout the history of the Pacific region and it has taken many different forms, but, as Kagan (2015) has emphasised, 'labour migration management remains underdeveloped' and the improvement of migration management has been identified as a regional and global goal to ensure decent work for migrants.[38]

This section highlights some of the main concerns and challenges to developing successful mobility programmes, and considers whether current mobility programmes may be adjusted to allow people affected by natural disasters, including environmental degradation, to move voluntarily from the affected settings.

First, there is a growing migration jigsaw puzzle, formed by the different programmes and schemes that are already in place, which can result in a fragmented normative environment and make the migration opportunities for PIC citizens very different and unequal. Most of the existing migration schemes take the form of unilateral and voluntary commitments, meaning that 'migrant-receiving governments establish rules that employers must follow in order to receive permission to have legal foreign workers admitted'.[39] In these frameworks, employers are gaining more and more control over administration of the schemes by asserting or attesting their need for foreign workers. In addition, as noted by Martin (2015), these temporary or guest foreign worker programmes aim at rotating temporary workers in and out of the countries of destination without adding permanent residents to the population.[40] In this context, the migration agreements developed by PICs with their neighbours, New Zealand and Australia, are of particular interest.

In 2007, New Zealand started the Recognised Seasonal Employer (RSE) programme, which allowed up to 8,000 persons annually temporary entry to work in seasonal agricultural jobs. The New Zealand Department of Labour (2007) stated that one main objective of this programme was to 'encourage economic development, regional integration and good governance within the Pacific, by allowing preferential access to workers who are citizens of eligible Pacific countries'.[41] According to the World Bank, 24,600 workers had participated in this scheme by 2014, and 'more than half of workers returned at least once, and 23 per cent of workers have participated in all seasons'.[42] The scheme is open to all countries, although there is a definite Pacific preference. As Burson and Bedford (2013) point out, according to this scheme, 'workers need to be recruited by New Zealand employers and the scheme is completely demand-driven'.[43] Recently, New Zealand decided to increase the annual cap from 8,000 to 9,500, which can be explained as a direct effect of Fiji's entry into the RSE programme and of the impact of the PACER Plus negotiations (see below). In consequence, the percentage of Pacific workers recruited under the scheme increased from "74 per cent in 2009–2010 to 85 per cent in 2014–2015".[44]

In 2012, Australia started the Seasonal Worker Programme (SWP) after the completion of the Pacific Seasonal Worker Pilot Scheme (PSWPS).[45] At first, 2,500 visas were offered to citizens from Papua New Guinea, Kiribati, Vanuatu, Tonga, Samoa, the Solomon Islands, Tuvalu, Nauru and East Timor for unskilled temporary work, mainly in the horticultural industry. The number of visas was subsequently increased.[46]

In 2008, an interesting study, designed by the World Bank with the New Zealand Department of Labour and the University of Waikato, raised some specific concerns about how the RSE was operating in practice.[47] In particular, the study highlighted poor knowledge of some specific conditions of the programme – for example, employers' obligations. Similar concerns about lack of knowledge were raised in a study of the Australian schemes.[48] In addition, available data have revealed increasing obstacles to implementing these schemes for technical reasons. For instance, high transportation costs from specific island nations, such as Vanuatu and Kiribati, may affect their citizens' ability to benefit from such schemes.

Speaking at a workshop attended by Pacific labour and trade officials in 2014, officials from New Zealand's Ministry of Business, Innovation and Employment indicated that the RSE programme was resource-intensive and costly, and that it would be difficult to extend it to other sectors.[49] For this reason, it was suggested that there is a need to explore additional labour mobility opportunities that could make a more significant contribution to combining the needs of the PICs and industrial labour.

Following on from this, significant progress has been made by the government of Australia, which adopted a White Paper in 2015 to remove existing caps on the number of migrant workers involved in temporary mobility schemes.[50] This instrument built on the government's previously stated intention to expand the SWP. The White Paper also proposed the establishment of a five-year pilot programme for 250 workers from Kiribati, Nauru and Tuvalu (that is, around 50 workers per year). This will introduce a multi-year visa for work in non-seasonal industries and occupations in Northern Australia.

With respect to the potential of these temporary programmes to deal with environmentally induced migration, it seems unlikely that they will resolve the issue because all of the schemes are 'completely demand-driven'. There is no option for a Pacific citizen to make an independent application; he or she must be recruited by an employer.[51] Also relevant is the absence of any option to transfer from temporary to long-term migration status in the country of destination. In this regard, the main countries of destination, such as Australia, could agree to foster labour mobility beyond the SWP – for instance, by introducing a Pacific Access Quota, as proposed by the World Bank.[52] The Pacific Access Category, adopted by New Zealand, has introduced a special quota for citizens from small island states (including their partners and children) to encourage permanent labour migration to New Zealand.[53]

The coverage of temporary movement of natural persons by trade agreements

Since 1981, PICs have been involved in trade negotiations at the regional levels.[54] However, only recently has the issue of labour mobility started to gain increasing relevance in the trade in services negotiation process. In fact, PICs are trying to increase and diversify their citizens' mobility options by including specific coverage of 'temporary movement of natural persons' in a variety of trade agreements.[55] This option could increase the number of opportunities available to cope with some of the impacts of climate change that are already happening, even if no formal linkages are made between labour mobility and environmental degradation.

As explained above, seasonal mobility schemes implemented by countries of destination, such as Australia and New Zealand, are limited. As highlighted by the Chief Trade Negotiator, Dr Edwini Kessie, the island nations are making specific demands first to increase the annual caps and then to extend the schemes to other sectors (e.g. care of the elderly, trade, mining, seafaring and tourism).[56]

Of great relevance in this context was the negotiation process for the adoption of the Pacific Agreement on Closer Economic Relations (PACER Plus) between the Pacific countries and Australia and New Zealand. The

Pacific countries identified labour mobility as a key priority.[57] As the Office of the Chief Trade Adviser (OCTA) argued:

> due to the economic differences between the parties and the fact that FICs [Forum Island Countries] stood to gain very little, if at all, from their liberalisation commitments in trade in goods, services and invest-ment, PACER Plus had to contain substantive commitments on labour mobility and development assistance.[58]

Edwini Kessie has noted that, to address the concerns raised by the government of Fiji, '[b]oth Australia and New Zealand have undertaken commitments which should facilitate the movement of skilled and semi-skilled workers in the PACER Plus area'.[59] The OCTA subsequently made a presentation in June 2016, during the sixth Non-State Actors' dialogue on the status of the PACER Plus negotiations, in which the focus was once again on labour mobility. The potential of this process to generate reciprocal advantages and facilitate the adoption of new forms of labour mobility was highlighted.[60]

Indeed, as Oxfam has stressed, a key element for Pacific countries regarding labour mobility for migrant workers under PACER Plus was the inclusion of binding obligations that will prevent Australia and New Zealand from unilaterally terminating programmes, as could happen with the seasonal schemes.[61] In fact, as Kelsey (2009) has highlighted, 'existing commitments on mode 4 and labour mobility show there are very limited precedents for binding and enforceable rights of access from the Pacific Islands, and none for workers with low skills or education'.[62]

A key question during the negotiations was whether the coverage of temporary movement of natural persons would include labour mobility for unskilled workers. Even if formal commitments under Mode 4 of the General Agreement on Trade in Services (GATS) in free trade agreements (FTAs) are traditionally confined to categories of high-skilled suppliers of services, there are some interesting precedents in recent FTAs concluded by Australia and New Zealand. In particular, the Association of Southeast Asian Nations (ASEAN)–Australia–New Zealand FTA (concluded in 2010) encompasses semi-skilled and technical workers by including the category of 'installers and services'.[63]

Furthermore, an interesting model is provided by the China–New Zealand FTA (concluded in 2008), in which commitments on temporary movement are contained in two separate annexes – the Annex on Temporary Employment Entry of Natural Persons and the Annex on Temporary Movement of Natural Persons – which provide opportunities to enter New Zealand for employment purposes in addition to the opportunities provided under the country's immigration policy.[64] In this agreement, categories of service suppliers include semi-skilled workers as well as skilled workers. Even if there is no agreed definition of this distinction, it was important for Pacific countries to ensure that access to New Zealand's and Australia's labour markets is offered not only to skilled migrants but also to lower-skilled service providers.

The temporary movement of natural persons has also been included in the negotiations for the Pacific Island Countries' Trade Agreement – Trade in Services to increase labour mobility and skills transfer in the region (PICTA TIS). The Pacific countries agreed to draft and adopt a scheme for the temporary movement of natural persons (the TMNP Protocol) with the the PICTA trade in services protocol (TIS).[65] This protocol covers the temporary mobility of highly skilled (Tier 1) but also skilled and semi-skilled (Tier 2) workers for temporary employment of up to three years.[66] As the Observatory on Migration (2013) has pointed out, this regulatory framework has the potential to increase circular mobility in the region by contributing to the establishment of a single regional labour market.[67] The protocol could thus assist in reducing vulnerability and enhancing the adaptive capacity of those faced with environmental degradation.

However, the Observatory on Migration's report also stresses that the scheme does not provide a comprehensive response to the 'protection gaps' raised by environment-induced migration. First, this model can facilitate the temporary mobility of skilled migrants, but this cannot be converted into permanent residence.[68] Second, the TMNP Protocol attempts to address social security issues, but additional steps must be taken at the bilateral level to draft and implement social security regimes. Finally, the scheme requires both the country of origin and the country of destination to play active roles, and some countries of origin may not have appropriate domestic regulations in place. In addition, the Pacific Island Forum Secretariat recommended the inclusion in PICTA of international provisions and standards to protect migrant workers' rights, as outlined within the International Labour Organization Convention and the United Nations' Convention on Migrant Workers and Member of Their Families.[69]

To conclude this overview, we should recall that the Melanesian Spearhead Group (MSG)[70] adopted a regional trade agreement. This was followed in 2012 by the Skills Movement Scheme's (SMS) Memorandum of Understanding, which addressed the temporary movement of highly skilled workers. The purpose of the SMS is to:

- strengthen regional cooperation and integration by providing access to employment opportunities and to facilitate the movement of MSG nationals among the parties;
- ensure and promote decent work practices among the parties; and
- bring mutual benefits to the parties by the movement of skilled nationals.[71]

This instrument has been recognised as the first 'intra-regional mobility scheme'.[72] It allows up to 400 citizens of committed members to move temporarily to another member state for work reasons.[73] Even if its relevance in the region has been defined as more 'symbolic than substantive' because of its low impact, it can be used as a frame of reference to improve the architecture of labour mobility at the inter-regional level and to meet skills shortages.

The Memorandum of Understanding contains some inspiring provisions for the temporary employment of migrant workers: Clause 6.2 requires parties to develop and objective criteria for its implementation; Clause 9.11 demands respect for the principle of non-discrimination in facilitating the entry and residence of migrant workers; and Clauses 12.1 and 12.2 encourage each member state to observe international human rights and labour protection standards.[74]

Conclusion

This analysis has provided a brief introduction to existing migration agreements in the Pacific region to explore the potential of migration as an adaptation strategy in response to environmental degradation. Concentrating on the mobility schemes developed by small island states, the chapter reveals a clear lack of comprehensive instruments that are able to provide specific responses in this context. The normative scenario is highly fragmented, and the current migration programmes will need to be revised to address limitations that risk impeding the mobility of potential environmental migrants. Temporary mobility schemes, such as seasonal programmes, remain the most widely adopted schemes for facilitating labour mobility, but challenges persist in consolidating them with Australia and New Zealand and translating them into binding agreements. For instance, the mechanisms in place will benefit from progressive flexibility in allocating quotas, as in the case of the government of Australia's latest programme. The core rationale of these schemes is to rotate foreign workers in and out to fill vacant positions without allowing them to become 'free agents' in the labour market, and this can have an impact on the adaptation efforts of affected populations. In fact, the schemes that are currently in place have allowed employers to make decisions on how and whether to recruit migrants beyond a country's borders.

In addition, the focus on labour mobility in the trade context, together with the TMNP Protocol, is a potential framework to facilitate the mobility of skilled migrant workers across the region. However, if the PACER Plus will not increase the cross-border mobility of less skilled workers, then new, alternative migratory mechanisms will have to be devised. Given the existing mechanisms' inability to absorb environmentally induced mobility, a key element when retooling or redesigning migratory schemes must be to ensure that the concerns and priorities of affected populations are paramount in the development of the international agenda.

Notes

1 SNSF Professor at the World Trade Institute, University of Bern. The chapter is based on the Global Knowledge Partnership in Migration and Development (KNOMAD) Working Paper 'The Future Role of Labour Mobility Mechanisms in the Context of Environmental Degradation: Building or Crumbling Adaptation Strategies' (forthcoming). The author is grateful for the invaluable comments of Dr Edwini Kessie. Contact: elisa.fornale@wti.org.

2 W. Kälin and N. Schrepfer, 'Protecting People Crossing Borders in the Context of Climate Change: Normative Gaps and Possible Approaches' (2012) UNHCR Legal and Protection Policy Research Series; Special Rapporteur on the Human Rights of Migrants, *Human Rights of Migrants* (United Nations 2012) UNGA A/67/299.

3 Intergovernmental Panel on Climate Change (IPCC), *Climate Change 2014: Impacts, Adaptation, and Vulnerability. Part A: Global and Sectoral Aspects, Contribution to the Fifth Assessment Report of the Intergovernmental Panel on Climate Change* (2014) www.ipcc.ch/report/ar5/wg2 accessed 25 October 2016.

4 Daria Mokhnacheva, Sieun Lee and Dina Ionesco, *Moving in the Right Direction? Assessing Progress in Doha: Migration in Climate Change Negotiations* (2013), Migration Policy Practice Vol. III N.1 11-14. http://unfccc.int/resource/docs/2012/cop18/eng/08a01.pdf.

5 The Conference of the Parties (COP), at its nineteenth session, established the Warsaw International Mechanism to address loss and damage associated with the adverse effects of climate change. The COP (2015), asked the Executive Committee of the Warsaw International Mechanism "to establish, according to its procedures and mandate, a task force to complement, draw upon the work of and involve, as appropriate, existing bodies and expert groups under the Convention including the Adaptation Committee and the Least Developed Countries Expert Group, as well as relevant organisations and expert bodies outside the Convention, to develop recommendations for integrated approaches to avert, minimise and address displacement related to the adverse impacts of climate change" Conference of the Parties, Twenty-first session, Agenda item 4b, Durban Platform for Enhanced Action (decision 1/CP/17), Adoption of the Paris Agreement (adopted 12 December 2015, entered into force 4 November 2016) FCCC/CP/2015/L.9/Rev.1).

6 The Nansen Initiative was conceived as 'a state-led consultative process to build consensus on a protection agenda addressing the needs of people displaced across borders in the context of disasters and the effects of climate change'. This process started in 2012 and ended in 2015 with the adoption of the 'Protection Agenda' (see note 8).

7 W. Kälin, 'From the Nansen Principles to the Nansen Initiative' (2012) 41 *Forced Migration Review* 48–49.

8 Nansen Initiative (the), *Agenda for the Protection of Cross-Border Displaced Persons in the Context of Disasters and Climate Change* (2015) Volume I 18.

9 European Commission (EC), 'Communication from the Commission to the European Parliament, the Council, the European Economic and Social Committee and the Committee of the Regions: An EU Strategy on Adaptation to Climate Change' (2013) COM (2013) 216 final 26; Albert Kraler, Tatiana Cernei, Marion Noack, *Climate Refugees' Legal and Political Responses to Environmentally Induced Migration* (2011) Study, European Parliament, Directorate-General for Internal Policies.

10 Advisory Group on Climate Change and Human Mobility (AGCCHM), 'Human Mobility in the Context of Climate Change: Recommendations from the Advisory Group on Climate Change and Human Mobility COP 20. Lima. Peru' (2015) https://www.iom.int/files/live/sites/iom/files/pbn/docs/Human-Mobility-in-the-context-of-Climate-Change.pdf accessed 25 October 2016 9.

11 Ibid.

12 UK Government Office for Science, *Foresight: Migration and Global Environmental Change: Final Project Report* (2011); R. McLeman, *Climate Change and Human Migration: Past Experiences, Future Challenges* (Cambridge University Press 2014); D. Ionesco, D. Mokhnacheva and F. Gemenne, *Atlas des migrations environnementales* (Presses de Science Po 2016).

13 In this chapter, we follow the definition adopted by the Nansen Initiative for 'migration', as the "preponderantly" voluntary decision ""to avoid or to adjust" deteriorating environmental conditions that could otherwise result in a humanitarian crisis and displacement in the future" (Nansen Initiative (the), *Agenda* para. 20).

14 G. Bettini, S. L. Nash and G. Gioli, 'One Step Forward, Two Steps Back? The Fading Contours of (In)Justice in Competing Discourses on Climate Migration' (2016) *Geographical Journal*, available at http://onlinelibrary.wiley.com/doi/10.1111/geoj.12192/full.

15 International Organization for Migration (IOM), *Climate Change, Environmental Degradation and Migration* (2012) International Dialogue on Migration No. 18.

16 EC, 'Communication from the Commission'; Kraler, Cernei, Noack, *Climate Refugees' Legal and Political Responses*.

17 J. McAdam, *Climate Change, Forced Migration, and International Law* (Oxford University Press 2012).

18 Kälin, 'Nansen Principles'.

19 AGCCHM, 'Human Mobility' 5.

20 Ibid.

21 Bettini *et al.*, 'One Step Forward, Two Steps Back?'.

22 Ibid.

23 Ibid.

24 F. Gemenne and J. Blocher, "How Can Migration Support Adaptation? Challenges to fleshing out a policy ideal" Geographical Journal, available on-line at http://onlinelibrary.wiley.com/doi/10.1111/geoj.12205/full.; C. Methmann and A. Oels, 'From "Fearing" to Empowering Climate Refugees: Governing Climate-Induced Migration in the Name of Resilience' (2015) 46(1) *Security Dialogue* 51–68.

25 G. Bettini and G. Gioli, 'Waltz with Development: Insights on the Developmentalization of Climate-Induced Migration' (2016) 5(2) *Migration and Development* 171–189; B. Burson and R. Bedford, *Opportunities and Challenges in Facilitating Voluntary Adaptive Migration in the Pacific in the Context of Climate Change* (2016) submitted to the Executive Committee of the Warsaw International Mechanism for Loss and Damage Associated with Climate Change Impacts.

26 A. Baldwin, 'Pluralising Climate Change and Migration: An Argument in Favour of Open Futures' (2014) 8(8) *Geography Compass* 516–528; R. Felli, 'Managing Insecurity by Ensuring Continuous Capital Accumulation: "Climate Refugees" and "Climate Migrants"' (2013) 18(3) *New Political Economy* 337–363.

27 Baldwin, 'Pluralising Climate Change' 520; Methmann and Oels, 'From "Fearing" to Empowering'; K. Ober, *Migration as Adaptation: Exploring Mobility as a Coping Strategy for Climate Change* (UK Climate Change and Migration Coalition 2015).

28 The Pacific Island Countries refer to 22 states: (Federated States of Micronesia, Fiji, French Polynesia, Guam, Kiribati, Marshall Islands, American Samoa, Cook Islands, Tokelau, Tuvalu, Vanuatu, Solomon Islands, Tonga, Papua New Guinea, Pitcairn Islands, Nauru, Niue, Northern Mariana Islands, Palau, and Wallis and Futuna) but for each legal instrument the states parties are listed in the next notes.

29 International Labour Organization (ILO), *Decent Work and Social Justice in Pacific Small Island Developing States: Challenges, Opportunities and Policy Responses* (2014).

30 S. Kagan, 'Making the Case for Preferential Access to Labour Markets for Kiribati and Tuvalu Migrants' (2015) http://devpolicy.org/making-the-case-for-preferential-access-to-labour-markets-for-kiribati-and-tuvalu-migrants-20140120/ accessed 25 October 2016; International Labour Organization (ILO), *Kiribati National Labour Migration Policy* (2015); International Labour Organization (ILO), *Tuvalu National Labour Migration Policy* (2015).

31 W. Eberhard, 'Of Tsunamis and Climate Change: The Need to Resettle? The Pacific Islands' (2012) paper presented at the European Science Foundation Conference 'Tracing Social Inequalities in Environmentally Induced Migration', University of Bielefeld.

32 ILO, *Decent Work and Social Justice*.

33 R. Bedford, B. Burson and C. Bedford, *Compendium of Legislation and Institutional Arrangements for Labour Migration in the Pacific Island Countries* (The Economic

and Social Commission for Asia and the Pacific and International Labour Organization 2014).

34 Kagan, 'Making the Case for Preferential Access'.

35 ILO, *Decent Work and Social Justice* 18.

36 ILO, *Kiribati National Labour Migration Policy*; ILO, *Tuvalu National Labour Migration Policy*; World Bank, *Well-Being from Work in the Pacific Island Countries* (2014).

37 ILO, *Decent Work and Social Justice*.

38 Ibid.

39 P. Martin, 'Low Skilled Labour Migration and Free Trade Agreements' in M. Panizzon, G. Zuercher and E. Fornalé (eds), *The Palgrave Handbook of International Labour Mobility* (Palgrave 2015) 205.

40 Ibid. 206.

41 New Zealand Department of Labour, *Recognised Seasonal Employer: Interagency Understanding: Vanuatu* (2007).

42 World Bank, *Well-Being from Work*. Eligible Pacific countries are: the Federated States of Micronesia, Fiji, Kiribati, Nauru, Palau, Papua New Guinea, the Republic of Marshall Islands, Samoa, the Solomon Islands, Tonga, Tuvalu, and Vanuatu.

43 B. Burson and R. Bedford, 'Clusters and Hubs: Toward a Regional Architecture for Voluntary Adaptive Migration in the Pacific' (2013) discussion paper, Nansen Initiative, 29.

44 R. Curtain *et al.*, *Pacific Possible, Labour Mobility: The Ten Billion Dollar Prize* (World Bank 2016), 9.

45 J. Gibson and D. McKenzie, *Australia's Pacific Seasonal Worker Pilot Scheme (PSWPS): Development Impacts in the First Two Years* http://siteresources.worldbank.org/DEC/Resources/Australia_Pacific_Seasonal_Worker_Pilot_Scheme.pdf accessed 25 October 2016.

46 Doyle, J., and S. Howes. 2015. "Australia's Seasonal Worker Program: Demand-Side Constraints and Suggested Reforms." Discussion paper, World Bank, Washington, DC.

47 D. McKenzie, P. Garcia Martinez and L. A. Winters, *Who is Coming from Vanuatu to New Zealand under the New Recognised Seasonal Employer Programme* (World Bank Development Research Group Finance and Private Sector Team 2008).

48 D. Hay and S. Howes, *Australia's Pacific Seasonal Worker Pilot Scheme: Why Has Take-Up Been So Low?* (Development Policy Centre, Australian National University 2012) Discussion Paper No. 17.

49 'Labour Mobility Workshop', 26–27 September 2014, Auckland, New Zealand.

50 Commonwealth of Australia, *Our North, Our Future: White Paper on Developing Northern Australia* (2015) http://industry.gov.au/ONA/WhitePaper/index.html accessed 25 October 2016.

51 McKenzie *et al.*, *Who is Coming from Vanuatu* 27.

52 World Bank, *Well-Being from Work*; F. Thornton, 'Regional Labour Migration as Adaptation to Climate Change? Options in the Pacific' in M. Leighton, S. Xiaomeng and K. Warner (eds), *Climate Change and Migration: Rethinking Policies for Adaptation and Disaster Risk Reduction* (United Nations University 2011) www.auca.kg/uploads/Source%20Pub%20Climate%20Change%20and%20Migration.pdf accessed 13 January 2017.

53 M. Becker, 'The Discourse about Legal Protection for Environmental Refugees: Re-constructing Categories – Rethinking Policies', in F. Gesing, J. Herbeck and S. Klepp (eds), *Denaturalizing Climate Change: Migration, Mobilities and Space* (Artec 2014).

54 In 1981, the Pacific countries (Cook Islands, Fiji, Nauru, Papua New Guinea, Samoa, Solomon Islands, Tonga, Tuvalu, Kiribati, and Niue) concluded a regional trade agreement with Australia and New Zealand: the South Pacific Regional Trade and Economic Cooperation Agreement (SPARTECA).

55 D. Ritter, 'Climate Change and Human Rights: The Imperative for Climate Change Migration with Dignity (CCMD)' in M. Di Paola and D. Kamal (eds), *Climate Change and Human Rights: The 2015 Paris Conference and the Task of Protecting People on a Warming Planet* (Global Policy 2015).

56 Office of the Chief Trade Adviser (OCTA). 2014. NSAs Workshop on the PACER Plus negotiations, Nadi, Fiji.

57 Ibid. The country involved in the process are Cook Islands, Federated States of Micronesia, Fiji, Kiribati, Nauru, Niue, Palau, Papua New Guinea, Republic of Marshall Islands, Samoa, Solomon Islands, Tonga, Tuvalu and Vanuatu.

58 Office of the Chief Trade Adviser (OCTA) speaking at the 'NSAs Workshop on the PACER Plus Negotiations', Nadi, Fiji, 2014.

59 F. Chaudharym, 'PACER Plus Concerns' (23 June 2016) *Fiji Times* www.fijitimes. com/story.aspx?id=359342 accessed 25 October 2016.

60 'OCTA Presentations during the Sixth Non-State Actors Dialogue Workshop on PACER Plus' (2016) www.octapic.org/wp-content/uploads/2016/06/Labour-Mobility-. pdf accessed 25 October 2016.

61 Oxfam, *PACER Plus and Its Alternatives: Which Way for Trade and Development in the Pacific?* (2009) 20.

62 J. Kelsey, *New Zealand's Commitments on Trade in Services and Labour Mobility* (Pacific Network on Globalisation 2009) 1; Oxfam, PACER Plus, 20.

63 See New Zealand Ministry of Foreign Affairs & Trade, 'ASEAN Australia New Zealand FTA (AANZFTA)' (n.d.) https://www.mfat.govt.nz/en/trade/free-trade-agreements/free-trade-agreements-in-force/aanzfta-asean-australia-new-zealand-fta/annexes/ accessed 25 October 2016.

64 See New Zealand Ministry of Foreign Affairs & Trade, 'NZ–China Free Trade Agreement' (n.d.) https://www.mfat.govt.nz/en/trade/free-trade-agreements/free-trade-agreements-in-force/china-fta/text-of-the-new-zealand-china-fta-agreement/ accessed 25 October 2016.

65 The PICTA TIS protocol, which was opened for signature in 2012, has been signed by Kiribati, Nauru, Samoa, the Solomon Islands, Tonga, Tuvalu, Vanuatu, Cook Islands, and the Federated States of Micronesia.

66 Tier 1 covers professionals who have a bachelor's degree and appropriate work experience, while Tier 2 covers semi-skilled professionals who have a diploma or certificate (Observatory on Migration, *South–South Labour Mobility in the Pacific: An Overview* (2013) 23).

67 Ibid.

68 Ibid.

69 Ibid.

70 The Melanesian Spearhead Group originated in 1986 among Papua New Guinea, Solomons Islands and Vanuatu, and in 1988, they adopted the Agreed Principles of Cooperation among Independent States of Melanesia.

71 Observatory on Migration, *South–South Labour Mobility* 24.

72 Ibid. 33.

73 Ibid.

74 Observatory on Migration, *South–South Labour Mobility* 24.

Part V

Conclusion

14 Conclusion

On the politics of climate change, migration and human rights

Andrew Baldwin

From 2011 to 2015, I had the good fortune to chair a major European research initiative called 'Climate Change and Migration: Knowledge, Law and Policy, and Theory'. Funded by COST, the project drew together a broad mix of social scientists and humanists from across Europe and around the world to map out the next generation of research in the rapidly expanding debate on climate change and migration. I must admit that when this project first took shape in 2010, my reading on the topic had been relatively limited, confined to just a few key texts and the odd media piece. Until then, the main focus of my research had concerned the interrelationships between race, nature, power and space,[1] without any real attention paid to migration. But once the COST project got under way, the intellectual universe opened up to me in ways I had never fully anticipated. Suddenly, I found myself in dialogue with legal scholars, environmental historians, political scientists, economists and international relations specialists, all of whom were speaking from their own disciplinary perspectives, and many of whom had been active participants in the climate change and migration debate for some time. This was a humbling experience, to say the least. Not only did it force me to pay much closer attention to how I communicate my research to non-disciplinary audiences. So, too, it made me far more sensitive to the inherent challenges of interdisciplinary research. We were all taking about 'climate change and migration', but were we in fact talking about the same thing? Needless to say, we did not agree on much (some might dispute this). But over the course of the project, I came to realise that this is precisely the value of interdisciplinarity: to debate, to challenge, to contest and to keep alive the democratic spirit of disagreement. On their own, climate change and migration are two of the most pressing political issues of our times. How we think about them *together* is of profound importance and worthy of our utmost scrutiny.

The essays gathered together in this volume represent a small but important slice of the wider COST dialogue on climate change and migration. The authors themselves were all active contributors to the COST project and share a commitment to thinking about climate change and migration through the lens of human rights. From a humanitarian perspective, this seems a pressing and obvious task. If current speculations about climate change are borne out, then people the world over will find themselves in increasingly precarious conditions which may or may not necessitate physical relocation. Ensuring that the human rights of those who relocate or may need to relocate because of climate change are protected seems not only responsible but urgent. This collection of essays is a modest contribution towards that end. But if there is one overarching lesson I learned from chairing the COST project on climate change and migration, it has to be that, however you slice it, the relation between climate change and migration is deeply political. What I mean by this is that, like all forms of knowledge, those that link climate change and migration, including texts such as this one, are never neutral and universal but are instead always partial and situated. This observation has been a standard truism in feminist philosophy and interpretive social science for well over three decades.[2]

Acknowledging that knowledge is situated has implications for how we comprehend the relationship between climate change, migration and human rights. Doing so can help clarify how knowledge relates to wider questions of power and inequality. It can also bring us closer to clarifying what might be called 'the politics of climate change and migration'. That is, it can help us better understand how specific actors with differential access to power and with specific interests can mobilise knowledge claims about climate change and migration for very specific purposes. This is especially so when such knowledge claims concern the human rights of those who are said to migrate because of climate change. In their universalism, human rights are often presumed to be above or apart from politics. Thus, the act of assuming responsibility for those who migrate because of climate change on the grounds that such a migration violates their human rights adopts a universal ethical responsibility in relation to the migrant. Such a universal act of responsibility appears indisputable. But the universality of such a claim to responsibility does not make it any less political. If anything, such universal claims merely veil their Eurocentric origins and thus their inherent political substance.[3] Or, more theoretically, such universalism presupposes the *a priori* nature of the universal itself. It neglects to recognise that whatever counts as 'universal' is not naturally occurring but contingent upon articulations of the *particular*.[4] More specifically, it fails to recognise that the particular is not just excluded from the universal, but, paraphrasing the feminist philosopher Judith Butler, that the particular is already 'inside' the universal as its own 'founding repudiation'.[5] As such, the universal is called into being only through the subordination of that which comes to be designated as particular. In this sense, it is important to recognise that even while the universal is heralded as a transcendent position, imagined to stand above and thus at a remove from and untainted by politics, the universal is itself always situated, forged from a knowledge located in European experience, history, philosophy and law. The non-European, in turn, comes to designate the particular, the situated and the emplaced.

Some readers might interpret this critique of the universal as excessively theoretical. After all, climate change stands to violate the human rights of actual people. People will be forced to relocate because of climate change even while they themselves are not responsible for climate change. The immediate injustice of this situation demands not excessively complicated theorisations but responsible action to ensure their rights are not jeopardised. But to discount the way in which the universalism of human rights discourse is shaped by issues of power and exclusion is to displace power from the frame of human rights altogether, a move that is symptomatic of the wider depoliticisation of climate change.[6] And this has important implications for how we conceive of responsible action in relation to the migration effects of climate change, whether such effects are real or imagined. Displacing considerations of power from the terrain of human rights delimits the very terms of responsible action. For example, it limits responsible action to ensuring the human rights of those who are forced to relocate from climate change, rather than including within the scope of responsible action efforts to expose how power functions in relation to knowledge claims about human rights, climate change and migration. Writing from a postcolonial perspective, which broadly acknowledges the way colonial and imperial power continues to shape all manner of development contexts, Patricia Noxolo, Parvati Ragurham and Clare Madge argue that 'responsible action is never free of its locational imperatives and its identifications so that the responsible agent is always tainted: there is no pure space within and from which responsibility can be enacted'.[7] This insight should give us pause to consider how power is implicated in constructions of knowledge of climate change and migration in terms of human rights – efforts that include, for example, anthologies such as the present volume. Indeed, when we take account of such power, we are led to ask a different set of questions. For whom is the discourse on climate change, migration and human rights? Whose knowledge is used in efforts to link climate change and migration to human rights? Whose interests does this knowledge serve? Where does this knowledge come from? And what are its effects?

In this volume, Silja Klepp and Johannes Herbeck rehearse elements of this argument when making their case for investigating the politics of climate change and migration in both the European Union and Oceania using the 'legal anthropology of emergence'. Implied in their argument is that the 'top-down' nature of the debate on climate change and migration in the European Union presupposes its universality. Klepp and Herbeck then provide a counter-narrative – one in which actors in Oceania refuse their implied particularity in favour of a more situated approach to the articulation of legal rights, and one that decentres Eurocentrism. But such questions of power and knowledge construction come into sharper relief when we compare Robin Bronen's chapter on the very real, material struggles of the Yup'ik in Newtok in Alaska with Anja Mihr's more abstract account of the relationship between migration, climate change and the concept of climate justice. The story Bronen tells concerns the structural impediments that the Yup'ik inhabitants of Newtok have faced in their attempt to resettle to a place free of coastal erosion and saline inundation. Bronen then uses the Yup'ik story to specify how human rights should be made a fundamental dimension of planned relocation due to climate change. There is much about this story that merits attention, but what makes it so important is that it is a *situated* form of knowledge – situated, that is, in a geographically located political struggle for indigenous self-determination. The meaning of human rights in this context derives from the fact that the Yup'ik are actively engaged in a struggle over land, a struggle that is only partly to do with climate change and much more to do with self-determination and overturning the structural conditions of settler colonialism. When the people of Newtok mobilise human rights in this context, they are making a territorial claim to the land to which they have historically been denied. What Bronen provides, then, is a very situated form of knowledge about the human rights dimensions of climate change and resettlement.

Now compare this with Anja Mihr's contribution. Writing from a universal subject position, Mihr carves out for herself an elevated, transcendent view that constructs a universal knowledge of climate change, migration and human rights. For her part, she articulates a role for human rights in ensuring something called 'climate justice', assumed throughout her essay as an abstract, universal concept. In formulating her argument, Mihr coins the concept of 'climate victims', a term she uses to describe 'marginalised or vulnerable groups that do not have legal status either domestically or internationally' due to the fact that they have had to migrate because of climate change. What Mihr seems to be arguing for is a human rights regime for those she claims are 'climate victims'. There are a number of problems with this account, not least the very causal use of climatic reductionism that runs through much of her argument, the assumption that climate causes mobility.[8] So, too, it is underpinned by a very ambiguous, even Eurocentric, geography which assumes that 'climate victims' will appear predominantly in 'poor and/or less democratic countries in Asia and Africa', even while acknowledging that such victims exist in 'peaceful and democratic countries'. But aside from these problems, what sets Mihr's analysis apart from Bronen's is that, whereas Bronen builds her human rights account from an actual, historically situated struggle over land, Mihr develops a universal form of knowledge abstracted from any specific historical circumstance and in which the category of 'climate victim' can be applied in a top-down manner. Or, in slightly different terms, we may say that Mihr's 'climate victim' is precisely the founding repudiation of the universal position from which she writes. In other words, Mihr must fabricate the concept of 'climate victim' in order for her universal position to appear as such. Mihr is not wrong to worry about 'climate justice' and clearly she offers her account with the best of intentions. But, in deriving her account from a set of abstract universal principles, she inadvertently masks the imperial assumptions that organise her intervention, such as the assumed right to label groups as vulnerable in ways that may well run counter to their own self-representation and political ambitions.

Two important observations can be drawn from the foregoing comparison between Bronen and Mihr. The first concerns the value of postcolonial theory in coming to terms with the politics of constructing climate change, migration and human rights as a universal site of knowledge formation. A postcolonial account of responsibility, such as that offered by Noxolo *et al.*,[9] is important, then, because it can help us appreciate how such claims of responsibility may in fact mobilise a kind of knowledge that is at cross-purposes with the political aims of those whom it is intended to assist.[10] If anything, the residents of Newtok are not 'climate victims', but victims of colonial dispossession; and, as such, their invocation of human rights is not based on their vulnerability to climate change, but on their historical knowledge of the land from which they have been forcibly displaced. In this sense, it is important to understand that when the villagers invoke human rights in their effort to resettle away from the detrimental effects of climate change, they do so in a manner that is consistent with their aims of indigenous self-determination. Not unlike Klepp and Herbeck, various commentators have also identified a similar dynamic in which various actors in Pacific island contexts have actively refused attempts by Western media and development authorities to label the inhabitants of the Pacific islands 'climate refugees',[11] a term not too dissimilar from Mihr's 'climate victims'.

But if postcolonial theory can help expose the gap between, on the one hand, the way that universalist knowledge particularises certain groups in the language of vulnerability, victimhood, remoteness, indigeneity and so forth, and, on the other, the self-representation of those very groups, then a postcolonial perspective offers additional value to the debate about climate justice by directing attention to the question of scale. Following arguments that are beginning to surface in my disciplinary home of geography,[12] it would seem that achieving something called 'climate justice' requires more than simply appealing to human rights in the abstract. So, too, it requires studious attention to the specific historical and geographic contexts within which and about which such claims to climate justice are made. In this respect, it is important to remember that scale matters in how we approach our understanding of climate justice. For example, claims to climate justice that are made in relation to REDD+ must be understood as substantively different from those formulated in urban contexts.[13] Both are separated by radically different political and economic contexts, thereby complicating any simple attempt to establish a set of solid foundations upon which universal legal principles like climate justice might be forged.

The second important observation that is at stake in the discussion about climate change, migration and human rights is that it contains a full-fledged politics of place. As might already be clear, this is partly a politics to do with struggles over the power to represent place. The claim that some places, by virtue of the migration effects of climate change, are in need of human rights – or that climate change will exacerbate existing or result in novel human rights violations – stands in contrast to the placeless quality that attaches to the universality of human rights. Places – whether Bangladesh (Ackerly, this volume) or Alaska (Bronen, this volume) – become marked by their absence of human rights or by the threat that climate change poses to those rights. Such places are subsequently made available to various forms of exogenous intervention on the promise of the installation or restoration of rights for those who move as a result of climate change. In this sense, the movements of otherwise emplaced people come to be understood in relation to human rights, which may or may not accord with their own styles of self-representation. Also at stake in this politics of place, however, is the power to dissimulate the emplaced nature of claims to universality. Whereas places designated as in need of human rights are said to be *particular* and thus emplaced, the Eurocentric origins of the universal concept that under-pins human rights are masked. That is, the place (Europe) from which the universal is derived is fully negated. As such, human rights are said to be universal even while they originate from the very particular history of Europe.

In this short conclusion, I have argued that the knowledge of climate change, migration and human rights is not universal but situated. My point, however, is not to negate the importance of this knowledge but merely to call attention to its contingent nature, to remind readers that even while climate change is a matter of pressing concern, to manage its migration effects through human rights law is a very particular and thus political undertaking. Acknowledging the contingent nature of this knowledge is, in turn, important because it allows us to widen the terms of responsible action. It allows us to pose questions about whether this form of knowledge is indeed best suited for managing the migration effects of climate change or whether other forms of knowledge, such as indigenous knowledge, might equally be up to the task. Indeed, if climate change demands that we ask fundamental questions about what it means to live in the world today or about what kind of life is possible as we stand on the threshold of profound global environmental change, then perhaps answers to these questions can be found in the experiences of human life and living that are not synonymous with what we understand to be modernity today.

Notes

1 Although now largely forgotten in the field of geography, these debates trace their origins to a set of now largely discredited discussions about migration, place and the environment that were popular from the nineteenth century until the 1950s.
2 D. Haraway, 'Situated Knowledges: The Science Question in Feminism and the Privilege of Partial Perspective' (1988) 14 *Feminist Studies* 575–599; D. Haraway, *Simians, Cyborgs and Women: A Reinvention of Nature* (Routledge 1991); S. Harding, *Whose Science? Whose Knowledge?* (Cornell University Press 1991).
3 J. Hobson, *The Eurocentric Conception of World Politics: Western International Theory, 1760–2010* (Cambridge University Press 2012); G. Bhambra, R. Shillian

and D. Orrells, 'Contesting Imperial Epistemologies: Introduction' (2014) 27 *Journal of Historical Sociology* 293–301; S. Buck-Morss, *Hegel, Haiti, and Universal History* (University of Pittsburgh Press 2009).

4 J. Butler, E. Laclau and S. Zizek, *Contingency, Hegemony, Universality: Contemporary Dialogues on the Left* (Verso 2000).

5 J. Butler, *Bodies that Matter* (Routledge 1993) 3.

6 G. Bettini, '(In)Convenient Convergences: "Climate Refugees", Apocalyptic Discourses and the Depoliticization of Climate-Induced Migration' in C. Methmann, D. Rothe and B. Stephan (eds), *Deconstructing the Greenhouse: Interpretive Approaches to Global Climate Governance* (Routledge 2013); W. Brown, 'Climate Change, Democracy, and the Crisis of Humanism' in A. Baldwin and G. Bettini (eds), *Life Adrift: Climate Change, Migration, Critique* (Rowman & Littlefield forthcoming).

7 P. Noxolo, P. Ragurham and C. Madge, 'Unsettling Responsibility: Postcolonial Interventions' (2012) 37 *Transactions of the Institute of British Geographers* 422.

8 M. Hulme, 'Reducing the Future to Climate: A Story of Climate Determinism and Reductionism' (2011) 26 *Osiris* 245–266.

9 Noxolo, Ragurham and Madge, 'Unsettling Responsibility'.

10 U. Kothari, 'Political Discourses of Climate Change and Migration: Resettlement Policies in the Maldives' (2014) 180 *Geographical Journal* 130–140.

11 C. Farbotko, 'Wishful Sinking: Disappearing Islands, Climate Refugees and Cosmopolitan Experimentation' (2010) 51 *Asia Pacific Viewpoint* 47–60; C. Farbotko and H. Lazrus, 'The First Climate Refugees? Contesting Global Narratives of Climate Change in Tuvalu' (2012) 22 *Global Environmental Change* 382–390; K. E. McNamara and C. Gibson, '"We Do Not Want to Leave Our Land": Pacific Ambassadors at the United Nations Resist the Category of "Climate Refugees"' (2009) 40 *Geoforum* 475–483.

12 S. Fisher, 'The Emerging Geographies of Climate Justice' (2015) 181 *Geographical Journal* 73–82.

13 H. Bulkeley, J. Carmin, V. Castan Broto, G. A. S. Edwards and S. Fuller, 'Climate Justice and Global Cities: Mapping the Emerging Discourses' (2013) 23 *Global Environmental Change* 914–925; H. Bulkeley, G. A. S. Edwards and S. Fuller, 'Contesting Climate Justice in the City: Examining Politics and Practice in Urban Climate Change Experiments' (2014) 25 *Global Environmental Change* 31–40.

Bibliography

ABC, 'World Sea Levels Set to Rise at Least One Metre over Next 100–200 Years, NASA Says' (26 August 2015) www.abc.net.au/news/2015-08-27/sea-levels-set-to-rise,-nasa-says/6728008?site=esperance accessed 25 October 2016.

'Abebe, A. M., 'The Kampala Convention and Environmentally Induced Displacement in Africa' (2011) paper presented at the IOM Intersessional Workshop on Climate Change, Environmental Degredation and Migration, Geneva www.iom.int/jahia/webdav/shared/shared/mainsite/microsites/IDM/workshops/climate-change-2011/SessionIII-Paper-Allehone-Mulugeta-Abebe.pdf accessed 25 October 2016.

Abhas, K. J., *Safer Homes, Stronger Communities: A Handbook for Reconstructing after Natural Disasters* (World Bank 2010).

Ackerly, B. A., 'Human Rights Enjoyment in Theory and Activism' (2011) 12(2) *Human Rights Review*.

Ackerly, B. A., *Just Responsibility: A Human Rights Theory of Global Justice* (Oxford University Press forthcoming).

Ackerly, B. A. and J. M. Cruz, 'Hearing the Voice of the People: Human Rights as if People Mattered' (2011) 33(1) *New Political Science*.

Ackerly, B. A., M. Anam and J. Gilligan, 'Environment, Migration and Adaptation: Evidence and Politics of Climate Change in Bangladesh' in B. Mallick and B. Etzold (eds), *Environment, Migration and Adaptation: Evidence and Politics of Climate Change in Bangladesh* (AHDPH 2015).

Ackerly, B. A., J. Gilligan and S. Goodbred, 'From Coastal Bangladesh: Climate Change, Migration and the Importance of Community Level Analysis for Using Human Rights to Guide "New" Legal Frameworks' (2012) paper prepared for COST Action programme IS1101.

Adams v. New Jersey Steamboat Co (1896), 151 NY 163, 45 NE 369.

Adeagbo, O. A. and J. M. Iyi, 'Post-Election Crisis in Kenya and Internally Displaced Persons: A Critical Appraisal' (2011) 4(2) *Journal of Politics and Law*.

Adger, W. N., J. M. Pulhin, J. Barnett, G. D. Dabelko, G. K. Hovelsrud, M. Levy, Ú. Oswald Spring and C. H. Vogel, 'Human Security' in C. B. Field, V. R. Barros, D. J. Dokken, K. J. Mach, M. D. Mastrandrea, T. E. Bilir, M. Chatterjee, K. L. Ebi, Y. O. Estrada, R. C. Genova, B. Girma, E. S. Kissel, A. N. Levy, S. MacCracken, P. R. Mastrandrea and L. L. White (eds), *Climate Change 2014: Impacts, Adaptation, and Vulnerability. Part A: Global and Sectoral Aspects. Contribution of Working Group II to the Fifth Assessment Report of the Intergovernmental Panel on Climate Change* (Cambridge University Press 2014).

Advisory Group on Climate Change and Human Mobility (AGCCHM), 'Human Mobility in the Context of Climate Change UNFCCC–Paris COP-21: Recommendations from the Advisory Group on Climate Change and Human Mobility' (2015) www. internal-displacement.org/assets/publications/2015/201511-human-mobility-in-the-context-of-climate-change-unfccc-Paris-COP21.pdf accessed 25 October 2016.

African Union, *Convention Governing Specific Aspects of Refugee Problems in Africa* (1969) www.achpr.org/instruments/refugee-convention/#1 accessed 10 January 2017.

African Union, *African Union Convention for the Protection and Assistance of Internally Displaced Persons in Africa* (adopted 22 October 2009).

Agnew:Beck Consulting, *Strategic Management Plan: Newtok to Mertarvik* (2012).

Agnew, R., 'Dire Forecast: A Theoretical Model of the Impact of Climate Change on Crime' (2012) 16 *Theoretical Criminology*.

Alaska Division of Community and Regional Affairs (DCRA), 'Newtok Planning Group Mertarvik Housing' (n.d.) www.commerce.alaska.gov/web/dcra/PlanningLand Management//NewtokPlanningGroup/MertarvikHousing.aspx accessed 25 October 2016.

Alaska Division of Homeland Security and Emergency Management, 'Home Page' (n.d.) http://ready.alaska.gov accessed 25 October 2016.

Ali, A. M. S., 'Rice to Shrimp: Land Use/Land Cover Changes and Soil Degradation in Southwestern Bangladesh' (2006) 23(4) *Land Use Policy*.

Alliance of Small Island States, *Malé' Declaration on the Human Dimension of Global Climate Change* (2007) www.ciel.org/Publications/Male_Declaration_Nov07.pdf accessed 25 October 2016.

Al Jazeera 'Where Will the Climate Refugees Go?' (23 December 2015) www.aljazeera. com/indepth/features/2015/11/climate-refugees-151125093146088.html accessed 31 December 2015.

Ammer, M., 'Climate Change and Human Rights: The Status of Climate Refugees in Europe' (Ludwig Boltzmann Institute of Human Rights 2009).

Anderson, C. A., 'Climate Change and Violence' in D. J. Christie (ed.), *The Encyclopedia of Peace Psychology* (Wiley Online Library 2012).

Andrijasevic, R. *et al.*, 'Turbulente Ränder: Konturen eines neuen Migrationsregimes im Südosten Europas' (2005) 35 *PROKLA: Zeitschrift für kritische Sozialwissenschaft*.

Arctic Slope Consulting Group (ASCG), 'Village of Newtok, Local Hazards Mitigation Plan' (2008) www.commerce.state.ak.us/dca/planning/pub/Newtok_HMP.pdf accessed 25 October 2016.

Armitage, D. and R. Plummer, 'Adapting and Transforming: Governance for Navigating Change' in D. Armitage and R. Plummer (eds), *Adaptive Capacity and Environmental Governance* (Springer 2010).

Auerbach, L. W. *et al.*, 'Flood Risk of Natural and Embanked Landscapes on the Ganges–Brahmaputra Tidal Delta Plain' (2015) 5 *Nature Climate Change*.

Awuor, C. B., V. A. Orindi and A. Ochieng Adwera, 'Climate Change and Coastal Cities: The Case of Mombasa, Kenya' (2008) 20(1) *Environment and Urbanization*.

Bacchus, J., 'What Does Climate Change Mean for Business?' (World Economic Forum 2014).

Bacon, D., 'The Right to Stay Home' (14 July 2008) *Truthout* www.truthout.org/article/ the-right-stay-home accessed 25 October 2016.

Baldwin, A., 'Pluralising Climate Change and Migration: An Argument in Favour of Open Futures' (2014) 8(8) *Geography Compass*.

Bardsley, D. and G. Hugo, 'Migration and Climate Change: Examining Thresholds of Change to Guide Effective Adaptation Decision-Making' (2010) 32 *Population and Environment*.

Barnett, J. and J. Campbell, *Climate Change and Small Island States: Power, Knowledge and the South Pacific* (Earthscan 2010).

Barnett, J. and M. Webber, 'Accommodating Migration to Promote Adaptation to Climate Change' (2009) policy brief prepared for the Secretariat of the Swedish Commission on Climate Change and Development and the World Bank World Development Report 2010 team.

Bassiouni, C. M., *Crimes against Humanity in International Criminal Law* (2nd edn, Kluwer Law International 1999).

Bates, D. C., 'Environmental Refugees? Classifying Human Migrations Caused by Environmental Change' (2002) 23 *Population and Environment*.

BBC, 'The President's Dilemma: Should Kiribati's President Anote Give In to Climate Change?' (2009) produced by the International Fund for Agricultural Development (IFAD), shown in *Life on the Edge*.

Beck, U., *World at Risk* (Polity Press 2009).

Becker, M., 'The Discourse about Legal Protection for Environmental Refugees: Re-constructing Categories – Rethinking Policies' in F. Gesing, J. Herbeck and S. Klepp (eds), *Denaturalizing Climate Change: Migration, Mobilities and Space* (Artec 2014).

Bedford, R. and C. Bedford, 'International Migration and Climate Change: A Post-Copenhagen Perspective on Options for Kiribati and Tuvalu' in B. Burson (ed.), *Climate Change and Migration: South Pacific Perspectives* (Institute of Policy Studies 2010).

Bedford, R., B. Burson and C. Bedford, *Compendium of Legislation and Institutional Arrangements for Labour Migration in the Pacific Island Countries* (International Labour Organization 2014).

Benneyworth, L. *et al.*, 'Drinking Water Insecurity: Water Quality and Access in Coastal South-Western Bangladesh' (2016) 26(5–6) *International Journal of Environmental Health Research*.

Berman, B. and J. Lonsdale, *Unhappy Valley: Conflict in Kenya & Africa* (Ohio University Press 1992).

Berry, H. L., K. Bowen and T. Kjellstrom, 'Climate Change and Mental Health: A Causal Pathways Framework' (2010) 55 *International Journal of Public Health*.

Bettini, G., 'Climate Barbarians at the Gate? A Critique of Apocalyptic Narratives on Climate Refugees' (2013) 45 *Geoforum*.

Bettini, G., '(In)Convenient Convergences: "Climate Refugees", Apocalyptic Discourses and the Depoliticization of Climate-Induced Migration' in C. Methmann, D. Rothe and B. Stephan (eds), *Deconstructing the Greenhouse: Interpretive Approaches to Global Climate Governance* (Routledge 2013).

Bettini, G. and G. Gioli, 'Waltz with Development: Insights on the Developmentalization of Climate-Induced Migration' (2016) 5 *Migration and Development*.

Bettini, G., S. Nash and G. Gioli, 'One Step Forward, Two Steps Back? The Fading Contours of (In)Justice in Competing Discourses on Climate Migration' (2016) 183(3) *Geographical Journal*.

Betts, A., 'Survival Migration: A New Protection Framework' (2010) 16 *Global Governance*.

Betts, A., 'Towards a "Soft Law" Framework for the Protection of Vulnerable Irregular Migrants' (2010) 22 *International Journal of Refugee Law*.

Betts, A., 'Substantive Issue Linkage and the Politics of Migration' in C. Bjola and M. Kornprobst (eds), *Arguing Global Governance* (Routledge 2012).

Bettis, R., 'The Iraqi Refugee Crisis' (2010) 19 *Transnational Law and Contemporary Problems*.

Bhambra, G., R. Shillian and D. Orrells, 'Contesting Imperial Epistemologies: Introduction' (2014) 27 *Journal of Historical Sociology*.

Biermann, F., 'Umweltflüchtlinge: Ursachen und Lösungsansätze' (2001) 12 *Aus Politik und Zeitgeschichte*.

Biermann, F. and I. Boas, 'Protecting Climate Refugees: The Case for a Global Protocol' (2008) *Environment: Science and Policy for Sustainable Development* www.environment magazine.org/Archives/Back%20Issues/November-December%202008/Biermann-Boas-full.html accessed 25 October 2016.

Biermann, F. and I. Boas, 'Preparing for a Warmer World: Towards a Global Governance System to Protect Climate Refugees' (2010) 10(1) *Global Environmental Politics*.

Bilsborrow, R. E., 'Rural Poverty, Migration and the Environment in Developing Countries: Three Case Studies' (1992) World Bank Policy Research Working Paper No. 1017.

Black, R., *Refugees, Environment and Development* (Longman 1998).

Black, R., 'Environmental Refugees: Myth or Reality?' (2001) UNHCR Working Paper on New Issues in Refugee Research No. 34.

Black, R. *et al.*, 'Migration and Global Environmental Change' (2011) 21 *Global Environmental Change*.

Bonanno, G. A. *et al.*, 'Weighing the Costs of Disaster: Consequences, Risks and Resilience in Individuals, Families and Communities' (2010) 11 *Psychological Science in the Public Interest*.

Boncour, P. and B. Burson, 'Climate Change and Migration in the South Pacific Region: Policy Perspectives' in B. Burson (ed.), *Climate Change and Migration: South Pacific Perspectives* (Institute of Policy Studies 2010).

Bourdieu, P., 'Sur le Pouvoir Symbolique' (1977) 32 *Annales Économies, Sociétés, Civilisations*.

Boyd, E., H. Osbahr, P. J. Ericksen, E. L. Tompkins, M. C. Lemos and F. Miller, 'Resilience and "Climatizing" Development: Examples and Policy Implications' (2008) 51 *Development*.

Brammer, H., 'After the Bangladesh Flood Action Plan: Looking to the Future' (2010) 9(1) *Environmental Hazards*.

Brammer, H., 'Bangladesh's Dynamic Coastal Regions and Sea-Level Rise' (2014) 1 *Climate Risk Management*.

Broderstad, E. G. and J. Dahl, 'Political Systems' in *Arctic Human Development Report* (Stefansson Arctic Institute 2004).

Bronen, R., 'Climate-Induced Community Relocations: Creating an Adaptive Governance Framework Based in Human Rights Doctrine' (2011) 35(2) *NYU Review of Law and Social Change*.

Bronen, R., 'Climate-Induced Community Relocations: Using Integrated Social-Ecological Assessments to Foster Adaptation and Resilience' (2015) 20(3) *Ecology and Society*.

Bronen, R. and F. S. Chapin, 'Adaptive Governance and Institutional Strategies for Climate-Induced Community Relocations in Alaska' (2013) *Proceedings of the National Academy of Sciences*.

Brookings Institution, Georgetown University and UNHCR, 'Guidance on Protecting People from Disasters and Environmental Change through Planned Relocation'

(2015) www.brookings.edu/research/planned-relocations-disasters-and-climate-change accessed 4 January 2017.

Brookings–LSE Project on Internal Displacement, *Climate-Induced Displacement of Alaska Native Communities* (2013).

Brookings–LSE Project on Internal Displacement, *Climate Change and Internal Displacement* (2014).

Brookings–LSE Project on Internal Displacement, *Resettlement in the Wake of Typhoon Haiyan in the Philippines: A Strategy to Mitigate Risk or a Risky Strategy?* (2015).

Brookings–LSE Project on Internal Displacement, *Planned Relocations, Disasters and Environmental Change* (2015) www.brookings.edu/about/projects/idp/planned-relocations accessed 25 October 2016.

Brown, A. *et al.*, 'Geomorphology of the Anthropocene: Time-Transgressive Discontinuities of Human-Induced Alluviation' (2013) 1 *Anthropocene*.

Brown, W., 'Climate Change, Democracy, and the Crisis of Humanism' in A. Baldwin and G. Bettini (eds), *Life Adrift: Climate Change, Migration, Critique* (Rowman & Littlefield forthcoming).

Buckel, S., R. Christensen and A. Fischer-Lescano, 'Einleitung: Neue Theoriepraxis des Rechts' in S. Buckel, R. Christensen and A. Fischer-Lescano (eds), *Neue Theorien des Rechts* (UTB, Lucius & Lucius 2009).

Buckley Vann Town Planning Consultants, *Newsletter, Climate Change Adaptation Planning for Choiseul Bay Township, Solomon Islands* (2014) www.buckleyvann.com.au/wp-content/uploads/2015/11/BV-Newsletter-20-Aug-14-Climate-change-adaptation-Solomon-Is.pdf accessed 25 October 2016.

Buck-Morss, S., *Hegel, Haiti, and Universal History* (University of Pittsburgh Press 2009).

Budayeva and Others v. Russian Federation (European Court of Human Rights 20 March 2008).

Bulkeley, H., J. Carmin, V. Castan Broto, G. A. S. Edwards and S. Fuller, 'Climate Justice and Global Cities: Mapping the Emerging Discourses' (2013) 23 *Global Environmental Change*.

Bulkeley, H., G. A. S. Edwards and S. Fuller, 'Contesting Climate Justice in the City: Examining Politics and Practice in Urban Climate Change Experiments' (2014) 25 *Global Environmental Change*.

Burger, M., *Towards an Integrated Approach to Disaster Risk Management and Climate Change Adaptation* (Sabin Center for Climate Change Law 2015).

Burson, B. and R. Bedford, 'Clusters and Hubs: Toward a Regional Architecture for Voluntary Adaptive Migration in the Pacific' (2013) discussion paper, Nansen Initiative.

Burson, B. and R. Bedford, *Opportunities and Challenges in Facilitating Voluntary Adaptive Migration in the Pacific in the Context of Climate Change* (2016) submitted to the Executive Committee of the Warsaw International Mechanism for Loss and Damage Associated with Climate Change Impacts.

Butler, J., *Bodies that Matter* (Routledge 1993).

Butler, J., E. Laclau and S. Zizek, *Contingency, Hegemony, Universality: Contemporary Dialogues on the Left* (Verso 2000).

Byravan, S. and S. C. Rajan, 'The Ethical Implications of Sea-Level Rise due to Climate Change' (2010) 24 *Ethics and International Affairs*.

Cameron, E., T. Shine and W. Bevins, 'Climate Justice: Equity and Justice Informing a New Climate Agreement' (World Resources Institute and Mary Robinson Foundation – Climate Justice 2013).

Canada (Attorney General) v. Ward (1993) 2 S.C.R. 689.

Caney, S., 'Human Rights, Responsibilities, and Climate Change' in C. R. Beitz and R. E. Goodin (eds), *Global Basic Rights* (Oxford University Press 2009).

Cannon, T., 'Reducing People's Vulnerability to Natural Hazards: Communities and Resilience' (United Nations University, World Institute for Development Economic Research 2008) Research Paper No. 2008/34.

Canzi, G., 'Q&A with Mary Robinson: What Is Climate Justice?' (2015), *The Road to Paris* http://roadtoparis.info/2015/07/29/qa-with-mary-robinson-what-is-climate-justice accessed 25 October 2016.

Castles, S., 'Environmental Change and Forced Migration: Making Sense of the Debate' (2002) UNHCR Working Paper on New Issues in Refugee Research No. 70.

Catley, A., J. Lind and I. Scoones, *Pastoralism and Development in Africa: Dynamic Change at the Margins* (Routledge 2013).

Center for Climate and Energy Solution, 'Outcomes of the UN Climate Change Conference in Paris' (2015).

Cernea, M. M., 'Internal Refugee Flows and Development-Induced Population Displacement' (1990) 3(4) *Journal of Refugee Studies*.

Chambwera, M. *et al.*, 'Economics of Adaptation' in C. B. Field, V. R. Barros, D. J. Dokken, K. J. Mach, M. D. Mastrandrea, T. E. Bilir, M. Chatterjee, K. L. Ebi, Y. O. Estrada, R. C. Genova, B. Girma, E. S. Kissel, A. N. Levy, S. MacCracken, P. R. Mastrandrea and L. L. White (eds), *Climate Change 2014: Impacts, Adaptation and Vulnerability Part A: Global and Sectoral Aspects. Contribution of Working Group II to the Fifth Assessment Report of the Intergovernmental Panel on Climate Change* (Cambridge University Press 2014).

Chappell, L., 'Drivers of Migration in Household Surveys' (2011) Foresight Report WP4.

Cha-Sartori, C., 'Environmental Refugees: The Latest Enterprise of Corporate Social Responsibility' (2011) 34(1) *Houston Journal of International Law*.

Chaturvedi, S. and T. Doyle, 'Geopolitics of Climate Change and Australia's "Re-engagement" with Asia: Discourses of Fear and Cartographic Anxieties' (2010) 45 *Australian Journal of Political Science*.

Chaudharym, F., 'PACER Plus Concerns' (23 June 2016) *Fiji Times* www.fijitimes.com/story.aspx?id=359342 accessed 25 October 2016.

Chimni, B. S., 'The Birth of a "Discipline": From Refugee to Forced Migration Studies' (2009) 22(1) *Journal of Refugee Studies*.

Chindarkar, N., 'Gender and Climate Change-Induced Migration: Proposing a Framework for Analysis' (2012) 7(2) *Environmental Research Letters*.

Christian Aid, *Human Tide: The Real Migration Crisis* (2007).

Clayton, A. and D. C. Savage, *Government and Labour in Kenya, 1895–1963* (Cass 1974).

Climate Change Portal of the Office of the President of Kiribati, *Climate Change in Kiribati* (2017) www.climate.gov.ki/ accessed 12 January 2017.

Climate and Clean Air Coalition to Reduce Short Lived Climate Pollutants, 'Home Page' (n.d.) www.ccacoalition.org accessed 25 October 2016.

Climate Vulnerable Forum, *Dhaka Ministerial Declaration* (2011).

ClimDev-Africa, 'Home Page' (2013) www.climdev-africa.org accessed 27 September 2016.

Cohen, R., 'Iraq's Displaced: Where to Turn?' (2008) 24 *American University International Law Review*.

Cohen, R., 'Lessons Learned from the Development of the Guiding Principles on Internal Displacement' (2013) www.brookings.edu/research/papers/2013/10/guiding-principles-on-internal-displacement-cohen accessed 25 October 2016.

Collier, J. S. and A. Lakoff, 'On Regimes of Living' in A. Ong and S. J. Collier (eds), *Global Assemblages: Technology, Politics, and Ethics as Anthropological Problems* (Blackwell 2005).

Colloquium on the International Protection of Refugees in Central America, Mexico and Panama, *Cartagena Declaration on Refugees* (1984) www.oas.org/dil/1984_Cartagena_Declaration_on_Refugees.pdf accessed 10 January 2017.

Commission for the Implementation of the Constitution (CIC), 'CIC Matrix on the Eviction and Resettlement Bill, 2014' (n.d.).

Committee on Petitions of the European Parliament, 'Notice to Members on Petition 1312/2009 by Andy Vermaut (Belgian) on Behalf of the Pimpampoentje (Ladybird) Climate and Peace Action Group, on Legal Recognition by the European Union of Climate Refugees' (2011).

Commonwealth of Australia, *Our North, Our Future: White Paper on Developing Northern Australia* (2015) http://industry.gov.au/ONA/WhitePaper/index.html accessed 25 October 2016.

Comprehensive Disaster Management Programme (CDMP II) and Ministry of Disaster Management and Relief (MoDMR), *National Strategy on the Management of Disaster and Climate Induced Internal Displacement* (2015).

Conot, R. E., *Justice at Nuremberg* (Harper & Row 1983).

Costi, A., 'Hybrid Tribunals as a Viable Transitional Justice Mechanism to Combat Impunity in Post-Conflict Situations' (2008) 22(2) *New Zealand Universities Law Review*.

Council of the European Union, 'Presidency Conclusions of the Brussels European Council, 15/16 December 2005' (2006) 15914/1/05. REV 1.

Cox, S., *An Overview of Erosion, Flooding, and Relocation Efforts in the Native Village of Newtok* (Alaska Department of Commerce, Community and Economic Development 2007).

CRED, EM-Database (2016) www.emdat.be/database accessed 9 June 2016.

CRIDEAU and CRDP, Faculty of Law and Economic Science, University of Limoges, *Revue Europeene de Droit de l'Environnement* (2008).

Cubie, D., 'Promoting Dignity for All: Human Rights Approaches in the Post-2015 Climate Change, Disaster Risk Reduction and Sustainable Development Frameworks' (2014) 8(1) *Human Rights and International Discourse*.

Curtain, R. et al., *Pacific Possible, Labour Mobility: The Ten Billion Dollar Prize* (World Bank 2016).

Dandekar, P., *Shrinking and Sinking Deltas: Major Role of Dams in Delta Subsidence and Effective Sea Level Rise* (South Asia Network on Dams, Rivers and People 2014).

De Schutter, O., *International Human Rights Law* (Cambridge University Press 2010).

de Sousa Santos, B. and C. A. Rodríguez-Garavito, *Law and Globalization from Below: Towards a Cosmopolitan Legality* (Cambridge University Press 2005).

de Moor, N. and A. Cliquet, 'Environmental Displacement: A New Challenge for European Migration Policy' (2009) paper prepared for the 'Protecting People in Conflict and Crisis: Responding to the Challenges of a Changing World' conference, Refugee Studies Centre, University of Oxford.

Dennis, M. and D. Stewart, 'Justiciability of Economic, Social and Cultural Rights: Should There Be an International Complaints Mechanism to Adjudicate the Rights to Food, Water, Housing and Health?' (2004) 98 *American Journal of International Law*.

Department of Defense, *Climate Change Adaptation and Resilience* (2016).

Department of Environment, Food and Rural Affairs (DEFRA), *Adapting to Climate Change: A Guide for Local Councils* (2010) www.gov.uk/government/uploads/system/uploads/attachment_data/file/218798/adapt-localcouncilguide.pdf accessed 25 October 2016.

DIDCE, 'Draft Convention on the International Status of Environmentally Displaced Persons' in J. Bétaille and M. Prieur (eds), *Les Catastrophes Écologiques et le Droit: Échecs du Droit, Appels au Droit* (Bruylant 2012).

Dietz, K., 'Prima Klima in den Nord–Süd-Beziehungen? Die Antinomien globaler Klimapolitik: Diskurse, Politiken und Prozesse' in H.-J. Burchardt (ed.), *Nord–Süd-Beziehungen im Umbruch: Neue Perspektiven auf Staat und Demokratie in der Weltpolitik* (Campus Verlag 2009).

Displacement Solutions, *Regulatory Obstacles to Rapid and Equitable Emergency and Interim Shelter Solutions after Natural Disasters* (2011).

Displacement Solutions, *The Peninsula Principles on Climate Displacement within States* (2013) http://displacementsolutions.org/wp-content/uploads/FINAL-Peninsula-Principles-FINAL.pdf accessed 25 October 2016.

Displacement Solutions, *Climate Displacement in Bangladesh: Stakeholders, Laws and Policies – Mapping the Existing Institutional Framework* (2014) http://displacementsolutions.org/wp-content/uploads/Mapping-Study-Climate-Displacement-Bangladesh.pdf accessed 25 October 2016.

Displacement Solutions, 'Bangladesh HLP Initiative: Updates and Developments' (2014) http://displacementsolutions.org/bangladesh-hlp-initiative-updates-and-developments accessed 25 October 2016.

Displacement Solutions, *Climate Displacement in Ontong Java, Solomon Islands* (2015) http://displacementsolutions.org/wp-content/uploads/2015/11/DIS4231-Ontong-Java-Photo-journal-v2_1-WEB.pdf accessed 25 October 2016.

Displacement Solutions, *Climate Displacement and Planned Relocation in Colombia: The Case of Gramalote* (2015) http://displacementsolutions.org/wp-content/uploads/2015/08/Colombia-final-Redux1.pdf accessed 25 October 2016.

Displacement Solutions, *Judicial Approaches to the Protection of Climate Displaced Persons: A Guide for the Legal Profession* (2016).

Displacement Solutions, *World Climate Displacement Map* (2016) http://displacementsolutions.org/world-displacement-map accessed 25 October 2016.

Displacement Solutions, *The Preventing and Resolving Climate Displacement: The Critical Role of Land Use Planning* (forthcoming).

Displacement Solutions and Young Power in Social Action, *Guidance Note on New Land for Climate Displaced Persons in Bangladesh* (2015) http://displacementsolutions.org/wp-content/uploads/2010/03/Guidance-Note-New-Land-for-Climate-Displaced-Persons-in-Bangladesh-FINAL.pdf accessed 25 October 2016.

Docherty, B., 'General Obligations in Repairing Domestic Climate Displacement' in S. Leckie and C. Huggins (eds), Repairing Domestic Climate Displacement: The Peninsula Principles (Routledge 2016).

Docherty, B. and T. Giannini, 'Confronting a Rising Tide: A Proposal for a Convention on Climate Change Refugees' (2009) 33 *Harvard Environmental Law Review*.

DPPS, 'Govt Gives IDPs Sh1bn, Orders Camps Closed' (4 February 2016) *Daily Nation* www.nation.co.ke/news/politics/Govt-gives-IDPs-Sh1bn-closes-camps/-/1064/3062636/-/3q74fl/-/index.html accessed 25 October 2016.

Dunne, J. P., R. J. Stouffer and J. G. John, 'Reductions in Labour Capacity from Heat Stress under Climate Warming' (2013) 3 *Nature Climate Change*.

Dwyer, G., *Climate Wars: The Fight for Survival as the World Overheats* (Oneworld Publications 2010).

EACH-FOR, *Synthesis Report* (2009).

Eberhard, W., 'Of Tsunamis and Climate Change: The Need to Resettle? The Pacific Islands' (2012) paper presented at the European Science Foundation Conference 'Tracing Social Inequalities in Environmentally Induced Migration', University of Bielefeld.

El-Hinnawi, E., *Environmental Refugees* (United Nations Environment Programme 1985).

Environmental Justice Foundation (EJF), *Climate Change Migration Human Rights* (2011).

Environmental Justice Foundation (EJF), *A Nation under Threat: The Impacts of Climate Change on Human Rights and Forced Migration in Bangladesh* (2012).

Ericson, J. P. *et al.*, 'Effective Sea-Level Rise and Deltas: Causes of Change and Human Dimension Implications' (2006) 50 *Global and Planetary Change*.

Esteban, M. and L. Yamamoto, 'Vanishing Island States and Sovereignty' (2010) 53 *Ocean and Coastal Management*.

EU Directorate-General on Development and Cooperation, 'Thematic Programme "Cooperation with Third Countries in the Areas of Migration and Asylum": 2011–2013 Multi-Annual Strategy Paper' (European Commission 2010).

EU High Representative, 'Climate Change and Security: Recommendations of the High Representative on Follow-Up to the High Representative and Commission Report on Climate Change and International Security' (2008) S412/08.

EU High Representative and the European Commission, 'Climate Change and International Security: Paper from the High Representative and the European Commission to the European Council' (2008) S113/08.

European Commission, 'Communication from the Commission to the Council and the European Parliament: Climate Change in the Context of Development Cooperation' (2003) COM (2003) 85 final.

European Commission, 'Adapting to Climate Change: Towards a European Framework for Action' (2009) COM (2009) 147 final.

European Commission, 'Communication from the Commission to the European Parliament, the Council, the European Economic and Social Committee and the Committee of the Regions: A Renewed EU Strategy 2011–14 for Corporate Social Responsibility' (2011) COM (2011) 681 final.

European Commission, 'Communication from the European Commission to the European Parliament, the Council, the European Economic and Social Committee and the Committee of the Regions: The Global Approach to Migration and Mobility' (2011) COM (2011) 743 final.

European Commission, 'Migration and Development: Commission Staff Working Paper' (2011) SEC (2011) 1353 final.

European Commission, 'Climate Change, Environmental Degradation, and Migration' (2013) SWD (2013) 138 final.

European Commission, 'Communication from the Commission to the European Parliament, the Council, the European Economic and Social Committee and the Committee of the Regions: An EU Strategy on Adaptation to Climate Change' (2013) COM (2013) 216 final.

European Commission, 'Priorities, Energy Union and Climate, Climate Action – Emission Reduction' (2016) in *COP21 UN Climate Change Conference, Paris* http://ec.europa.eu/priorities/energy-union-and-climate/climate-action-emission-reduction/cop21-un-climate-change-conference-paris_en accessed 25 October 2016.

European Commission, 'European Climate Change Programme' (2016).

European Council, 'The Stockholm Programme: An Open and Secure Europe Serving and Protecting Citizens (2010/C 115/01)' (2010) 53 *Official Journal of the European Union*.

Fair, H., 'Not Drowning but Fighting: Pacific Islands Activists' (2015) 49 *Forced Migration Review*.

Farbotko, C., 'Wishful Sinking: Disappearing Islands, Climate Refugees and Cosmopolitan Experimentation' (2010) 51 *Asia Pacific Viewpoint*.

Farbotko, C., 'Skilful Seafarers, Oceanic Drifters or Climate Refugees? Pacific People, News Value and the Climate Refugee Crisis' in K. Moore, B. Gross and T. Threatgold (eds), *Migrations and the Media* (Peter Lang Publishing 2012).

Farbotko, C. and H. Lazrus, 'The First Climate Refugees? Contesting Global Narratives of Climate Change in Tuvalu' (2012) 22 *Global Environmental Change*.

Felli, R., 'Managing Insecurity by Ensuring Continuous Capital Accumulation: "Climate Refugees" and "Climate Migrants"' (2013) 18(3) *New Political Economy*.

Felli, R. and N. Castree, 'Neoliberalising Adaptation to Environmental Change: Foresight or Foreclosure?' (2012) 44 *Environment and Planning A*.

Feng, S., A. B. Krueger and M. Oppenheimer, 'Linkages among Climate Change, Crop Yields and Mexico–US Cross-Border Migration' (2010) 107(32) *Proceedings of the National Academy of Sciences*.

Ferris, E., 'Climate Change Is Displacing People Now: Alarmists vs. Skeptics' (21 May 2014) www.brookings.edu/blogs/planetpolicy/posts/2014/05/21-climate-change-displacement-ferris accessed 25 October 2016.

Ferris, E., *On Climate Change, Migration and Policy* (Center for Migration Studies 2015) http://cmsny.org/climate-change-migration-policy accessed 25 October 2016.

Field, C. B., V. R. Barros, D. J. Dokken, K. J. Mach, M. D. Mastrandrea, T. E. Bilir, M. Chatterjee, K. L. Ebi, Y. O. Estrada, R. C. Genova, B. Girma, E. S. Kissel, A. N. Levy, S. MacCracken, P. R. Mastrandrea and L. L. White (eds), *Climate Change 2014: Impacts, Adaptation, and Vulnerability. Part A: Global and Sectoral Aspects. Contribution of Working Group II to the Fifth Assessment Report of the Intergovernmental Panel on Climate Change* (Cambridge University Press 2014).

Final Act of the UN Conference of Plenipotentiaries on the Status of Refugees and Stateless Persons (1951).

Fischer, E. M., K. W. Oleson and D. M. Lawrence, 'Contrasting Urban and Rural Heat Stress Responses to Climate Change' (2012) 39 *Geophysical Research Letters*.

Fischer, M. M. J., 'Technoscientific Infrastructures and Emergent Forms of Life: A Commentary' (2005) 107 *American Anthropologist*.

Fisher, S., 'The Emerging Geographies of Climate Justice' (2015) 181 *Geographical Journal*.

Fornalé, E., 'The Future Role of Labour Mobility Mechanisms in the Context of Environmental Degradation: Building or Crumbling Adaptation Strategies' (forthcoming) KNOMAD Working Paper.

Forsyth, T., 'Climate Justice Is Not Just Ice' (2014) 54 *Geoforum*.

Frynas, J. G., 'Corporate Social Responsibility or Government Regulation? Evidence on Oil Spill Prevention' (2012) 17 *Ecology and Society*.

Gamble, J. L. and J. J. Hess, 'Temperature and Violent Crime in Dallas, Texas: Relationships and Implications of Climate Change' (2012) 13 *Western Journal of Emergency Medicine*.

Gassner, M., *Prävention irregulärer Migration im integrierten Gesamtansatz zur Migrationsfrage: Entwicklungszusammenarbeit im Dienst der europäischen Migrationspolitik am Beispiel Marokko* (Diplomarbeit, Philologisch-Kulturwissenschaftliche Fakultät, Universität Wien 2010).

Gemenne, F., *Environmental Changes and Migration Flows: Normative Frameworks and Policy Responses* (2009) Doctorate in Political Sciences, Institut d'Etudes Politiques de Paris and the University of Liege.

Gemenne, F., 'Climate-Induced Population Displacements in a 4°C+ World' (2011) 369 *Philosophical Transactions of the Royal Society A: Mathematical, Physical and Engineering Sciences.*

Gemenne, F., 'Migration Doesn't Have to Be a Failure to Adapt: An Escape from Environmental Determinism' in J. Palutikof *et al.* (eds), *Climate Adaptation Futures* (John Wiley & Sons Ltd 2013).

Gemenne, F., 'One Good Reason to Speak of Climate Refugees' (2015) 49 *Forced Migration Review.*

Gemenne, F. and J. Blocher, 'How Can Migration Support Adaptation? Different Options to Test the Migration–Adaptation Nexus' (2014) paper presented at the COST Workshop on Environmental Migration, World Trade Institute.

Georgi, F., 'Kritik des Migrationsmanagements: Historische Einordnung eines politischen Projekts' (2009) 2 *Juridikum: Zeitschrift für Politik / Recht / Gesellschaft.*

GIBB Africa, 'Olkaria IV (Domes) Geothermal Project in Naivasha District: Resettlement Action Plan for Olkaria IV Power Station' (2012) www-wds.worldbank.org/external/default/WDSContentServer/WDSP/IB/2012/07/27/000333037_20120727015 202/Rendered/PDF/RP8830v110P1030IA0IV0RAP0JULY002012.pdf accessed 25 October 2016.

Gibb, C. and J. Ford, 'Should the United Nations Framework Convention on Climate Change Recognize Climate Migrants?' (2012) 7(4) *Environmental Research Letters.*

Gibson, J. and D. McKenzie, *Australia's Pacific Seasonal Worker Pilot Scheme (PSWPS): Development Impacts in the First Two Years* (2011) http://siteresources.worldbank.org/DEC/Resources/Australia_Pacific_Seasonal_Worker_Pilot_Scheme.pdf accessed 25 October 2016.

Giddens, A., *The Politics of Climate Change* (John Wiley & Sons 2009).

Godfery, M., 'New Zealand Refuses Climate Change Refugees: Mass Action Is Now Needed' (5 December 2014) *Guardian* www.theguardian.com/commentisfree/2014/may/12/new-zealand-refuses-climate-change-refugees-mass-action-is-now-needed accessed 27 March 2016.

Goodwin-Gill, G. S. and J. McAdam, *The Refugee in International Law* (3rd edn, Oxford University Press 2007).

Gooley, B., 'Nuremberg or the South African TRC: A Comparison of the Retributive and Restorative Models of Justice' (2012) University of Connecticut Honors Scholar Thesis Paper.

Government of Kenya (GOK), *National Disaster Management Policy of Kenya: Final Draft* (2010) http://de.scribd.com/doc/136662332/National-Disaster-Management-Policy-of-Kenya-Final-Draft-Oct-2010#scribd accessed 25 October 2016.

Grasso, M., *Justice in Funding Adaptation under the International Climate Change Regime* (Springer 2010).

Gray, C. L. and V. Mueller, 'Natural Disasters and Population Mobility in Bangladesh' (2012) 109(16) *Proceedings of the National Academy of Sciences.*

Green Climate Fund, 'Home Page' (2016) www.greenclimate.fund/home accessed 27 September 2016.

Greens/EFA Group, *Declaration on Climate Migration* (2008).

Griffin, D. R., *Unprecedented: Can Civilization Survive the CO_2 Crisis?* (Clarity Press 2015).

Grinsted, A., J. C. Moore and S. Jevrejeva, 'Reconstructing Sea Level from Paleo and Projected Temperatures 200 to 2100 AD' (2010) 34 *Climate Dynamics*.

Gromilova, M. and N. Jägers, 'Climate Change Induced Displacement and International Law' in J. Verschuuren (ed.), *Research Handbook on Climate Change Adaptation Law* (Edward Elgar 2013).

Gunda, T., L. Benneyworth and E. Burchfield, 'Exploring Water Indices and Associated Parameters: A Case Study Approach' (2015) 17(1) *Water Policy*.

Gupta, D., 'Climate of Fear: Environment, Migration and Security' in F. Dodds, A. Highham and R. Sherman (eds), *Climate Change and Energy Insecurity* (Earthscan 2009).

Guterres, A., *Climate Change, Natural Disasters and Human Displacement: A UNHCR Perspective* (UNHCR 2009).

Haines, P., K. Rolley, S. Albert and S. McGuire, 'Empowering Solomon Islands Communities to Improve Resilience to Climate Change' (2015) 55(1) *Queensland Planner, Journal of the Planning Profession*.

Hakijamii, 'Draft Eviction and Resettlement Guidelines and Draft Bill, 2012: An Abridged Version' (2012) www.escr-net.org/sites/default/files/Final%20evictions%20booklet.pdf accessed 25 October 2016.

Haraway, D., 'Situated Knowledges: The Science Question in Feminism and the Privilege of Partial Perspective' (1988) 14 *Feminist Studies*.

Haraway, D., *Simians, Cyborgs and Women: A Reinvention of Nature* (Routledge 1991).

Hardin, R., 'From Bodo Ethics to Distributive Justice' (1999) 2 *Ethical Theory and Moral Practice*.

Harding, S., *Whose Science? Whose Knowledge?* (Cornell University Press 1991).

Harris, J. R. and M. P. Todaro, 'Migration, Unemployment and Development: A Two-Sector Analysis' (1970) 60 *American Economic Review*.

Hartmann, B., 'Rethinking Climate Refugees and Climate Conflict: Rhetoric, Reality and the Politics of Policy Discourse' (2010) 22 *Journal of International Development*.

Hathaway, J. C., 'A Reconsideration of the Underlying Premise of Refugee Law' (1990) 31 *Harvard International Law Journal*.

Hathaway, J. C., 'Reconceiving Refugee Law as Human Rights Protection' (1991) 23 *Journal of Refugee Studies*.

Hau'ofa, E., 'Our Sea of Islands' in V. Naidu and E. Waddell (eds), *A New Oceania: Rediscovering Our Sea of Islands* (University of the South Pacific 1993).

Hay, D. and S. Howes, *Australia's Pacific Seasonal Worker Pilot Scheme: Why Has Take-Up Been So Low?* (Development Policy Centre, Australian National University 2012) Discussion Paper No. 17.

Heltberg, R., P. B. Siegel and S. L. Jorgensen, 'Social Policies for Adaptation to Climate Change' in R. Mearns and A. Norton (eds), *Social Dimensions of Climate Change: Equity and Vulnerability in a Warming World* (World Bank 2010).

Herbeck, J. and M. Flitner, '"A New Enemy Out There"? Der Klimawandel als Sicherheitsproblem' (2010) 65 *Geographica Helvetica*.

Heyward, C., 'Climate Change as Cultural Injustice' in *New Waves in Global Justice* (Palgrave Macmillan 2014).

Hillerbrand, R., *Technik, Ökologie und Ethik* (Mentis Verlag 2006).

Hirokawa, K. H. and J. Rosenbloom, 'Climate Change Adaptation and Land Use Planning Law' in J. Verschuuren (ed.), *Research Handbook on Climate Change Adaptation Law* (Edward Elgar 2013)

Hiskes, R. P., *The Human Right to a Green Future: Environmental Rights and Intergenerational Justice* (Cambridge University Press 2008).

Hobson, J., *The Eurocentric Conception of World Politics: Western International Theory, 1760–2010* (Cambridge University Press 2012).

Hodgkinson, D., T. Burton, H. Anderson and L. Young, '"The Hour When the Ship Comes In": A Convention for Persons Displaced by Climate Change' (2010) 36(1) *Monash University Law Review*.

Hoffmann, A., *Getting Ahead of the Curve: Corporate Strategies that Address Climate Change* (Pew Center on Global Climate Change 2006) www.c2es.org/publications/getting-ahead-curve-corporate-strategies-address-climate-change accessed 11 January 2017.

Hollifield, M., M. T. Fullilove and S. E. Hobfoll, 'Climate Change Refugees' in I. Weissbecker and A. Marsella (eds), *Climate Change and Human Well-Being* (Springer 2011).

Houghton, J. T., G. J. Jenkins and J. J. Ephraums (eds), *Climate Change: The IPCC Scientific Assessment* (1990) report prepared for the IPCC by Working Group I.

Houthakker, H. S., 'An International Comparison of Household Expenditure Patterns, Commemorating the Centenary of Engel's Law' (1957) 25(4) *Econometrica, Journal of the Econometric Society*.

Hsiang, S. M., M. Burke and E. Miguel, 'Quantifying the Influence of Climate on Human Conflict' (2013) 341 *Science*.

Hufford, G. and J. Partain, *Climate Change and Short-Term Forecasting for Alaskan Northern Coasts* (National Weather Service 2005).

Hugo, G., 'Environmental Concerns and International Migration' (1996) 30(1) *International Migration Review*.

Hulme, M., 'Reducing the Future to Climate: A Story of Climate Determinism and Reductionism' (2011) 26 *Osiris*.

Human Rights and Equal Opportunity Commission (HREOC), *Background Paper: Human Rights and Climate Change* (2008).

Hyndman, J. and A. Mountz, 'Another Brick in the Wall? Neo-Refoulement and the Externalization of Asylum by Australia and Europe' (2008) 43 *Government and Opposition*.

ICIMOD Foundation, 'Help Save the Third Pole' (2016) www.icimod.org/?q=3491 accessed 27 September 2016.

IFAD, *Rural Poverty Report 2011* (2011).

Ikobe, C. and E. O. Abuya, 'Wasted Lives: Internally Displaced Persons Living in Camps in Kenya' (2010) 1(2) *Journal of International Humanitarian Legal Studies*.

Immigration New Zealand, 'Pacific Access Category' (n.d.) www.immigration.govt.nz/migrant/stream/live/pacificaccess/ accessed 25 October 2016.

Inter-Agency Standing Committee (IASC), *IASC Operational Guidelines on the Protection of Persons in Situations of Natural Disasters* (Brookings–Bern Project on Internal Displacement 2011).

Intergovernmental Panel on Climate Change (IPCC), *Climate Change: The IPCC Scientific Assessment: Final Report of Working Group I* (Cambridge University Press 1990).

Intergovernmental Panel on Climate Change (IPCC), 'Glossary A–D' in *Climate Change 2007: Working Group II: Impacts, Adaptation and Vulnerability* www.ipcc. ch/publications_and_data/ar4/wg2/en/annexessglossary-a-d.html accessed 25 October 2016.

Intergovernmental Panel on Climate Change (IPCC), 'Summary for Policymakers' in C. B. Field *et al.* (eds), *Managing the Risks of Extreme Events and Disasters to Advance Climate Change Adaptation: A Special Report of Working Groups I and II of the Intergovernmental Panel on Climate Change* (Cambridge University Press 2012).

Intergovernmental Panel on Climate Change (IPCC), 'Summary for Policymakers' in T. F. Stocker *et al.* (eds), *Climate Change 2013: The Physical Science Basis: Contribution of Working Group I to the Fifth Assessment Report of the Intergovernmental Panel on Climate Change* (Cambridge University Press 2013).

Intergovernmental Panel on Climate Change (IPCC), *Climate Change 2014: Synthesis Report* (2014).

Intergovernmental Panel on Climate Change (IPCC), 'Summary for Policymakers' in C. B. Field, V. R. Barros, D. J. Dokken, K. J. Mach, M. D. Mastrandrea, T. E. Bilir, M. Chatterjee, K. L. Ebi, Y. O. Estrada, R. C. Genova, B. Girma, E. S. Kissel, A. N. Levy, S. MacCracken, P. R. Mastrandrea and L. L. White (eds), *Climate Change 2014: Impacts, Adaptation, and Vulnerability. Part A: Global and Sectoral Aspects. Contribution of Working Group II to the Fifth Assessment Report of the Intergovernmental Panel on Climate Change* (Cambridge University Press 2014).

Internal Displacement Monitoring Centre (IDMC), 'Kenya: Too Early to Turn the Page on IDPs, More Work Is Needed' (2014) www.internal-displacement.org/ sub-saharan-africa/kenya/2014/kenya-too-early-to-turn-the-page-on-idps-more-work-is-needed accessed 25 October 2016.

Internal Displacement Monitoring Centre (IDMC), 'A Review of the Normative Framework in Kenya Relating to the Protection of IDPs – in the Context of the Kampala Convention and Other Supranational Frameworks' (2015) www.internal-displacement.org/assets/publications/2015/20150827-af-kenya-review-of-normative-framework-relating-to-protection-of-idps-en.pdf accessed 25 October 2016.

Internal Displacement Monitoring Centre (IDMC), 'Global Report on Internal Displacement 2016' (2016) www.internal-displacement.org/globalreport2016/#home accessed 10 January 2017.

International Bar Association (IBA), 'Achieving Justice and Human Rights in an Era of Climate Disruption' (2014) Climate Change Justice and Human Rights Task Force Report 147.

International Centre for Migration Policy Development (ICMPD), *Climate Refugees' Legal and Political Responses to Environmentally Induced Migration* (2011).

International Commission on Intervention and State Sovereignty (ICISS), *Responsibility to Protect* (International Development Research Centre 2001).

International Federation of Red Cross and Red Crescent Societies (IFRC), *What Is VCA? An Introduction to Vulnerability and Capacity Assessment* (2006).

International Federation of Red Cross and Red Crescent Societies (IFRC), 'Background Report Law and Regulation for the Reduction of Risk from Natural Disasters in Kenya: A National Law Desk Survey' (2012) http://drr-law.org/resources/Kenya-Desk-Survey.pdf accessed 25 October 2016.

International Federation of Red Cross and Red Crescent Societies (IFRC), *Integrating Climate Change and Urban Risks into the VCA: Ensure Effective Participatory Analysis and Enhanced Community Action* (2014).

International Federation of Red Cross and Red Crescent Societies (IFRC) and UN Development Programme (UNDP), *Effective Law and Regulation for Disaster Risk Reduction: A Multi-Country Report* (2013).

International Institute for Environment and Development (IIED), 'AdMit' (2016) www.iied.org/admit#about accessed 27 September 2016.

International Labour Organization (ILO), *Decent Work and Social Justice in Pacific Small Island Developing States: Challenges, Opportunities and Policy Responses* (2014).

International Labour Organization (ILO), *Kiribati National Labour Migration Policy* (2015).

International Labour Organization (ILO), *Tuvalu National Labour Migration Policy* (2015).

International Law Commission, *Draft Articles on the Protection of Persons in the Event of Disasters* (2014) A/CN.4/L.831.

International Organization for Migration (IOM), *Discussion Note: Migration and the Environment* (2007) MC/INF/288.

International Organization for Migration (IOM), *Climate Change, Environmental Degradation and Migration* (2012) International Dialogue on Migration No. 18.

International Organization for Migration (IOM), *Moving in the Right Direction? Assessing Progress in Doha: Migration in Climate Change Negotiations* (2013).

International Organization for Migration (IOM), 'Brief 5: State of Knowledge on Migration, Environment and Climate Change' in IOM, *Outlook on Migration, Environment and Climate Change* (2014).

International Organization for Migration (IOM), 'Migration and Climate Change' (2015) www.iom.int/migration-and-climate-change-0 accessed 27 September 2016.

International Organization for Migration (IOM), *Migration Governance Framework* (2015) C/106/40.

International Organization for Migration (IOM), Environmental Migration Portal www.environmentalmigration.iom.int accessed 25 October 2016.

International Tribunal for the Prosecution of Persons Responsible for Serious Violations of International Humanitarian Law Committed in the Territory of Former Yugoslavia since 1991 (ICTY), *Prosecutor v. Blagoje Simić, Miroslav Tadić, Simo Zarić* (judgement 17 October 2003).

International Tribunal for the Prosecution of Persons Responsible for Serious Violations of International Humanitarian Law Committed in the Territory of Former Yugoslavia since 1991 (ICTY), *Statute of the International Tribunal for the Prosecution of Persons Responsible for Serious Violations of International Humanitarian Law Committed in the Territory of the Former Yugoslavia since 1991* (concluded 25 May 1993).

Inuit Circumpolar Conference, *Petition to the Inter-American Commission on Human Rights Seeking Relief from Violations Resulting from Global Warming Caused by Acts and Omissions of the United States* (2005).

Ionesco, D., D. Mokhnacheva and F. Gemenne, *Atlas des migrations environnementales* (Presse de Science Po 2016).

IRIN, 'Drought Response Faces Funding Shortfall' (2009) www.irinnews.org/news/2009/11/24/drought-response-faces-funding-shortfall accessed 20 October 2016

Jacobson, J. L., 'Environmental Refugees: A Yardstick of Habitability' (1988) 8 *Bulletin of Science, Technology and Society*.

Jakobeit, C. and C. Methmann, *Klimaflüchtlinge: Die verleugnete Katastrophe* (Greenpeace e.V. 2007).

Jakobeit, C. and C. Methmann, '"Climate Refugees" as Dawning Catastrophe? A Critique of the Dominant Quest for Numbers' in J. Scheffran *et al.* (eds), *Climate Change, Human Security and Violent Conflict* (Springer 2012).

Jamieson, D., 'Climate Change, Responsibility, and Justice' (2010) 16 *Science and Engineering Ethics*.

Jeffries, M. O., J. Richter-Menge and J. E. Overland, *Arctic Report Card* (NOAA 2015).

Johnson, C. A., 'Governing Climate Displacement: The Ethics and Politics of Human Resettlement' (2012) 21 *Environmental Politics*.

Kagan, S., 'Making the Case for Preferential Access to Labour Markets for Kiribati and Tuvalu Migrants' (2015) http://devpolicy.org/making-the-case-for-preferential-access-to-labour-markets-for-kiribati-and-tuvalu-migrants-20140120/ accessed 25 October 2016.

Kahl, C. H., 'Population Growth, Environmental Degradation, and State-Sponsored Violence: The Case of Kenya, 1991–93' (1998) 23(2) *International Security*.

Kälin, W., *Guiding Principles on Internal Displacement: Annotations* (American Society of International Law 2008).

Kälin, W., 'A Human Rights-Based Approach to Building Resilience to Natural Disasters' (2011) www.brookings.edu/research/a-human-rights-based-approach-to-building-resilience-to-natural-disasters/ accessed 12 January 2017.

Kälin, W., 'From the Nansen Principles to the Nansen Initiative' (2012) 41 *Forced Migration Review*.

Kälin, W. and N. Schrepfer, 'Protecting People Crossing Borders in the Context of Climate Change Normative Gaps and Possible Approaches' (2012) UNHCR Legal and Protection Policy Research Series.

Kamungi, P. M., 'The Current Situation of IDPs in Kenya' (Jesuit Refugee Service 2001) http://jrs.net/Assets/Publications/File/ken-idp.pdf accessed 25 October 2016.

Kamungi, P. M., 'The Politics of Displacement in Multiparty Kenya' (2009) 27(3) *Journal of Contemporary African Studies*.

Kamungi, P. M., 'Municipalities and IDPs Outside of Camps: The Case of Kenya's "Integrated" Displaced Persons' (2013) www.brookings.edu/~/media/research/files/reports/2013/05/kenya-displacement/idp-municipal-authorities-kenya-may-2013-final.pdf accessed 25 October 2016.

Karanja, S. K., 'Land Restitution in the Emerging Kenyan Transitional Justice Process' (2010) 28 *Nordic Journal of Human Rights*.

Kartha, S. and P. Baer, 'Zero Carbon Zero Poverty, the Climate Justice Way: Achieving an Equitable Phase-Out of Carbon Emissions by 2050 while Protecting Human Rights' (Mary Robinson Foundation – Climate Justice 2014) www.mrfcj.org/wp-content/uploads/2015/02/MRFCJ-Zero-Zero-short-doc-v3.pdf accessed 20 October 2016.

Kauffeld, B. D., *Analysis and Recommendations to Enhance Development–Military Cooperation* (USAID and DoD 2014).

Kelman, I., 'Beyond Disaster, beyond Diplomacy' in M. Pellman (ed.), *Natural Disasters and Development in a Globalizing World* (Routledge 2003).

Kelman, I., 'Tsunami Diplomacy: Will the 26 December, 2004 Tsunami Bring Peace to the Affected Countries?' (2005) 10 *Sociological Research Online*.

Kelsey, J., *New Zealand's Commitments on Trade In Services and Labour Mobility* (Pacific Network on Globalisation 2009).

Kempf, W., 'A Sea of Environmental Refugees? Oceania in an Age of Climate Change' in E. Hermann, K. Klenke and M. Dickhardt (eds), *Form, Macht, Differenz: Motive und Felder ethnologischen Forschens* (Universitätsverlag Göttingen 2009).

Kenya National Bureau of Statistics (KNBS), 'Kenya Population and Housing Census 2009: Counting Our People for the Implementation of Vision 2030: Volume IC: Population Distribution by Age, Sex and Administrative Units' (2010) www.knbs.or. ke/index.php?option=com_phocadownload&view=category&download=584:volume-1c-population-distribution-by-age-sex-and-administrative-units&id=109:population-and-housing-census-2009&Itemid=599 accessed 25 October 2016.

Kenyan Ministry of Environment and Mineral Resources, *National Environmental Policy: Revised Draft #4* (2012) http://theredddesk.org/sites/default/files/national-environment-policy-may-2012_1.pdf accessed 9 June 2016.

Kenyan Ministry of Lands, 'Sessional Paper No. 3 of 2009 on National Land Policy' (2009).

Keridis, D., 'Earthquakes, Diplomacy and New Thinking in Foreign Policy' (2006) 30 *Fletcher Forum of World Affairs*.

Kiama, L. and F. Koome, 'Internal Displacement in Kenya: The Quest for Durable Solutions' (2014) 45 *Forced Migration Review*.

Kibreab, G., 'Environmental Causes and Impact of Refugee Movements: A Critique of the Current Debate' (1997) 21 *Disasters*.

Kiln, 'The Carbon Map' (2013) www.carbonmap.org/#Extraction accessed 27 September 2016.

Kimani-Murage, E. W., L. Schofield, F. Wekesah, S. Mohamed, B. Mberu, R. Ettarh, T. Egondi, C. Kyobutungi and A. Ezeh, 'Vulnerability to Food Insecurity in Urban Slums: Experiences from Nairobi, Kenya' (2014) 91(6) *Journal of Urban Health*.

Klepp, S., 'A Contested Asylum System: The European Union between Refugee Protection and Border Control in the Mediterranean Sea' (2010) 12 *European Journal of Migration and Law*.

Klepp, S., *Europa zwischen Grenzkontrolle und Flüchtlingsschutz: Eine Ethnographie der Seegrenze auf dem Mittelmeer* (Transcript Verlag 2011).

Klepp, S. and J. Herbeck, 'The Politics of Environmental Migration and Climate Justice in the Pacific Region' (2016) 7 *Journal of Human Rights and the Environment*.

Klinenberg, E., 'Denaturalizing Disaster: A Social Autopsy of the 1995 Chicago Heat-Wave' (1999) 28 *Theory and Society*.

Klinenberg, E., *Heat-Wave: A Social Autopsy of Disaster in Chicago* (University of Chicago Press 2003).

Klopp, J. and P. M. Kamungi, 'Failure to Protect: Lessons from Kenya's IDP Network' (2007) 28 *Forced Migration Review*.

Klopp, J. and N. M. Sheekh, 'Can the Guiding Principles Make a Difference in Kenya?' (2008) Special Issue *Forced Migration Review*.

Knox, J. H., 'Report of the Independent Expert on the Issue of Human Rights Obligations Relating to the Enjoyment of a Safe, Clean, Healthy and Sustainable Environment' (General Assembly of the United Nations 2012) A/HRC/22/43.

Kolmannskog, V. and F. Myrstad, 'Environmental Displacement in European Asylum Law' (2009) 11 *European Journal of Migration and Law*.

Kothari, U., 'Political Discourses of Climate Change and Migration: Resettlement Policies in the Maldives' (2014) 180 *Geographical Journal*.

Kungu, D. M., 'The Dilemma of Integration: Internally Displaced Persons in Uasigishu County, Kenya' (2015) 11(16) *European Scientific Journal*.

Kurian, G. T., Encyclopaedia of the Third World (4th edn, Facts on File 1992).

Lambert, J., Refugees and the Environment: The Forgotten Element of Sustainability (The Greens/European Free Alliance in the European Parliament 2002).

Lavenex, S. and E. M. Uçarer, 'The External Dimension of Europeanization' (2004) 39 Cooperation and Conflict.

Lazrus, H., 'The Governance of Vulnerability: Climate Change and Agency in Tuvalu, South Pacific' in S. Crate and M. Nuttal (eds), Anthropology and Climate Change: From Encounters to Actions (Left Coast Press 2009).

Le Billon, P. and A. Waizenegger, 'Peace in the Wake of Disaster? Secessionist Conflicts and the 2004 Indian Ocean Tsunami' (2007) 32 Transactions of the Institute of British Geographers.

Leckie, S., 'Climate-Related Disasters and Displacement: Homes for Lost Homes, Lands for Lost Lands' in J. M. Guzmán et al. (eds), Population Dynamics and Climate Change (UNFPA 2009).

Leckie, S. and E. Simperingham, 'Focusing on Climate-Related Internal Displacement' (2015) 49 Forced Migration Review.

Leo, C., 'The Failure of the "Progressive Farmer" in Kenya's Million-Acre Settlement Scheme' (1978) 16(4) Journal of Modern African Studies.

Levi, E. H., An Introduction to Legal Reasoning (University of Chicago Press 1948).

Levine, S. et al., The Relevance of 'Resilience'? (Overseas Development Institute 2012) Humanitarian Policy Group Policy Brief 49.

Lewis, W. A., 'Economic Development with Unlimited Supplies of Labour' (1954) 20 Manchester School of Economics and Social Studies.

Limon, M., 'Human Rights and Climate Change: Constructing a Case for Political Action' (2009) 33 Harvard Environmental Law Review.

Lock, S. et al., 'Secondary Stressors and Extreme Events and Disasters: A Systematic Review of Primary Research from 2010–2011' (2012) 4 PLoS Currents.

Locke, J. T., 'Climate Change-Induced Migration in the Pacific Region: Sudden Crisis and Long-Term Developments' (2009) 175 The Geographical Journal.

Lonsdale, J. and B. Berman, 'Coping with the Contradictions: The Development of the Colonial State in Kenya, 1895–1914' (1979) 20(4) Journal of African History.

Lubkemann, S. C., 'Involuntary Immobility: On a Theoretical Invisibility in Forced Migration Studies' (2008) 21(4) Journal of Refugee Studies.

Mahongo, S. B., 'The Changing Global Climate and Its Implication in Sea Level Trends in Tanzania and the Western Indian Ocean Region' (2009) 8(2) Western Indian Ocean Journal of Marine Science.

Mandela, N., Long Walk to Freedom: The Autobiography of Nelson Mandela (Little, Brown & Company 1994).

Manji, A., 'The Politics of Land Reform in Kenya 2012' (2014) 57(1) African Studies Review.

Martin, P., 'Low Skilled Labour Migration and Free Trade Agreements' in M. Panizzon, G. Zuercher and E. Fornalé (eds), The Palgrave Handbook of International Labour Mobility (Palgrave 2015).

Martin, S. F., 'Climate Change, Migration, and Governance' (2010) 26 Global Governance.

Mary Robinson Foundation – Climate Justice, various, www.mrfcj.org.

Massey, D. S. et al., 'Theories of International Migration: A Review and Appraisal' (1993) 19(3) Population and Development Review.

Maurer, B., 'Introduction to "Ethnographic Emergences"' (2005) 107 American Anthropologist.

Mayer, B., 'The International Legal Challenges of Climate-Induced Migration: Proposal for an International Legal Framework' (2011) 22 *Colorado Journal of International Environmental Law and Policy*.

Mayer, B., 'Fraternity, Responsibility and Sustainability: The International Legal Protection of Climate (or Environmental) Migrants at the Crossroads' (2012) 56 *Supreme Court Law Review* [Canada].

Mayer, B., 'Environmental Migration in Asia and the Pacific: Could We Hang Out Sometime?' (2013) 3(1) *Asian Journal of International Law*.

Mayer, B., 'Environmental Migration: Prospects for a Regional Governance in the Asia-Pacific Region' (2013) 16 *Asia Pacific Journal of Environmental Law*.

McAdam, J., *Complementary Protection in International Refugee Law* (Oxford University Press 2007).

McAdam, J., 'Swimming against the Tide: Why a Climate Change Displacement Treaty Is Not the Answer' (2011) 23(1) *International Journal of Refugee Law*.

McAdam, J., *Climate Change, Forced Migration, and International Law* (Oxford University Press 2012).

McAdam, J., 'No "Climate Refugees" in New Zealand' (13 August 2014) *Brookings Planet Policy Blog* www.brookings.edu/blogs/planetpolicy/posts/2014/08/13-climate-refugees-new-zealand-mcadam accessed 25 October 2016.

McAdam, J. and B. Saul, 'Displacement with Dignity: International Law and Policy Responses to Climate Change Migration and Security in Bangladesh' (2010) Sydney Law School, Legal Studies Research Paper No. 10/113.

McBarnet, D., 'Corporate Social Responsibility beyond Law, through Law, for Law: The New Corporate Accountability' in A. Voiculescu, T. Campbell and D. McBarnet (eds), *The New Corporate Accountability: Corporate Social Responsibility and the Law* (Cambridge University Press 2009).

McCorquodale, R., 'Corporate Social Responsibility and International Human Rights Law' (2009) 87 *Journal of Business Ethics*.

McKenzie, D., P. Garcia Martinez and L. A. Winters, *Who is Coming from Vanuatu to New Zealand under the New Recognised Seasonal Employer Programme* (World Bank Development Research Group Finance and Private Sector Team 2008).

McLeman, R. and B. Smit, 'Migration as an Adaptation to Climate Change' (2006) 76 *Climatic Change*.

McLeman, R. and B. Smit, *Climate Change and Human Migration: Past Experiences, Future Challenges* (Cambridge University Press 2014).

McNamara, K. E. and C. Gibson, '"We Do Not Want to Leave Our Land": Pacific Ambassadors at the United Nations Resist the Category of "Climate Refugees"' (2009) 40 *Geoforum*.

McNeil, A., 'Solomon Islands Planners' Four-Day Intensive' (2015) 55(1) *Queensland Planner, Journal of the Planning Profession*.

MECLEP Project – Migration, Environment and Climate Change: Evidence for Policy (2016) www.environmentalmigration.iom.int/migration-environment-and-climate-change-evidence-policy-meclep accessed 25 October 2016.

Merry, S. E., 'Legal Pluralism' (1988) 22(5) *Law and Society Review*.

Merry, S. E., 'Legal Pluralism and Transnational Culture: The Ka Ho'Okolokolonui Kanaka Maoli Tribunal, Hawai'i, 1993' in R. A. Wilson (ed.), *Human Rights, Culture and Context* (Pluto Press 1997).

Merry, S. E., 'Transnational Human Rights and Local Activism: Mapping the Middle' (2006) 108 *American Anthropologist*.

Merryman, J. H., 'Comparative Law and Social Change: On the Origins, Style, Decline and Revival of the Law and Development Movement' (1977) 25 *American Journal of Comparative Law.*

Merton, R. K., 'The Self-Fulfilling Prophecy' (1948) 8 *The Antioch Review.*

Methmann, C. and A. Oels, 'From "Fearing" to Empowering Climate Refugees: Governing Climate-Induced Migration in the Name of Resilience' (2015) 46(1) *Security Dialogue.*

Mezzadra, S., 'The Right to Escape' (2004) 4 *Ephemera: Theory and Politics in Organization.*

Mezzadra, S., 'Kapitalismus, Migrationen, soziale Kämpfe: Vorbemerkungen zu einer Theorie der Autonomie der Migration' in M. Pieper *et al.* (eds), *Empire und die biopolitische Wende: Die internationale Diskussion im Anschluss an Hardt und Negri* (Campus 2007).

Migrants in Countries in Crisis (MICIC), *Migrants in Countries in Crisis* (2016) https://micicinitiative.iom.int accessed 25 October 2016.

Mimura, N. *et al.*, 'Small Islands' in M. L. Parry *et al.* (eds), *Climate Change 2007: Working Group II: Impacts, Adaptation and Vulnerability* (Cambridge University Press 2007).

Montevideo Convention on the Rights and Duties of States (adopted 13 July 1934, entered into force 26 December 1934).

Morrissey, J., 'Environmental Change and Forced Migration: A State of the Art Review' (2009) paper prepared for the Refugee Studies Centre, Oxford Department of International Development.

Moulier Boutang, Y., 'Europa, Autonomie der Migration, Biopolitik' in M. Pieper *et al.* (eds), *Empire und die biopolitische Wende: Die internationale Diskussion im Anschluss an Hardt und Negri* (Campus 2007).

Moyn, S., *The Last Utopia: Human Rights in History* (Harvard University Press 2010).

Mueller, V., C. Gray and K. Kosec, 'Heat Stress Increases Long-Term Human Migration in Rural Pakistan' (2014) 4 *Nature Climate Change.*

Murakami, H., M. Sugi and A. Kitoh, 'Future Changes in Tropical Cyclone Activity in the North Indian Ocean Projected by the New High-Resolution MRI-AGCM' in M. Mohapatra *et al.* (eds) *Monitoring and Prediction of Tropical Cyclones in the Indian Ocean and Climate Change* (Springer 2014).

Musembi, C. N. and P. Kameri-Mbote, 'Mobility, Marginality and Tenure Transformation in Kenya: Explorations of Community Property Rights in Law and Practice' (2013) 17(1) *Nomadic Peoples.*

Myers, N., 'Environmental Refugees in a Globally Warmed World' (1993) 43 *BioScience.*

Myers, N., 'Environmental Refugees' (1997) 19 *Population and Environment.*

Myers, N., 'Environmental Refugees: A Growing Phenomenon of the 21st Century' (2002) 357 *Philosophical Transactions of the Royal Society: Biological Sciences.*

Nansen Initiative, *The Nansen Initiative: Disaster-Induced Cross-Border Displacement* (2015) www.nanseninitiative.org accessed 25 October 2016.

Nansen Initiative, *Agenda for the Protection of Cross-Border Displaced Persons in the Context of Disasters and Climate Change* (2015).

Naser, M. M., 'Climate Change and Forced Displacement: Obligation of States under International Human Rights Law' (2010) 22(2) *Sri Lanka Journal of International Law.*

National Snow and Ice Data Center (NSIDC), 'Arctic Sea Ice News & Analysis' (2016) https://nsidc.org/arcticseaicenews/2016/03/ accessed 25 October 2016.

National Trust, *Shifting Shores* (2015).

Newland, K., *Climate Change and Migration Dynamics: Improving US and EU Immigration Systems* (Migration Policy Institute 2011).

New Zealand Department of Labour, *Recognised Seasonal Employer: Interagency Understanding: Vanuatu* (2007).

New Zealand Ministry of Foreign Affairs & Trade, 'ASEAN Australia New Zealand FTA (AANZFTA)' (n.d.) www.mfat.govt.nz/en/trade/free-trade-agreements/free-trade-agreements-in-force/aanzfta-asean-australia-new-zealand-fta accessed 25 October 2016.

New Zealand Ministry of Foreign Affairs & Trade, 'NZ–China Free Trade Agreement' (n.d.) www.mfat.govt.nz/en/trade/free-trade-agreements/free-trade-agreements-in-force/china-fta accessed 25 October 2016.

Ngecu, W. M., C. M. Nyamai and G. Erima, 'The Extent and Significance of Mass-Movements in Eastern Africa: Case Studies of Some Major Landslides in Uganda and Kenya' (2004) 46(8) *Environmental Geology*.

Nicholls, R. J. and A. Cazenave, 'Sea-Level Rise and Its Impact on Coastal Zones' (2010) 328 *Science*.

Nicholson, C. T. M., 'Is the "Environmental Migration" Nexus an Analytically Meaningful Subject for Research?' (Center on Migration, Citizenship and Development 2011).

Norwegian Refugee Council, *Climate Changed: People Displaced* (2009).

Norwegian Refugee Council/Internal Displacement Monitoring Centre (NRC/IDMC), *Global Estimates 2015: People Displaced by Disasters* (2015).

Noxolo, P., P. Ragurham and C. Madge, 'Unsettling Responsibility: Postcolonial Interventions' (2012) 37 *Transactions of the Institute of British Geographers*.

Nurse, L. A. *et al.*, 'Small Islands' in V. R. Barros *et al.* (eds), *Climate Change 2014: Working Group II: Impacts, Adaptation and Vulnerability. Part B: Regional Aspects* (Cambridge University Press 2014).

Nyaoro, D., J. Schade and K. Schmidt, 'Migration, Environment and Climate Change: Understanding the Nexus in Kenya' (International Organization for Migration forthcoming).

Obama, B., 'Nobel Peace Prize Lecture' (2009) www.nobelprize.org/nobel_prizes/peace/laureates/2009/obama-lecture.html accessed 25 October 2016.

Ober, K., *Migration as Adaptation: Exploring Mobility as a Coping Strategy for Climate Change* (UK Climate Change and Migration Coalition 2015).

Observatory on Migration, *South–South Labour Mobility in the Pacific: An Overview* (2013).

'OCTA Presentations during the Sixth Non-State Actors Dialogue Workshop on PACER Plus' (2016) www.octapic.org/wp-content/uploads/2016/06/Labour-Mobility-.pdf accessed 25 October 2016.

OECD, *Integrating Climate Change Adaptation into Development Co-operation* (2009).

OECD, 'OECD Guidelines for Multinational Enterprises' (2011) http://dx.doi.org/10.1787/9789264115415-en accessed 27 September 2016.

Oels, A., 'Saving "Climate Refugees" as Bare Life? A Theory-Based Critique of Refugee Status for Climate-Induced Migrants' in *Papers Prepared for the ESF-ZiF-Bielefeld Conference on 'Environmental Degradation and Conflict: From Vulnerabilities to Capabilities'* (Center for Interdisciplinary Research 2010).

Okeke, I. N., 'Towards a New Growth Path in Africa: A Study of National Urban Policy Responses to Urbanisation' (2014) South African Cities Network Working

Paper 20 http://sacitiesnetwork.co.za/wp-content/uploads/2014/09/2014-08_sacn_national_urban_policy_in_africa_working_paper.pdf accessed 25 October 2016.

Olsson, L. *et al.*, 'Cross-Chapter Box on Heat Stress and Heat Waves' in C. B. Field, V. R. Barros, D. J. Dokken, K. J. Mach, M. D. Mastrandrea, T. E. Bilir, M. Chatterjee, K. L. Ebi, Y. O. Estrada, R. C. Genova, B. Girma, E. S. Kissel, A. N. Levy, S. MacCracken, P. R. Mastrandrea and L. L. White (eds), *Climate Change 2014: Impacts, Adaptation, and Vulnerability. Part A: Global and Sectoral Aspects. Contribution of Working Group II to the Fifth Assessment Report of the Intergovernmental Panel on Climate Change* (Cambridge University Press 2014).

Olsson, L. *et al.*, 'Why Resilience Is Unappealing to Social Science: Theoretical and Empirical Investigations of the Scientific Use of Resilience' (2015) 1(4) *Science Advances*.

O'Mahony, C., 'There Is No Such Thing as a Right to Dignity' (2012) 10(2) *International Journal of Constitutional Law*.

Öneryildiz v. Turkey (European Court of Human Rights 30 November 2004).

Orlitzky, M., D. S. Siegel and D. A. Waldman, 'Strategic Corporate Social Responsibility and Environmental Sustainability' (2011) 50 *Business and Society*.

Oxfam, *PACER Plus and Its Alternatives: Which Way for Trade and Development in the Pacific?* (2009).

Pacific Islands Forum Secretariat, 'Pacific Island Countries Trade Agreement (PICTA) Temporary Movement of Persons' (2014) paper presented at the 'Labour Mobility Workshop', Auckland, New Zealand.

Park, S. and United Nations High Commissioner for Refugees, 'Climate Change and the Risk of Statelessness: The Situation of Low-Lying Island States' (2011) PPLA/2011/04.

Parks, B. C. and J. T. Roberts, 'Climate Change, Social Theory and Justice' (2010) 27 *Theory, Culture and Society*.

Parliamentary Select Committee on the Resettlement of Internally Displaced Persons (PSC), 'Report of the Parliamentary Select Committee on the Resettlement of Internally Displaced Persons' (2012) www.knchr.org/portals/0/reports/psc_final_idps_report_2012-2.pdf accessed 25 October 2016.

Parnell, J., 'Island States Appeal for COP17 Ministers to Avert "Climate Genocide"' (2011) www.rtcc.org/policy/island-states-appeal-for-cop17-ministers-to-avert-%E2%80%9Cclimate-genocide%E2%80%9D/ accessed 25 October 2016.

Parry, M. L., O. F. Canziani, J. P. Palutikof, P. J. van der Linden and C. E. Hanson (eds), 'Impacts, Adaptation and Vulnerability, Appendix 1: Glossary' in *Contribution of Working Group II to the Fourth Assessment Report of the Intergovernmental Panel on Climate Change* (Cambridge University Press 2007).

Patrick, S. and K. Brown, 'The Pentagon and Global Development: Making Sense of the DoD's Expanding Role' (2007) https://papers.ssrn.com/sol3/papers.cfm?abstract_id=1101526 accessed 17 December 2016.

Pearce, F., *When the Rivers Run Dry: What Happens When Our Water Runs Out?* (Random House 2012).

Penz, P., 'International Ethical Responsibilities to "Climate Change Refugees"' in J. McAdam (ed.), *Climate Change and Displacement: Multidisciplinary Perspectives* (Oxford University Press 2010).

Pethick, J. and J. D. Orford, 'Rapid Rise in Effective Sea-Level in Southwest Bangladesh: Its Causes and Contemporary Rates' (2013) 111 *Global and Planetary Change*.

Piguet, E., 'From "Primitive Migration" to "Climate Refugees": The Curious Fate of the Natural Environment in Migration Studies' (2013) 103 *Annals of the Association of American Geographers*.

Pillwein, S., *Climate Refugees: Klimawandel und Migration am Beispiel des Inselstaates Tuvalu im Pazifik* (Diplomica Verlag 2013).

Polya, G., 'Climate Racism, Climate Injustice and Climate Genocide: Australia, US and EU Sabotage Copenhagen COP15' (2009) http://bellaciao.org/en/spip.php?article 19422 accessed 25 October 2016.

Porter, J. R. *et al.*, 'Food Security and Food Production Systems' in C. B. Field, V. R. Barros, D. J. Dokken, K. J. Mach, M. D. Mastrandrea, T. E. Bilir, M. Chatterjee, K. L. Ebi, Y. O. Estrada, R. C. Genova, B. Girma, E. S. Kissel, A. N. Levy, S. MacCracken, P. R. Mastrandrea and L. L. White (eds), *Climate Change 2014: Impacts, Adaptation, and Vulnerability. Part A: Global and Sectoral Aspects. Contribution of Working Group II to the Fifth Assessment Report of the Intergovernmental Panel on Climate Change* (Cambridge University Press 2014).

Practical Action, 'Corporate Social Responsibility and Our Changing Climate' (2014) http://practicalaction.org/climate-change-3 accessed 27 September 2016.

Preston, I. *et al.*, 'Climate Change and Social Justice: An Evidence Review' (Joseph Rowntree Foundation – Centre for Sustainable Energy 2014).

Principles for Responsible Investment (PRI), 'Information on the UN-Backed Principles for Responsible Investment' www.unpri.org accessed 25 October 2016.

Quisumbing, A., R. Meinzen-Dick, J. Njuki and N. Johnson (eds), *Gender, Agriculture and Assets: Learning from Eight Agricultural Development Interventions in Africa and South Asia* (IFPRI 2013).

Rahmstorf, S., 'New View on Sea Level Rise' (2010) 4 *Nature Reports Climate Change*.

Refugee Status Appeals Authority, New Zealand, Refugee Appeal Nos. 72189/2000, 72190/2000, 72191/2000, 72192/2000, 72193/2000, 72194/2000, 72195/2000 (judgement 17 August 2000).

Renaud, F., J. J. Bogardi, O. Dun and K. Warner, 'Control, Adapt or Flee: How to Face Environmental Migration?' (UNU Institute for Environment and Human Security 2007).

Reuters, 'Solomons Town First in Pacific to Relocate Due to Climate Change' (15 August 2014).

Risse, M., 'The Right to Relocation: Disappearing Island Nations and Common Ownership of the Earth' (2009) 23 *Ethics and International Affairs*.

Ritter, D., 'Climate Change and Human Rights: The Imperative for Climate Change Migration with Dignity (CCMD)' in M. Di Paola and D. Kamal (eds), *Climate Change and Human Rights: The 2015 Paris Conference and the Task of Protecting People on a Warming Planet* (Global Policy 2015).

Rizki, R. M., *Report of the Independent Expert on Human Rights and International Solidarity* (United Nations 2010) A/HRC/15/32.

Robinson, M., 'Climate Justice: Human Rights Informing Climate Action – Development that Also Grows Those at Risk and Those in Poverty' (10 December 2014) *Stakeholder Forum* www.stakeholderforum.org/fileadmin/files/OUTREACHCOP2 0DAY8.pdf accessed 12 January 2017.

Rolnik, R., *Report of the Special Rapporteur on Adequate Housing as a Component of the Right to an Adequate Standard of Living, and on the Right to Non-Discrimination in This Context* (United Nations 2010) A/HRC/16/42.

Rome Statute of the International Criminal Court (concluded 17 July 1998, entered into force 1 July 2002).

Rop, B. K., 'Landslide Disaster Vulnerability in Western Kenya and Mitigation Options: A Synopsis of Evidence and Issues of Kuvasali Landslide' (2011) 5(1) *Journal of Environmental Science and Engineering*.

Rouviere, C. *et al.*, 'Human Settlement; the Energy, Transport and Industrial Sectors; Human Health; Air Quality; and Changes in Ultraviolet-B Radiation' in W. J. M. Tegart, G. W. Sheldon and D. C. Griffiths (eds), *Climate Change: Working Group II: Impacts Assessment of Climate Change* (Australian Government Publishing Service 1990).

Rudiak-Gould, P., 'Climate Change and Anthropology: The Importance of Reception Studies' (2011) 27 *Anthropology Today*.

Ruggie, J., *Just Business: Multinational Corporations and Human Rights* (W. W. Norton & Company 2013).

Rutten, M. and S. Owuor, 'Weapons of Mass Destruction: Land, Ethnicity and the 2007 Elections in Kenya' (2009) 27(3) *Journal of Contemporary African Studies*.

Sand, P. H., 'Diego Garcia: British–American Legal Black Hole in the Indian Ocean?' (2009) 21 *Journal of Environmental Law*.

Saunders, P. L., 'Environmental Refugees: The Origins of a Construct' in P. Scott and S. Sullivan (eds), *Political Ecology: Science, Myth and Power* (Arnold 2000).

Schade, J., 'Land Matters: The Role of Land Policies and Laws for Environmental Migration in Kenya' (2016) Migration, Environment and Climate Change Policy Brief Series 2(1) https://publications.iom.int/books/migration-environment-and-climate-change-policy-brief-series-issue-1-vol-2-january-2016 accessed 25 October 2016.

Schade, J., 'Kenya Case Study Report: ClimAccount – Human Rights Accountability of the EU and Austria for Climate Policies in Third Countries and Their Possible Effects on Migration' (forthcoming) COMCAD Working Paper.

Schade, J. *et al.*, 'Climate Change and Climate Policy Induced Relocations: A Challenge for Social Justice – Recommendations of the Bielefeld Consultation' (2015) Migration, Environment and Climate Change Policy Brief Series 1(10) http://publications.iom.int/system/files/pdf/policy_brief_series_issue10_0.pdf accessed 9 June 2016.

Schmedding, T., *Environmental Migration: A Global Issue under European Union Leadership?* (Centre international de formation européenne, Institut européen des hautes études internationales, Academy of Nice 2011).

Semenza, J. C. *et al.*, 'Heat-Related Deaths during the July 1995 Heat-Wave in Chicago' (1996) 335 *New England Journal of Medicine*.

Sherbinin, A. *et al.*, 'Preparing for Resettlement Associated with Climate Change' (2011) 334 *Science*.

Sherwood, S. C. and M. Huber, 'An Adaptability Limit to Climate Change due to Heat Stress' (2010) 107 *Proceedings of the National Academy of Sciences*.

Shulski, M. and G. Wendler, *The Climate of Alaska* (University of Alaska Press 2007).

Silva, J., 'Purposes of Trust in Trust Law' (2016) www.climate-justice-now.org/purposes-of-trust-in-trust-law/ accessed 11 January 2017.

Simmons, B. A., *Mobilizing for Human Rights: International Law in Domestic Politics* (Cambridge University Press 2009).

Simperingham, E., 'The Urgent Need for Rights Based Solutions to Climate Displacement in Bangladesh' (10 October 2015) *Dhaka Tribune* www.dhakatribune.com/feature/2015/oct/10/urgent-need-rights-based-solutions-climate-displacement-bangladesh accessed 25 October 2016.

Simperingham, E., 'The Responsibilities of States to Protect Climate Displaced Persons' in S. Leckie and C. Huggins (eds), *Repairing Domestic Climate Displacement: The Peninsula Principles* (Routledge 2016).

Sitkin, A. and N. Bowen, *International Business: Challenges and Choices* (Oxford University Press 2013).

Sjaastad, L. A., 'The Costs and Returns of Human Migration' in H. W. Richardson (ed.), *Regional Economics* (Springer 1970).

Smith, A. O., 'Introduction' in A. O. Smith (ed.), *Development and Dispossession: The Crisis of Forced Displacement and Resettlement* (Santa Fe School for Advanced Research Press 2009).

Smith, E. W., 'Land in Kenya' (1936) 35(140) *Journal of the Royal African Society*.

Soltau, F., *Fairness in International Climate Change Law and Policy* (Cambridge University Press 2009).

Somerville, W., *Environmental Migration Governance: Debate in the European Union* (Foresight 2011).

Special Rapporteur on the Human Rights of Migrants, *Human Rights of Migrants* (United Nations 2012) UNGAA/67/299.

Stark, O. and D. E. Bloom, 'The New Economics of Labor Migration' (1985) 75 *American Economic Review*.

Statute of the International Criminal Tribunal for the Former Yugoslavia (concluded United Nations Security Council 25 May 1993) SC Res. 827.

Stern, N. H., *The Economics of Climate Change: The Stern Review* (Cambridge University Press 2007).

Storey, D. and S. Hunter, 'Kiribati: An Environmental "Perfect Storm"' (2010) 41 *Australian Geographer*.

Straussa, B. H., S. Kulpa and A. Levermann, 'Carbon Choices Determine US Cities Committed to Futures below Sea Level' (2015) *Proceedings of the National Academy of Sciences* www.pnas.org/content/early/2015/10/07/1511186112.full.pdf accessed 25 October 2016.

Suckalla, N., E. Fraser and P. Forster, 'Reduced Migration under Climate Change: Evidence from Malawi Using an Aspirations and Capabilities Framework' (2016) *Climate and Development* www.tandfonline.com/doi/full/10.1080/17565529.2016.1149441 accessed 25 October 2016.

Suhrke, A., 'Environmental Degradation and Population Flows' (1994) 47 *Journal of International Affairs*.

Sydney Morning Herald, 'Escaping the Waves: A Fijian Village Relocates' (3 October 2015).

Syvitski, J. et al., 'Sinking Deltas due to Human Activities' (2009) 2 *Nature Geoscience*

Syvitski, J. and S. Higgins, 'Going Under: The World's Sinking Deltas' (2012) 216 *New Scientist*.

Tabucanon, G. M. and B. Opeskin, 'The Resettlement of Nauruans in Australia: An Early Case of Failed Environmental Migration' (2011) 46(3) *Journal of Pacific History*.

Tanner, T. and J. Allouche, 'Towards a New Political Economy of Climate Change and Development' (2011) 42 *IDS Bulletin*.

Tawatsupa, B. et al., 'Heat Stress, Health and Well-Being: Findings from a Large National Cohort of Thai Adults' (2012) 2 *British Medical Journal Open*.

Teitiota v. Chief *Executive of the Ministry of Business Innovation and Employment* (2014) NZCA 173, NZAR 688.

Thomalla, F. *et al.*, 'Reducing Hazard Vulnerability: Towards a Common Approach between Disaster Risk Reduction and Climate Adaptation' (2006) 30(1) *Disasters.*

Thornton, F., 'Regional Labour Migration as Adaptation to Climate Change? Options in the Pacific' in M. Leighton, S. Xiaomeng and K. Warner (eds), *Climate Change and Migration: Rethinking Policies for Adaptation and Disaster Risk Reduction* (United Nations University 2011) www.auca.kg/uploads/Source%20Pub%20Climate %20Change%20and%20Migration.pdf accessed 13 January 2017.

Thorp, T., *Climate Justice: A Voice for the Future* (Palgrave Macmillan 2014).

Todaro, M. P., 'Internal Migration in Developing Countries: A Survey' in R. A. Easterlin (ed.), *Population and Economic Change in Developing Countries* (University of Chicago Press 1976).

Tomlinson, S. A., 'No New Orleanians Left Behind: An Examination of the Disparate Impact of Hurricane Katrina on Minorities' (2005) 38 *Connecticut Law Review.*

Tompson, T. *et al.*, *Resilience in the Wake of Superstorm Sandy* (Associated Press–NORC Centre for Public Affairs Research 2013).

Truth, Justice and Reconciliation Commission (TJRC), 'Report of the Truth, Justice and Reconciliation Commission' (2013) http://digitalcommons.law.seattleu.edu/tjrc accessed 25 October 2016.

Tsianios, V., *Imperceptible Politics: Rethinking Radical Politics of Migration and Precarity Today* (Department Sozialwissenschaften, Universität Hamburg 2007).

Tsing, A. L., *Friction: An Ethnography of Global Connection* (Princeton University Press 2005).

UK Government Office for Science, *Foresight: Migration and Global Environmental Change: Final Project Report* (2011).

UK Government Office for Science, *Migration and Global Environmental Change: Future Challenges and Opportunities* (2011).

UN Commission on Human Rights, Sub-Commission on Prevention of Discrimination and Protection of Minorities, *Report on the Right to Adequate Food as a Human Right Submitted by Mr Asbjørn Eide, Special Rapporteur* (1987) E/CN.4/Sub.2/1987/23.

UN Committee on Economic, Social and Cultural Rights, 'Fact Sheet No. 16' (1945).

UN Committee on Economic, Social and Cultural Rights, *General Comment No. 7: The Right to Adequate Housing (Art.11.1): Forced Evictions* (1997) E/1998/22.

UN Committee on Economic, Social and Cultural Rights, *General Comment No. 12: The Right to Adequate Food* (1999) E/C.12/1995/5.

UN Committee on Economic, Social and Cultural Rights, *General Comment No. 14: The Right to the Highest Attainable Standard of Health* (2000) E/C.12/2000/4.

UN Committee on Economic, Social and Cultural Rights, *General Comment No. 14: The Right to Water* (2002) E/C.12/2002/11.

UN Development Programme (UNDP), *Fighting Climate Change: Human Solidarity in a Divided World* [Human Development Report] (2007).

UN Development Programme (UNDP), *Work for Human Development* [Human Development Report] (2015).

UN Development Programme (UNDP), 'Kenya Natural Disaster Profile' (n.d.) retrieved from the Global Risk Information Platform (GRIP) www.gripweb.org/ gripweb/sites/default/files/disaster_risk_profiles/Preliminary%20Natural%20Hazard %20Risk%20Profile%20of%20Kenya.pdf accessed 25 October 2016.

UN Economic and Social Council, *Final Report of the Special Rapporteur, Paulo Sérgio Pinheiro: Principles on Housing and Property Restitution for Refugees and Displaced Persons* (2005) E/CN.4/Sub.2/2005/17.

UN Economic and Social Council, *Specific Groups and Individuals: Mass Exoduses and Displaced Persons, Report of the Representative of the Secretary-General on the Human Rights of Internally Displaced Persons, Walter Kálin* (2006) E/CN.4/2006/71.

UNFCCC, *Cancun Agreements Adopted by COP16 of the UNFCCC* (2010) http:// unfccc.int/meetings/cop_16/items/5571.php accessed 25 October 2016.

UNFCCC, *Paris Agreement Concluded at the 21st Conference of the Parties to the UN Framework Convention on Climate Change* (adopted 12 December 2015, entered into force 4 November 2016) FCCC/CP/2015/L.9/Rev.1.

UN General Assembly, Resolution 8(I) (adopted 12 February 1946) [Annex III of the *Constitution of the International Refugee Organization*].

UN General Assembly, Resolution 60/1 (adopted 24 October 2005).

UN General Assembly, *World Summit Outcome Document* (2005).

UN General Assembly, *Convention for the Safeguarding of the Intangible Cultural Heritage* (2006).

UN General Assembly, *Universal Declaration on the Rights of Indigenous Peoples* (2007).

UN General Assembly, 'Agenda Item 2' (2009) A/HRC/10/61 HRC.

UN General Assembly, 'Chapter IX: Protection of Persons in the Event of Disasters' in *Sixty-Sixth Session, Supplement No. 10* (2011) A/66/10.

UN General Assembly, 'One Humanity: Shared Responsibility. Report of the Secretary-General for the World Humanitarian Summit' (2016) A/70/709.

UN Habitat, *Land and Natural Disasters: Guidance for Practitioners* (2010).

UNHCR, *Climate Change, Natural Disasters and Human Displacement: A UNHCR Perspective* (2009).

UNHCR, *Legal and Protection Policy* (2011) PPLA/2011/04.

UNHCR, *Summary of Deliberations on Climate Change and Displacement* (2011) www. unhcr.org/542e95f09.html accessed 25 October 2016.

UNHCR, 'Summary of Deliberations on Climate Change and Displacement' (2011) 23(3) *International Journal of Refugee Law*.

UNHCR, *Planned Relocations, Disasters and Climate Change: Consolidating Good Practices and Preparing for the Future* (2014) background document for San Remo consultation.

UNHCR, *Climate Change and Disasters* (2015) www.unhcr.org/pages/49e4a5096.html accessed 25 October 2016.

UNHCR, IOM and NRC, *Climate Change and Statelessness: An Overview – Submission to the 6th Session of the Ad Hoc Working Group on Long-Term Cooperative Action (AWG-LCA 6) under the UN Framework Convention on Climate Change (UNFCCC)* (2009).

UN Human Rights Council, *The Right to Food* (2011) A/HRC/RES/16/27.

UN Human Rights Council, *Human Rights and Climate Change* (2015) A/HRC/29/L.21.

UN Human Rights Council, *11th Report of the Commission of Inquiry on Syria* (2016) A/ HRC/31/68.

UNICEF, *The Impact of Climate Change on Children* (2015).

UNISDR, *The Human Cost of Weather Related Disasters 1995–2015* (2015).

United Nations, *Constitution of the International Refugee Organization* (adopted 15 December 1946).

United Nations, 'Record of the Third Meeting of the Ad Hoc Committee on Statelessness and Related Problems Held on 17 January 1950 at 3pm', E/AC.32/SR.3.

United Nations, *Convention Relating to the Status of Refugees* (adopted 28 July 1951, entered into force 22 April 1954) 189 UNTS 137.

United Nations, *International Covenant on Economic, Social and Cultural Rights* (adopted 16 December 1966, entered into force 3 January 1976) 993 UNTS 3.

United Nations, *Protocol Relating to the Status of Refugees* (adopted 31 January 1967, entered into force 4 October 1967) 606 UNTS 267.

United Nations, *Rio Declaration on Environment and Development* (1992) A/CONF.151/26.

United Nations, *Framework Convention on Climate Change* (UNFCCC) (concluded 9 May 1992, entered into force 21 March 1994).

United Nations, *Guiding Principles on Internal Displacement* (1998).

United Nations, *The Cancun Agreements: Outcome of the Work of the Ad Hoc Working Group on Long-Term Cooperative Action under the Convention* (2011) FCCC/CP/2010/7/Add.1.

United Nations, *Protection of and Assistance to Internally Displaced Persons* (adopted 19 December 2011, distributed 22 March 2012) A/RES/66/165.

United Nations, *Doha Decision on Loss and Damage* (2013) FCCC/CP/2012/8/Add.1.

United Nations, 'UN Climate Summit 2014' (2014) www.un.org/climatechange/summit/ accessed 27 September 2016.

United Nations, *Sendai Framework for Disaster Risk Reduction 2015–2030* (2015) A/CONF.224/CRP.1.

United Nations, *UN 2030 Agenda for Sustainable Development* (adopted 21 October 2015).

United Nations, 'Goal 13: Take Urgent Action to Combat Climate Change and Its Impacts' (2016) www.un.org/sustainabledevelopment/climate-change-2/ accessed 27 September 2016.

United Nations, Department of Social and Economic Affairs (DESA), 'Recommendations on Statistics, Revision 1' (1998) http://unstats.un.org/unsd/publication/SeriesM/seriesm_58rev1e.pdf accessed 25 October 2016.

United Nations, Department of Social and Economic Affairs (DESA), 'Population Facts: Trends in International Migration' (2015) www.un.org/en/development/desa/population/migration/publications/populationfacts/docs/MigrationPopFacts 20154.pdf accessed 25 October 2016.

United Nations Environment Programme (UNEP), 'Kenya: Atlas of Our Changing Environment' (2009) www.unep.org/pdf/Kenya_Atlas_Full_EN_72dpi.pdf accessed 25 October 2016.

United Nations Mandate on Human Rights and the Environment (John H. Knox, UN Special Rapporteur), 'UN Documents' (n.d.), http://srenvironment.org/un-documents accessed 25 October 2016.

United Nations, Office for the Coordination of Humanitarian Affairs (UNOCHA), 'Syria Drought Response Plan 2009–2010' (2009) www.unocha.org/cap/appeals/syria-drought-response-plan-2009-2010 accessed 20 October 2016.

United Nations, Office of the High Commissioner for Human Rights (OHCHR), 'Forced Evictions: Commission on Human Rights Resolution 1993/77' (1993) http://ap.ohchr.org/Documents/E/CHR/resolutions/E-CN_4-RES-1993-77.doc accessed 25 October 2016.

United Nations, Office of the High Commissioner for Human Rights (OHCHR), *Consultation on Human Rights and Access to Safe Drinking Water and Sanitation* (2007).

United Nations, Office of the High Commissioner for Human Rights (OHCHR), *Consultation on the Relationship between Climate Change and Human Rights* (2008).

United Nations, Office of the High Commissioner for Human Rights (OHCHR), *Guiding Principles on Internal Displacement* (2008) E/CN.4/1998/53/Add.2.

United Nations, Office of the High Commissioner for Human Rights (OHCHR), *Human Rights and Climate Change* (2008) Resolution 7/23.

United Nations, Office of the High Commissioner for Human Rights (OHCHR), *Report of the Office of the UN High Commissioner for Human Rights on the Relationship between Climate Change and Human Rights* (2009) A/HCR/10/61.

United Nations, Office of the High Commissioner for Human Rights (OHCHR), *UN Guiding Principles on Business and Human Rights* (2011).

United Nations, Office of the High Commissioner for Human Rights (OHCHR), *Towards Freedom from Fear and Want: Human Rights in the Post-2015 Agenda* (2012).

United Nations, Office of the High Commissioner for Human Rights (OHCHR), *The Core International Human Rights Instruments and Their Monitoring Bodies* (2014) www.ohchr.org/EN/ProfessionalInterest/Pages/CoreInstruments.aspx accessed 25 October 2016.

United Nations, Office of the High Commissioner for Human Rights (OHCHR), 'Human Rights and the Environment: Our Generation Must Meet the Great Challenge – UN Experts' (5 June 2015) www.ohchr.org/EN/NewsEvents/Pages/DisplayNews.aspx?NewsID=16052&LangID=E accessed 21 October 2016.

United Nations, Office of the High Commissioner for Human Rights (OHCHR), *Recommended Principles and Guidelines on Human Rights at International Borders* (2015).

United Nations, Office of the High Commissioner for Human Rights (OHCHR), 'Human Rights and Climate Change' (2016) www.ohchr.org/EN/Issues/HRAndClimateChange/Pages/HRClimateChangeIndex.aspx accessed 27 September 2016.

United States Congress Bicameral Task Force on Climate Change, *Implementing the President's Action Plan: US Department of the Interior* (2013).

UN Security Council, 'The Rule of Law and Transitional Justice in Conflict and Post-Conflict Societies' (2004) report of the Secretary-General, S/2004/616.

UN University (UNU), *Climate Change and Migration in the Pacific: Links, Attitudes and Future Scenarios in Nauru, Tuvalu and Kiribati* (2015).

US Army Corps of Engineers (USACE), *Alaska Village Erosion Technical Assistance Program: An Examination of Erosion Issues in the Communities of Bethel, Dillingham, Kaktovik, Kivalina, Newtok, Shishmaref and Unalakleet* (2006).

US Army Corps of Engineers (USACE), 'Section 117 Project Fact Sheet' (2008) www.commerce.state.ak.us/dca/planning/pub/Newtok_Sec_117.pdf accessed 25 October 2016.

US Army Corps of Engineers (USACE), 'Revised Environmental Assessment: Finding of No Significant Impact: Newtok Evacuation Center: Mertarvik, Nelson Island, Alaska' (2008) www.commerce.state.ak.us/dca/planning/pub/Newtok_Evacuation_Center_EA_&_FONSI_July_08.pdf accessed 25 October 2016.

USAID, 'Fact Sheet on Typhoon Haiyan/Yolanda in Philippines' (2014) http://iipdigital.usembassy.gov/st/english/texttrans/2013/11/20131112286248.html#ixzz3yyeFWGPR accessed 25 October 2016.

USAID, 'New Policy Guides: USAID's Cooperation with Department of Defense' (2015) https://blog.usaid.gov/2015/06/new-policy-guides-usaids-cooperation-with-department-of-defense/ accessed 25 October 2016.

Valencia-Ospina, E., *Preliminary Report on the Protection of Persons in the Event of Disasters* (United Nations 2008) A/CN.4/598.

Valencia-Ospina, E., *Sixth Report on the Protection of Persons in the Event of Disasters* (United Nations 2013) A/CN.4/66.

Veit, P., 'History of Land Conflicts in Kenya' (2008) www.focusonland.com/download/52076c59cca75 accessed 25 October 2016.

Vidal, J., 'Climate Change Brings New Risks to Greenland, Says PM Aleqa Hammond' (23 January 2014) *Guardian* www.theguardian.com/environment/2014/jan/23/climate-change-risks-greenland-arctic-icecap accessed 25 October 2016.

von Benda-Beckmann, F., K. von Benda-Beckmann and A. Griffiths, 'Mobile People, Mobile Law: An Introduction' in F. von Benda-Beckmann, K. von Benda-Beckmann and A. Griffiths (eds), *Mobile People, Mobile Law: Expanding Legal Relations in a Contracting World* (Ashgate 2005).

Wahlström, M., 'Chair's Summary' (2011) Nansen Conference on Climate Change and Displacement in the 21st Century, Oslo.

Walsh, J. E. *et al.*, 'Cryosphere and Hydrology' in *Arctic Climate Impact Assessment* (Cambridge University Press 2015).

Warner, K., 'Climate Change Induced Displacement: Adaptation Policy in the Context of the UNFCCC Climate Negotiations' (2011) UNHCR Legal and Protection Policy Research Series.

Warner, K., 'Climate and Environmental Change, Human Migration and Displacement: Recent Policy Developments and Research Gaps' (United Nations University 2011) UN/POP/MIG-9CM/2011/10.

Westra, L., *Environmental Justice and the Rights of Ecological Refugees* (Earthscan 2009).

Wewerinke, M., 'The Role of the UN Human Rights Council in Addressing Climate Change' (2014) 8(1) *Human Rights and International Legal Discourse*.

White, G., *Climate Change and Migration: Security and Borders in a Warming World* (Oxford University Press 2011).

White House, *President's State, Local and Tribal Leaders' Task Force on Climate Preparedness and Resilience, Recommendations to the President* (2014).

Wijnberg, H. and S. M. Leiderman, *The Toledo Initiative on Environmental Refugees and Ecological Restoration* (Living Space for Environmental Refugees and Environmental Refugees & Environmental Restoration Environmental Response/4th World Project 2004).

Wilson, C., S. Goodbred, C. Small, J. Gilligan and S. Sams, 'Widespread Infilling of Tidal Channels and Navigable Waterways in Human-Modified Delta Plain of Southwest Bangladesh' submitted to *PNAS Sustainability Science*.

Wolf, A. T., 'Conflict and Cooperation along International Waterways' (1998) 1(2) *Water Policy*.

Wong, P. P. *et al.*, 'Coastal Systems and Low-Lying Areas' in C. B. Field, V. R. Barros, D. J. Dokken, K. J. Mach, M. D. Mastrandrea, T. E. Bilir, M. Chatterjee, K. L. Ebi, Y. O. Estrada, R. C. Genova, B. Girma, E. S. Kissel, A. N. Levy, S. MacCracken, P. R. Mastrandrea and L. L. White (eds), *Climate Change 2014: Impacts, Adaptation, and Vulnerability. Part A: Global and Sectoral Aspects. Contribution of Working Group II to the Fifth Assessment Report of the Intergovernmental Panel on Climate Change* (Cambridge University Press 2014).

World Bank, *Well-Being from Work in the Pacific Island Countries* (2014).

World Meteorological Organization (WMO), *State of the Climate Report 2015* (2015) http://public.wmo.int/en/media/press-release/state-of-climate-record-heat-and-weather-extremes accessed 25 October 2016.

Wouters, K., *International Legal Standards for the Protection from Refoulement: A Legal Analysis of the Prohibitions on Refoulement Contained in the Refugee Rights and the Convention against Torture* (Intersentia 2009).

Yavinsky, R. W., 'Women More Vulnerable than Men to Climate Change' (Population Reference Bureau 2012).

Yim, E. S. *et al.*, 'Disaster Diplomacy: Current Controversies and Future Prospects' (2009) 24 *Prehospital and Disaster Medicine*.

Zander, K. K. *et al.*, 'Heat Stress Causes Substantial Labour Productivity Loss in Australia' (2015) 5 *Nature Climate Change*.

Zerilli, F. M., 'The Rule of Soft Law: An Introduction' (2010) 56 *Focaal*.

Zetter, R., 'The Role of Legal and Normative Frameworks for the Protection of Environmentally Displaced People' in F. Laczko and C. Aghazarm (eds), *Migration, Environment and Climate Change: Assessing the Evidence* (IOM 2009).

Zetter, R., 'Protecting People Displaced by Climate Change: Some Conceptual Challenges' in J. McAdam (ed.), *Climate Change and Displacement: Multi-Disciplinary Perspectives* (Hart 2010).

Zetter, R., *Protecting Environmentally Displaced People: Developing the Capacity of Legal and Normative Frameworks* (Refugees Studies Centre, University of Oxford 2011).

Index

References to Notes will contain the letter 'n' followed by the Note number.